A R E

PRACTICES / PROJECTS / SPACES

Artist-Run Europe

Practice / Projects / Spaces

Artist-Run Europe:
Practice/Projects/Spaces

SET MARGINS' 14
ISBN: 978-90-832706-6-1

EDITORS
Gavin Murphy & Mark Cullen

COPY EDITING
Lucy Watts & Gavin Murphy

PUBLISHER
Set Margins', Eindhoven

CONTRIBUTORS
Pallas Projects/Studios, *Dublin*
Triangle - Astérides, *Marseille*
Transmission Gallery, *Glasgow*
Onomatopee, *Eindhoven*
Catalyst Arts, *Belfast*
Eastside Projects, *Birmingham*
Pink Cube, *Oslo*
Secession, *Vienna*
Dienstgebäude, *Zurich*
Supermarket, *Stockholm*
126 Artist-Run Gallery, *Galway*
The Artist-led Archive, *Ireland*

AUTHORS
Jason E. Bowman, AA Bronson, Noelle Collins, Valerie Connor, Mark Cullen, Céline Kopp & Alun Williams, Joanna Laws, Freek Lomme, Megs Morley, Gavin Murphy, Transmission Gallery, Gavin Wade, Katherine Waugh.

ARTIST-RUN EUROPE INDEX
Devised by Gavin Murphy & Mark Cullen.
Researched and compiled by Róisín Hackett, Lucy Watts, Tadhg Ó Cuirrín and Elizabeth Lyne, with additional research by Daniel Birmingham and Niamh Reynolds.
Second edition updated by Gavin Murphy, with Viktorija Kacanauskaite, Louise Dolan, Aisling Clark, Adela Cerezo

DESIGN
Designed in Ireland by WorkGroup

PRINT
Printed in the Netherlands by Booxs

TYPE
Bitstream Gothic 720, Monotype Grotesque & Monotype Letter Gothic

PALLAS PROJECTS CLG IS A COMPANY LIMITED BY GUARANTEE NOT HAVING A SHARE CAPITAL, REGISTERED UNDER THE LAWS OF IRELAND. REGISTERED NUMBER 503645 AND HAVING ITS REGISTERED OFFICE AT:

PALLAS PROJECTS/STUDIOS
115–117 THE COOMBE
DUBLIN 8, IRELAND

WWW.PALLASPROJECTS.ORG
INFO@PALLASPROJECTS.ORG

FIRST PUBLISHED 2016, ONOMATOPEE, EINDHOVEN

SECOND REVISED EDITION 2023, SET MARGINS', EINDHOVEN

Contents

Gavin Murphy

What makes artist-run spaces different? (And why it's important to have different art spaces)

I

Artist-Run Europe – Practice/Projects/Spaces is part how-to manual, part history, and part socio-political critique of the conditions, organisational models, and role of artist-led practice within contemporary art and society. The aim is to show how artist-run practice manifests itself, how artist-run spaces are a distinctive and central part of visual art culture, and how they present a complex, heterogeneous, and necessary set of alternatives to the art institution, museum and commercial gallery.

The artist-run model and ethos is one which perpetuates alternative – and often non-hierarchical – modes of organisation and economies of exchange (knowledge and resources). A non-commercial approach to producing art and culture, it supports and develops experimental or unrepresented forms of practice and discourse, and proposes a model of social and cultural interaction that could be seen to eschew the roles of producer and consumer. Artist-run spaces play a vital role in supporting artists' practices at the early stages of their careers, and often have a key stake (albeit a precarious one) in the revitalisation of derelict urban areas.

In a self-reflexive, critically questioning process, *Artist-Run Europe* aims to allow a fuller understanding of the characteristics and roles of artist-run spaces, discussing and analysing areas such as: What position do artist-run spaces occupy within the field of contemporary art today? Should they stand in opposition to museums and commercial galleries, or in parallel to other art-world structures? How is value ascribed to these often transitory practices, and is this value recognised within the field? How are these spaces organised, and can artist-run spaces develop and be sustained in the longer term without becoming institutionalised? How important, intrinsic, or problematic is the voluntary nature of much artist-run practice? What do artist-run spaces add to the ecology of the civil society? What are the main practical issues or problems faced by artist-run spaces? Does precarity have to be a defining feature? Can recognition of the alternative and specific type of value that artist-run spaces provide allow for a specific approach to the funding and support of these organisations? What can we say about future (or hoped for) trajectories?

—

Alternative and artist-run culture as we know it today can be said to have its roots in 1960s and 70s counter-culture. This culture, that gave rise to a wave of spaces in the 60s and 70s, was anti-establishment in its rejection of dominant structures, which either ignored cutting-edge contemporary art, new-media art, female artists, experimental and performance art, or were commercial and driven primarily by sales. Crucially, rather than just acting as a *movement* of individuals, the proponents of this culture of self-determination and collectivisation opted to locate themselves as *groups* in *spaces*: spaces for production, thought, exhibition, and debate, and spaces which lay outside prescribed commercial or cultural zones – both ideologically and often literally – situating themselves in run-down inner-city areas which were, like the art forms, largely ignored by commercial, cultural, and political interests of the time.

The common denominator among all of these groups and spaces is that they arose out of a deficit – i.e. there was something missing in the cultural landscape: artists were dissatisfied with, or unable to access, the established venues, forums, or modes of presentation, and convened to create a new kind of space that addressed their needs. In North America the spaces that emerged in the 1970s "proved to be active contemporary witnesses involved in the start-up of the global media society which was emerging during 1960s, a period highly politicised by the Vietnam War, the rise of feminism and gay rights, as well as civil rights…"[1]

Here in Ireland, a number of notable examples emerged from this deficit. Project Arts Centre began life in 1966, as a three-week festival of experimental music, visual arts, seminars, and children's theatre, concluding with a debate on censorship. Set up "by visual artists and theatre practitioners […] as an alternative to the established institutions of the day as a place where artists could control their working situation"[2], the response was such that the founders cooperated to establish a permanent alternative centre for the performing and visual arts. In 1967, Project Gallery opened in Lower Abbey Street and by 1969 film screenings and plays were introduced to the programme.[3] By the 80s a need for workspaces led to the establishment in 1983 of Temple Bar Gallery & Studios by a group including Brian Maguire, Paddy Graham, and Jenny Haughton (who had just retuned from a stint at Franklin Furnace/Archive in New York)[4]. The activities of its artists – studios, exhibition space, cafe, and a sculptor's annex – influenced the creative and distinctly underground atmosphere of Temple Bar in the 1980s, establishing the area's reputation as a cultural hub and contributing

---

[1] Gabriele Detterer, 'The Spirit and Culture of Artist-Run Spaces' in *Artist-Run Spaces. Nonprofit Collective Organizations in the 1960s and 1970s*, Eds. Gabriele Detterer & Maurizio Nannucci, p. 13

[2] 'Artists/Groups', curated by Grant Watson, Project Arts Centre, 2003. http://projectartscentre.ie/event/artists-groups/

[3] http://projectartscentre.ie/about-us/

[4] Jenny Haughton, 'Why on earth ask someone other than an artist about an artist's space?' in *Generation: 30 Years of Creativity at Temple Bar Gallery + Studios*, Dublin, 2013, p. 29–35

to its eventual regeneration as Dublin's Cultural Quarter[5]. The artists who started both of these spaces, negotiated their leases, fixed up the premises, and fought against all odds to keep them going, created legacies which today allow the general public, tourists, art-lovers, and art professionals to experience contemporary art in what are now visible public institutions. They also created whole swathes of culture in the process, establishing careers, supporting emerging and experimental art forms, broadening and enlightening their audiences, helping to create a new culture in Ireland: an open, inclusive, and outward-looking society.

The conditions that led to a surge in artist-run spaces in Ireland in the 1990s and 2000s could be attributed to a number of factors. The warming of economic conditions had allowed a new generation of artists to stay in the country, yet a gulf existed between these artists and established galleries and museums, with few studio spaces to produce work, and fewer galleries showing emerging or experimental art. The property boom, while in its infancy, saw a proliferation of run down and as-yet-undeveloped properties around the city, with some landlords being prepared to let space out to groups of enterprising artists (often on short leases of less than five years) while the value of their sites rose. The confluence of the socio-economic backdrop and the prevailing cultural conditions into which artists emerge, have at various stages acted to fuel a particular agency for those who were interested in taking things into their own hands to actively opt-in to a process of self-determination. The activity and support for artists produced through this agency could lead one to argue that artist-led practice should take equal billing – alongside the emergence of ambitious postgraduate programmes, increased government supports, reinvigorated programming within institutions, and a small but progressive commercial scene – in the emergence of a thriving, critically engaged and increasingly international contemporary art landscape that flourished here in the 2000s.

—

Despite this history, it is clear that artist-run spaces are still a largely undervalued 'cog' within the field of contemporary art practice. Often going under the radar, run on a voluntary basis, and by-and-large of a transient or precarious nature (with notable exceptions), their importance and value to the wider viability of critically-engaged contemporary art is overlooked. Equally, the role of these spaces in sustaining the practices of artists, often in the crucial formative stages, goes largely un-remarked. The energy invested in maintaining these initiatives is often used up quickly in the face of a lack of resources (burn-out is rife), and the finite ability to maintain activities through an economy of sharing and predominantly

[5] http://www.templebargallery.com/info/about/history

free labour. As such, the continued though constantly changing presence of an artist-run field of practice, and its value, is by its very nature difficult to quantify and record.

This has been redressed to a degree over recent years, and internationally the subject of artist-led practice is now being seen as worthy of further study and debate, with a number of notable publications, to date largely focused on Canada and the USA. Recent examples include *Decentre – Concerning Artist-run Culture* (YYZBOOKS, 2008); *Alternative Histories: New York Art Spaces, 1960-2010* (Exit Art and MIT Press, 2012); *Artist-Run Spaces – Nonprofit Collective Organizations in the 1960s and 1970s* (JRP | Ringier, Les presses du reel & Zona Archives, 2012); and the *Institutions by Artists* conference in Vancouver and subsequent publication (Fillip Editions, 2012), all of which have added greatly to current discourse. As well as these, *Self-Organised* (Open Editions, 2013) is a welcome and important addition looking at the wider role of 'not-just artist-run' spaces. Artist-run events such as *Artist Run* (festival), Copenhagen, *Supermarket Art Fair* in Stockholm, and *Sluice Art Fair* in London, who, in using the outward structure of the art fair – something the wider public (and funding bodies) can more readily understand – have had an impact in drawing together international pockets of artist-run practice, and rather than actually focussing on sales, afford artist-run and independent spaces from different countries a locus to meet and connect.

More often, the artist-run presence becomes visible in the wider (art) world only in cases where large institutions and museums have sought to collaborate with artist-run spaces, or include them in survey-type exhibitions in order to present a 'whole picture' of a period or art scene. The exhibition *Life/Live* at the Musee d'Art Moderne de la Ville de Paris, 1996, curated by Hans-Ulrich Obrist and Laurence Bosse, included spaces such as Glasgow's Transmission and London's City Racing. For the 2002 Gwangju Biennale in Korea, curated by Wan-Kjung Sung, Charles Esche and Hou Hanru, the inclusion of artist-run spaces, suggests Rebecca Gordon-Nesbitt, "conferred a freedom through stylistic choices that perhaps the curators did not feel able to take themselves. In an attempt to foreground the inclusion in the biennial of 26 artist-run spaces from Asia, Europe and beyond, Hou Hanru championed artist-led activity as a counterpoint to pervasive Empire, the local influencing the global". Gordon-Nesbitt goes on to cite Charles Esche's *Baltic Babel* in which eight cities were represented through their artist-led initiatives, a project that "was accompanied by the most explicit understanding yet of the role of artist-led initiatives in local communities and their political potential".[6]

---

[6] Rebecca Gordon-Nesbitt, 'Harnessing the Means of Production', in *New Institutionalism*. Ed. Jonas Ekeberg. Oslo, Office for Contemporary Art Norway, 2003.

In Ireland, Dublin City Gallery The Hugh Lane invited Pallas Studios to curate an exhibition in its main galleries in 2005, for which Pallas opted to present Irish and international artists, commissioning new or showing current work, as opposed to presenting a survey of projects to date. Again in Ireland, The Model, Sligo, under the direction of Seamus Kealy, conceived of the exhibition *Dorm* to re-launch their refurbished galleries in 2010, which featured twenty-one international and Irish collectives and artist-run spaces (including Pallas Projects, Catalyst Arts, IRWIN, General Idea, and RAQS Media Collective).

Other instances have afforded further currency to spaces, in so far as presenting current work, if in some cases not paying them at all. Tate Modern's "highly unconventional celebration"[7] of its first decade *No Soul for Sale – A Festival of Independents* is perhaps the most high profile and large scale of these (with over 70 groups contributing), yet was deeply problematic in not paying any of the contributors, and according to Stine Herbert in *Self-Organised*: "received harsh criticism for its barely-concealed exploitative undertones"[8]. She goes on to point out, however, "that most of the participants so readily accepted these terms demonstrated [...] an important lesson about how the institutional art world sustains itself."[9]

While it seems clear that institutions gain from drawing from the artist-run well – and equally what attracts the spaces to participate (institutional support, bigger budgets, exposure) – these crossovers have done little to alter the precariousness of the position of the artist-run. Often seen as dispensable, perhaps because of a perceived notion that they are inherently short-lived as a defining feature (supported by the likelihood that another artist-run alternative will surely pop up to carry on the work), or because of their voluntary nature, the value of their labour remains difficult to quantify.

[7] Stine Herbert in *Self-Organised*, Eds. Stine Herbert & Anne Szefer Karlsen, Open Editions, 2013, p. 13

[8] Ibid., p. 14

[9] Ibid., p. 13

II

"Artist organisations choose the form of the organisation."
—Banners hung over the stage at the 'Artists Organisations International' congress, Berlin, 2015

In his essay 'On De-Organisation', Barnaby Drabble points to the structural diversity of the artist-run: "the diversity of [descriptive] terms alone reminds us just how broad a spectrum of activities the term self-organised has come to be applied to", which in turn describes the flexibility of form by which these spaces mould, incorporate, or invent their organising structures. Differentiation is key to this; artist-run spaces choose their own form in answer to their own needs, and the needs of the culture as they see it at a particular time. The question of time, duration, and its relationship to structure and precarity is also at the crux of the problematic issue of artist-run sustainability.

The recent report that resulted from the Footfall Research project, conducted by 126 Artist-Run Gallery, states:

> It was proposed during the discussion that precarity may be 'situational', in that precarity may be needed for artist led spaces to come about. However, it was qualified that artists do not need to be poor [...] With short-term artist led spaces being the 'default stance', it was agreed that a broader conceptual base for thinking about sustainability is urgently required.[10]

---

[10] Joanne Laws, FOOTFALL: Articulating the Value of Artist Led Organizations in Ireland, 126 Artist-Run Gallery, Galway, 2015, p. 58. "Notions of precarity being 'necessary' for 'creativity, risk and edginess' were raised on several occasions, signaling debate on whether creativity can be stifled by 'too much funding', presumably referring to the bureaucratic restraints which accompany the funding processes. This position was unilaterally disregarded by the assembled group. The idea that good art comes out of struggle and constant reinvention due to capricious funding is 'highly damaging' for artist led organizations, with one contributor stating: It is dangerous to aspire to, fetishize or idealize precarity."

If an artist-run space is to sustain itself, more often than not the voluntary roles that brought it into being need to be phased out, as voluntary labour in the long term is unsustainable in most models. If voluntary labour is removed, funding or other revenue streams are required to replace it, and to a large degree, if funding is applied, a new level of bureaucracy and a standardisation of organisational structure is generally insisted upon. Therein lies the catch-22 of duration and the artist-run. In most cases, for an artist-run space to be sustainable, it needs to homogenise its structure and appoint a director, curator, administrator, and technical staff, artists may retain some oversight or advisory role, or may be jettisoned entirely. To succeed in the duration stakes, artist-run spaces often have to cease to exist as artist-run. By current metrics, a successful artist-run space is one that 'grows up' to become an institution. As noted in *Institutions by Artists*, "the 'failure of the self-determination paradigm' became apparent once artists [...] no longer seemed to have control over the institutions they created", an eventuality predicted by artist AA Bronson in his 1983 essay 'The Humiliation of the Bureaucrat: Artist-Run Centres as Museums by Artists'.[11]

The question, or conceptualisation of the institution is approached by Jeff Khonsary and Kristina Lee Podesva, in their introduction to *Institutions by Artists* citing Andrea Fraser's 'From the Critique of Institutions to an Institution of Critique' (2005)[12]: "it's not about being against the institution: We are the institution. It's a question of what kind of institution we are, what kind of values we institutionalise, what forms of practice we reward, and what kind of rewards we aspire to." This position, as distinguished from Raunig's alternative of 'instituent practices' discussed elsewhere in this volume, poses some interesting problems for the artist-led. In Barnaby Drabble's essay 'Assembled Thoughts on Artist-Led Culture in Zurich', he cites a 2006 article by critic and curator Burkhard Meltzer, "in which he argued that Zurich's artist-run spaces were no longer fulfilling their critical [subcultural] role but instead simply emulating commercial and institutional spaces, albeit in a "micro" format."[13] This potential "shift in thinking about the institution of art... wresting it from the gallery and museum"[14], re-situating the idea of the institution for and by artists, becomes problematic in light of the tendency to turn 'successful' artist-run spaces towards established structures, thus aping the institution in miniature.

A further problem occurs when speaking of the artist-run in terms of the institution. To define artist-run practice as 'institutional' brings with it modes of evaluation that are plainly unsuitable for smaller arts organisations. Anne Szefer Karlsen is correct in saying that the

---

[11] Jeff Khonsary and Kristina Lee Podesva, *Institutions by Artists: Volume One*, Fillip Editions, 2012, p. 15–16

[12] Andrea Fraser, Artforum, New York: September 2005. Vol. 44, Issue 1, p. 278

[13] Barnaby Drabble, 'Assembled Thoughts on Artist-Led Culture in Zurich, Part two: We are the Artists!' in *Institutions by Artists: Volume One*, p. 212

[14] Jeff Khonsary and Kristina Lee Podesva, Op. Cit., p. 13

"field of self-organisation is [...] more complex than the conventional separatist approach entails. It has moved beyond a process of simply dissolving boundaries between institutional and non-institutional platforms to create new possibilities." However, purposefully taking alternative positions to recognisable institutional forms can still provide a necessary and useful distinction for what artist-run practice is (and isn't). An enforced perspective in which artist-run spaces are required to emulate other 'defined' institutions in order to ensure sustainability is a real problem – though not necessarily of artists' own making – and one that has yet to be adequately addressed.

—

The issue of representation, recognition, and the visibility of artist-run spaces and their contributory value (rather than marketing visibility), is tied into the question of what artist-run spaces add to our culture. In *Self-Organised*, Anne Szefer Karlsen points to the growing number of books and seminars showing an active engagement with the historicisation of the artist-run field by the very same people involved in it, suggesting, "[a]n absence of competing accounts has allowed the practitioners to write themselves into history – ironically, often employing the same strategies as their institutional cousins."[15] One might ask the question, 'if not us, then who?', an example being Gabriele Detterer and Maurizio Nannucci's *Artist-Run Spaces*, which has its genesis in Zona/Zona Archives, Florence – of which Nannucci was co-founder – and gathers together extensive research on international pioneering examples vital to a broader understanding of contemporary art practice and its indebtedness to alternative, artist-run spaces. Detterer and Nannucci's suggestion however that spaces today are run with the "primary goal of marketing emerging artists" is unfortunate, in that it ignores the reality of the disparate non-commercial, communal actions, and discursive self-determination that exists within an admittedly different scene, one that crosses-over with the commercial and institutional, but by no means desires as a whole to be assimilated into the status quo. If anything it perpetuates the idea of the artist-run space as a 'stop gap', where artists hope to find eventual commercial or critical reward, without affording much value to what alternative spaces offer in today's increasingly commercial (art) world.

According to Sarah Thelwall writing for Common Practice's *Size Matters: Notes towards a Better Understanding of the Value, Operation and Potential of Small Visual Arts Organisations*, "small organisations act as an unofficial support mechanism" to the wider field of contemporary art and its institutions, while "research exposes the inapplicability of current metrics to measuring this 'deferred value', which means that smaller organisations will appear less successful, since the majority of

[15] *Self-Organised*, Op. Cit., p. 12

the value that they create is not visible".[16] The follow-up conference to *Size Matters*, entitled *Value, Measure, Sustainability: Ideas towards the future of the small-scale visual arts sector*, equally found issues with some of the language that defines and typecasts the role of organisations at 'different levels':

> "Size Matters had used the term 'ecology' to describe the relevant field. This was problematised by some, on the basis that it naturalised the existing order, potentially delimiting critical analysis of a notionally stable system, and thereby inhibiting its disruption. Unreflexive use of ecological metaphors has recently served to suggest that only those organisations able to adapt – particularly to corporate or philanthropic models of organisational development – will survive the austerity measures being imposed in response to the financial crisis."[17]

The study found problematic the perception that "small arts organisations form a natural and fitting part of a continuum of development [that] implies a linear progression up the rungs of a ladder". It also admitted that in the case of the *Size Matters* research, which looked primarily at small arts organisations such as the members of Common Practice[18], this ladder metaphor left the role of artists and artist-run organisations to "function as the proverbial 'bottom rungs'".[19]

—

[16] Sarah Thelwall, *Size Matters: Notes towards a Better Understanding of the Value, Operation and Potential of Small Visual Arts Organisations*. Commissioned and published by Common Practice, London, July 2011, p. 6–7

[17] Rebecca Gordon-Nesbitt, *Value, Measure, Sustainability: Ideas towards the future of the small-scale visual arts sector*. Commissioned and published by Common Practice, London, December 2012, p. 5

[18] Common Practice members are Afterall, Chisenhale Gallery, Electra, Gasworks, LUX, Matt's Gallery, Mute Publishing, The Showroom, Studio Voltaire. See: www.commonpractice.org.uk

[19] *Value, Measure, Sustainability*, Op. Cit., p. 6

III

Why another publication on artist-run spaces? As Freek Lomme in his Netherlands study in this volume reflects:

> "Over the past decade, I've been given quite a number of books by artist-run and independent art spaces, published on the occasion of their X-year existence, meant as calls-to-authority to policy makers and as relation gifts to the network. Hardly ever do matters reach another level: that of collective organisation, exchange of knowledge and so forth. People are simply happy celebrating yet another X-years of existence [impeded by a] financial and time-wise lack to go beyond."

It is the intention of this publication to go beyond, to reach out to the field of the artist-run and the wider field of contemporary practice, to encourage and facilitate discourse, collaboration, connections, and make a case for the alternative. This book began with a number of questions, or, one obstacle and one big question; the obstacle was a lack of information on artist-run spaces in general, and the difficulty in determining and locating spaces in other countries – something which we felt was a barrier to discourse, collaboration, and the understanding of these spaces and the broader field. The second part was the 'big question', which was of particular relevance to PP/S in nearing 20 years in operation: how does an artist-run space develop and continue to be artist-run, and how can we think about this and address it? A further impetus was the many instances over the years of other groups and spaces approaching us for advice on 'what to do next', asking how has our model been sustained and developed. We intend that this book will give an insight into not only the workings of PP/S, but a range of models, situations, and applied knowledge.

In producing a book about artist-run spaces we didn't want to focus on the archival – as seductive as this is – and so have limited the space for histories and nostalgia, preferring to use these pages as a working study of current practices, and current spaces (not so straightforward given the hitherto mentioned attrition rate): to produce a useful object, an active object, a tool for 'doing' artist-run practice as much as showing it. It was also important that the participants not be part of an existing hub or club, or a group of spaces already in dialogue, but draw in a positive way on the peripheral position that Ireland holds – both geographically and in the contemporary art world – in bringing an outsider's viewpoint to gather together a disparate set of examples that demonstrate the polyphony of artist-run models.

Artist-Run Europe has been written in collaboration with a number of artist-run and artist-initiated spaces, projects, initiatives, and authors. The *practice* – the activity, politics, concepts, philosophies and histories of the artist-run – is addressed in a number of newly commissioned essays and case studies. Jason E. Bowman's essay reflects on *Midwest* (2003–2008), its ethoi and the methods employed by the project towards the development of an artist-led infrastructure, focussing on the non-art-making aspects of practice. AA Bronson's 'Notes from Berlin' shifts between the beginnings of Art Metropole in Canada in the early 70s, the emergence of artists' organisations in the Germanic countries in the 1800s, and the artist-run scene of present day Berlin, touching upon the intimate, the communal, and the cooperative essence of artists' collaboration and its public life. Valerie Connor asks us to reconsider the relentless reproduction of popular representations of the artist in their studio, that hinder a better understanding of what 'artist-run' could mean in terms of a more radical and interventionist approach to self-representation. The essay uses two photographs that allow for a reflection on Pallas Studios' development in particular, and the longer historical relationship between 'studio' and 'project'. In her essay 'Delicate Yet Deadly', Katherine Waugh looks at recent theoretical and political analyses of the complicated relationship between capitalism, subjectivity and artist-run spaces, and questions the philosophical foundations and impact of commercially driven PR rationalities on such organisations and their possible futures.

Illustrated case studies look at different models of spaces: Transmission Gallery, Glasgow (run on a model of a rotating board of volunteers) present a collectively authored text that addresses the organisation's structure, history and modes of communication; Céline Kopp, director of Triangle France, Marseille, discusses that organisation's artist-led beginnings and development from the Triangle Workshops of the early '80s, to posing questions for Triangle France and artist-run practice today. In the case of Pallas Projects/Studios, co-founder Mark Cullen charts the development of the organisation through multiple sites in a 20-year nomadic journey, and through Dublin city centre's regeneration, giving frank and practical insights into motivations, changing strategies, challenges and actions undertaken. Gavin Wade of Eastside Projects, Birmingham appears in conversation with PP/S discussing the artist-run space as 'public gallery'. Further case studies – Pink Cube, Oslo; Dienstgebäeude, Zurich; and Secession, Vienna – allow an idea of the diversity of spaces and models in Europe today. Expanding the parameters from that of individual spaces, Noelle Collins provides a study of Limerick city, the issue of sustainability and recent challenges for artist-led initiatives in securing space, while Onomatopee publisher and curator Freek Lomme contributes an impassioned look at the current situation for independent spaces in the Netherlands. Artist-run projects feature in the form of Supermarket Art Fair, Stockholm, and Catalyst Arts' FIX festival (one of Europe's longest running live art and performance biennials). Artist and curator Megs Morley discusses her project the *Artist-led Archive*, a touring artwork and resource which has collected and catalogued 40 years of Irish artist-run projects, and Joanne Laws provides a report on the 'Footfall' conference organised by 126 Artist-Run Gallery, Galway.

The final part of the publication is an expansive and detailed 'Directory' of artist-run spaces in Europe, featuring spaces from 36 countries. While accepting it gives only a momentary picture of the ever-changing artist-run presence, it provides an idea of the level of activity, gives information on organisational make-up, and acts as a resource for contact and collaboration. By enlisting contributions from the spaces presented in this book, the commissioned essays, and the exhaustive (but we're sure by-no-means fully complete) index, it is hoped that many other questions can be asked, answered, obstacles recognised and overcome. The publication is, we feel, timely and unique. With no such study available in a European context, and no available history of European spaces, we hope to provide both a resource for academics and students, and a practical tool for those running or wishing to set up artist-run spaces.

Within this volume there will be mixed signals of what an artist-run space is, or is supposed to be: a cacophony of ideas. The idea of the cacophony of 'doing' artist-run spaces will be familiar to many who do it, where the matter of survival becomes a persistent ringing in the ears.

> Who am I working for:
> Myself? My peers? The common good?! Funders?
>
> And why am I doing it:
> I can't remember, I'm too busy doing it!

It is important to remember that artist-run spaces are at their core, as Gabriele Detterer reminds us in *Artist-Run Spaces*, "mutually supportive organisations" that mitigate an artist's isolation in social and economic terms[20], and in the words of Jason E. Bowman, "challenge exclusion [and] circumnavigate the market-driven art-world"[21]. In essence, an alternative.

---

[20] Gabriele Detterer, 'The Spirit and Culture of Artist-Run Spaces', Ibid., p. 20

[21] Jason E. Bowman, keynote address at the FOOTFALL Symposium, 21st November 2014. The symposium, which took place during TULCA Festival of Visual Art, Galway, was coordinated by Megs Morley and 126 and included presentations from invited contributors, Jason E. Bowman (Midwest UK; University of Gothenburg, Sweden), Valerie Connor (NCFA chairperson, independent curator) and Mikael Löfgren (writer and activist, Unga Klara Theatre, Stockholm). In the afternoon, a discursive 'Plenary Session' was devised and facilitated by Ailbhe Murphy and Ciaran Smyth of Vagabond Reviews.

It must also be acknowledged that alongside the many examples of the artist-run in this volume are hundreds of others, underground or under the radar, defunct or forgotten, who nonetheless do, or have done their part in creating, supporting, and sustaining our visual art culture from the ground up. In that previously and often-used analogy, whereby your place in the art-world can be gauged as being on a certain 'rung' of the ladder, artist-run spaces tend to be seen as the 'bottom rung'. If, however, we were to upend that analogy, we could look at those artist-run spaces as in fact embodying the living, vibrant substance of that archetypal wooden ladder's make-up. These spaces could then instead be described as being the strong and vital roots upon which everything else can be borne and sustained.

NAME
Triangle France - Astérides*, centre d'art contemporain d'intérêt national

LOCATION
Marseille, France

WEBSITE
www.trianglefrance.org

YEAR
1994 to present

STRUCTURE
Artist-Run, non-profit organisation with a voluntary board

LEGAL STATUS
Association by the 1901 law

TEAM
1 permanent director–curator,
1 permanent administrator,
1 permanent curator in charge of residencies,
1 permanent assistant,
2 part-time staff

MISSION
Triangle France - Astérides develops a yearly program of exhibitions, public events, and new commissions, as well as residencies and studio programs dedicated to Marseille-based, French, and international artists; supporting artistic research, experimentation and production. In 28 years, the organisation has hosted more than 650 artists in residence and produced more than 130 exhibitions, with a focus on equal representation, open debate, and multiple viewpoints regardless of gender, race, class, or creed. An active member of Triangle Network, an international network of over 90 arts organisations in 41 countries

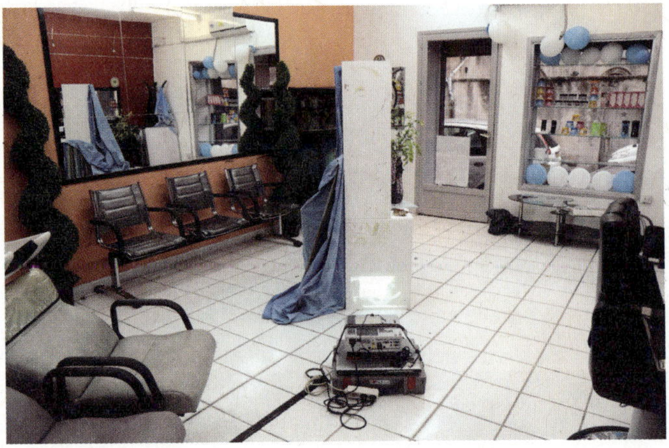

CORE FUNDING
Triangle France - Astérides is supported by Ministère de la Culture, Direction Régionale des Affaires Culturelles Provence-Alpes-Côte d'Azur, Ville de Marseille, Région Sud, Conseil Départemental 13, and SCIC Friche la Belle de Mai.

PREMISES
Triangle France - Astérides is a tenant of the Friche Belle de Mai

SELECTED PROJECTS
Carlos Kusnir (2018), *Vos désirs sont les nôtres* (2018), *CREVÉ*, Jesse Darling (2019), *OOLOI*, Paul Maheke (2019), *Sur pierres brûlantes* (2020), *En attendant*, Omar Gatlato (2021), Lydia Ourahmane, *Barzakh* (2021)

*Since our first publication, Triangle France merged with Astérides (in 2018), pooling the mission, programs and know-how of each of the two structures while respecting and continuing their unique histories in order to sustain their development.

A Brief History of Triangle France

Céline Kopp & Alun Williams

← 0,00€ – A project by Jean-Alain Corre
Rue Espérandieu – 13001 Marseille
27 April – 19 May, 2013
Renaud Jerez, ***DEAD SPEL HO EYES***, 2013
Photograph courtesy of the artist and Galerie Crevecoeur, Paris

An exhibition conceived by Jean-Alain Corre during his residency at Triangle France. Ten artists were invited to convince small business owners to let them exhibit works in their shops. Conversations happened and bakers, hairdressers, sandwich makers, became curators and gallery invigilators so that artworks could in turn integrate the shops and the daily life of this small neighbourhood community.

Triangle's mother organisation was created in New York in 1982 by two Englishmen, the collector, Robert Loder and the sculptor, Anthony Caro. The original idea and formula had the intention of stimulating a sort of visual arts laboratory by bringing together about 25 artists for two weeks in a fairly remote setting in the upstate New York countryside – providing them with lodgings, food, drink, work spaces and the accompaniment of a few thinking heads, such as Clement Greenberg, the champion of American abstract painting, as well as Anthony Caro, Karen Wilkin and Michael Fried, among others.

This first 'Triangle Workshop' had no long-term goals, it was merely an experiment in dialogue about process, and if its participants hadn't responded with such a high degree of enthusiasm, Triangle might never have gone beyond that first edition. The name 'Triangle' was coined in reference to the fact that the artists involved in 1982 all came from three countries, namely the US, UK and Canada. By the following year, this was no longer the case, as artists from France and South Africa had already expanded the roster, as well as beginning to diversify artistic disciplines and practices, a trend that has continued throughout Triangle's history.

The intensity of the 1982 experience meant that there was an immediate desire to organise a second edition, then a third, and so on, with participating artists coming from an ever increasing range of countries and origins. Triangle Workshops had already spread to South Africa by 1985, thanks to participants from New York wanting to take the formula back home. Over the next thirty years, the Triangle Network developed in this organic way, with artists who participated in one or other of the affiliated venues spreading the idea to their own countries.

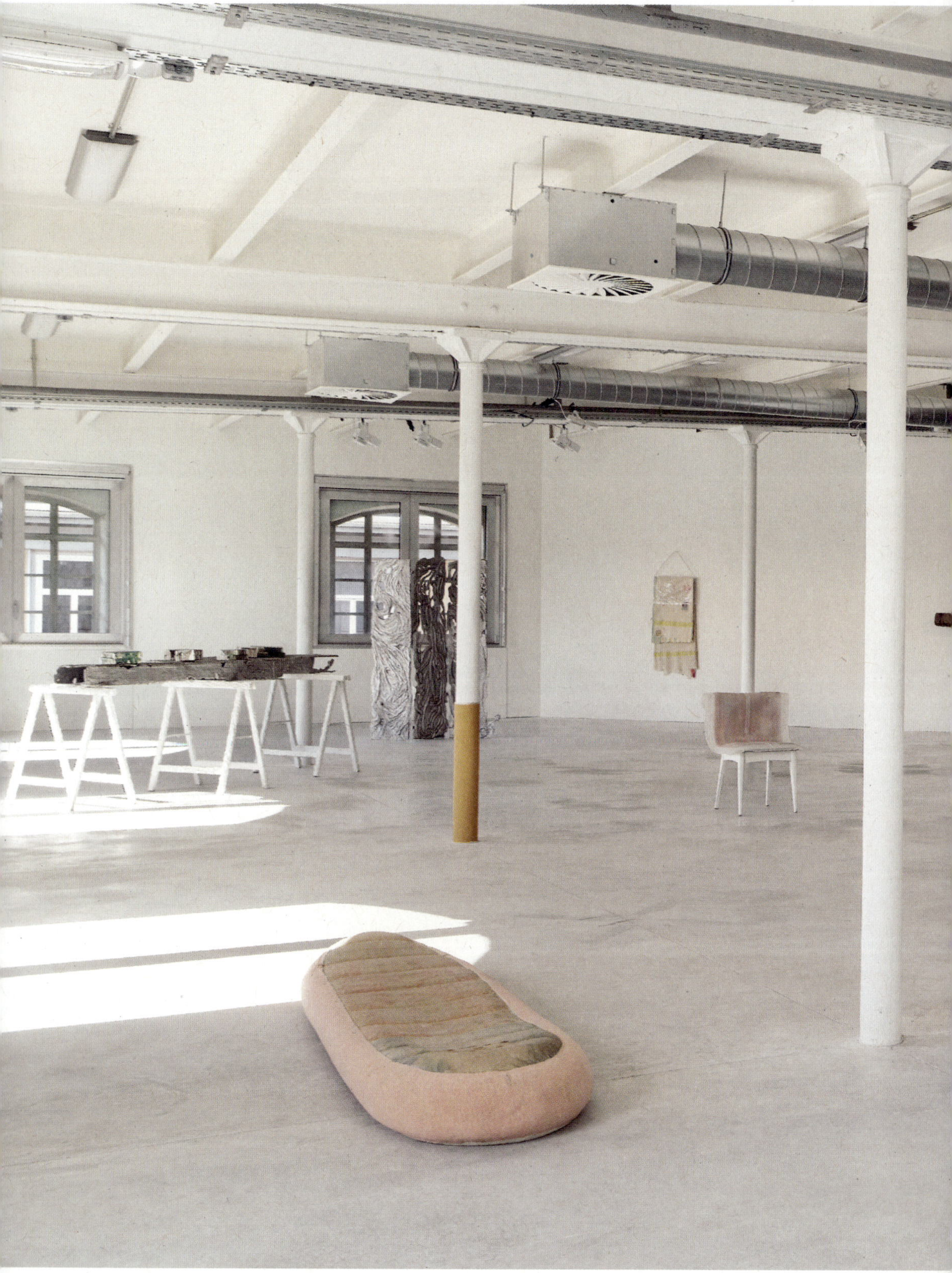

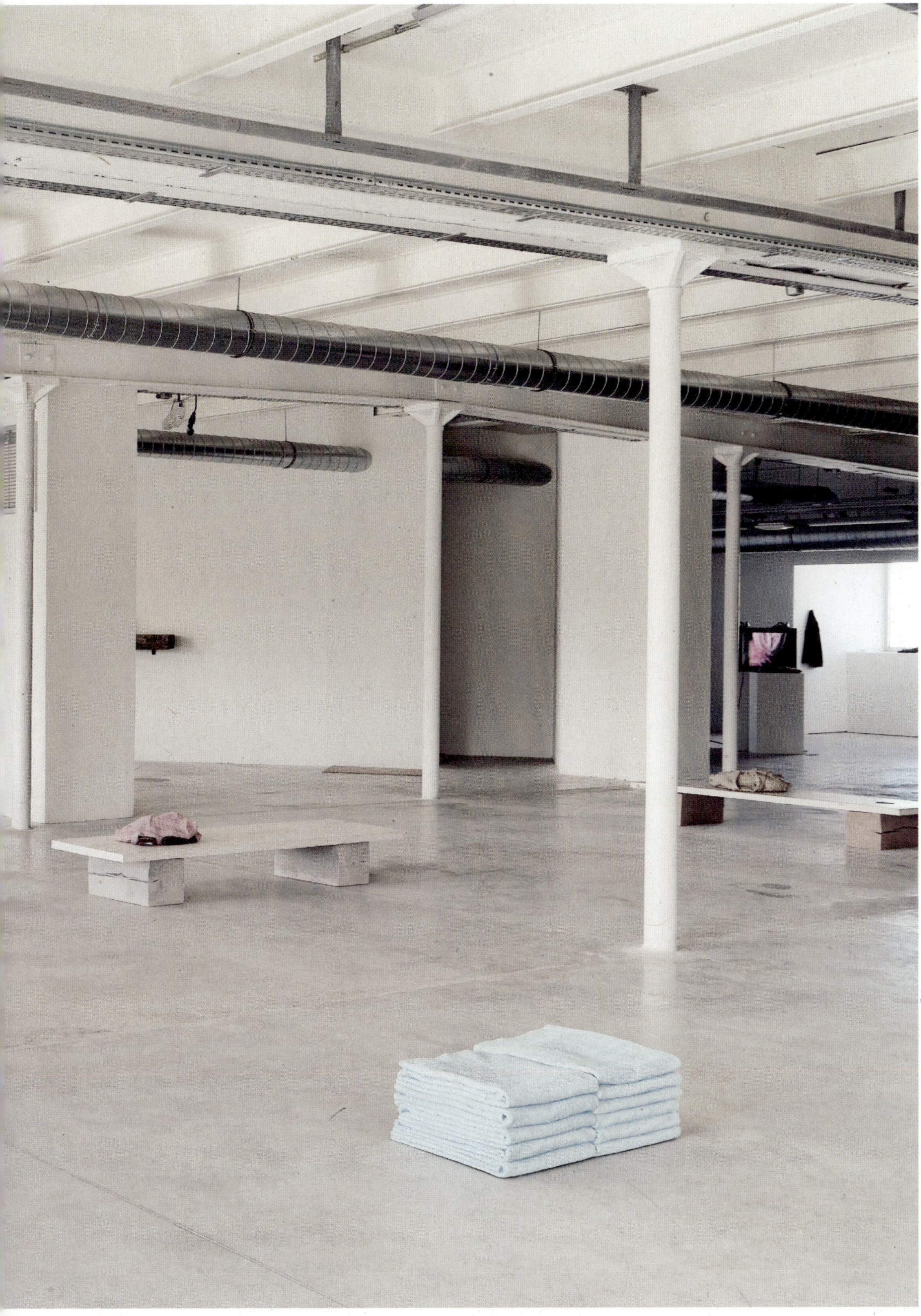

CÉLINE KOPP & ALUN WILLIAMS

↖ **No Fear, No Shame, No Confusion**
Solo exhibition of Liz Magor with new commissions by Jean-Marie Appriou, Andrea Büttner, and Laure Provost
Triangle France
12 October 2013 – 2 February 2014
Photograph by Aurélien Mole

During the 1990s in particular, Triangle Workshops took place in a number of African countries, as well as in Asia and South America. Inevitably, the enormous need for artists' studios saw the first year-round Triangle residency programme being established in Johannesburg in 1991, and further permanent studio programmes emerged, for example at Gasworks, London (1994), Kenya (1995), Marseille (1996), Brazil and India (1997), Capetown (1998) and Pakistan (1999). The spread of the Triangle Network has continued with Triangle Workshops and Residencies taking place in over 40 countries to date, with over 30 affiliated organisations currently active.

The story of Triangle's arrival in Marseille is a particular one, since it came on the heels of the last Triangle Artists' Workshop at the original venue in Pine Plains, New York, where it had taken place every year since 1982. When it became clear in 1994 that the Pine Plains venue could no longer be used, the search for alternatives began. The Triangle Board was adamant that a solution had to be found for 1995, and the call for candidates was put out so that the selection of artists could take place even though there was no confirmed venue. It was at this time that discussions with the new director of the École Supérieure des Beaux-Arts in Marseille, Michel Enrici, identified the school, with its purpose-built studios, cafeteria and student housing, as a potential host venue for a Triangle Workshop for the summer of 1995.

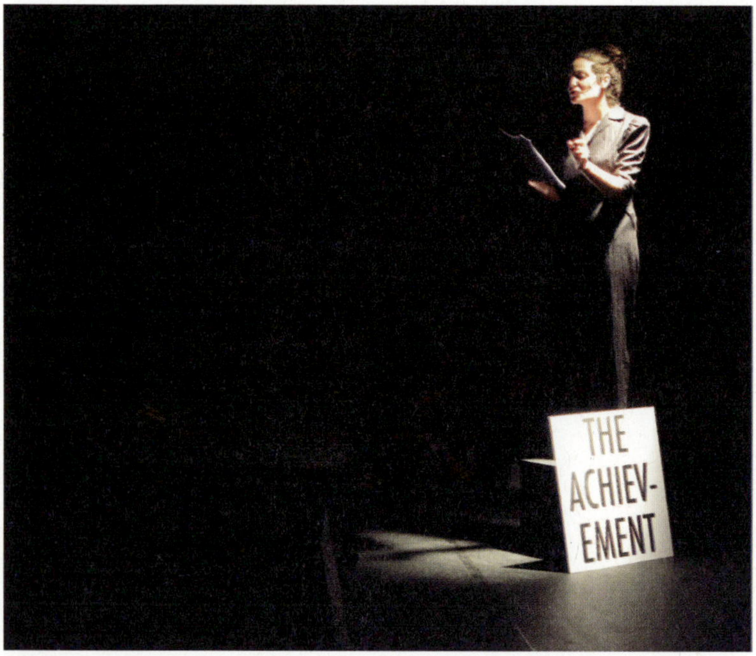

A Six Stage Manifesto On Action – Part 2
Performance written and directed by Cally Spooner
Devised with and performed by Dulcie Lewis. Musical Arrangement by Peter Joslyn Accompanied by Christophe Castan, Stéphane Zef Richard, Davis Timsit
3 October 2012
Triangle France
Coproduction: International Project Space, Birmingham / Triangle France / Actoral.12
Photograph by Céline Kopp

Towards the end of 1994, Triangle France was constituted as a French non-profit association, and work began in conjunction with the Board of Directors in New York to export a special edition of the Triangle Workshop to France. In a quirk of this unfolding history, a number of the 1995 participating artists submitted their applications in the hope that they'd be selected for New York, and instead they found themselves sitting on a Marseille fishing boat, being ferried to a small castle on a tiny island off the coast of Marseille where they were to share the Triangle Workshop inaugural dinner with a group of diverse artists from across the world. The 1995 workshop at the Marseille art school in Luminy, on the outskirts of the city, was as energetic as ever, and it was graced by a dynamic roster of accompanying personalities, including the ever-faithful Anthony Caro. A series of exhibitions were organised at the end of 1995 in diverse venues including the contemporary art museum, regional government galleries, as well as other municipal, non-profit and commercial galleries in Marseille.

Even before the dust had settled over the 1995 workshop and its resulting exhibitions in Marseille, it seemed clear that the city and its cultural community could benefit from maintaining its newly established links with Triangle's international network. The relative introspection of the lively Marseille art world had a real need to extend its reach, and as Triangle now had an identity in France, as well as rapidly established relations with local funders, it seemed like an obvious step to explore possibilities for a permanent presence. Developments at the Friche Belle de Mai, a sprawling former government tobacco factory behind the railway station in Marseille, meant that proposals for new cultural tenants were being studied. Triangle France proposed a new residency programme, with the mandate of bringing selected overseas artists to Marseille, as well as providing opportunities for Marseille-based artists, both at home and abroad.

While there has not been another Triangle Workshop in Marseille, the commitment to artists' needs spawned by Triangle's history and the Workshop spirit remained the hallmark of Triangle's ongoing activities at the Friche. In the years following the arrival of the first artists in residence in early 1996, Triangle continued to give particular attention to supporting artists' projects however possible. As Triangle France began to produce exhibitions, publications, performance events and other initiatives, as well as maintaining its residency programme, the strong commitment to providing artists with specific and tailor-made support to accompany them in their research and projects always seemed as much a part of the DNA of Triangle in Marseille, as it was in upstate New York in 1982, when food, drink, time and space were the most simple but vital offerings.

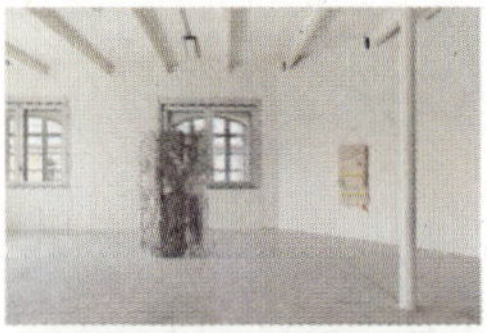

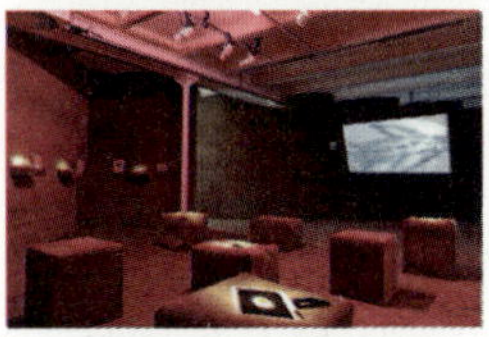

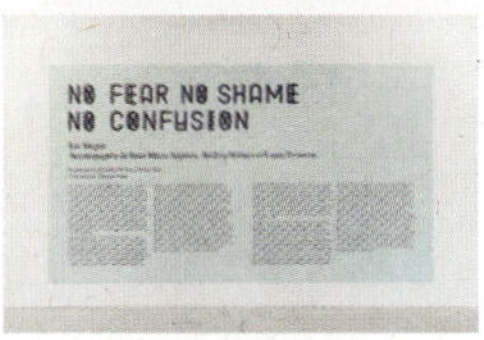

No Fear, No Shame, No Confusion
Triangle France
12 October 2013 – 2 February 2014
Photographs by Aurélien Mole

TOP:
Jean Marie Appriou, ***Mages***, 2013.
Courtesy the artist.
Liz Magor, ***Alberta/Quebec***, 2013
Courtesy Marcelle Alix, Paris et Catriona Jeffries Gallery

MIDDLE:
Laure Prouvost, ***Grandma's Dream***, 2013
Coproduction Triangle France and FNAGP.
Courtesy of the artist and MOTINTERNATIONAL London and Bruxelles.

BELOW:
Exhibition wall text

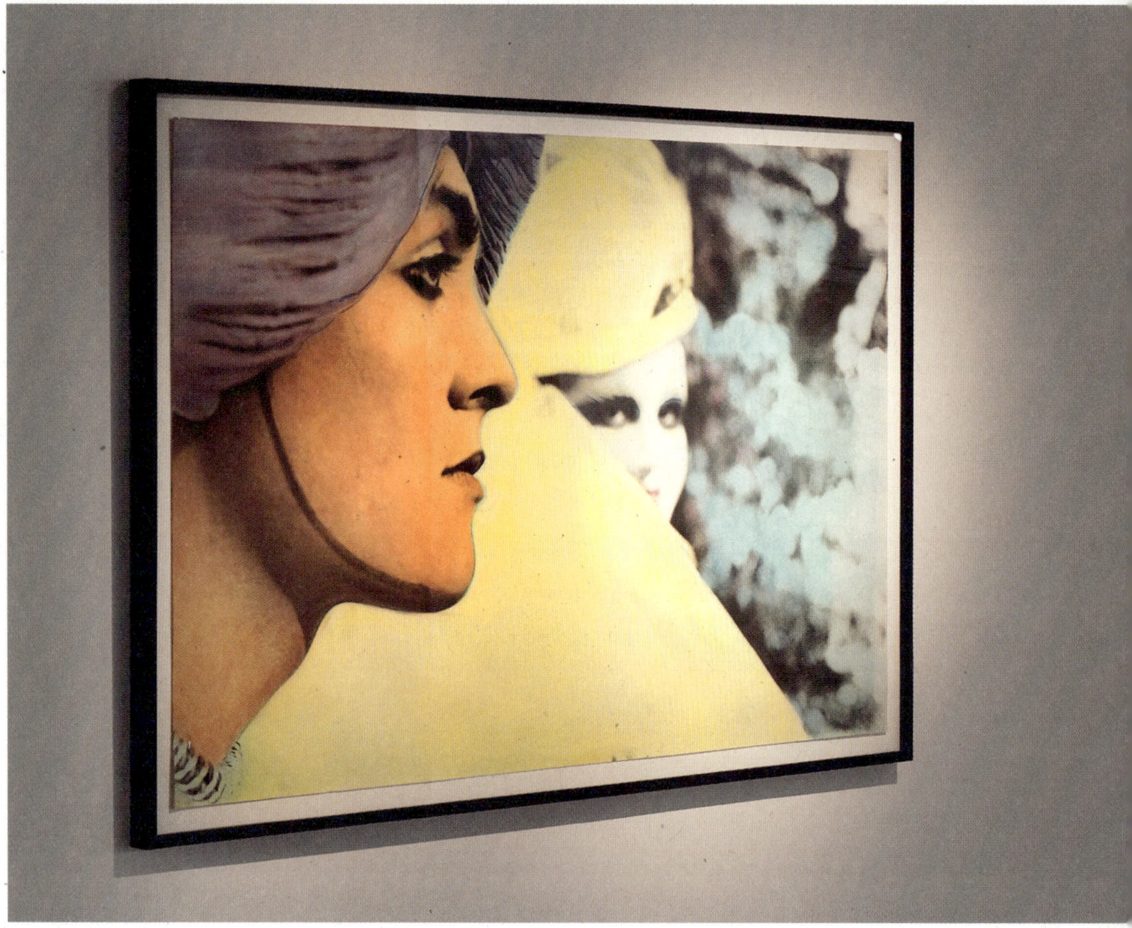

Twenty years later, Triangle France is still based in La Friche la Belle de Mai and faithful to its DNA. The organisation runs an internationally renowned residency programme with high quality studios, accommodation, as well as an ambitious curatorial programme of exhibitions, events, and publications. In a French institutional landscape where National Museums are a dead zone for young curators (permanent employment is essentially accessible only to state employees), and where art centres and FRACs are called institutions, one can wonder about the long term position of an organisation with an alternative identity: how can we evolve and stay true to our core values when we are funded by exactly the same public entities as any other French art centre? What does it mean after twenty years of existence when we are operating under the same bureaucratic laws and subjected to the same pressure as any other art institutions? Also, the short-term format and the emphasis on process of the original workshops, as well as the artists' need for exchange and mobility, have to now be re-evaluated in light of the Internet era. Early on, in 1995,

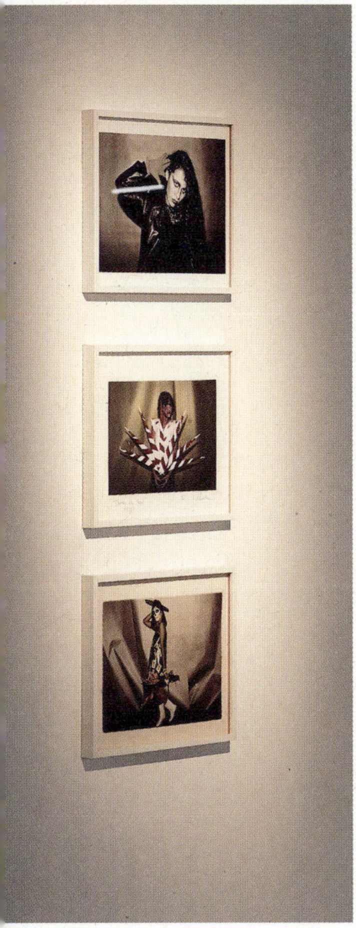

← **Asco and Friends: Exiled Portraits**
Triangle France
8 March – 6 July 2014
WORKS CLOCKWISE, L–R: Patssi Valdez, ***Cyclona and Victor Herrera***, 1980, courtesy of the artist; Ricardo Valverde, ***Dia de los Muertos (Paper Fashion Show) with Diane Gamboa***, 1983; ***Lotería de los Muertos***, 1983/1993; ***Teresa de Paper (Paper Fashion Show)***, 1982/1991, all courtesy of Esperanza Valverde and Christopher J. Valverde.
Photograph by Aurélien Mole

↓ ***Asco, Decoy Gang War Victim***, 1974, photograph by Harry Gamboa, Jr.
Asco and Friends: Exiled Portraits
Triangle France
8 March – 6 July 2014
Courtesy of Harry Gamboa, Jr.
Photograph by Aurélien Mole

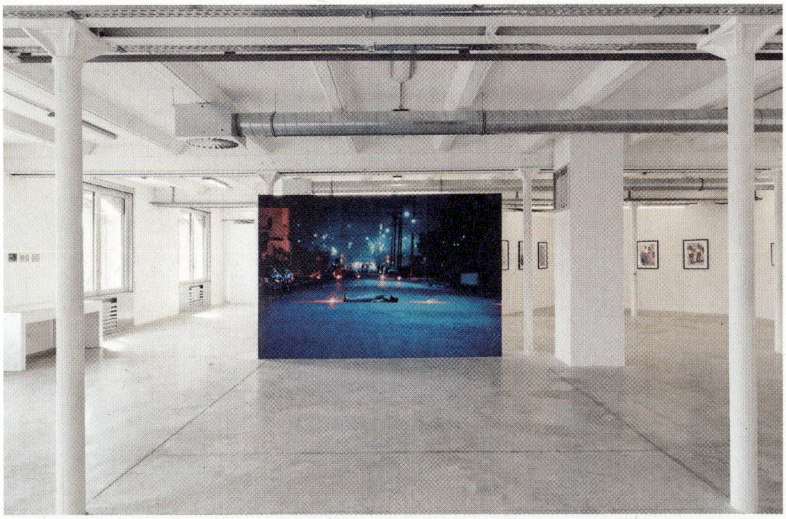

the funders of Triangle France made the decision to involve a curator to lead the organisation. As artists, they favoured their presence within the organisation's board and presidency and chose to collaborate with young curators to avoid what AA Bronson famously called "the humiliation of the bureaucrat". Thus, they could stay away from practical contingencies while being involved in discussing the vision of the organisation, focusing on ethics and development. Consequently, curatorial experimentation and an affirmed proximity between artists and curators have been an important part of the original profile of Triangle France.

Maybe, rather than entering a rabbit hole in search of an ideal alternative format (sometimes at the cost of content), the success of an artist-run space should be judged for what it accomplishes rather than for the structural model and original statement it follows. What does "alternative" mean? The generic idea of the perfect artist-run space that seems to prevail today is something where structure and activities display a perfect alternative to the power inequities of the art world: it operates outside the market; it is an alternative to institutions; it is independent from local politics while publicly funded; it avoids bureaucracy; it is outside the main centres; it is not an instrument of gentrification; it supports local artists while also being part of a peer network on the global scale; it is happy, desirable, the programme is amazing and diverse, and it operates beyond pyramidal forms of decision making — a sort of mythical animal that one can never really see in its entirety. And it lives near the Fountain of Youth. Never changing, staying forever young.

Time is a major element that is too often forgotten. Can an artist-run space become adult? When time is actually acknowledged within the original statement of an artist-run space, it is generally to underline the preconceived end-point of the project's lifespan. An example could be *ESL | Esthetics as a Second Language*, a great project created in the mid 2000s in Los Angeles by artists Mario Garcia Torres, Nate Harrison and Hugo Hopping. The initiative aimed to create a discursive space for socially motivated artworks through a migratory series of one-day exhibitions and events (10 artists, 10 one-day projects, every month over 10 months). It was funded by donations from other artists, and the end of the project was announced up front. It was highly successful both in terms of content, intergenerational participants, financial independence, and as a comment on the energy and commitment needed to maintain the existence of such initiatives. Too often, a point is reached where a project succumbs to inertia and an organisation loses its reason for existing, only existing to exist. When it is not only fed by pure energy and will, but also funded and a source of employment (as in the case for Triangle France), it seems that there is a risk to become an institution in the worst meaning of the term: something that only feeds its structure and aims at surviving. Compromise is the gateway to inertia. However, there is a difference between evolution and compromise.

↗ 0,00€ – A project by Jean-Alain Corre
Anne Bourse, ***Croissant***, 2013
Rue Espérandieu – 13001 Marseille
27 April – 19 May, 2013
Photograph courtesy of the artist

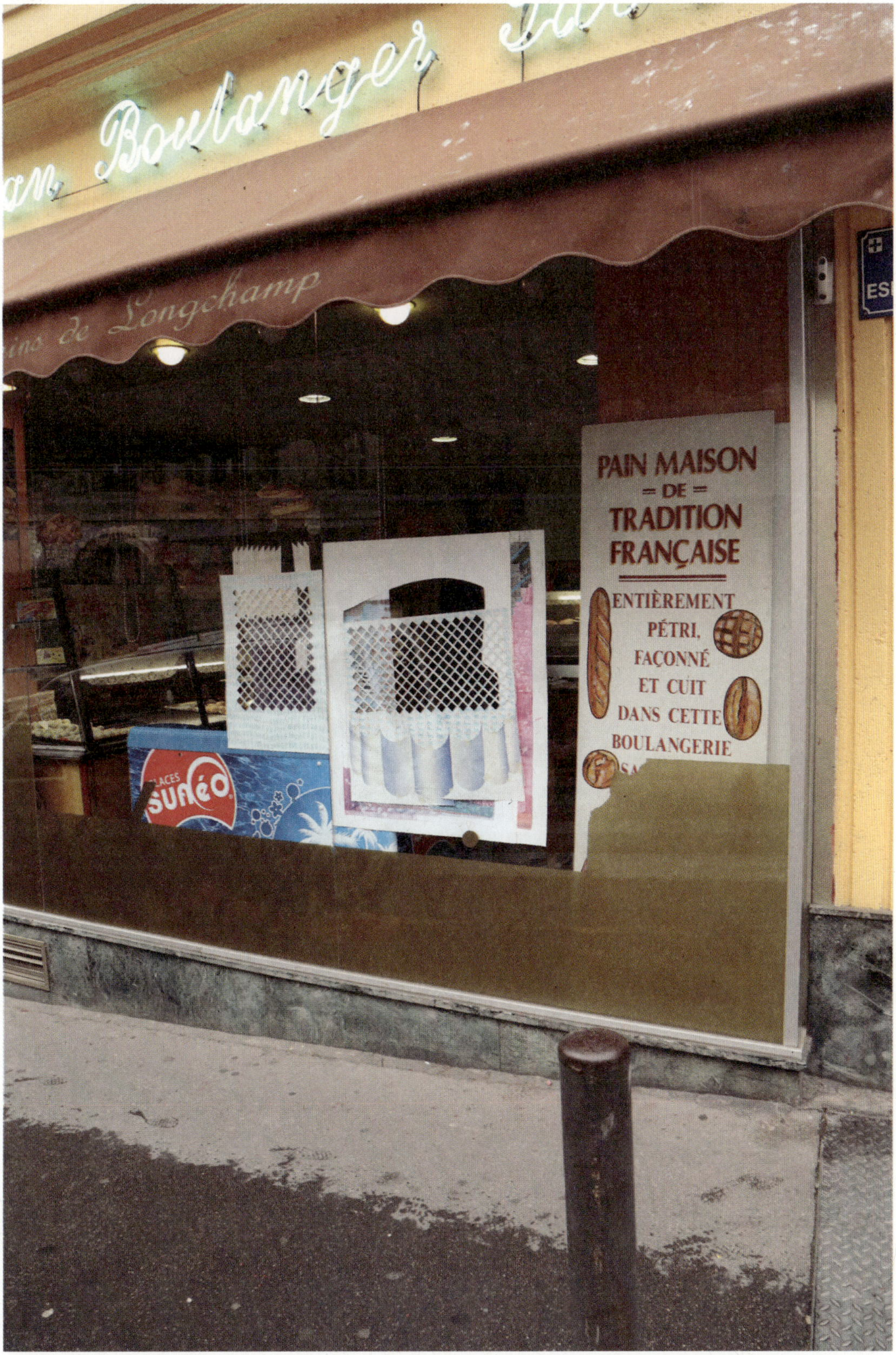
Boulanger
de Longchamp
PAIN MAISON
DE
TRADITION
FRANÇAISE
ENTIÈREMENT
PÉTRI,
FAÇONNÉ
ET CUIT
DANS CETTE
BOULANGERIE

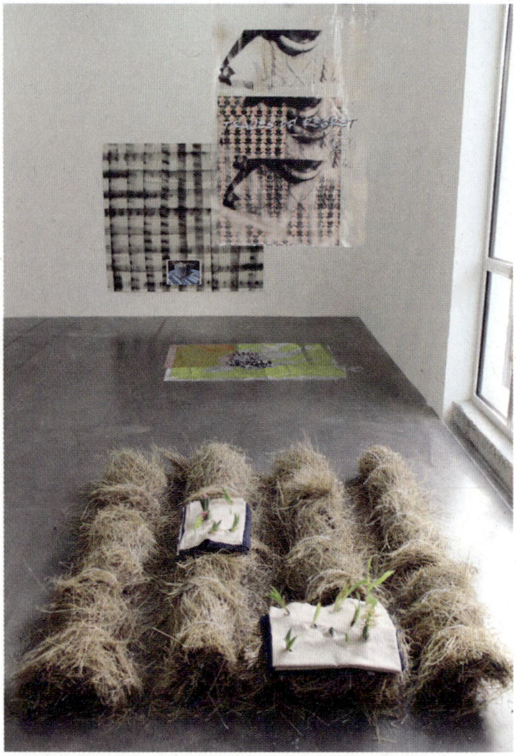

← **Les Drames 3D grillagés**
Benjamin Blaquart, Kevin Gallagher et Camilla Wills
4 April – 3 May 2015
Triangle France
Detail of works by Camilla Wills (from foreground to background): ***Combusted Scarecrow / Saint Sebastian / new life***, 2015; ***Went back into this, its shows regret. Analogy: like returning into a room after saying bye, reveals a lack of resolve***, 2015; ***Carrier of a mood***, 2015
Photograph courtesy of the artist and Gaudel de Stampa, Paris. Production Triangle France

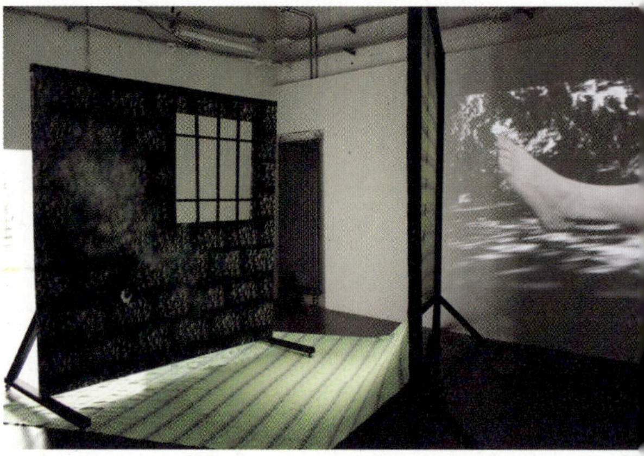

Triangle France passed the twenty-year mark and is actively thinking about what it means to grow up, about its commitments and role, locally, nationally and internationally. It does not necessarily mean more square metres, more money or people (although money rarely hurts initiatives like ours). It is a matter of experience, a capacity to read our original mission, and adjust its format and activities to the current context. It needs to be right and tuned to the artists it supports. The project leads the way, and what was right at the specific moment always needs to be reevaluated. Supporting artists is our fundamental mission. Passing the twenty-year mark also means that the need for Triangle France's existence never faded, and was passed on: studios, critical answers to the work, providing networks, exchanges, opportunities, exhibitions, events, publications. Let's be honest: a structure like ours never really risked falling asleep because of too much comfort.

In our current context, we are more than ever committed to our residency programme. Like workshops, residencies are one of the toughest activities to fund. Research, experimentation and the need for closed doors are not a fashionable object to explain to funders, for whom it is easier to think that one can visit an artist in a studio like a zoo. A studio is a place of intimacy, work, and reflection. A residency is a time where works might not be ready for a public life and where artists might need to be left alone. It takes a lot of commitment to maintain a residency programme. New models of public programmes have to be conceived of with respect to an ethical vision of residencies, not obligating artists to do something else other than thinking and making their works. Similarly, one of our hardest commitments to maintain is the open call; because residencies are so complex to fund, an easy answer is to get funding where it is available, and turn towards national programmes of cultural exchanges.

More and more residencies are based on nationality and are exclusive to artists originating from countries with the resources or the philanthropic tradition for such programmes. Each year, Triangle France receives more than 300 applications originating from about 40 different countries. Selection is based on the quality of the work only and often brings artists to Marseille who would never be able to come otherwise. Triangle France is actively part of "Arts en Résidence", the French national network of residency programmes, writing guidelines and providing tools for an ethical vision of such programmes. Our understanding of residencies, values research and process, and is not necessarily linked to an exhibition opportunity. Sometimes it takes several years to push the work and offer the perfect conditions for its public debut. Time, again, against the logic of funding prevails.

← Benjamin Blaquart
The Pilgrim, ver. 0,90, 2015
HD video, wood, polyester resin, laser print, textile, paint, variable dimension
Les Drames 3D grillagés
4 April – 3 May 2015
Triangle France
Photograph courtesy of the artist.
Production Triangle France

What we are actually trying to communicate on a faster pace is the urgency for a better defence of the artists' economy. Today in France, like in many other countries, artists are rarely paid for their projects and exhibitions. While larger institutions should set the example, it is unfortunately not happening and artist-run spaces like Triangle France have to take on that role. Even if amounts end up being symbolic, the importance is equity and regularity: no exceptions, whether young or established. We also accompany our young residents and help them set their paperwork straight and understand tax laws and status. Organisations like W.A.G.E. have no equivalent in France and curators have no official status either.

One question to ask when looking at alternative models and artist-run spaces also concerns the audience: who is it for? A lot of artist initiatives are devoted to avant-garde practices and essentially to a peer audience, leaving public programmes and education to institutions. However, when looking at models that have reached a certain duration, it seems that the question of a general audience is (or had to be) acknowledged. Is a consciousness of the public what separates independent artists' initiatives to more established art centres? Obviously the answer is a lot more complex than that sentence, but in France, an organisation cannot join the national network of art centres (DCA) without having developed a specific vision and politics towards its public, and having at least one position in their organisation chart essentially devoted to this mission. In the end, it is a matter asking what guidelines must be kept in mind when conceiving of public programmes and interpretations of projects. While the audience needs regular schedules,

→ Allison Gibbs
Our Extra-Sensory Selves: A development Circle for Radical Subjectivity
4 weekly sessions, 18 November – 9 December 2014
Triangle France
Production Triangle France

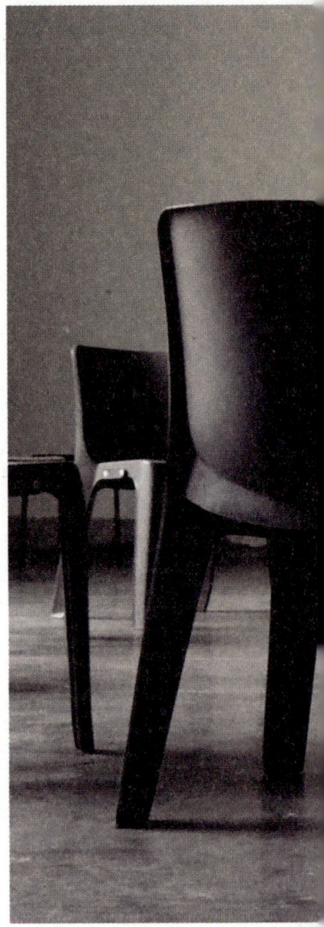

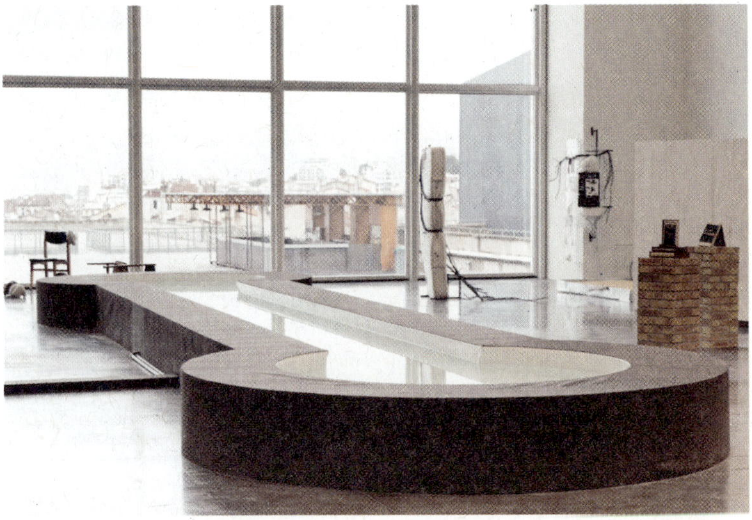

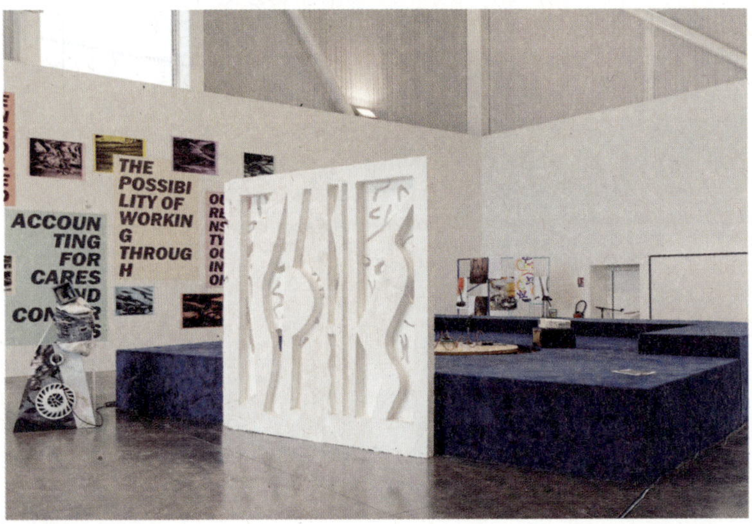

Moucharabieh
Exhibition views
13 February – 19 April 2015
Triangle France
Photograph by Aurélien Mole

↖ Centre installation by Clémence Seilles, ***Moucharabieh***, 2015, Courtesy Torri, Paris

← Works by L–R: Mónica Restrepo, Jean-Alain Corre, Clémence Seilles, Lina Viste Grønli, and Gail Pickering

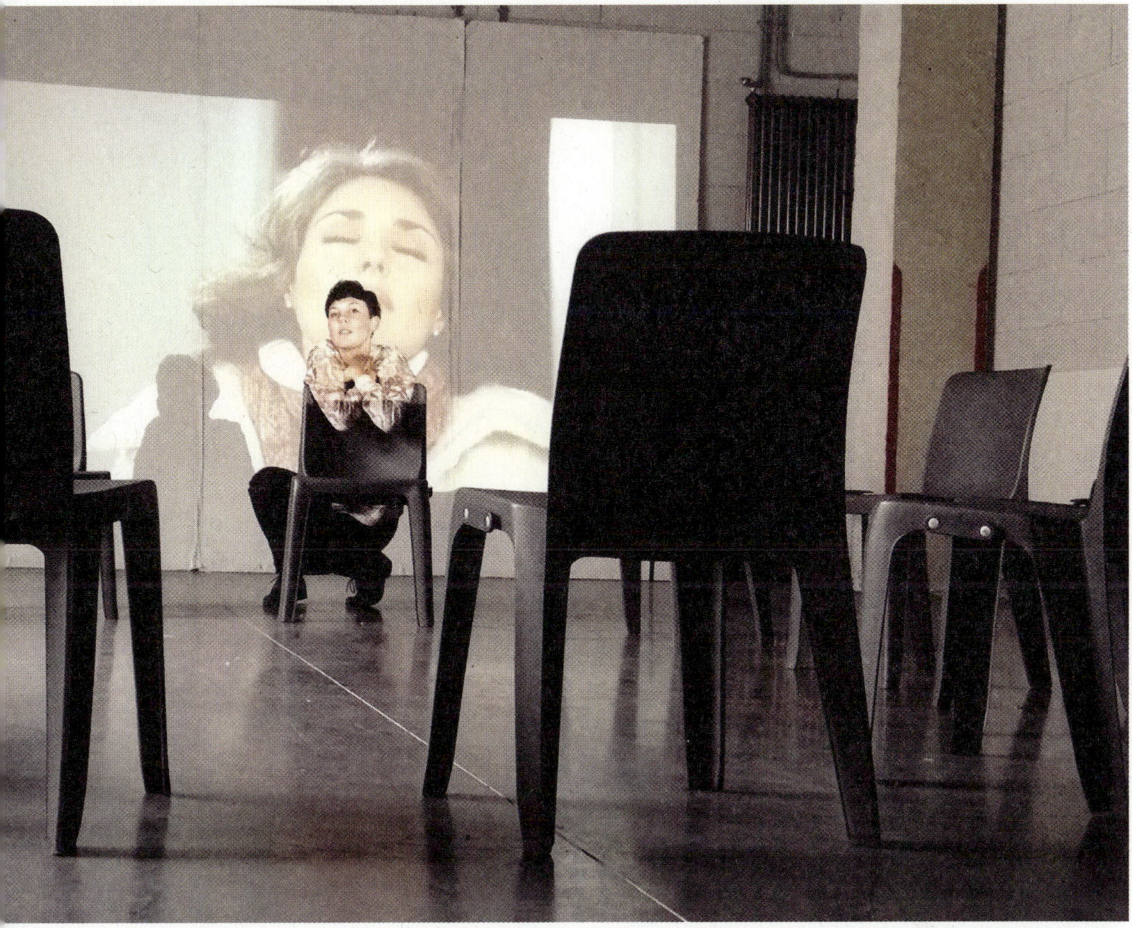

CÉLINE KOPP & ALUN WILLIAMS

formats have to be adapted to each project, and be developed together with the artists whenever this is an area of interest for them, or even a place of extension for the project itself. Being conscious of public life in what is shown and done in an artist-run space does not mean it will stop being a place of critical exchange and discussion amongst peers.

Since the beginning of the Triangle Network in the 1980s, there has been a awareness of diversity and a desire to connect people outside of the western art world and the main art centres. This is still very much part of what is done today. Over the past decades, Triangle France has been heavily involved in a feminist, or even a womanist approach to programming. Currently we conceive of our exhibition programme with the endeavour of not replicating the patterns of the global art world where the same emerging artists get invited fromart centre to art centre. We enable emerging or under-represented artists to make significant steps and pursue important new directions in their practice through new production and critical presentation of their past works. New commissions, exhibitions, events and publications ought to pursue an intergenerational vision, to push new narratives and diverse voices.

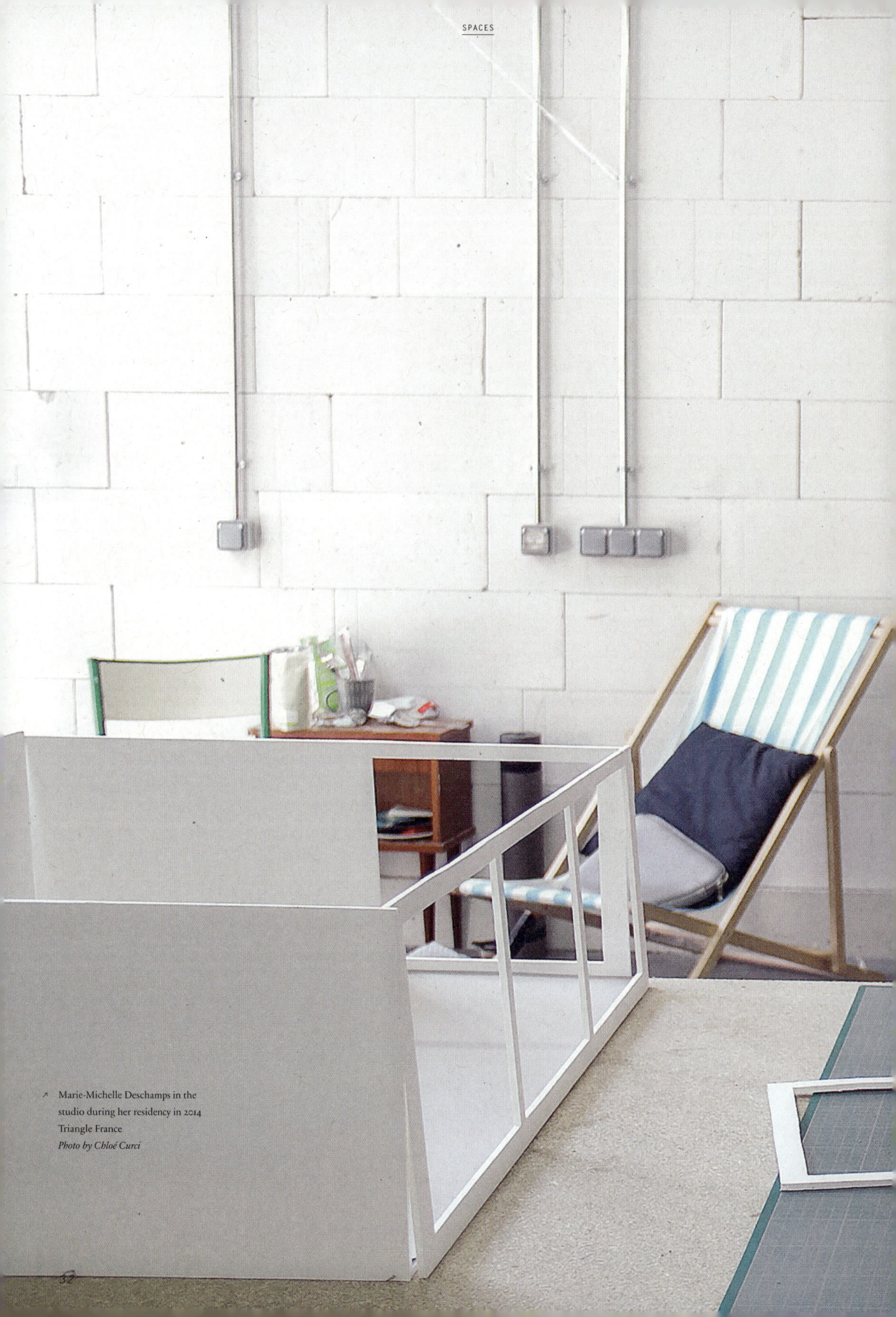

↗ Marie-Michelle Deschamps in the studio during her residency in 2014 Triangle France
Photo by Chloé Curci

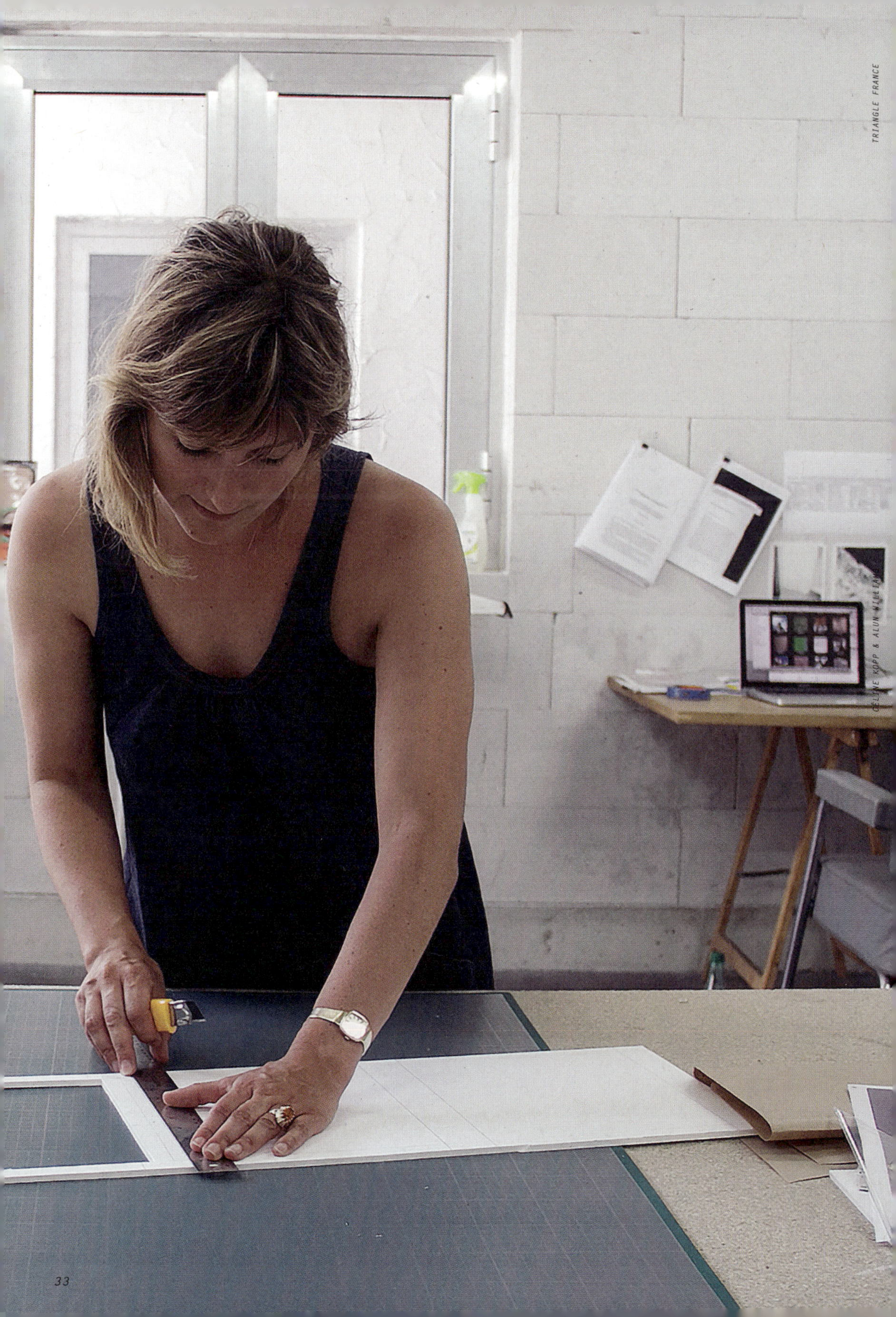

CÉLINE KOPP & ALUN WILLIAMS

NAME
Catalyst Arts / FIX Live Art Biennale

LOCATION
Belfast, Ireland

WEBSITE
www.catalystarts.org.uk

YEAR
1993–Present

STRUCTURE
Artist-led, members-based organisation run voluntarily by a board of co-directors

LEGAL STATUS
Company limited by guarantee and a registered charity

TEAM
Between 4–10 co-directors (part-time), volunteers

MISSION
To advance and support the careers of national and international contemporary artists in Belfast and Northern Ireland through onsite exhibitions at Catalyst Arts Gallery, offsite projects, residencies and exchanges, critical resources, networking and international opportunities

CORE FUNDING
Primary public funding from Arts Council of Northern Ireland, Belfast City Council, British Council & AIVCNI Volunteer fund. Project funding from trusts and foundations, and income generation through fundraising events, membership, donations with occasional sponsorship

PREMISES
Commercial lease, private landlord & estate agent, subsidized by Arts Council Northern Ireland

SELECTED PROJECTS
Transmission in Belfast (1993), Exchange Resource (1995), Art Rebels (1996–2010), David Shrigley (1996), On the buses (1997), Cinilingus (2000), The Max Factory (2000), Precinct (2002), C-Zine (2004), David Sherry (2006), Fata Morgana (2012), Underconstruction (2013), Wildscapes (2014), Amanda Beech (2014), OUTPOST EXCHANGE (2015), Artist-at-Sea (2015) FIX International Live Art & Performance Biennial (1994–2015)

Catalyst Arts is an artist-led organisation based in Belfast, Northern Ireland. Since its inception by a multidisciplinary collective of the same moniker, a relentless current of co-directors, artists, members, friends, family, and community of contributors have helped build a reputation as a space which embraces experimentation and artistic risk, through its gallery programme, public projects, commissions, the pioneering *FIX* – one of Europe's longest running live art and performance biennials – and various accompanying printed projects. An early exchange with Transmission in Glasgow led to the organisation becoming constituted in 1994, gaining charitable status and allowing it to pursue funding for its programme. This was a seminal step, integrally changing the means by which Catalyst could continue to provide resources and opportunities to artists and members. Following on from its statement of commitment to remain a valve for creative output in Belfast, a relentless relay of overlapping committees continued to get involved on a rolling two-year basis, managing every aspect of the organisation as a collective to deliver the programming.

To allude to the folklore of its murky beginnings in the early 90s through to present day, as it always has a mutable, mythical idea, too slippery to define, passed on by way of storytelling, repeating its mistakes and propelled by

...ART'S FEAR OF ART
(artifobia, artefobia) claustrophobia (closure, enclosure)
FEAR OF CLOSING
FEAR OF CLOSING THE MOUTH...[1]

Catalyst's ever-changing committee lent itself to a high-paced and multi-faceted programming output, and it quickly developed a community excited by their activations of the city: live events, gigs, screenings, dinners, readings and performances, offering a way private and public spaces could be accessed and altered through artistic use. Unsurprisingly, these affiliations as an aperture to hybridised underground culture were cemented through artist-led exchanges (Transmission in Belfast, 1993), public interventions (Exchange Resource, 1995), music (club curious), experimental film (Cinilingus, 2000; The Max Factory, 2000), punk publications (C-Zine, 2004), time capsules (Art Rebels, 1996–2010), solo shows for emerging new talents (David Shrigley, 1996; David Sherry, 2006), freewheeling tours (On the buses, 1997), residency opportunities (OUTPOST 2015; Artist-at-Sea, 2015), and its most enduring legacy, international live art and performance biennial FIX (1994–2015).

"FIX...I am thinking of why it seemed like...in the first place...Art and Research Exchange... Alastair MacLennan...you couldn't walk down a corridor... without tripping over some performance piece...a lot of the first directors... Síofra Campbell...opening up the possibilities... an experimental platform...this was going to

Essi Kausalainen
Tuning (Belfast), 2013
FIX 13
Image courtesy of the artist and Catalyst Arts

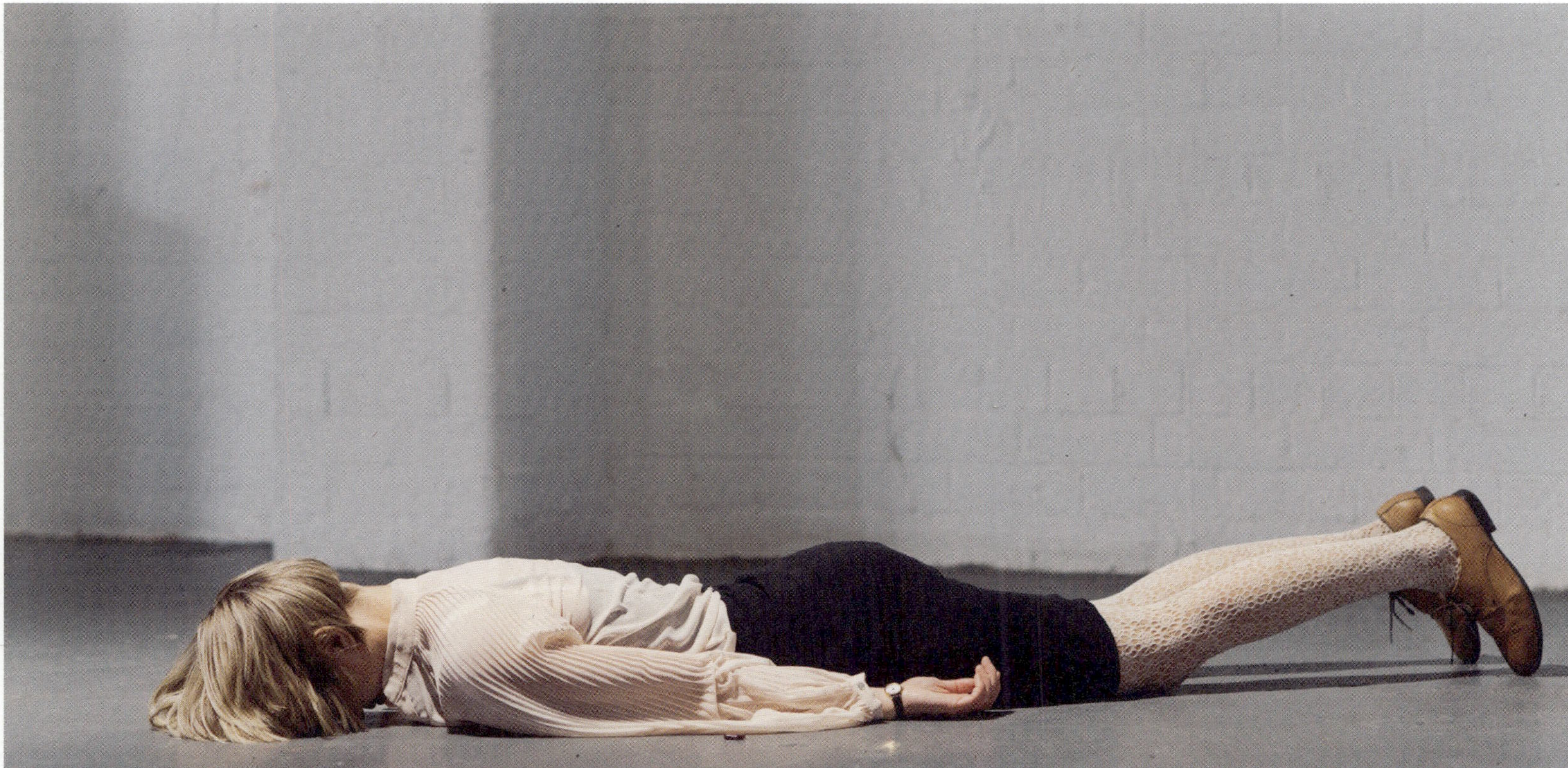

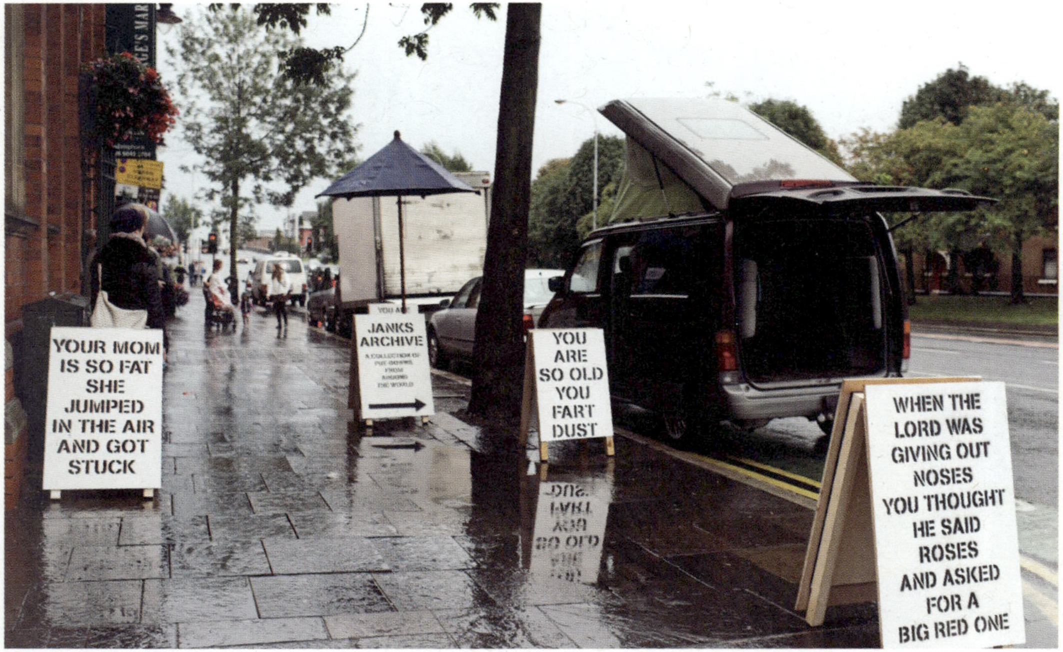

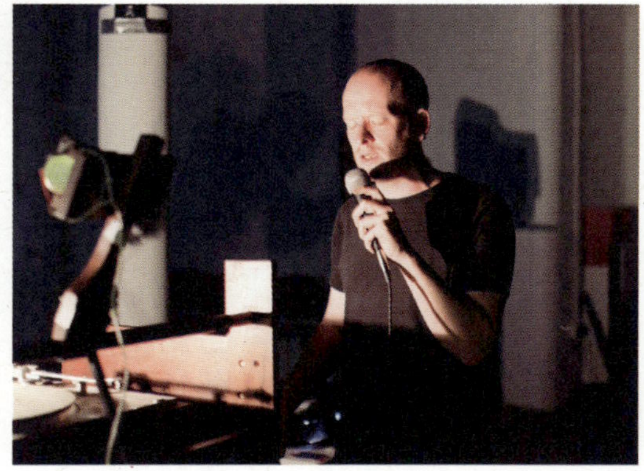

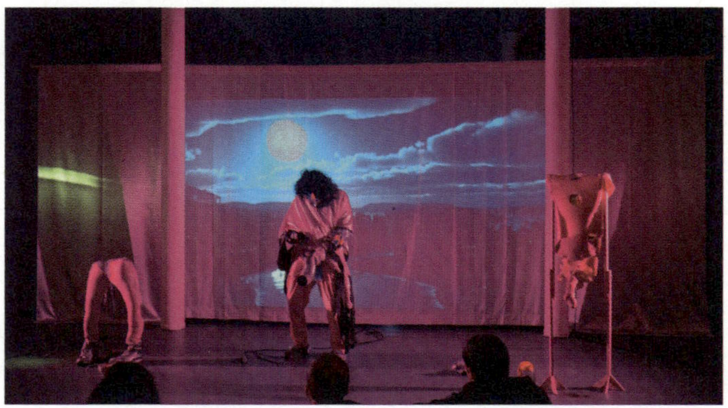

↑ Janks Archive
Belfast Connection, 2013
FIX 13
Image courtesy of the artist and Catalyst Arts

→ Cian Donnelly
Bleachbox, 2015
FIX 15
Image courtesy of the artist and Catalyst Arts

↑ Remi Voche
Nearby trees, 2013
FIX 13
Image courtesy of the artist and Catalyst Arts

↓ David Sherry
Total Crap, 2015
FIX 15
Image courtesy of the artist and Catalyst Arts

remedy the lack of…FIX…we used a red cross, first-aid style…I can see that the female sitting at the desk…Jennifer Dempsey…female … around the stones…Niamh O'Malley…images of the lit figure behind the polythene curtain… Theo was smoking and sawing the leg off his chair…Just like Catalyst itself…Club Curious… dreamt-up…[2]

Despite their inherent flexibility and resilience, all artist-led spaces are acutely aware of the precarious situation they operate under on an annual or even daily basis. None more so than Catalyst, where cautionary tales abound and we've made a pet of the wolf at the door. While the Catalyst archive remains the proof of its efforts, its memory is short and it will only be defined by what it continues to do. The defining feature of the artist-led space is its commitment to improving the conditions for art, artists and audiences when frustrated by a lack of opportunity. This refusal of complacency, inertia and apathy is at the root of every Catalyst project, no more evident than in the spirit of FIX – now in its 21st year of celebrating live art and performance – seeming to define all that has been great, experimental and exciting about why it all seemed like a good idea in the first place.[3]

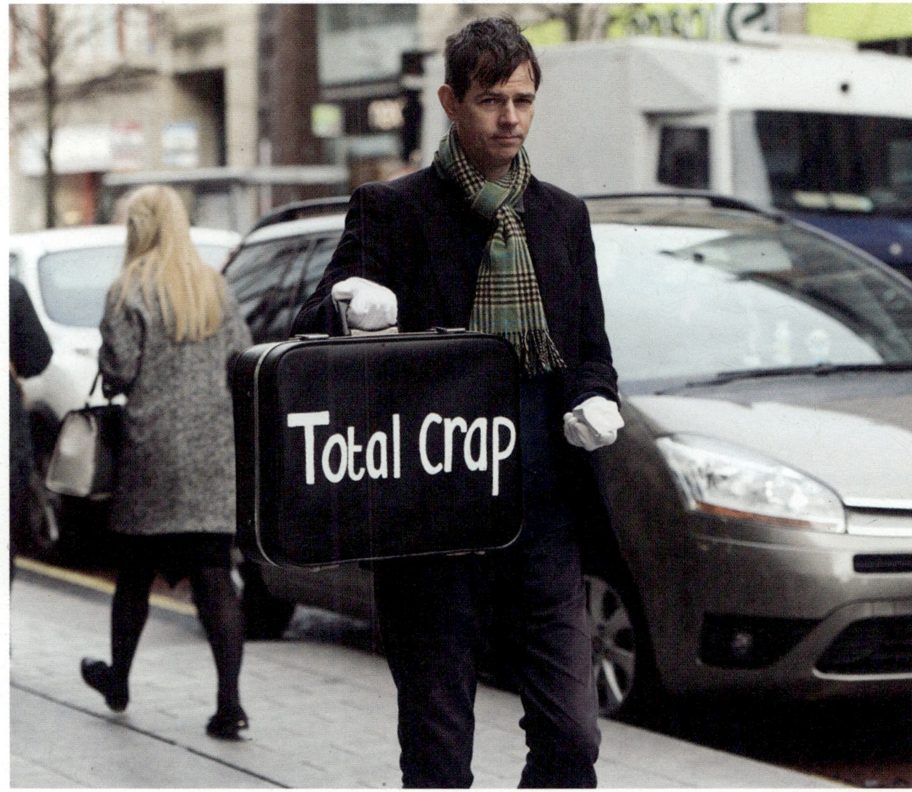

[1] Artur Tajber, 'DESOLAcTION', Performance, Exchange Resource, exhibition catalogue, 15th November 1995, (Catalyst Arts) Belfast
[2] Dougal McKenzie, (Catalyst Arts Co-director 1994–1996) excerpts from email correspondence with Catalyst Arts,' Memories of FIX' (August 2015) Belfast
[3] Ibid.

NAME
DIENSTGEBÄUDE Art Space

LOCATION
Zurich, Switzerland

WEBSITES
www.dienstgebaeude.com
www.artspaceguide.ch

YEAR
2008 to present

STRUCTURE
Artist-run space, collaboration with artists and curators

LEGAL STATUS
None (Operated by Andreas Marti alongside his art practice)

TEAM
Director: Andreas Marti, Assistants: Patrizia Mazzei, Sandra Schudel

MISSION
Promoting the young emerging art scene by realizing exhibitions, collaboration with artists, editing artists editions

FUNDING
City and County of Zurich, private funds, "Cari Amici" (Membership)

PREMISES
Private lease

SELECTED PROJECTS
Marianne Engel, Isabelle Krieg, Andreas Marti, Cat Tuong Nguyen, 2008 (inaugural exhibition); Bob Gramsma, 2010 (first solo show at DIENSTGEBÄUDE); Silvie Zürcher, *Hi, how are you*, 2011 (first show at new space); *Young British Art II*, 2012, curated by Ryan Gander; Pascal Schwaighofer, *Sketches for a Sundial*, 2012; Colin Guillemet, *Half full. Half empty.* 2014; Catch of the Year, 100 Artists / 100 Works, 2009 to present; Zurich Art Space Guide, guide for the independent art scene (Anne-Laure Franchette, Andreas Marti)

DIENSTGEBÄUDE Art Space is an artist-run space based in Zurich since September 2009. DIENSTGEBÄUDE is not organised as an artist group: it is a collaboration with invited artists and curators, with a small team directing, organising and connecting with the artists and offering a vibrant platform. A selection of artist editions has been edited since 2012.

The first exhibition took place in the former service building of the train company that the organisation's name comes from. Exhibiting artists were Marianne Engel, Isabelle Krieg, Andreas Marti and Cat Tuong Nguyen, some of whom had their studios in the same building. Over 200m² exhibition space was used to invite artists and curators to realize exhibitions, featuring both emerging artists as well as from established artistic positions. Directed by artist Andreas Marti, the independent art space became well-known in the local and national art scene, and the annual show 'Catch of the Year' – with one hundred invited artists – has become a well-known (and well-visited) exhibition. At the beginning of our activity we were one of five independent art spaces in Zurich. Today, seven years later, Zurich has an active independent scene with around 40 different spaces and small initiatives.

From September 2011 a new larger 250m² space with three exhibition spaces (140m², 70m², 25m²), and three artists' studios, was a new opportunity to continue the activity. The programme became more focused on solo exhibitions of young and emerging artists. Invitations to and participation in art fairs in Zurich, Stockholm, Athens and Warsaw gave DIENSTGEBÄUDE the chance to present our activity to an international audience. With exchange projects with other independent spaces (Piano Nobile, Geneva and Artpartment Hong Kong) and collaborations with some institutions (MASI Lugano) we gained new opportunities.

A collaboration with Anne-Laure Franchette and Andreas Marti, the Zurich Art Space Guide was launched for the first time in January 2014. A printed fold-out and website about independent projects in Zurich is an attempt to list an overview, to show their importance to the culture of the city and to make our activities more public.

Andreas Marti
slasdlalsflakdfgjalkdjglak, 2013
Installation view
18 July – 24 August 2013
Photograph courtesy of DIENSTGEBÄUDE

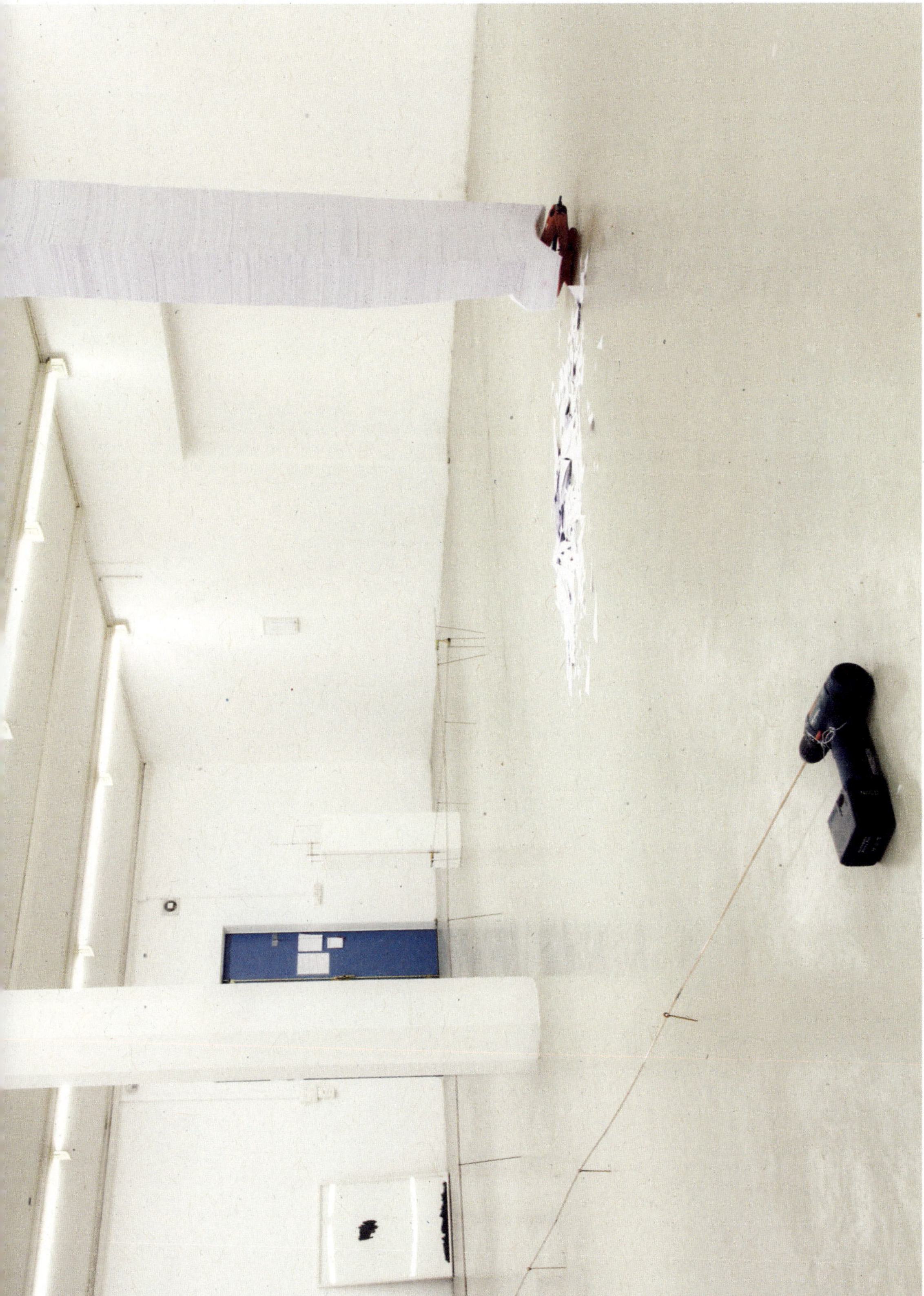

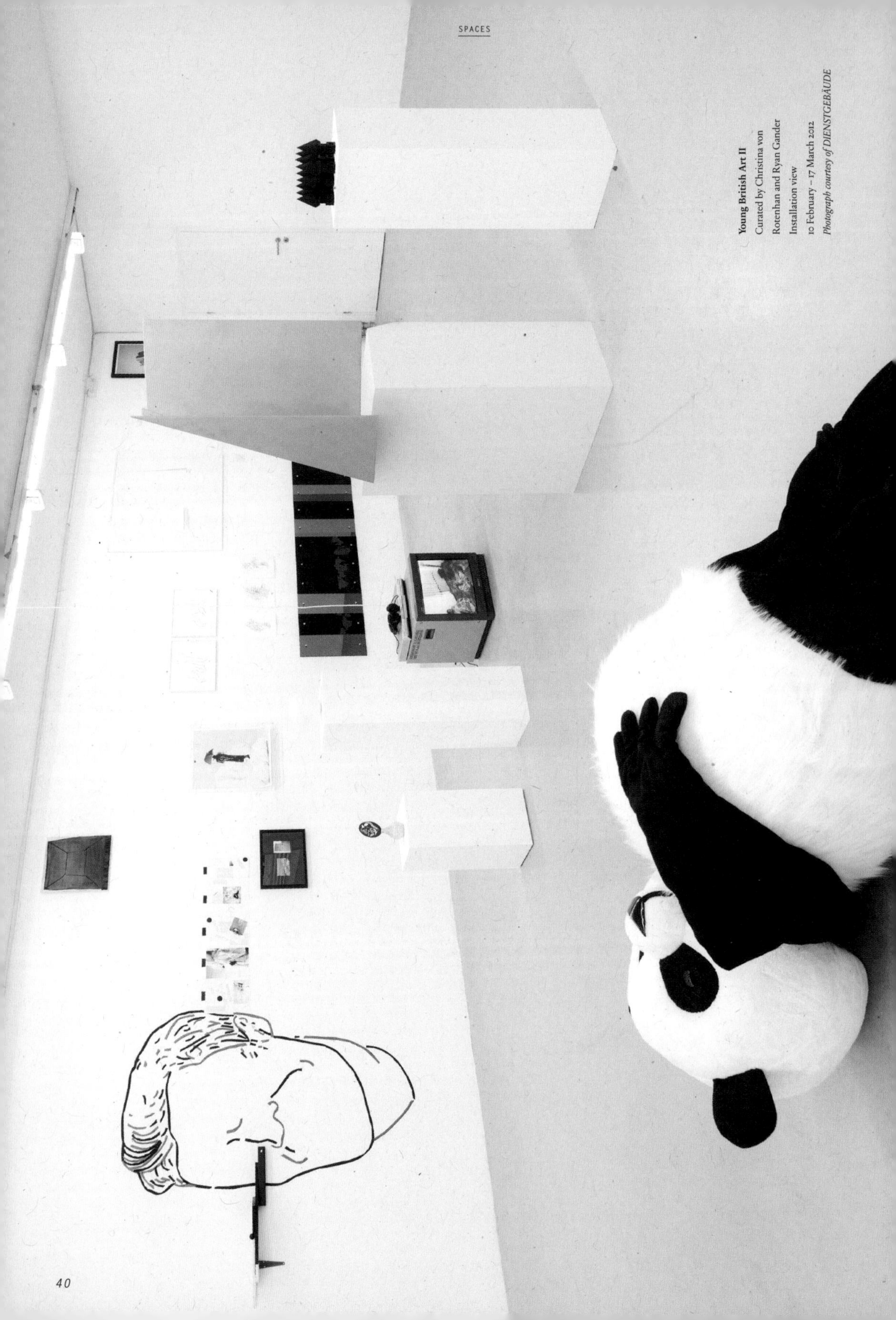

Young British Art II
Curated by Christina von Rotenhan and Ryan Gander
Installation view
10 February – 17 March 2012
Photograph courtesy of DIENSTGEBÄUDE

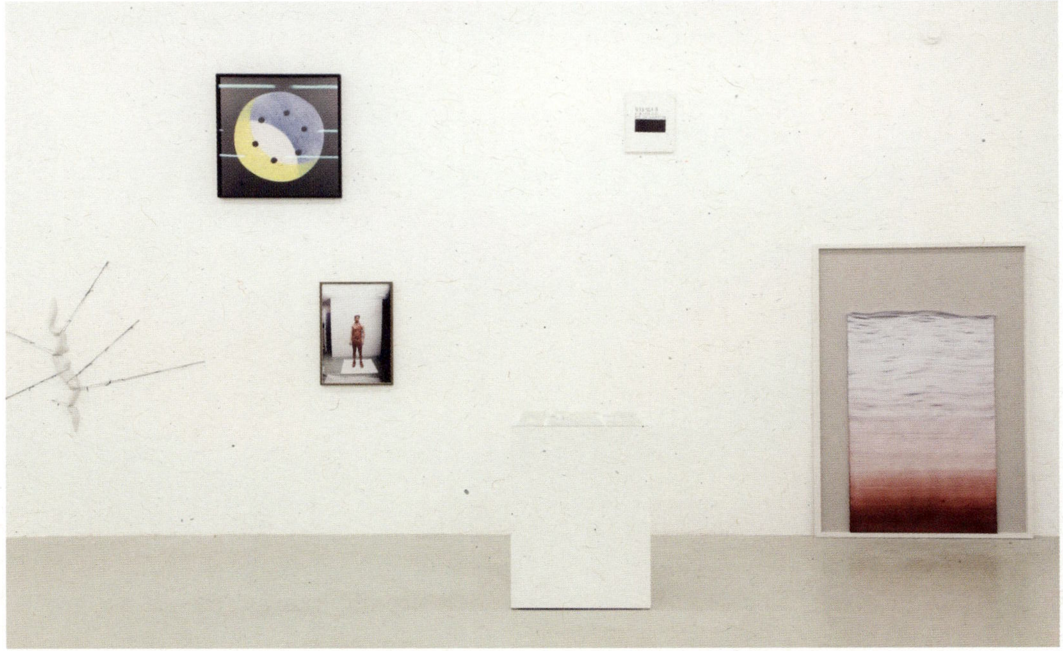

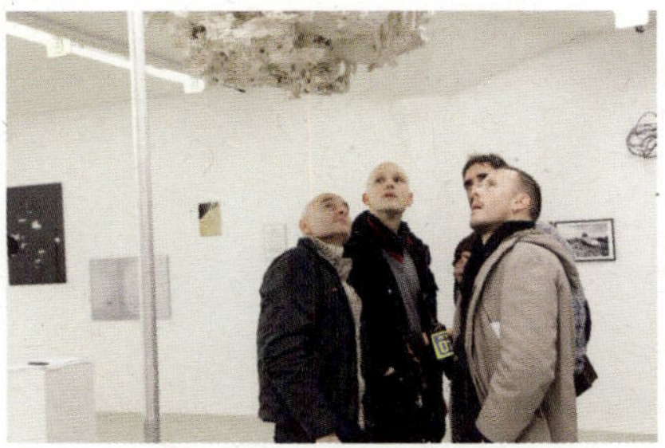

↑ **Catch of the Year,** 2014
100 Artists / 100 Works
29 November 2014 – 24 January 2015
Photograph courtesy of DIENSTGEBÄUDE

← **Catch of the Year,** 2012
100 Artists / 100 Works
Opening
Photograph courtesy of DIENSTGEBÄUDE

NAME
Pink Cube

LOCATION
Oslo, Norway

WEBSITE
www.pinkcube.no

YEAR
2011 to present

STRUCTURE
Artist-run, non-profit organisation, voluntary

LEGAL STATUS
Incorporated as part of artist Anja Carr's practice and one-person company

TEAM
1 permanent artistic-director-curator, guest-curators, assistant and volunteers

MISSION
PINK CUBE is a pink artist-run space dedicated to offer an alternative to the sterile white cube and its inherent power structures, with a better gender balance and a flat structure. Situated first at Grünerløkka and later at Grønland, Oslo until 2016, it is now a nomadic space, with the possibility of traveling to different venues and countries with its unique wall-paint

FUNDING
Arts Council Norway and
The Municipality of Oslo,
The Agency for Cultural Affairs

OTHER FUNDING
Pink Cube has previously received grants and support for individual projects from The Municipality of Bergen, Section for Arts and Cultural Affairs and Arts Council Norway

PREMISES
Commercial lease with private landlord, no subsidy

SELECTED PROJECTS
22 «battles» in the the battle-series (2011–to present)

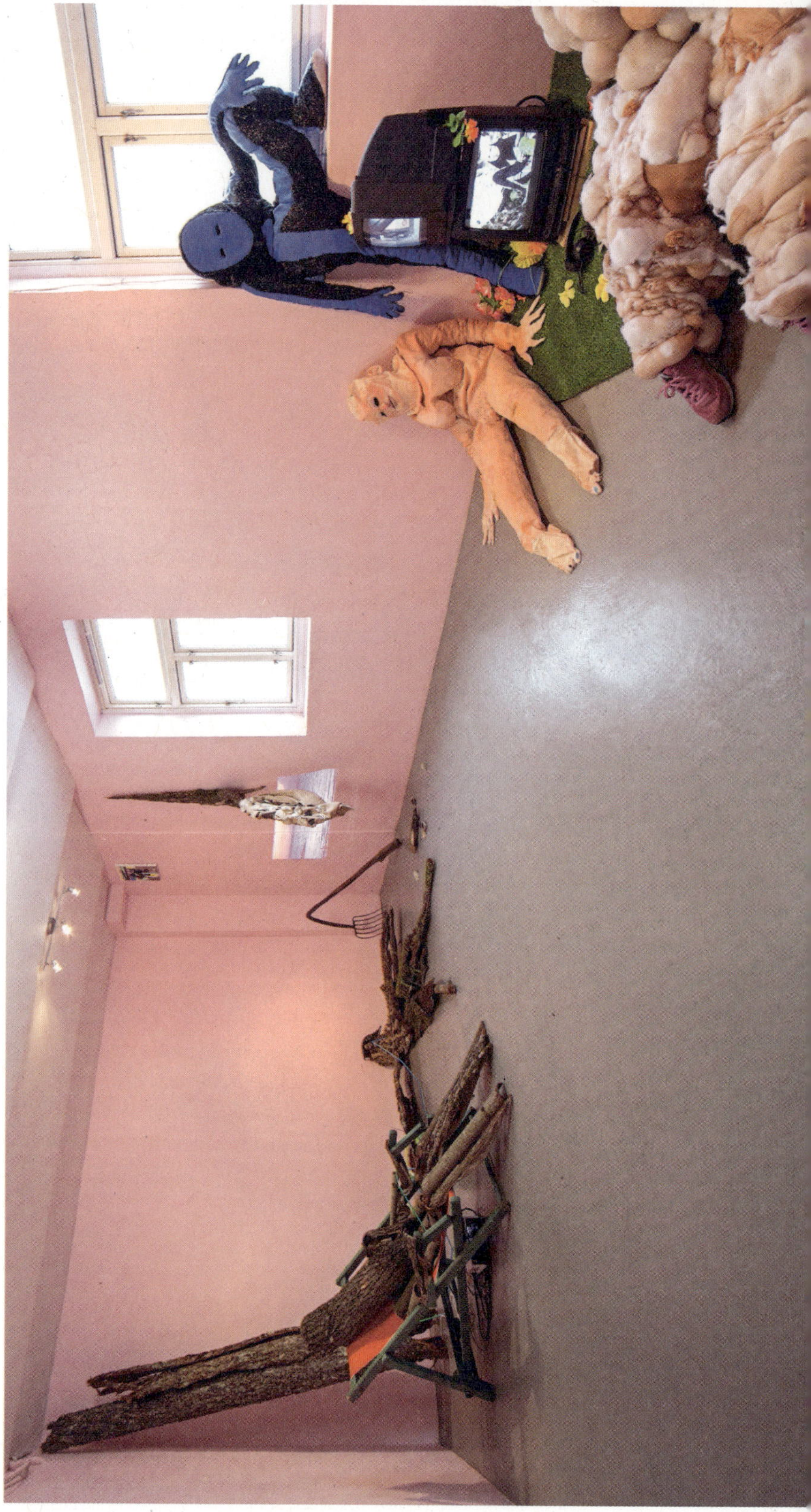

Pink Cube is an intimate, non-profit art space with a pink wall-paint containing body fluids. Artist and director Anja Carr started Pink Cube in January 2011 with an aim to create a space with a good gender balance that challenged the idea of the white cube as a neutral and ideal space for art. Unlike the commercial «shopping-window galleries» Pink Cube's entrance is located in a backyard in the neighborhood of Grønland, central Oslo, up some stairs and through a labyrinth of corridors. The body fluids on the walls, and the fact that finding the entrance is an adventure in its own right, underlines Pink Cube's focus on the physical experience of the events and the space: the bodily experience and the live situation as opposed to the more common experience of art today – through a computer screen. The inclusion of body fluids also points to the history of performance art and the French philosopher Julia Kristeva's idea of «the abject» (what lies between the subject and the object), while the pink colour represents another continuation of Carr's own art production, where the vulnerable distinctions between genders – as well as the child and adult spheres – are among the core interests.

All the exhibitions at Pink Cube are art-battles between two artists(-groups). This duel-format aims to boost fruitful artistic dialogue across genres and generations, and gives artists the opportunity to test their artistic strengths in a new way. The battle-exhibitions usually last 1–3 weekends and include up-and-coming as well as established artists working with all kinds of media; for Battle #11 Janna Thöle-Juul filled the space with 2 tonnes of hay, and for Battle #13 Bård Ask created paintings containing sperm. Previous battles include artists from Norway, Sweden, Denmark, Australia, Israel, Brazil, Scotland, Canada, Germany and the USA. For each battle Carr invites artists that have some common interests, but can challenge each other in different ways. The planning and the mounting of the works is a collaboration between the director and the exhibitors. A group of 4–6 artists work as volunteers at the event openings.

By the end of 2015 there has been 20 art-battles at Pink Cube and the space has gained a great deal of attention from national newspapers, magazines, journals and television, as well as international press like *Dazed and Confused* Magazine (UK), *Frieze* Magazine (UK), *Måg* Magazine (UK), *La Monda* Magazine (ES) and *Travel + Leisure* Magazine (NY). In 2012 PINK CUBE won the Oslo-prize for «Best art of the year» together with artists Unni Askeland (NO) and Tommy Olsson (SE) for Battle #8. For the 2014 programme Pink Cube had a special focus on live-performance and invited two co-curators: Maaike Gouwenberg (NL) and Charlotte Jansen (UK). Also in 2012 Pink Cube was part of Fredrikstad Independent Art Fair (NO), and in April 2015 Battle #18 took place at SUPERMARKET Stockholm Independent Art Fair (SE). The concept of the space can be moved as long as the walls are painted with the same unique pink paint.

↑ **Battle 19: Bakketun/Ballo/Norum** (NO) **vs. Brookman/White** (CO/IL)
Andrea Bakketun, Petter Ballo, Christian Tony Norum, Hannah Brookman, Becca White
3 – 12 July 2015
Pink Cube, Oslo
WORKS L–R: Performative installations with costumes by Bakketun/Ballo/Norum and Brookman/White
Photograph by Anja Carr

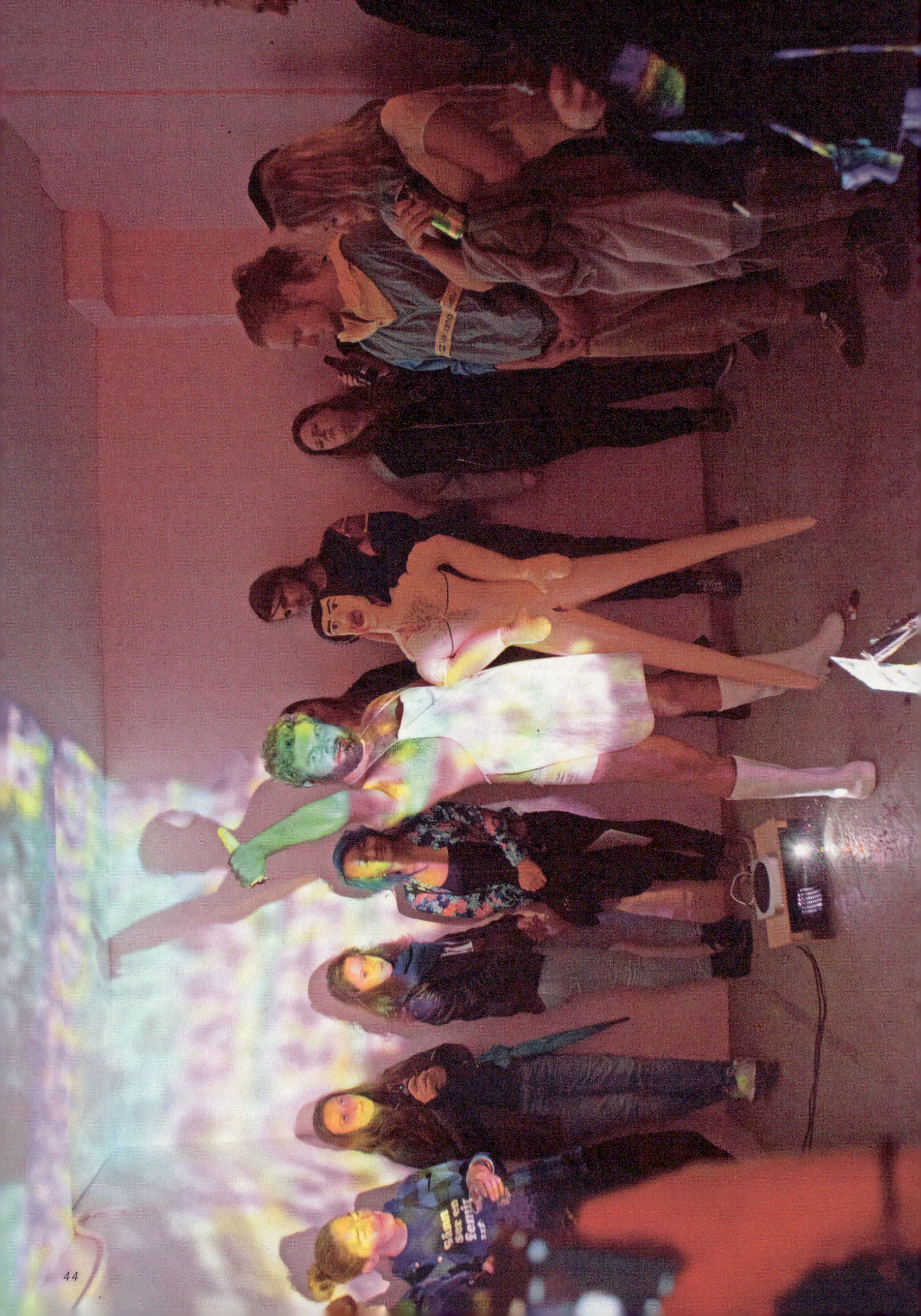

↓ **Exhibition poster**, 2015
Anja Carr
29.7 × 21 cm
Battle 18: Trollkrem (NO) vs. Kirsty Kross (AU)
SUPERMARKET – Stockholm Independent Art Fair 2015, Svarta Huset, Telefonplan, Stockholm
Image courtesy of the artist

↑ **Battle 16: Olivia Dunbar (CA) vs. Henrique Saidel (BR)**
Olivia Dunbar and Henrique Saidel
22 August – 7 September 2014
Pink Cube, Oslo co-curated with Maaike Gouwenberg (NL)
Live-performance by Saidel, video installation by Dunbar
Photograph by Anja Carr

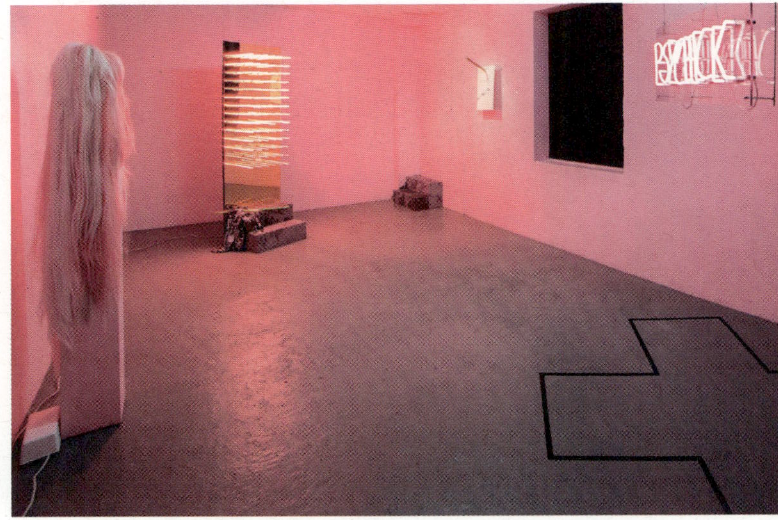

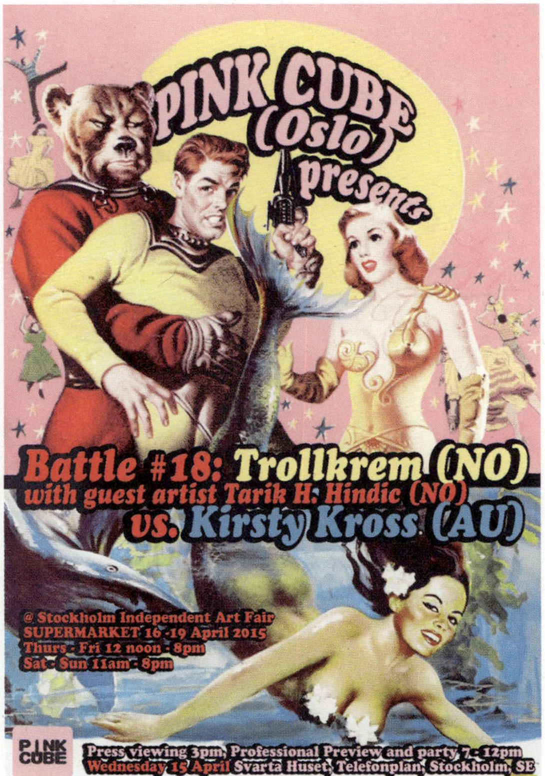

↑ **Battle 17: Josefine Lyche vs. Richard Øiestad**
Josefine Lyche and Richard Øiestad
30 January – 15 February 2015
Pink Cube, Oslo
Sound sculpture with hair by Lyche (left), neon-light-installations by Øiestad (middle) and Lyche (right)
Photograph by Anja Carr

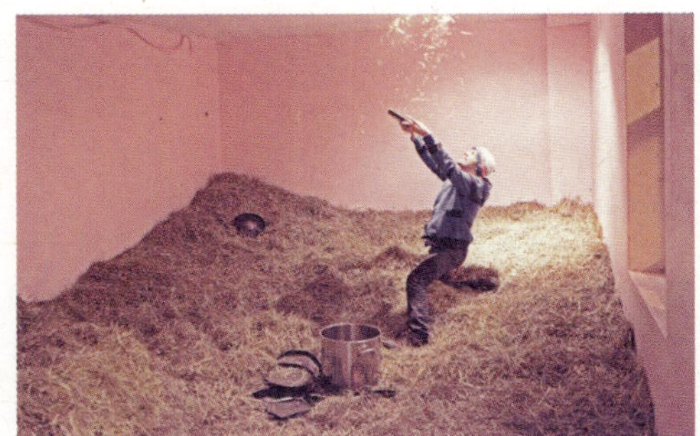

← **Battle 10: Janna Thöle-Juul (NO) vs. Fast Forward (NY)**
Janna Thöle-Juul (NO) and Fast Forward
2 – 4 November 2012
Pink Cube, Oslo
Interactive installation by Thöle-Juul, props from performance by Forward, audience interacting
Photograph by Anja Carr

Valerie Connor
'Brown Studies' and Artist-Led Enthusiasm

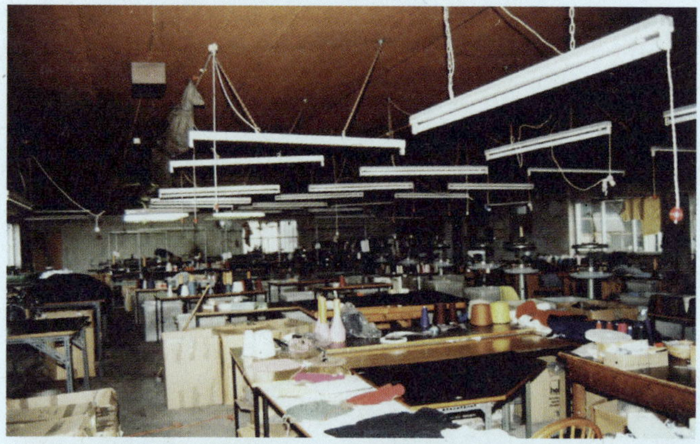

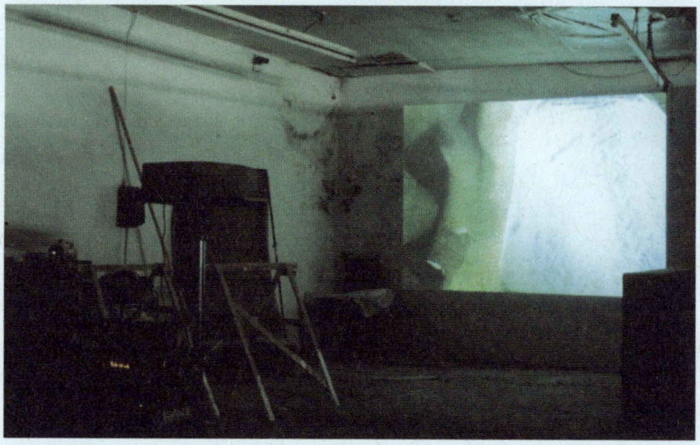

Photograph affixed to property viewing leaflet, Vincent Finnegan Ltd. Auctioneers, Valuers & Estate Agents, circa 1989
Courtesy of Valerie Connor/Blue Funk

work-seth/tallentire
trailer, 1998
Project Arts Centre, Off Site Programme, Pallas Studios, 4 December 1998
Photograph by Valerie Connor

Is 'artist-led' an assertion of artistic autonomy, or a pragmatic description of any self-organised activity by artists? What about the semantics of 'artist-driven' or 'artist-centred'? The latter usually a formal organisation not led or run by artists, but a mission to support artists in the production and presentation of art. In practice the artist-led, driven, centred and run work together as is the case with the Artist-Led Archive, a collection of ephemera and information about such initiatives in Ireland that is an artist-led project in itself, physically housed in an artist-centred collection.[1] More broadly, the structures and temporalities of the artist-led that are reflected in this book show how artists organise themselves, using examples from across Europe. In all cases self-identifying as artist-led must mean standing for something and standing apart. It is easy to assume that artist-led means not-for-profit, yet this may not be a part of such an initiative's actual or aspirational status. Functioning as a sign for all things artist, the studio is a culturally potent representation of the conditions that produce creative and cultural work, and informs the placing of this in hierarchies of need for fair and decent working conditions. The idea and image of the studio acts as a container of meaning and depicts the kind of life that is led by an artist, as well as the type of life that art will lead you into if you follow in its path. Isn't the studio, obviously, the archetype of the 'artist-led'?

2:00 Landshoff
+ still life of table
total failure
I was here waiting

[1] M. Morley, Artist-Led Archive, collection of the National Irish Visual Arts Library, NCAD, Dublin.

The four short lines above are from Eva Hesse's private papers, collected after her death. Writing about this personal note, art historian Kirsten Swenson has proposed it was most likely connected to an arrangement made with fashion and people photographer Hermann Landshoff, as the two did (at some point) make a set of photographs together in the mid-1960s in the artist's studio in New York[2]. In one, Hesse is horizontal on a daybed amid a number of items that have, like her, been arranged to camera. A table has been prepared. Small vessels, exhibition invite cards, photographs of sculpture, typed notes are spread like notation across and between the black lines of a squared-off grid underneath the paraphernalia. The objects and items are artworks by the artist herself and by friends. Hesse and Landshoff's mise-en-scène presents a set of relations to us that we can read as both signifiers of the art scene of which she was a part and a sign of her 'everyday', the daily living and working life of the artist. Outside, beyond the frame, through writing, movement and moving image, and so on, co-authorship, collectivity and collaboration were re-imagining the ownership of the culture, similarly made visible in workers and civil rights movements.

Looking at the photograph feels a lot like looking at a quite didactically styled exhibition; on show, an artist-led social system where artists' self-possession over what it is that they do is the primary organisational logic seen in the picture to make the photograph meaningful. Landshoff's photography for young women's fashion magazines at this time is notable for its naturalistic style and looser modeling techniques not typically associated with more static techniques from the photography studio. The photograph of Hesse that especially holds Swenson's eye has a metaphysical atmosphere that has something to do with a visual effect caused by the controlled placement and organisation of objects in the room: spatially, carefully placed; strange possessions. The artworks, ephemera and furniture, and even the optics of the photograph, look possessed; likewise, Landshoff's (unseen) invisible position in the room. However, the gaze of the positively self-possessed Hesse, lying with a pile of rope effortlessly gathered onto herself, could believably be the source of all the kinetic forces pictured. The rope could be keeping her from levitating off her couch. The same poltergeist zeitgeist is true of other photographs of Hesse, where we see details of part of a room and the artist holding and touching assorted things nearby. Enthusiastic, Hesse smiles.

Possession is a state of being that is sometimes attributed to the artist. This conjures up the most extreme melancholy and devotional stereotypes. But whereas possession is not so valued as relatable, social and useful, something like it is enthusiasm. Directly linked to the labours of devotion and melancholy, enthusiasm is the overt and extrovert tendencies of these contemplative practices; a pathology of

---

[2] K. Swenson, *Portrait of the Artist with Work: Eva Hesse* in Wouter Davidts & Kim Paice (Eds.), The Fall of the Studio, Amsterdam, Valiz/Antenna, 2009.

success in the sales arena but considered a dangerous aberration in the spiritual arena. A consideration of this condition might stimulate further understanding of the ontology of the artist-led today and produce some clues as to why it can seem hard to get a fix on its defining attributes.

At some level, Landshoff knew, or inadvertently reproduced in Hesse's appearance of idleness and happiness, a performance to camera that has an important commercial function in his work for fashion editorials. For one thing, the image breaks with the old chestnut of the artist at the precipice of deep introspection, simultaneously filled with fear and pleasure, once called the 'brown study'. And we have context: Hesse is part of a group of people, artists, working at the same time and around the same city and here she is organising to have herself photographed with their art objects, making the sociality of (these) artists visible; artists seeking to posses their own potentiality and control the realities of their art lives. It also introduces the viewer to images of work that look like leisure, or not work. This prefigures the appearance of the 'cognariat' labouring in the sharing economy and the instrumental use of down-time, for example, in adding value to oneself (through the curated consumption of digital media) and monetising of mass 'browsing' patterns. The cognitive work of the artist and the 'browser' are so alike. The brown study is 'off site', wireless, connected, socialised in commercial spaces fashioned with signifiers of community that individuals can cluster around.

Recent nostalgia for the imagery and sentiment of civil disobedience, embodied opposition and arts activism has blossomed in a period when enthusiasm is everything for the artist, social entrepreneur, media freelancer and independent cultural producer[3]. The work of enthusiasm is the 'affective labour' that sustains and reproduces core characteristics of the artist-led. "Hopeful signs" is how the setting up of a new art studio in Dublin is described in an Irish Times article in the collections at the National Irish Visual Arts Library (NIVAL). The artists leading this enterprise look forward to a future where, specifically, Dublin Corporation, the private sector and the Arts Council of Ireland can have an authentic experience of self-realisation by virtue of their patronage of the arts and care for the city centre of Dublin. Described by the artists interviewed as a place for the exchange of ideas and residencies with artists from other countries, the artists' intention and prediction for the new studio was that it would be the end of their struggle to beat the gallery system. Replying to a question about what will be catered for, the answer is the usual fine arts, plus weaving, etching, silk-screening – and photography. Who that has set up a shared or group studio in the last forty years could remain unmoved? The article was published in 1978.[4]

---

[3] G. Bachmann and A. Wittel, 'Enthusiasm as Affective Labour: On the Productivity of Enthusiam in the Media Industry' in M/C Journal, Vol 12, no. 2, 2009, http://journal.media-culture.org.au/index.php/mcjournal/article/view/147

[4] E. Gillespie, 'A New Arts Workshop', Irish Times, 28 February, 1978, clipping accessed at National Irish Visual Arts Library.

A year later Daniel Buren's *The Function of the Studio* was published in English, having first circulated in French eight years earlier[5]. Buren's analysis of the "cave without heating" eagerly anticipated the extinction of the studio, belittling it as little more than a commercial depot, or boutique of ready-to-wear art. If anything, the studio's value in the performance of privilege may count more than ever: the alchemy of the studio visit and transformation of the artist's humdrum workaday activities into a high value transactional experience. Even if the spatial and temporal occupation of the artist's space and time during the 'studio visit' is never welcomed, such occupations are largely tolerated. Undeniably, enthusiasm has become one of the most effective and highly prized kinds of affective labour an artist can now engage in. This is complimented by the work of embodying and performing enthusiasm in multiple situations and across a range of media, making this immaterial labour symbolically manageable and commercially available. The exclusivity and the febrile energy attached to the production of real or artificial intimacy produces a very special economy of signs that includes the more ridiculous images of artists. It takes nothing to find some very recent publishing ventures promoting art from such-and-such a country (step forward America and Britain) that deploy the worst kinds of visual clichés in their photography picturing artists in their studios[6]. In these times of transnational economic and humanitarian crises the choice to disseminate these kinds of images fulfils Buren's prophecy of extinction in a way. These uninteresting photographs are reactionary, and awful.

When Buren was writing, radically or nominally self-organised groupings from theological dissenters to others across the women's, workers and civil rights movements were mobilising. Occupations and marches saw classrooms and congregations literally or symbolically on the move. In art, the studio had already became mobile as the artist journeyed into other actual and symbolic spaces, to make work in wider and sometimes more local social contexts, in which the studio was hitherto foreseen as within, but essentially separate from, and the 'audience' become portable. As for studio art, Buren described an inescapable studio logic so imprinted that the artwork could never escape its "first frame" or "first limit". Latent within it, when it leaves its place of production studio art suffers a rupture or tear in its logic, which is repaired by the suturing institutional customs and practices of art museums, galleries and their equivalents, where the connection to audiences is mediated[7]. Buren, of course, was an artist who aimed to work 'outside' this problem, positioning himself as an interventionist in relation to public space and the built environment.

---

[5] D. Buren, *The Function of the Studio*, translated from French by T. Repsensek, in October Vol 10, Autumn, 1979.

[6] For example, M. Eisler (Ed.), Art Studio America, London, Thames and Hudson, 2013; M. Eisler (Ed.), Sanctuary: Britain's Artists and their Studios, 2012.

[7] For a current perspective on institutional practices see E. Kluitenberg, *Tactical Media and the Politics of the Archive* in Legacies of Tactical Media, Network/Notebooks 5, Amsterdam, Institute of Network Cultures, 2011.

The trajectory of thinking about the studio leads to a consideration of post-studio practice and the art history of the project in art within modernist and post-modernist cultural practices: a manifest rejection of the shtick of the 19th century artist's studio; an action against the cloistering or kenneling the artist in real life and in the popular or official cultural imagination. We know that the hegemony of 'the studio' was strongly restated in the ruined and rising centres of art in Europe and the United States in the period after the Second World War. This was in part done through some of the most reactionary images of artists, and certainly the types most fetishized, produced in the 20th century. The appearance of a new media iconography of singular devotional melancholics and the frame-by-frame exertions of vocational maniacs was aided greatly by photographers like Hans Namuth. They look comical now but the legacy of these archetypical images associated with the studio artist may yet be with us in the guise of the enthusiasm that the artist-led requires in order to work and be functionally affective. Also as part of the post-studio practices and project thinking that has journeyed with artists into participatory and public art projects. Qualities of responsiveness, performativity, the embrace of contingency and public-ness present in these contexts are *de facto* social, in clear contrast to the cryptic anti-sociality of the studio and the devotional and melancholic image of the artist.

trailers for sale or rent
rooms to let for fifty cents
no phone, no pool, no pets[8]

In 1989, I was part of a group of artists looking for somewhere to start a studio in Dublin, where artists could make work in video, film and photography, "with the prospect of Dublin being the cultural capital of Europe in 1991"[9]. As it happened, we changed our strategy and collaborated on projects for several years instead. Despite this, along the way we learned about the exodus of manufacturers to the outskirts of the city, which buildings were in investment portfolios, and where abroad absentee owners kept registered offices. We heard that something was wrong with the size of the new apartments on the city quays, and there was – they were far too small to comfortably live in for any length of time. But when we started to chase that studio dream, we viewed a building "close to the centre" of the city, where on the day the estate agent gave us the specifications on two A4 sheets of paper with a colour photograph of part of the interior glued to the first page. The floor we viewed didn't look very different from the photograph. Spools of thread, fabric swatches, sweeping brush, fluorescent tubes for lighting. No people in the room when the photograph was taken though, no-one sewing or cutting, nobody working. The photograph was amateurish in appearance, likely taken

---

[8] R. Millar, 'King of the Road', song lyrics, 1964.

[9] *Blue Funk, n. Inf., chiefly Brit. A state of great terror,* Aims and Objectives for 1990–1992, Printed Manifesto, n.d

by a letting and sales agent. This functional visual document records an important moment in the circumstances of the workforce and the city. Meant as a simple common reference as to the facts of what was on offer at the time of the viewing, some reflection on the inexpert photograph got us thinking about regeneration, and how visible or invisible the displacement of manufacturing out of cities can be, and the shrinking likelihood of living and working locally. If the dual function of the photographic document is to record the presence of something real in physical space and simultaneously evoke everything that is visually outside it, to establish context, that is available in reading this photograph.

On a winter's night in 1998, I was again in the same building on Foley Street. In the intervening years an artists' studios had been established: Pallas Studios. In all, Pallas have run studios or project spaces at eleven different addresses, all but the current one on the north side of the city. A risky and tiring trail, no doubt, but such a unique view of the city over a period of immense social and infrastructural change. Where can we see what Pallas saw outside – in each changing neighbourhood – and what does that tell us?

I was back because Pallas Studios was one of ten places in the city where a collaborative project by work-seth/tallentire was taking place. Artists Anne Tallentire and John Seth had been commissioned by Project Arts Centre as part of a programme of commissioned projects run in buildings and structures in Dublin and Galway during a major re-development aided by European structural funding. This was the Project Art Centre's third address, where it had been for almost twenty-five years, at that stage. The building being knocked to make way for the re-build had originally also been a small industry building, a printing works. I started working with the arts centre as the old building was decommissioned. The off-site project by work-seth/tallentire was called *trailer*[10]. The locations were chosen because of their distinct functions in the city. Audiences called a freephone number each day for information about where the screenings would take place. A website archived still images from the work carried out earlier each day. That night in Pallas Studios at Foley Street I took some photographs before the audience arrived. The small TV sets and video projection used for the screening at Pallas can be seen of course, and a couple of technicians who worked on the project. Then there is the staircase, lit from outside by sodium streetlights, the individual studio spaces themselves lit with single tube fluorescent fittings hung at right angles, and white-painted partitions almost to the ceiling. Plastic boxes, cardboard packages, handwritten labels, small paintings, easels, palettes, sweeping brushes, large plastic bottles filled with different colours inside, a hat and books, mirror, gas canisters, cardigans, hand-saw, cotton sheets, spirit level, timber, handmade greeting card, Calvin Klein, milk carton, paint-covered table, pencil, and some folded photocopies.

---

[10] For more information, see The Project Arts Centre Papers, Collection List No 152, prepared by Barry Houlihan, assisted by Máire Ní Chonalláin and Luke Kirwan.

Almost none of the artist-led, run, driven, centred or cultural tenants who hosted screenings as part of 'trailer' are still in the same buildings. Neither are the property development companies that owned or occupied others.

The photographs of 'trailer' at Pallas, and the other off-site project sites, include visual information that is surplus to the purpose of documenting the artwork. This excess is not meaningless. Successive years of alteration to the city through intensive property development are conceptually framed by the peregrinations of that project-based mobile arts programme, and visible beside and behind the objects and actions documented. By cultivating a 'camera consciousness' and having due diligence to the politics of representation, the ontology of the artist-led will be better developed by closer inspection of their strategies of self-representation[11]. Otherwise, does this increase the risk that artist-led initiatives will reproduce the models they claim to dislike and be unlike?

Writing about 'trailer', Uriel Orlow describes a "provisional series of attempts" to find a response to some of "the city's almost invisible signs" at the threshold of vision and the urgent necessity of entering into relation with these signs, of becoming "practically (as opposed to conceptually) involved in their tiny mechanisms of material signification", and compares this to a "process of handling (rather than showing), literally of touching and moving [...] a process of transformation"[12]. The artist-led (studio, project, publication) is not only a state of being or a feeling, it is also an optic and, for that matter, a listening device. If the artist-led amounts to no more than a concept for a type of boutique service, it is the same as any accessible campus style serviced offices delivering the necessaries to the creative industries and social enterprise.

If shifting the paradigm will be slow, the analysis can begin quickly. It is a struggle to persuade arts and cultural researchers to use visual methodologies, although the chauvinism underpinning this is being challenged, if imperfectly, as the more ethnographic and anthropologically-minded reach out to artists. In 'The Yellow Wallpaper' written in 1892 by the American writer Charlotte Perkins Gilman, the eponymous paper hangs in a rented room, in a rented house[13]. The protagonist, captive to powerful stereotypes of the day, is compelled to go there daily and forbidden to "work". She has been told she is ill and fed with ale, cod liver oil, tonics, wine, and rare meat, accompanied by long spells of lying down. The wallpaper smooches and marks her clothes and the odour, the yellow smell, carries in her hair, even after she can leave the room. She searches the wallpaper's surface pattern of "printed grotesques", "sprawling outlines", and "slanting waves of optic horror" when, one day, something catches her eye. Re-focusing, she sees a sub-pattern, a multitude. She examines it, then joins it, freeing herself from her melancholy, moving the story toward its conclusion.

---

[11] N. Papastergiadis, 'The Elastic Metaphor, Cultural Identity, Place and Photography' in Spatial Aesthetics: Art, Place, and the Everyday, Theory on Demand 5, Amsterdam, Institute of Network Cultures, 2010.

[12] U. Orlow, trailer, LUX ONLINE, 1999, http://www.luxonline.org.uk/articles/trailer(1).html

[13] C. Perkins Gilman, *The Yellow Wallpaper*, 1892.

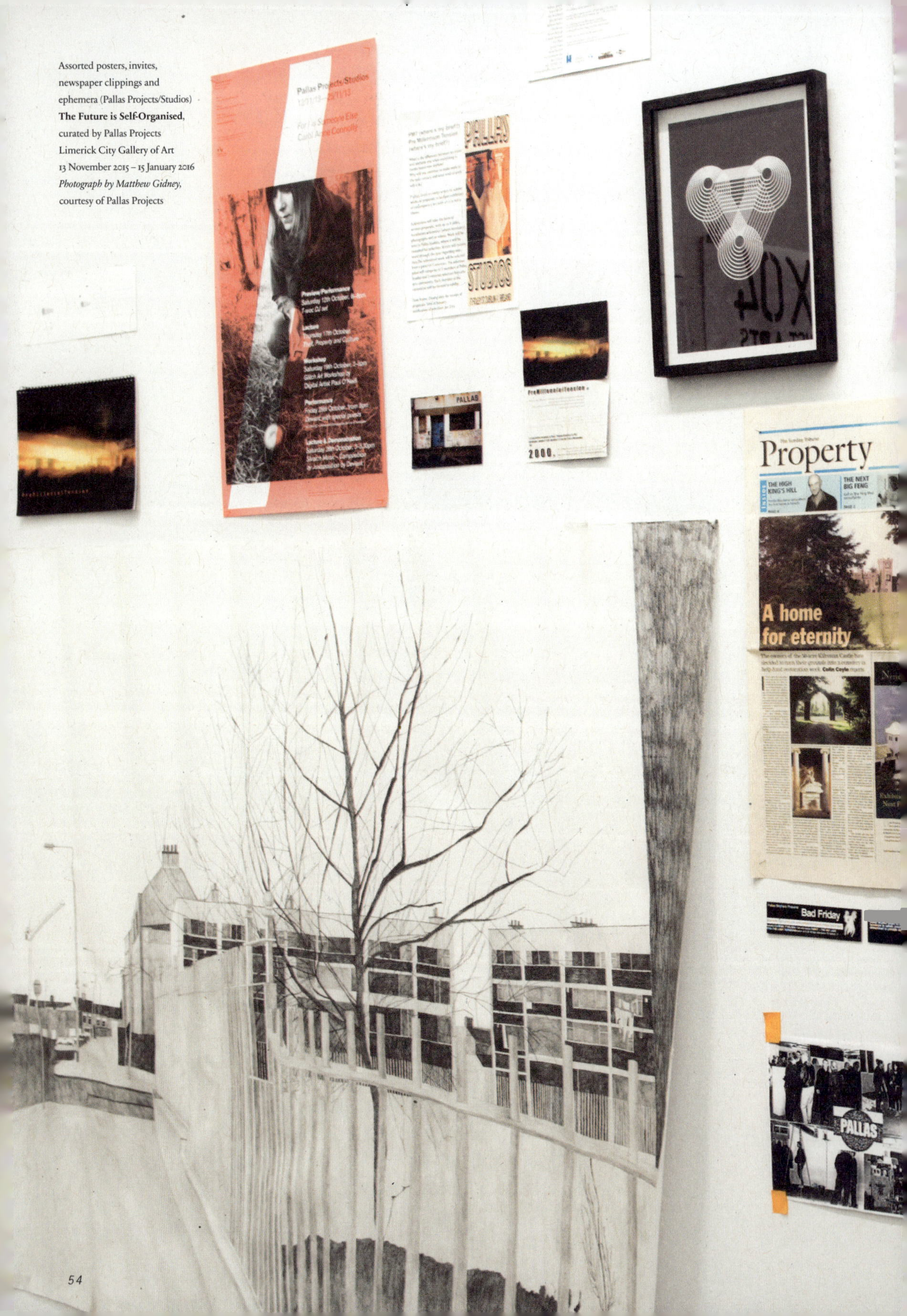

Assorted posters, invites, newspaper clippings and ephemera (Pallas Projects/Studios) **The Future is Self-Organised**, curated by Pallas Projects Limerick City Gallery of Art 13 November 2015 – 15 January 2016 *Photograph by Matthew Gidney*, courtesy of Pallas Projects

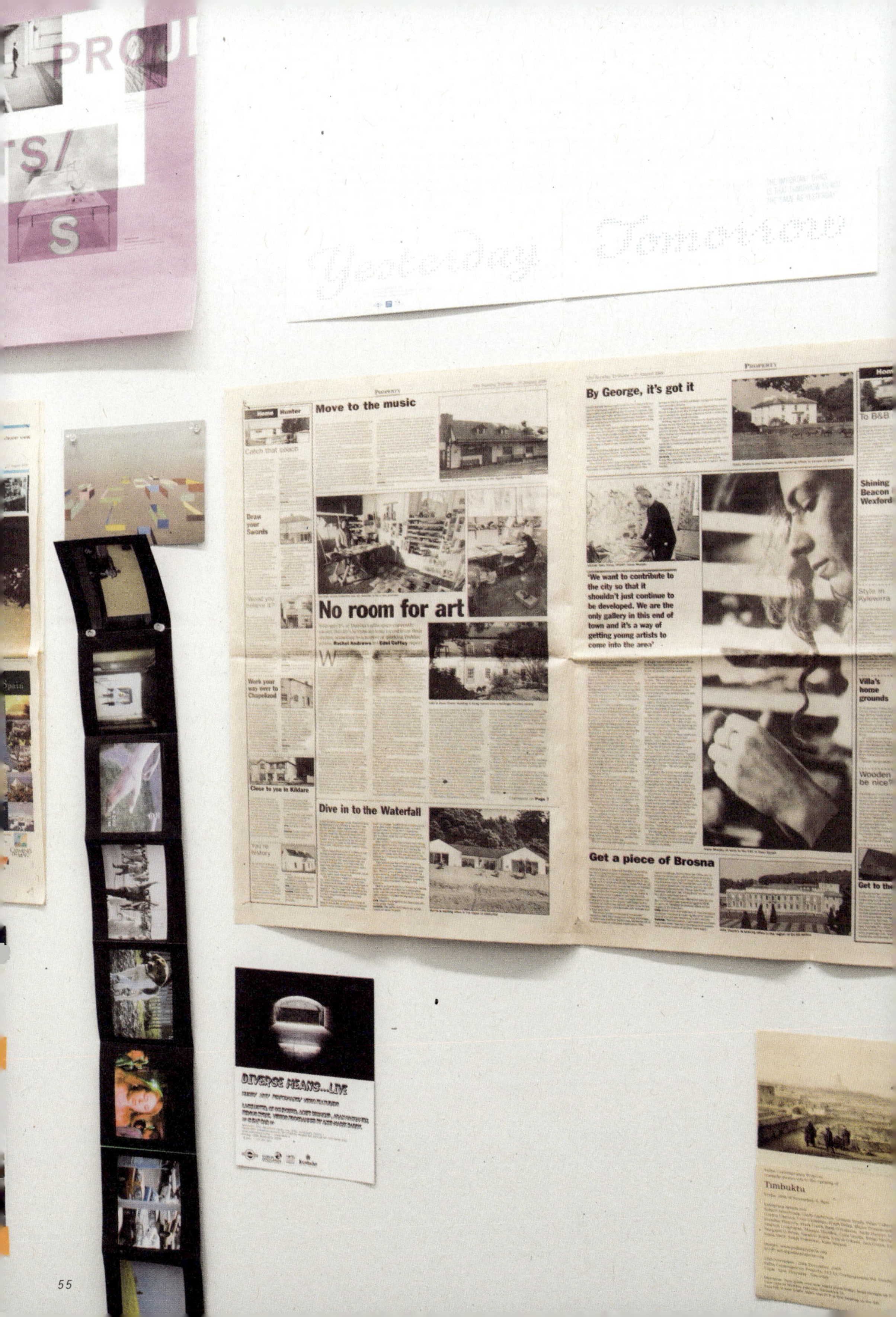
PROU
TS/
S
Yesterday
Tomorrow
Property
Move to the music
Catch that coach
Draw your Swords
No room for art
Work your way over to Chapelizod
Close to you in Kildare
Dive in to the Waterfall
By George, it's got it
'We want to contribute to the city so that it shouldn't just continue to be developed. We are the only gallery in this end of town and it's a way of getting young artists to come into the area'
Get a piece of Brosna
To B&B
Shining Beacon Wexford
Style in Kylemira
Villa's home grounds
Wooden be nice?
Get to the
Spain
DIVERSE MEANS...LIVE
Timbuktu

NAME
Pallas Projects/Studios

LOCATION
Dublin, Ireland

WEBSITE
www.pallasprojects.org

YEAR
1996 to present

STRUCTURE
Artist-run organisation
with a voluntary board

LEGAL STATUS
Pallas Projects CLG is incorporated as a non-profit company limited by guarantee

TEAM
2 permanent artist–director/curators, 1 assistant director/programme producer, 3–4 part-time staff, volunteers, Erasmus students and international interns

MISSION
PP/S is an artist-run organisation dedicated to the facilitation of artistic production and discourse, via the provision of affordable artists' studios, curated projects and cooperative exchanges, and by conducting research and advocacy on artist-run practice and studio provision

CORE FUNDING
Arts Council: Arts Grant (annual)

OTHER FUNDING:
PP/S has received grants and support for individual projects from the following: Goethe-Institut Irland; Mondriaan Fund; Culture Ireland; British Council; Dublin Docklands Development Authority. Dublin City Council: Annual Revenue funding 2007–2015; Project Funding 2016–2020

PREMISES
Commercial leases with private landlord, and the Digital Hub Development Agency

SELECTED PROJECTS
Pre Millennial Tension, Pallas Studios (1999); *Precinct*, off-site locations, Dublin (2001) and Belfast (with Catalyst Arts, 2002); *Offside*, Dublin City Gallery The Hugh Lane (2005); Pallas Heights (2003–2006); *Automatic*, Auto Italia South East, London (2009); Manon de Boer & Hito Steyerl, Pallas Contemporary Projects (2009); *E.S.P. TV* – live, Pallas Projects (2012); *Periodical Review* (2011–to present); *The Future is Self-Organised*, Limerick City Gallery of Art (2015–16); Artist-Initiated Projects programme (2018–present); *'Dubliners'*, 6th Biennial of Painting, Zagreb (2021)

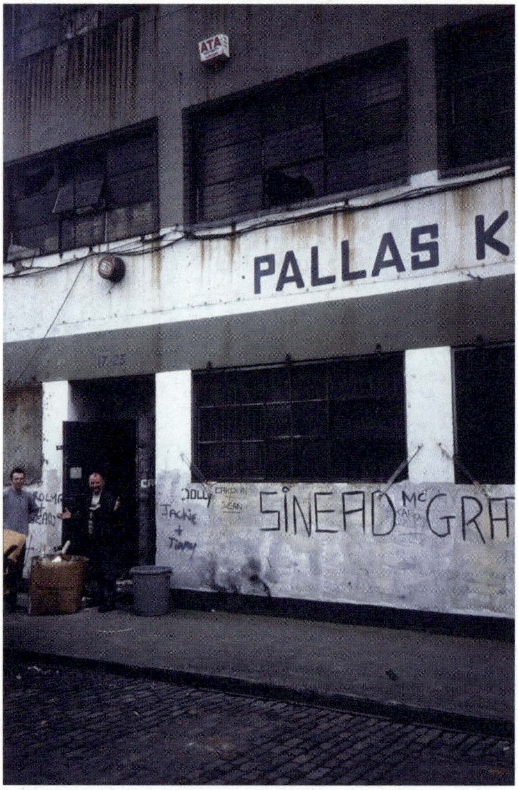

Zones of Contention – two decades in the life of Pallas

Mark Cullen

Pallas Studios (Formerly Pallas Knitwear) Foley Street, Dublin 1
PICTURED: Gavin Murphy, other unknown, circa 1998
Image courtesy of Mark Cullen, from 35mm slide

Pallas, set up in 1996 by Mark Cullen and Brian Duggan, latterly joined by Gavin Murphy in 2006, began as an impulse to create a space for both working together and working within, in parallel or in a community with other artists, and it has survived to witness a wide intermeshing of an artistic community that is interconnected across Ireland. This is a cultural community that is underrepresented and marginalised in Irish society to a point whereby its consideration is not given due regard, nor nourished through reasonable levels of state or private support.

Pallas Projects/Studios provides a valuable platform for supporting the emerging grassroots, alternative and non-commercial practices of this widespread community of peers. The initial impulse to self-organise grew and extended to become an interest in what it could be achieved outside of itself – projecting out into the wider artistic and social milieu to stimulate activity and cultural meaning. Having a predilection towards collaboration as a strategic response to a lack of resources in a monied society brought benefits in community-building. We actively sought out partners beyond ourselves, working with most other artist-run organisations in Ireland, along with many others internationally.[1] We ignored notions of hierarchy in developing collaborations and were as much willing to work with institutions as with independent practitioners.

---

[1] Gertrude Contemporary, Melbourne; Project 304, Bangkok; ESP TV, New York; Suburban, Rotterdam; VTO Gallery, London; Root, London; Auto Italia South East, London; The Black Mariah, Cork; Lismore Castle Arts, Waterford; 126 Artist-Run Gallery, Galway; The Model, Sligo; Catalyst Arts, Belfast; Irish Museum of Modern Art, Dublin; Dublin City Gallery The Hugh Lane; Fire Station Artists' Studios, Dubin; The LAB, Dublin; Common Ground, Dublin; Irish Architecture Foundation, Dublin; NCAD Gallery, Dublin.

This proclivity for reaching out to other organisations has been a real strength that has helped Pallas enrich and revitalise its own project, with every partnership exchange entered into, providing possibilities for learning and creative expression.

The name Pallas was taken from the previous occupier of the organisation's first building, Pallas Knitwear. As the goddess of the muses, the intellect, (and war), it was an appropriate choice: famed for her ability to transform, Pallas Athena suited an organisation whose perseverance is defined by its capacity to adapt. Over the course of 20 years, Pallas has occupied 14 premises and many other exhibition locations, out of a necessity to stay one step ahead of the developers in a Celtic Tiger-bubble economy. By 2012, the stagnant property market that followed the 2007/08 global banking meltdown ultimately allowed Pallas to obtain a relatively long-term lease – that which was almost a holy grail in that nomadic pre-crash period. And yet in writing these words there is still a marked sense of the precariousness of its position as the property developers begin heating up the market for another round of amnesiac development, to take up where they left off.[2]

Pre Millennial Tension, 1999
Pallas Studios
WORKS L–R: Clive Murphy, Mark Cullen, David Timmons
Image courtesy of Mark Cullen, from 35mm slide

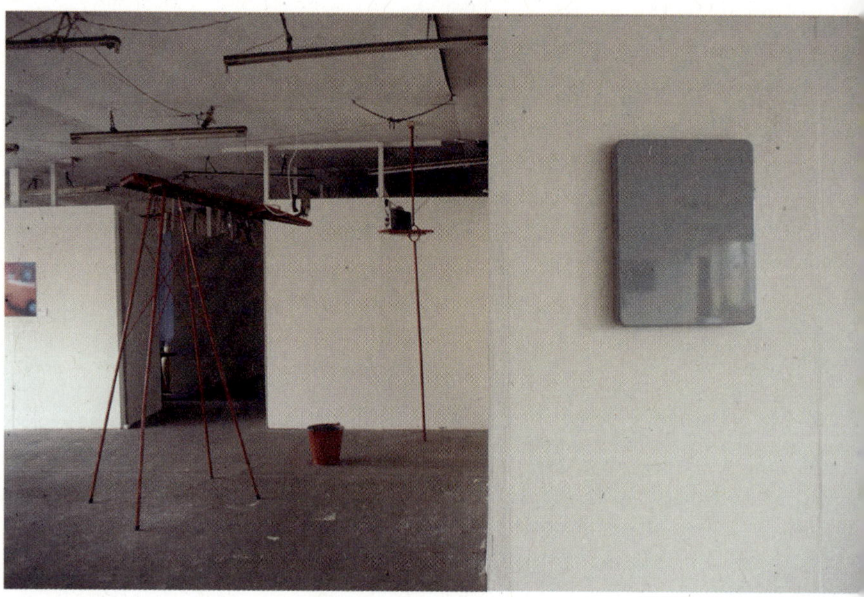

[2] John Mulligan, 'Confidence returning to the boom time developers. Those builders who survived the crash are back, and they have big ideas', published 15/06/2014. Accessible on: http://www.independent.ie/business/irish/confidence-returning-to-the-boomtime-developers-30354470.html

Pallas Studios

7 BUILDINGS OVER 20 YEARS:
THE FIRST AND THIRD – 2 ADJACENT FLOORS OF A FORMER KNITWEAR FACTORY: 16 AND 14 STUDIOS.
THE SECOND – AN UNUSED AND MILDLY DILAPIDATED OUTPOST OF A BUSINESS PARK: 9 STUDIOS.
THE FOURTH – ABOVE A FORMER MILKING PARLOUR: 4 STUDIOS.
THE SIXTH – FORMER OFFICES OF ENGINEERS OF FIRE-ENGINES, CONVERTED FROM TWO TERRACED HOUSES: 9 STUDIOS.
THE SEVENTH – A CONVERTED 19TH CENTURY CONVENT SCHOOL: 18 STUDIOS.

The question of finance

There is the issue of funding an arts organisation – where it comes from and what one must do in order to get it. Most artists (in Ireland as elsewhere) do not make their money solely from the sale of artworks or from receiving fees. Artists engage in myriad jobs that enable them to continue their practice. We were chefs and builders at different times, others are teachers, invigilators, installers, administrators. When either of the directors were awarded public art commissions through our own practices, we channeled 70% of the profits through the studio to keep it buoyant. Every year we applied for Arts Council revenue funding. The first 4 years of our existence we survived without it, apart from small exhibitions grants. Consequently, we had part-time jobs to keep the show going. As we got more funding we concentrated more of our time on the artistic programme at Pallas, and as we did that we got still more funding, which plateaued in 2007 then began a nose dive in 2011. We would like to think that we have the vitality to survive without public funding, but I fear that is not the case, as cultural organisations such as Pallas do not operate in the same manner as ordinary commercial businesses, and there is not enough significant interest from the private sector to keep the game going by investing in culture. The Celtic Tiger's cubs haven't learned to spend their money on art or to re-invest in society: personal gain in property investments and displays of wealth in flashy vehicles are the more common expressions of newly found affluence. And so the cycle is renewed in 2015 with a new property bubble forming in Dublin, while artist-run spaces are going through a period of contraction following rapid post-crash growth when the grip of bankrupt developers on the city was loosened.

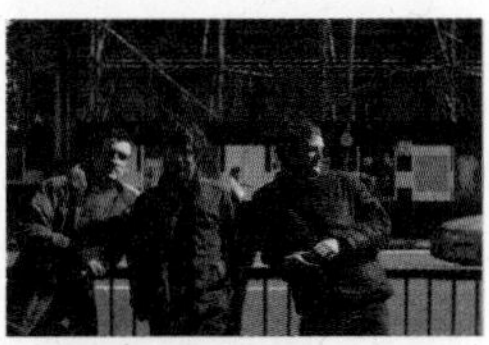

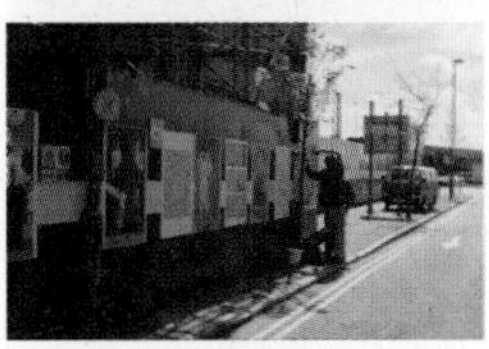

Precinct, 2002
Pallas Studios & Catalyst Arts, Belfast
TOP: Mark Cullen, Clive Murphy, Brian Duggan
BOTTOM: Cris Neumann
Images courtesy of Mark Cullen, from 35mm slide

During the early years we looked at ways to enable Pallas to become sustainable. Dressed in entrepreneurial cloaks to support art's self-determination, we formed a co-op of three members that received support from the Co-operative Development Unit (CDU)[3] to produce a feasibility study and a business plan with three-year strategic objectives. A successful plan secured employment grants from the CDU and Enterprise Set-up Employment Provision from the Department of

[3] The Co-operative Development Unit (CDU) was a Government Agency with a remit to stimulate the growth of co-operative business models that was dismantled by the right-wing Fianna Fáil/Progressive Democrats coalition government enacting its neo-liberal deregulatory tendencies in the late 1990s. We were one year into a three-year contract with them when this happened. The contract was upheld with the addition of more red-tape.

Social Welfare in the form of yearly support that was reduced by 25% to zero over a four-year period. In 1999 we began lobbying the local area office of Dublin Corporation – now Dublin City Council (DCC) – about the need for the provision of studios, as our first lease of four years and nine months (the longest we could get without gaining rights of tenure under the regulations then in place) was coming to a conclusion, and empty properties in the city were at a premium. Our talks with DCC about support for the provision of studios for artists in Dublin yielded a temporary solution in the form of vacant flats in Sean Tracey House, a social housing project that had been scourged by a heroin epidemic throughout the 1980s and 1990s. These flats enabled us to present a yearly programme for the first time in our existence, and the programme was of such significance to the emerging art scene in Dublin that the Arts Council doubled our small revenue grant twice and added a further 25% over the course of three years. This enabled the directors to concentrate on running Pallas, with time to develop their own artwork, and give up their part-time jobs.

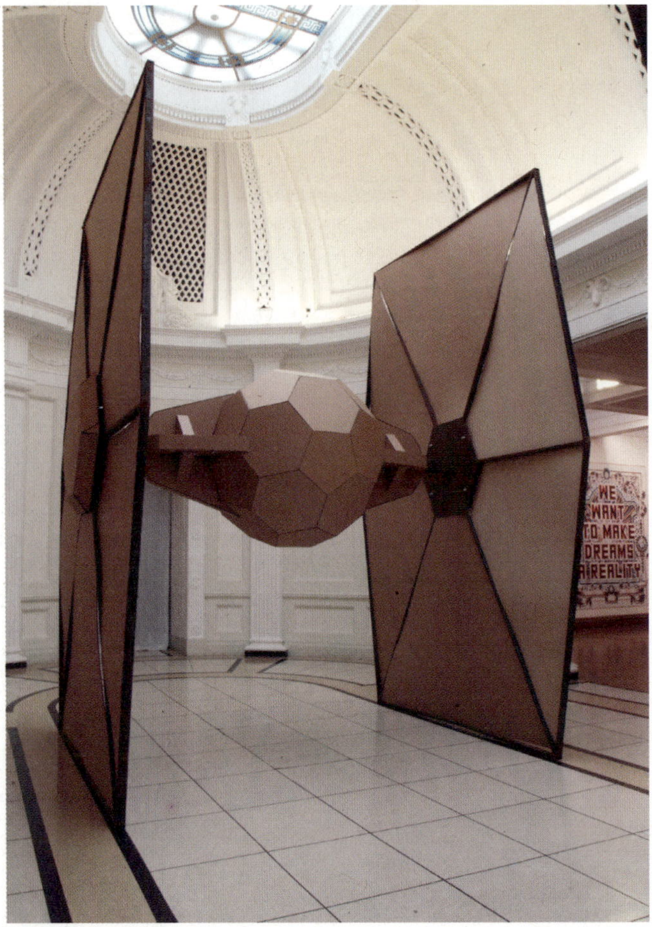

← **Offside**, 2005
Dublin City Gallery The Hugh Lane,
curated by Pallas Studios
WORKS L–R Nina McGowan, Mark Titchner
9 July – 2 October 2005
Photograph by Alex McCullagh

→ **Salon**, 1999
Pallas Studios
Exhibition view
Image courtesy of Mark Cullen,
from 35mm slide

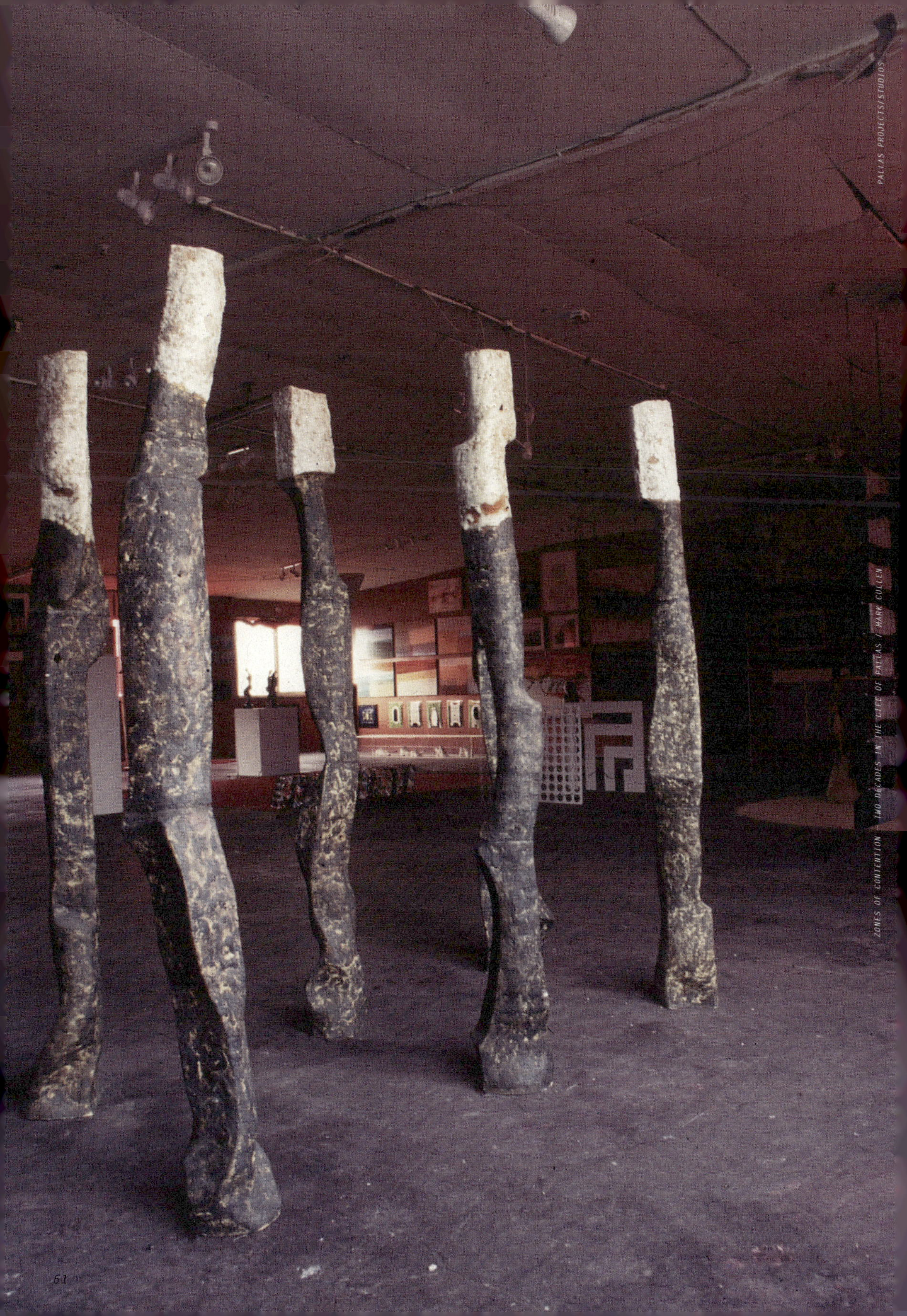

PALLAS PROJECTS/STUDIOS

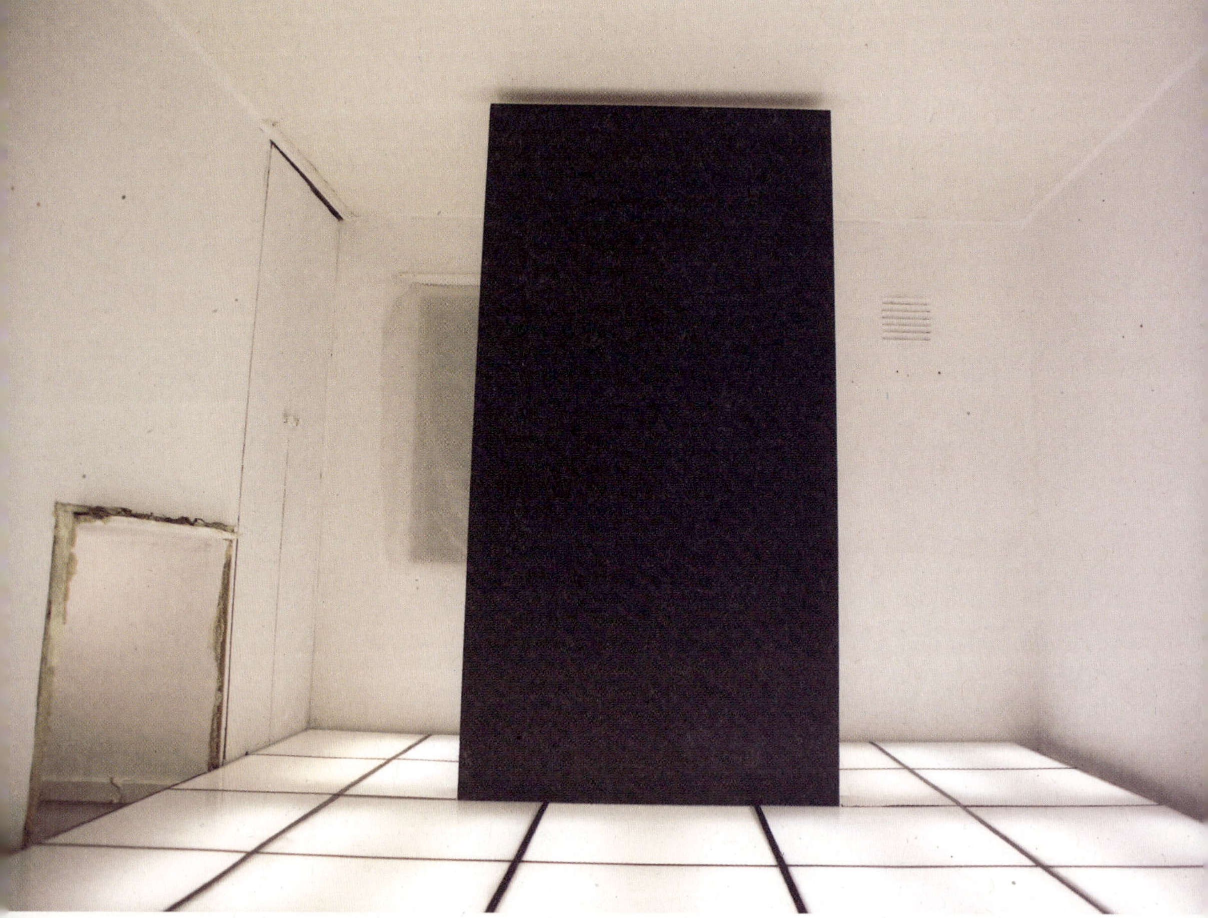

↑ Brendan Earley
Arrival, 2003
Pallas Heights
24 October – 3 December 2003
Photograph courtesy of the artist and mothers tankstation

Pallas Heights: 2002–2007

APT 11, APT 12, APT 17, & APT 18 SEAN TRACEY HOUSE, BUCKINGHAM ST. 2 PROJECT SPACES IN 2 APARTMENTS, AND 6 STUDIOS IN THE OTHER 2 APARTMENTS – REDUCED TO 5 DUE TO STRANGE DARK LIQUID LEAKING IN FROM ROOF AND COLONISATION OF INEDIBLE FUNGAL GROWTHS ON WINDOW SURROUNDS.

The space that came out of the talks with DCC – Pallas Heights – gave artists a chance to work outside standard gallery conventions in an environment that had particular relevance to the growth of a changing city; one that seemed separate from the trajectory of urban renewal and the dynamics of the Celtic Tiger. A space that was outside and offside, existing in a limbo between decay and renewal: four empty flats repurposed for art, in a disintegrating social housing block, a building being slowly vacated of its people and families.

Into this context, artists applied their time and creativity, making comment through their art on issues whether oblique or immediately pertinent to the site. Pallas Heights gave artists the space and time to intervene on-site in the manner that was most suitable to their practice. In certain cases this involved extended periods of time working in situ prior to the exhibitions. In other cases artists brought their work to the location. No common thread of artistic practice was sought in choosing artists to respond to the flats in Sean Tracey House, and as a consequence each show had a unique interpretation of possibility for the site. What emerged through the programme were projects that re-imagined the site as zones of contention, allowing its histories, its extended contexts, and its inevitable future demise become relevant to the concerns of the exhibiting artists.

Pallas Heights featured 18 unique exhibitions of new work by solo artists coming from Ireland and abroad, and a small number of group shows generated out of various connections with London. We created our first major (award winning) publication 'Pallas Heights 2003–2006' as legacy to this project. It came to a conclusion when DCC asked that the flats be vacated in 2007. They remained empty for a further 2 years before the final demolition occurred.

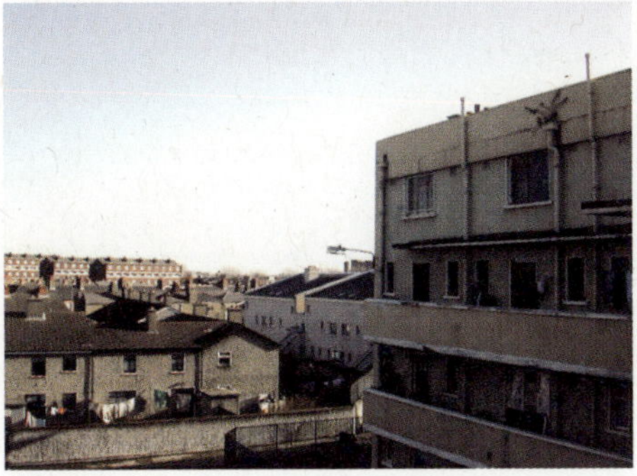

Pallas Heights
Sean Tracey House,
Buckingham Street, Dublin 1
Photograph by Mark Cullen

Pallas enters the Museum

When asked by Barbara Dawson and Christina Kennedy of Dublin City Gallery The Hugh Lane to programme the main galleries for the summer of 2005, we wanted to continue our engagement with some of the various artists we had worked with in previous projects and others that we hoped to work with in the future, with a commitment to raising the bar of expectation for cultural activity in Dublin through supporting the rise of Irish artists, counter-balanced by showing international works throughout the programme.

For *Offside* we were conscious of the opportunity a museum show presents, so we wanted to extend this opportunity to a sizeable group of artists. We didn't want to confine the works to the gallery, nor did we want to just show 'gallery' art. Four projects were sited outside the gallery: Rhona Byrne's poster attached to the gable end of an adjacent building; John Dummet used the concourse outside the museum; Garrett Phelan activated the expansive atrium of Dublin City Council's Civic Offices; and Niamh McCann's work was sited in an empty shop unit in the newly redeveloped Docklands, beside the IFSC financial district and close to the site of our first studios. We wanted to extend the possibilities of the museum to consider its role as a prime space in the city where cultural activity can take place, while challenging the traditional timeframe of museum opening times that offer limited potential to that expression and reception of culture, as in Ireland, they tend to be open mainly during standard working hours. In this regard two *OFFSIDE LIVE* events were co-programmed with artist Fergus Byrne, wherein wider artistic fields of music and performance could mingle and be expressed in the halls of the museum. These events made use of the space as a venue late into the night.

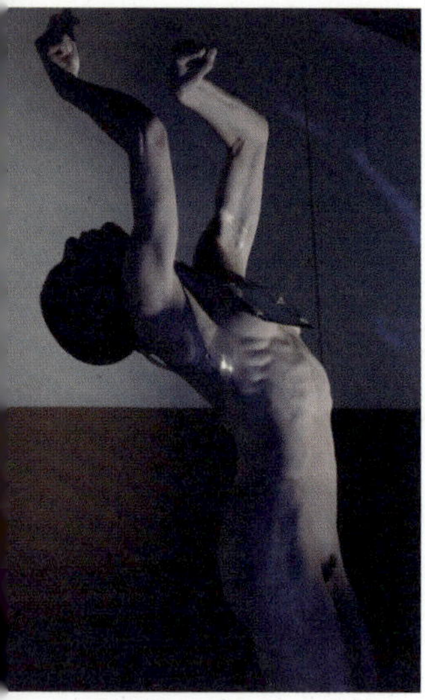

↑ **Offside Live**, 2005
Performance by Anne Seagrave
Dublin City Gallery The Hugh Lane,
curated by Pallas Studios
Photograph by Futoshi Sakauchi

→ **Offside**, 2005
Dublin City Gallery The Hugh Lane,
curated by Pallas Studios
Installation by Nathaniel Mellors
9 July – 2 October 2005
Photograph by Alex McCullagh

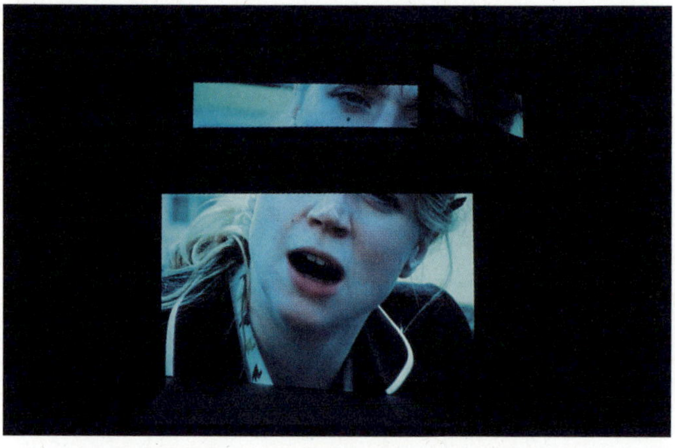

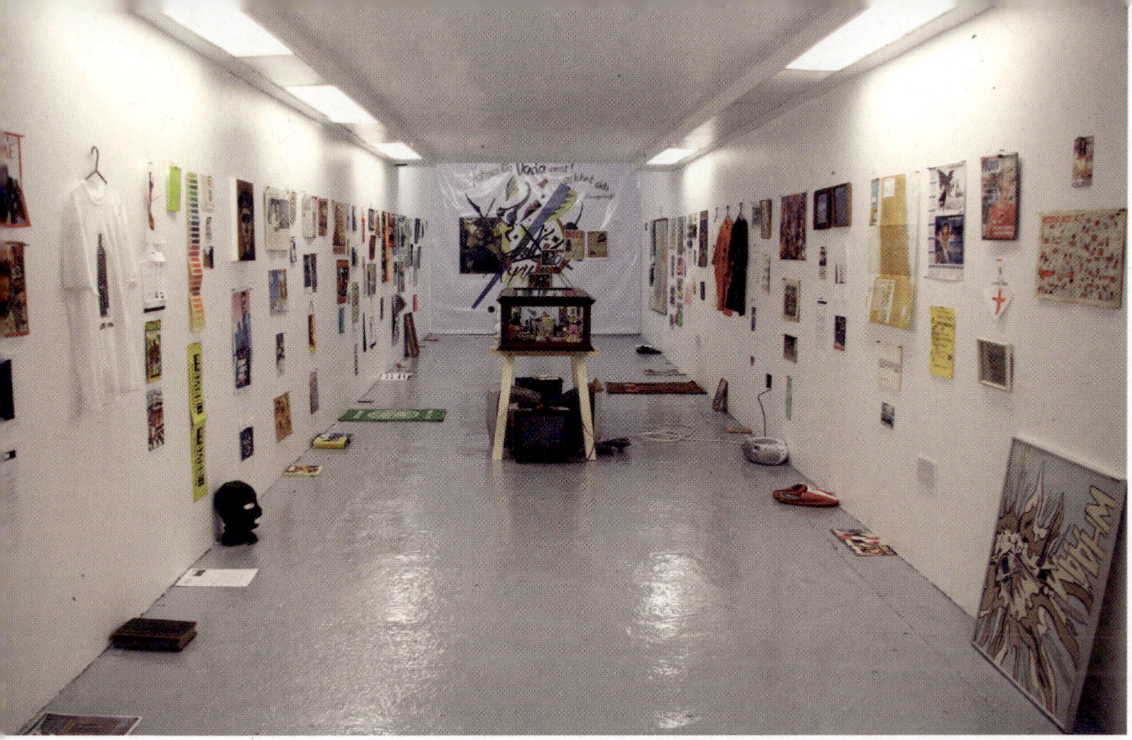

Jim Ricks
Synchromaterialism, 2010
Exhibition view
Pallas Contemporary Projects
16 October – 13 November 2010
Photograph courtesy of the artist and Pallas Projects

Nomads inhabit O'Doherty's 'White Cube' (well, sort of). Pallas Contemporary Projects

111A UPPER GRANGEGORMAN RD (DOWNSTAIRS): 2007 – 2011
GALLERY – WHITE CUBOID (5 TIMES LONGER THAN IT WAS WIDE).
GAVIN MURPHY JOINS THE DIRECTORIAL TEAM.
PALLAS INITIATES ITS FIRST ADVISORY BOARD.
FOUNDER BRIAN DUGGAN HANGS UP HIS EXECUTIVE BOOTS FOR A SEAT ON THE BOARD.
OUR INTERN AND VOLUNTEERS PROGRAMME IS COMMENCED.

Following the sustained period of programming in the heavily subjective context of Pallas Heights we knew the challenge to explore the dynamics of the white cube would be an interesting new departure, so we set about seeking out a place we could transform into the notionally neutral space for presenting art. However, in the selection of a former milking parlour-cum-mechanics garage, we fitted out a space that was closer to an elongated bunker than a traditional white cube. As such, the conventional neutrality we sought out for this stage of the project was ultimately subverted by this strangely shaped building. The ceiling tapered and the floor rose to compress the room height from a little less than three metres to little more than two metres. The walls, starting at about 3.3 metres wide at the entrance to the gallery, tapered to about three metres wide forcing the sense of perspectival length to an odd extreme. Not a great gallery for hanging works on the walls, but it excelled in prescribing artists to create total site-reactive installations that revelled in this long dark tunnel.

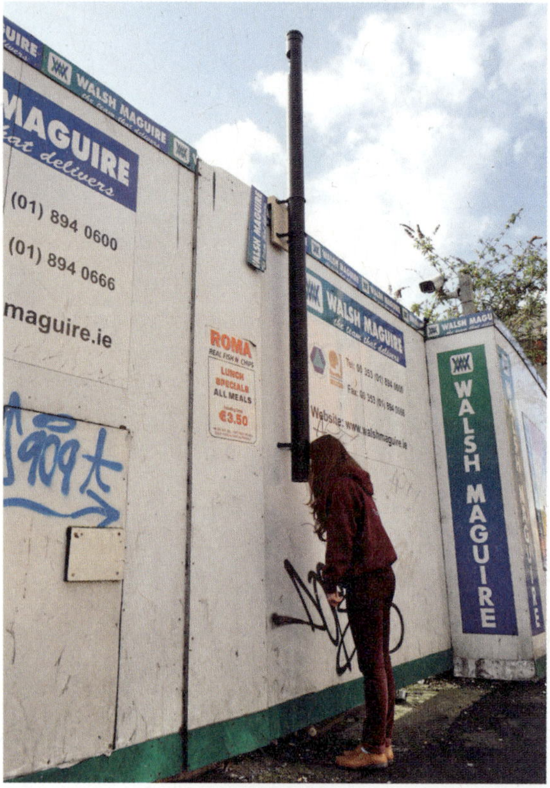

Ruth Clinton & Niamh Moriarty
Rotator
2 March – 6 April 2013
Pallas Projects/Studios
Wormhole (drainpipe), 2013, installed offsite on The Coombe, Dublin 8
Photograph by Florence Paule G

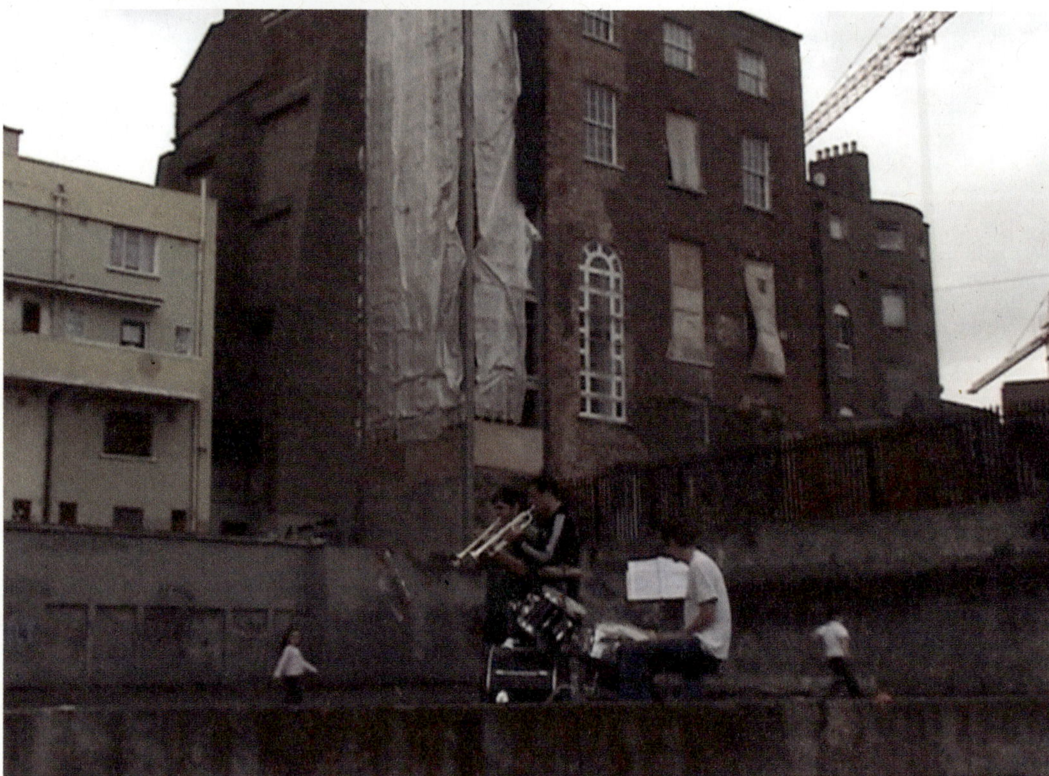

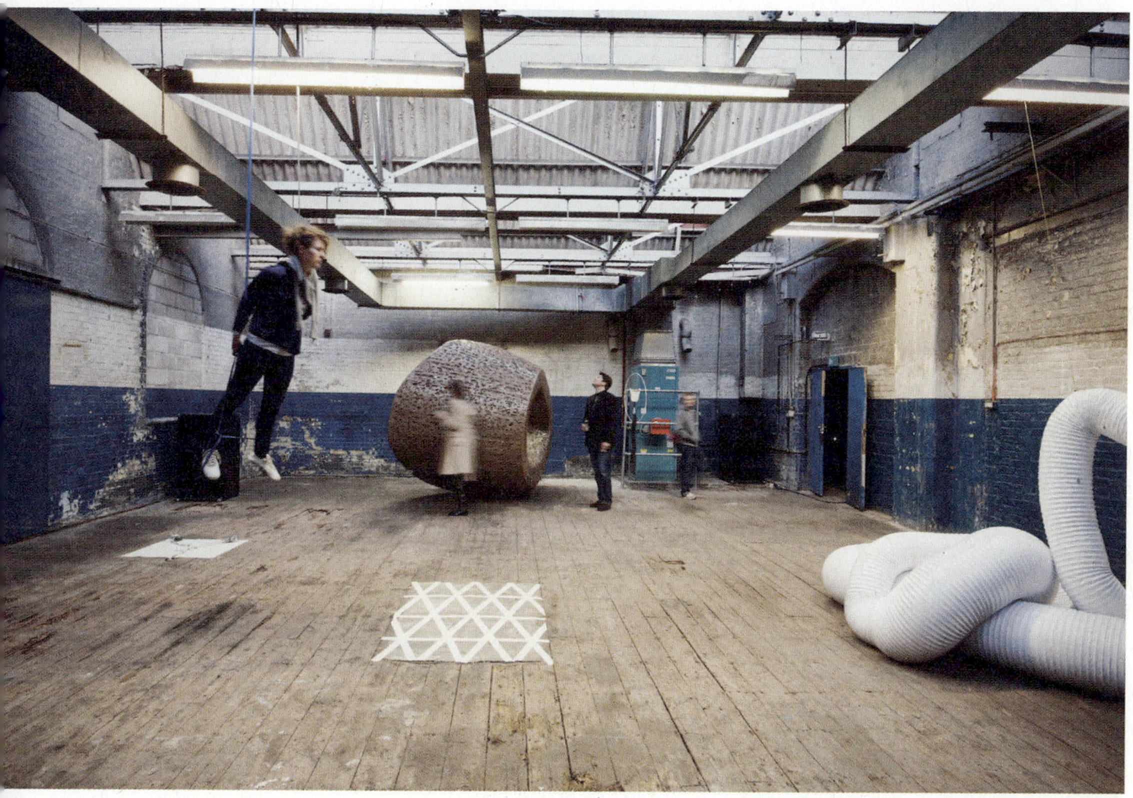

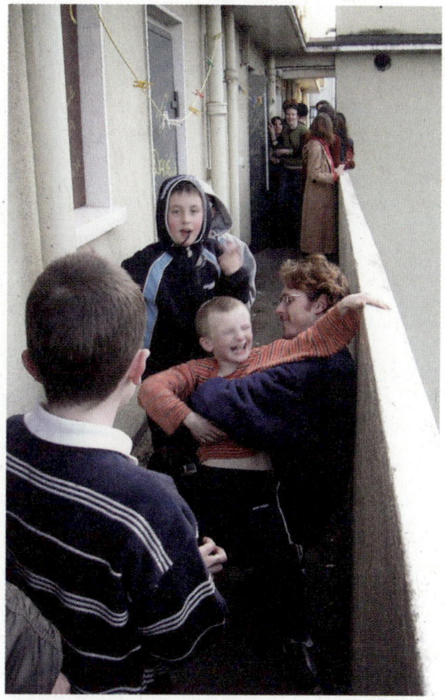

↑ ***Automatic***, 2009
Curated by Gavin Murphy & Chris Fite-Wassilak
Auto Italia South East, London &
Pallas Contemporary Projects
9–26 September 2009
Opening performance by Alicia Frankovich
WORKS L–R: Alicia Frankovich, Ruth Proctor, Gereon Krebber, Karl Burke, Berndnaut Smilde, (Candice Jacobs, Linda Quinlan, not pictured)
Photograph by Theo Cook

← Jesse Jones
On The Waterfront, 2005
Video film of a live performance, recorded in the courtyard of Sean Tracey House
Pallas Heights
1 July – 15 August 2005
Image courtesy of the artist

→ Pallas Heights
Local children attempt to storm the exhibition opening, held back by artist Fergus Byrne
APT 30
Slavek Kwi, Seoidin O'Sullivan and Gillian Kane
Pallas Heights
16 April – 12 May 2004
Photograph by Mark Cullen

Pallas Projects

23 LOWER DOMINICK ST: 2011-2012
GALLERY IN GROUND FLOOR OF 18TH CENTURY GEORGIAN BUILDING.
A NEW COMPANY LIMITED BY GUARANTEE IS FORMED WITH THE NAME CHANGED TO PALLAS PROJECTS/STUDIOS.
A SYMPATHETIC ACCOUNTANT IS CONTRACTED.[4]

Operating grandly in one of the former jewels of Georgian Dublin, this down-at-heel Dublin mansion brought with it an inevitable shortness to our term there, with the bank foreclosing on our overstretched landlords the day after we signed a year long lease. No potential to renew beyond a year was likely, so our sights continued to rove to find a longer-term home. Meanwhile on the other side of town our main studios on Lower Grangegorman Road were burnt out by young hoodlums, causing a major strain on our operations and our morale, occurring as it did on the same week as the opening of the new gallery. (We had ultimately planned to leave behind these studios and gallery in Grangegorman, but more preferably on our own terms when a suitable replacement was found.)

An eventful programme in these two ground floor rooms opened with the UK artist John Smith and concluded with the first of our now annual survey of contemporary visual art practice in Ireland, *Periodical Review 1*. It had a different atmosphere from our previous locations and being so near to the city centre it attracted a transient audience of art-goers coming to and from Dublin City Gallery The Hugh Lane, which was in the neighbourhood. It also marked the start of a fruitful relationship with design studio Conor & David who created a new logo and website for the newly branded Pallas Projects/Studios, along with publishing three of an ongoing series of booklets that featured work by artists in our programme.

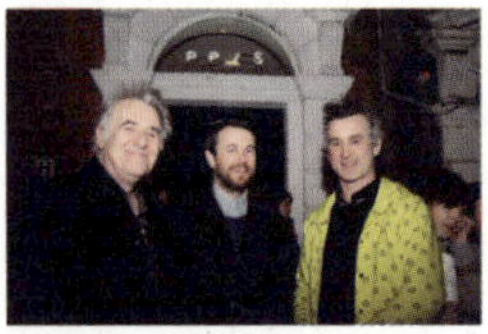

John Smith
The world seems a long way away
(Exhibition opening)
Pallas Projects
2 March 2011
L–R: John Smith, Gavin Murphy, Mark Cullen
Photograph by Roya Miller

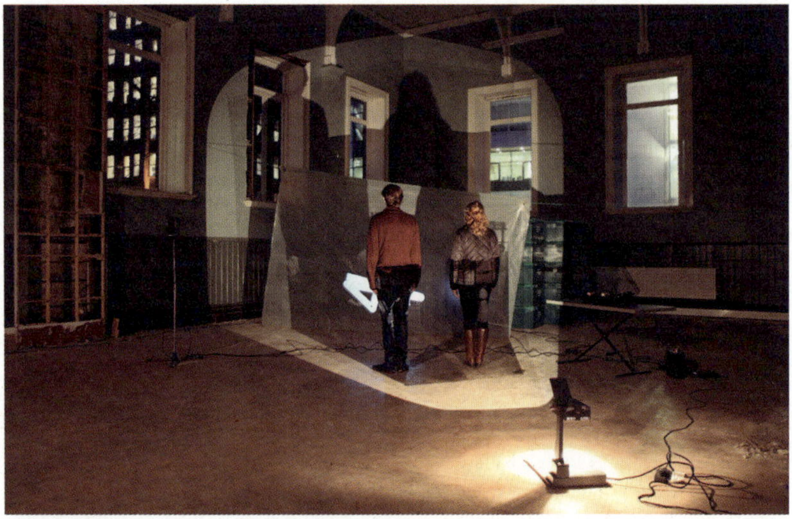

→ Dennis McNulty
A cloud of soft equations
(Rehearsal image)
4, 5, 7, 11 February 2014
A promenade performance scripted for two performers, with costumes, lighting and various media technologies, sited in the former Pathology Department of UCD, Earlsfort Terrace, Dublin. Presented as part of Periodical Review #3, produced with the support of Pallas Projects/Studios, Irish Architecture Foundation and The Arts Council of Ireland.
Photograph by Senija Topcic, courtesy of the artist

[4] Following a few incompatables the importance of a sympathetic accountant was made more obvious when we finally managed to find one in the form of Donall Curtin & BCK.

Pallas Projects/Studios

115–117 THE COOMBE: 2012–2022
A VICTORIAN CONVENT SCHOOL – A PLAYGROUND, A HALL.
A PROJECT SPACE AND STUDIOS COMBINE.

In 2011 we began our most recent, and most likely not our last, search for a long-term premises. We identified an old school building on the edge of the Liberties area of the city centre as an ideal location for a gallery and studios. Following a torturous nine-month period of lease negotiations, we began a ten-year lease on our best premises to date. The generously proportioned classrooms provided spacious studios, the old assembly room ideal as a gallery project space. Nestled off the street and down a lane, the building offers a certain peaceful atmosphere that is very conducive to making art and instigating situations where it can be experienced. Positioned in an area that is surrounded by schools and community groups, and armed with the longer-term lease than we have previously enjoyed, we are in a position to engage our neighbours though active programmes, occasional outreach, and we have been able to develop many ancillary aspects to the programme such as talks, workshops, performance events and gigs that open out the activities of Pallas to wider groups, audiences and participators. So far this has borne fruit through collaborative projects with the likes of: Common Ground, Open House, Irish Architecture Foundation, the National College of Art & Design, and ESP TV, New York. The temporal security has enabled Pallas the potential for thinking ahead and for initiating expanded international engagements such as this ongoing *Artist-Run Europe* project.

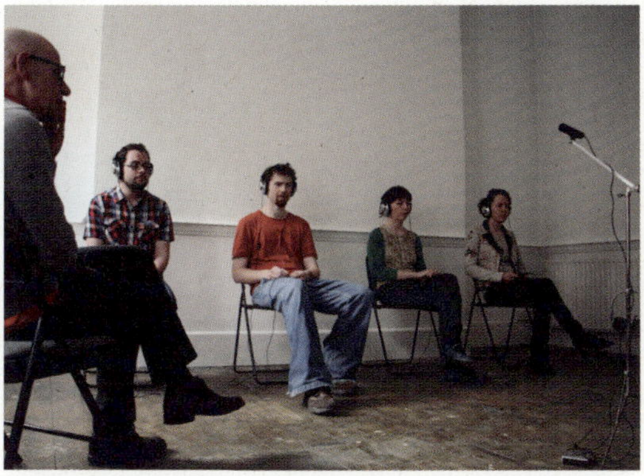

Toine Horvers
Copying as a Ritual Act
(performance documentation)
Pallas Projects
7 – 23 April 2011
Photograph by Roya Miller

Post script

As I write for this second edition, after 26 years of operating and many successes, the situation for artist-run spaces is still as precarious as ever, as inevitably another property boom has seized the city. Since 2016, a further 20 artist-run gallery and studio spaces have closed in Dublin alone. However, collective lobbying to Dublin City Council has yielded new conditions in the City Plan requiring developers to consider cultural space as part of their developments. This planning aspect is due to be strengthened further with a clause that requires existing arts organisations to be included in any redevelopment of their buildings. This potentially game-changing condition could have saved many arts organisations, and time will tell how it plays out in reality.

Arts spending has effectively doubled during the COVID years, however Ireland is still below the EU average. It has seen our funding increase significantly (set against a similarly big drop following the post 2008 crash), allowing us the stability to develop a funded programme of Artist Initiated Projects and international partnerships such as a fruitful relationship with HDLU, Zagreb, and this second edition. In the meantime we are on borrowed time in our current building, and massively increased rents will gobble a disproportionate amount of our grant in 2023. As such we continue to research, lobby, advocate, and focus on securing a long-term home for our studios and projects – a holy grail of artist-run culture.

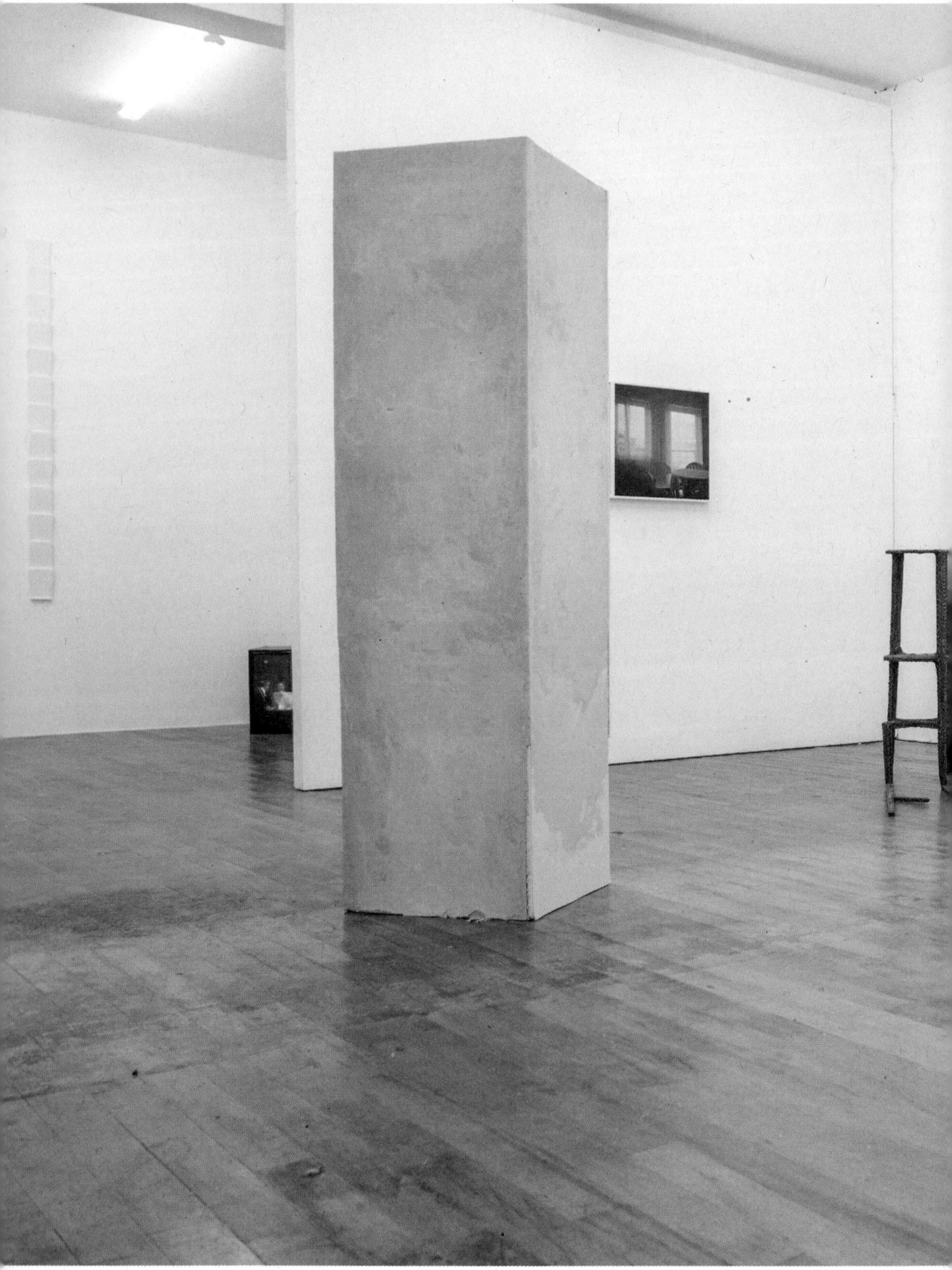

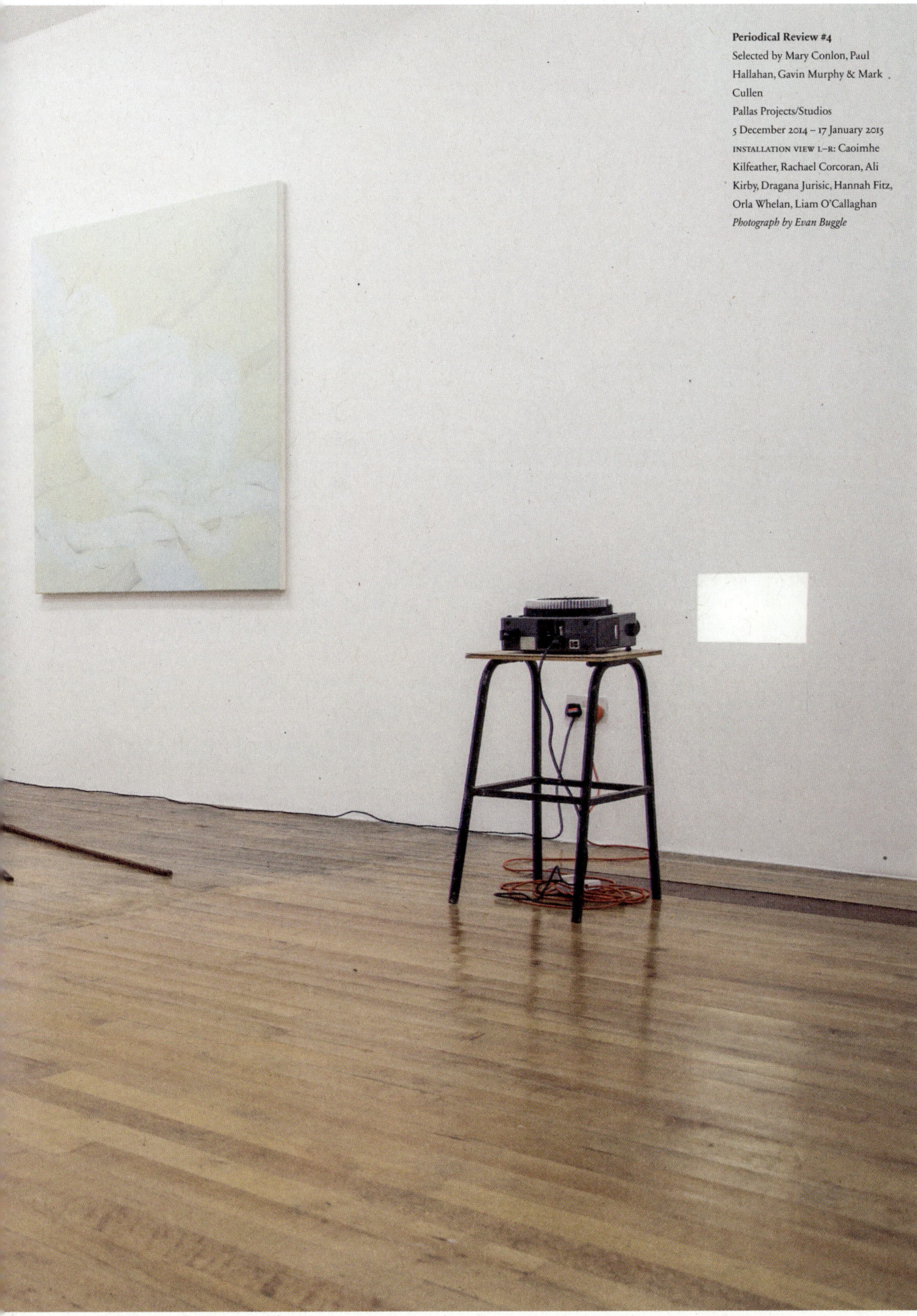

Periodical Review #4
Selected by Mary Conlon, Paul Hallahan, Gavin Murphy & Mark Cullen
Pallas Projects/Studios
5 December 2014 – 17 January 2015
INSTALLATION VIEW L–R: Caoimhe Kilfeather, Rachael Corcoran, Ali Kirby, Dragana Jurisic, Hannah Fitz, Orla Whelan, Liam O'Callaghan
Photograph by Evan Buggle

The Artist-led Archive

Sustainable Activism and the Embrace of Flux

Megs Morley

The *Artist-led Archive* is an artist-led initiative that began in 2006, as an attempt to intervene into a perceived pressing lack, or 'gap', in collective knowledge, about the contexts, histories and developments of artist-led culture in Ireland. In order to reflect and house a multiplicity of voices, perspectives, ideologies and genealogies, the creation of an archive aimed to form a knowledge commons created by multiple authors, where various perspectives and narratives could potentially emerge. Also conceived as an exhibition, the *Artist-led Archive* used the exhibition space as a site of visibility, to pose or broadcast both an alternative position and the potential of an alternative history, or multiplicity of histories, on this largely undocumented and less visible practice in Ireland.

Taking the approximate period from the 1970s to the present day – a period marking one of the most turbulent periods of economic, social and political change in Ireland – the *Artist-led Archive* aims to decipher the social and political contexts and conditions of artist-led initiatives, their economic independence (or lack thereof), their organisational structures, and how all of these factors affect their activities and life spans.

As the *Artist-led Archive* exhibition toured Ireland from 2006 to 2008[1], a variety of discussions were initiated to activate the terms of reference surrounding the critical ideas, pragmatic issues and socio-political contexts of artist-led culture in Ireland, particularly in relation

---

[1] The ALA exhibition toured (2006–2008) to Galway Arts Centre, The Lab Dublin, Catalyst Arts Belfast. The archive has also toured in other contexts – as part of the Model Sligo dialogues in 2009, Occupy Limerick in 2012, and 126's Footfall 2014. Most recently the ALA was exhibited in the Irish Museum of Modern Art's 'More than One Maker' exhibition and 'The Future is Self-Organised', curated by Pallas Projects in Limerick City Gallery of Art, in 2015.

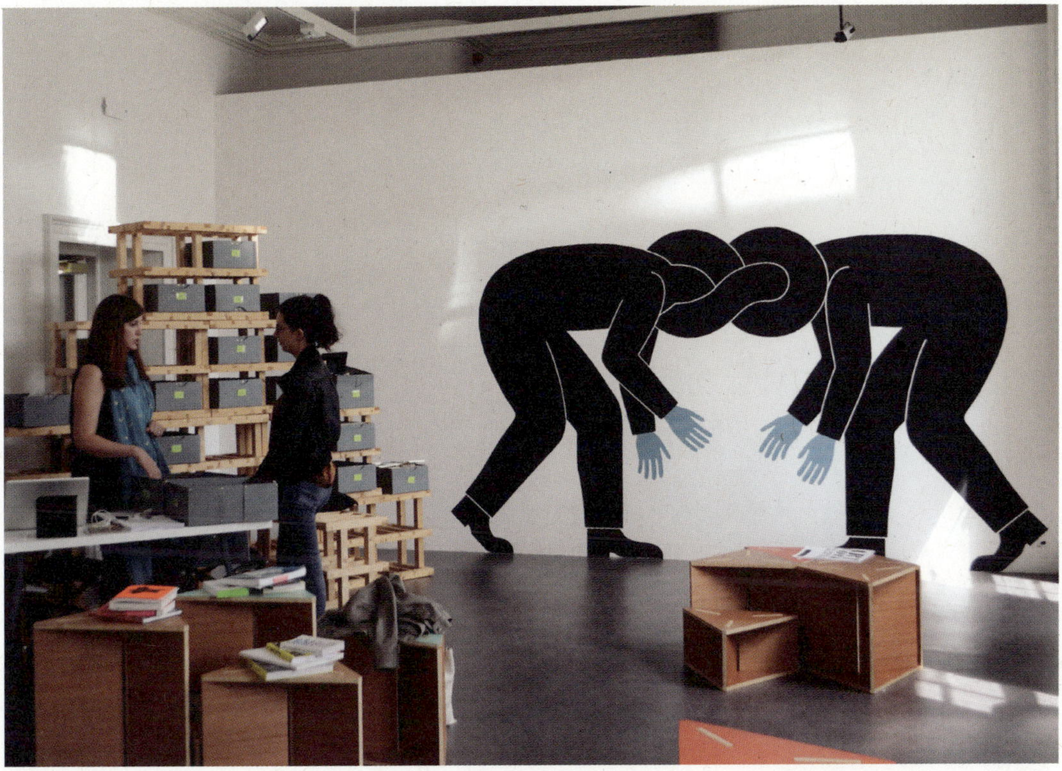

The Artist-led Archive –
Reactivation: Megs Morley
13 & 14 June 2015
Part of the exhibition **More than One Maker**
Irish Museum of Modern Art
28 May – 12 July 2015
Megs Morley pictured with Michaela Butler of Catalyst Arts, mural in background by The Project Twins
Photograph courtesy of Catalyst Arts

to other international artist-led cultures[2]. Alongside this, artists and groups responded to the archive creating further interventions, performances, sound pieces, and installations. Contributions from any group or individual who described or self-defined their activity as artist-led were collected; any documents or materials, including artworks, personal accounts and word-of-mouth were also accepted into the archive.

Now housed in the Special Collections of the National Visual Arts Library (NIVAL) in the National College of Art and Design (NCAD), Dublin, the *Artist-led Archive* currently contains materials relating to over 90 Irish artist-led initiatives from both North and South of the country, over the past 40 years. The materials range from publications, videos and films, photography, sonic works, correspondences, artworks, posters, and constitutive documents, providing a unique insight into the variations and similarities between initiatives operating at different periods and within distinct contexts across Ireland, acknowledging past initiatives' work and also exposing the artist-led roots of some of our oldest cultural vehicles and institutions.

[2] Multiple focus groups, panel discussions and symposia were coordinated including contributing talks by Julie Ault (Group Material), Julie Crawshaw (Midwest), Mick Fortune and Aileen Lambert (Real Art Project), Fergal Gaynor and Dobz O'Brien (Art not Art), Ben Geoghegan and Niall Moore (126), Daniel Jewesbury and Brian Kennedy (Art & Research Exchange), Sean Lynch and Deirdre O'Mahony (X-PO) and Lise Skou (U.K.K. – the Young Danish Artworkers Union).

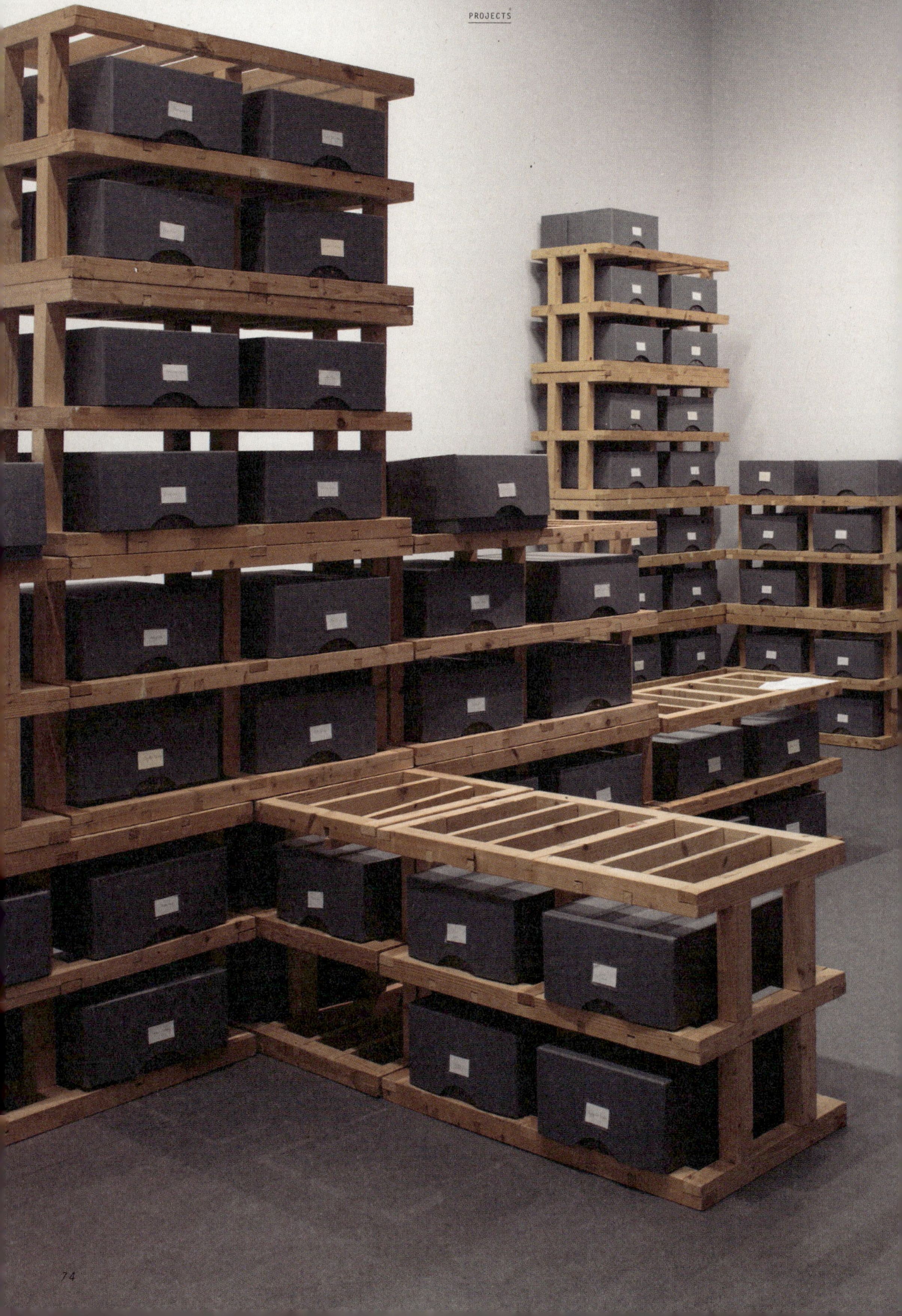

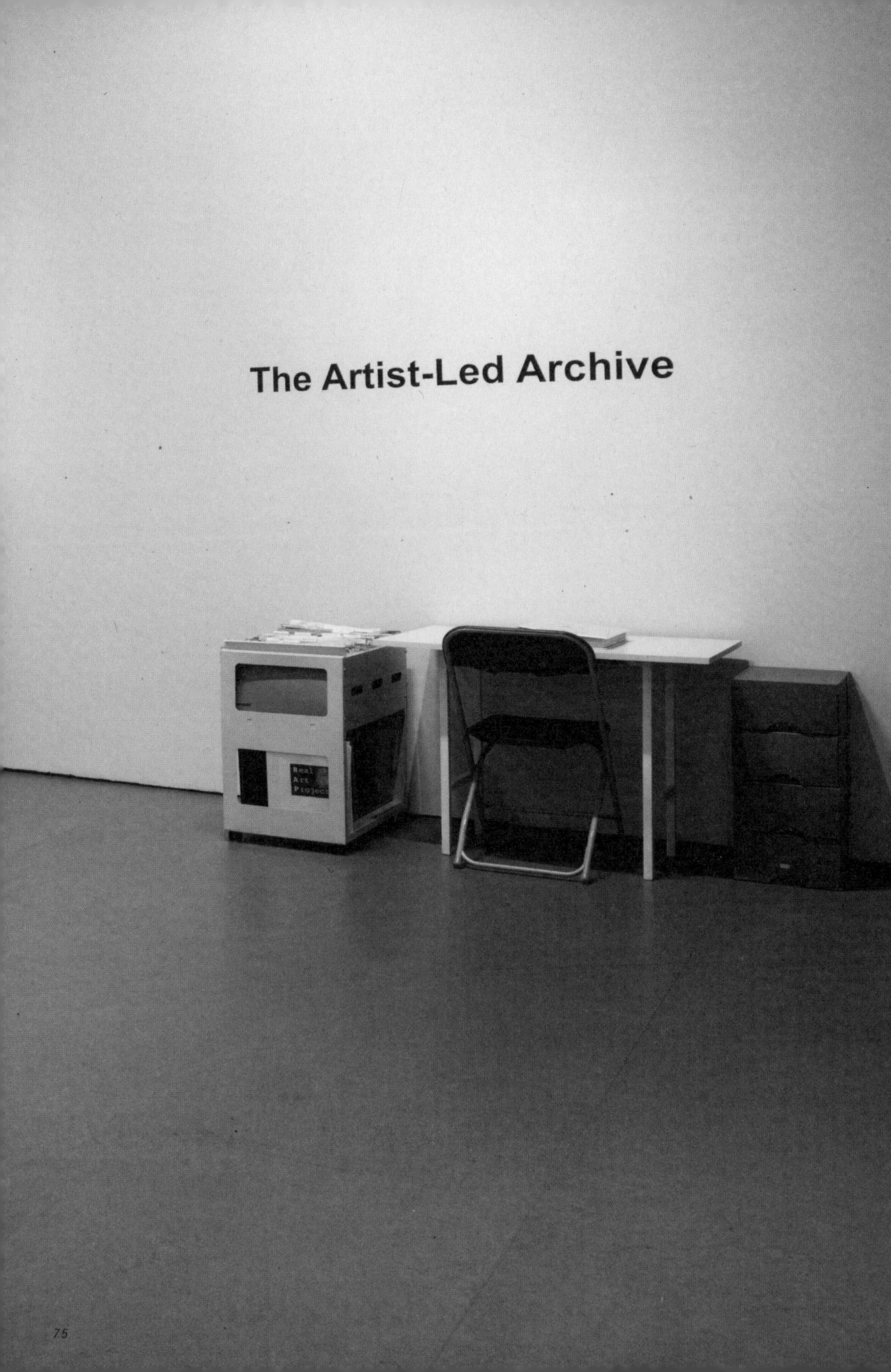
The Artist-Led Archive
Real
Art

↖ ***The Artist-Led Archive***
2006–ongoing
The Future is Self-Organised,
curated by Pallas Projects
Limerick City Gallery of Art
13 November 2015 – 15 January 2016
Photograph by Matthew Gidney, courtesy of the National Irish Visual Arts Library (NIVAL)

Emerging from decades of cultural censorship, from the 1970s on, through the *Artist-led Archive* we can start to see the beginning of the development of a growing, more independent or self-organised art scene in Ireland, wherein artists began to collaborate and claim space for experimentation, cross-disciplinarity, and in solidarity with social and political aims and objectives. While not specifically a counter to institutions as such, these artist-led initiatives certainly attempted to secure space for alternative practices that, in the context of a post-revolution malaise and religious oppression, had become culturally insular and suffocating for artists, to the extent that "those who had eyes to see and the heart to feel, was rebellious."[3]

Broadly speaking, many artist-led initiatives in the '70s and '80s in Ireland, for example Beuys' Northern Ireland workshop of the Free International University, known as Art and Research Exchange (ARE) in Belfast, Blue Funk, City Arts, and Women Arts Action Group (W.A.A.G.), were working in line with the politically oriented international artists groups from that period that operated in solidarity with social and political movements, such as civil rights, feminism and anti-war movements.

Equally, art forms such as media art, video art, live art and performance found a platform through artist-initiated spaces and groups such as Project Arts Centre, Triskel Arts Centre, Real Art Project, and Catalyst Arts' FIX Festival. As we entered the subsequent decades however, the Irish State began to perceive the arts as a way of projecting an image of Ireland that was modern, progressive and successful. This, along with the rise of the Celtic Tiger[4], meant there was much more State support for the arts. Artist-led groups in the '90s and '00s began to focus largely on the development of the infrastructure for contemporary Irish artists to create, produce and exhibit work, with spaces such as Pallas Studios in Dublin, and Catalyst Arts (Belfast), 126 Artist-Run Gallery (Galway), Cork Artists Collective (Cork), and Ground Up Collective (Clare), among many others, establishing a wide range of studio, production and residency facilities across Ireland that had largely been absent for artists outside of the capital.

Along with this, artists' organisations such as the Artists Collective of Northern Ireland, the Artists Association of Ireland and the Sculptors Society of Ireland (now Visual Artists Ireland, or VAI) were formed to collectively represent artists' concerns, and to improve the professional status and working conditions of artists working in all media in Ireland and Northern Ireland. It was also about this time that many of the more experimental spaces of previous decades began to adopt more

---

[3] Mervyn Wall – the Irish Authour and Secretary of the Arts Council for 1957–75, 'Some Questions about the Thirties', Mervyn Wall in conversation with Michael Smith (Ed.), The Lace Curtain 4, Summer 1971, pp 77–86.) cited in "Dreams and Responsibilities, The State and the Arts in Independent Ireland" a report by Brian P Kennedy, commissioned by the Arts Council in 1990.

[4] Celtic Tiger is a term referring to the economy of the Republic of Ireland between 1995 and 2000, a period of rapid real economic growth fuelled by foreign direct investment, and a subsequent property price bubble which rendered the real economy uncompetitive.

institutional models and roles as well, notably Project Arts Centre, Temple Bar Gallery & Studios, and the National Sculpture Factory, which had been started by artists in 1967, 1983 and 1989 respectively.

In recent years, during the recession, as elsewhere internationally, there has been a burgeoning of artist-led activity, particularly in urban centres across Ireland due to the availability of cheaper rents, with some Local Authority Economic Development Planning departments also actively seeking to regenerate urban centres through the presence of the creative industries. But with rumours of an economic upturn, many spaces have already closed their doors within the last few months in Dubin and elsewhere (Broadstone Studios, Faber Studios, Basic Space, and Block T to name but a few)[5]. While local authorities are happy to support creativity and the creative industries, the current preference is for temporary, and pop-up galleries and creative enterprises – to provide a kind of temporary fix in the wait for a more lucrative customer, or to generate that illusive 'creative economy'.

Regardless of the political affinity or genealogy of artist-led initiatives in Ireland, through self-organising and working collectively in the attempt to alter the conditions for initiating new frameworks for the production, dissemination and role of art, what the archive reveals is that many of these groups come face to face not only with the politics of self-organisation itself – as well as the struggle to find new and more democratic forms of organisation – but in the attempt to claim space for alternative critical practices, they inevitably become entangled within the dense web of local and national politics, policies, and agendas of local government and nation state. How the artist-led/self-organised strategise and negotiate their position or counter-position within this entanglement has ultimately sown the seeds for the longevity of many organisations, and by extension, their associated communities. Many more find themselves having to reinvent the wheel, where the learning and strategies developed by predecessors and now-defunct groups are sometimes lost, rather than being passed on or shared, meaning the same problems – precarity of labour, funding and venues – are encountered over and over again.

Over the course of the *Artist-led Archive*'s existence many such discussions around the sustainability of artist-led initiatives have taken place, and it is hoped that through the many shared cases and stories that are housed in it, further research, analysis and advocacy will continue to be generated towards creating a more supported, diverse and valued artist-led culture in Ireland.

[5] Block T are still open at time of writing, but announced in a press release dated the January 26th, 2016 that they will be vacating their premises in Smithfield on the 31st March 2016, which currently houses over 70 creative studios and workshop facilities, citing the impact of economic recovery on the property market as the main reason for their eviction (www.blockt.ie).

Producing the contemporary along the hegemony of a past-day elite and a present silent majority

A perspective on independent art spaces in the Netherlands

Freek Lomme

Over the past decade, I've been given quite a number of books by artist-run and independent art spaces, published on the occasion of their X-year existence, meant as calls-to-authority to policy makers and as relation gifts to the network. Hardly ever do matters reach another level: that of collective organisation, exchange of knowledge and so forth. People are simply happy celebrating yet another X-years of existence. It's also for this financial and time-wise lack to go beyond, that this text will not turn out a thought-through analysis of the Dutch situation, of contrasts between regions and nations, continents and cultures, but rather a kind or oral impression of the Dutch side – possibly the Noord-Brabant provincial side – that is to say my side of the story… for whatever that might be worth.

I came to work in the 'independent' arts in 2003 as a curator working for the artist-run space Lokaal 01, at the time based in Breda (NL) and Antwerp (BE). No idea why they hired me: I was just a bit of a 'want-to-figure-himself-out' kid, still studying arts and science at the University (not even an artist), who only just before, via artist friends, came about some art spaces, somewhere off centre in nearby cities. The people who ran it started it back in the late '70s–early '80s or came in after studying at art school and having started a career in the arts. Even though I was a bit of a strange duck to the organisation, I learned pretty much all I needed to know to work in the arts at Lokaal 01 – even more than at the university where I graduated a little later in arts policy (a particular history proven worthless to me while producing the future and having to cope with the day-to-day blindness of cultural policy's prophecies) and cultural identity (good) – and even more working at the Van Abbemuseum some years later, where learning about the arts was more about familiarising myself with forms of meetings.

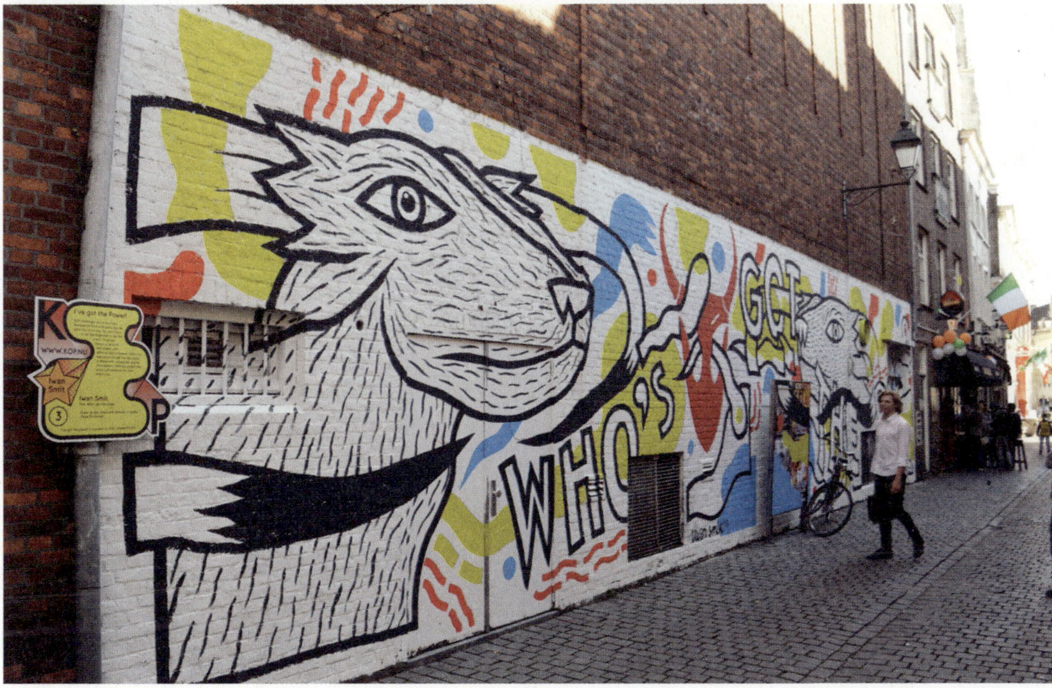

KOP, Breda
Iwan Smit
I've Got The Power!, 2015
Photograph by Michelle Vleugebls

What I learned at Lokaal 01, a knock-out for me at the time, is that there are certain people who go about discovering really particular stuff by their own conditions, not so much through conceptual written analysis (philosophy), or by test and check and double-check (natural sciences), or fiction (literature), but rather by creating experiences that through matter enter our environment and our sociability, and thus become present. These people (many call them artists) were to be respected, for who is a specialist in that particular unknown but that person, and how better to respect that experimental domain than by respecting the integrity of that person, and how better to position and promote that domain than by using the only way to manifest it besides the encounter of the work (which is the responsibility of the artist): by using ugly words? In love with speculative wonder, I suddenly felt I had found my place. This bunch of inarticulate individuals offered me a home.

—

The 1970s and early 1980s was a time when the economy went down while the welfare state was establishing itself, under guidance of the typical Dutch compartmentalisation of society through top-down political governance, wherein all Catholics and Protestants, the Socialists and the – at the time minor – Liberals, submitted to the few political parties who ran the nation together. In the enduring, yet slowly dying, spirit of a post-war urge to stimulate cultural uplifting, the late 80s and early 90s became a time wherein any graduate self-proclaimed artist could get a

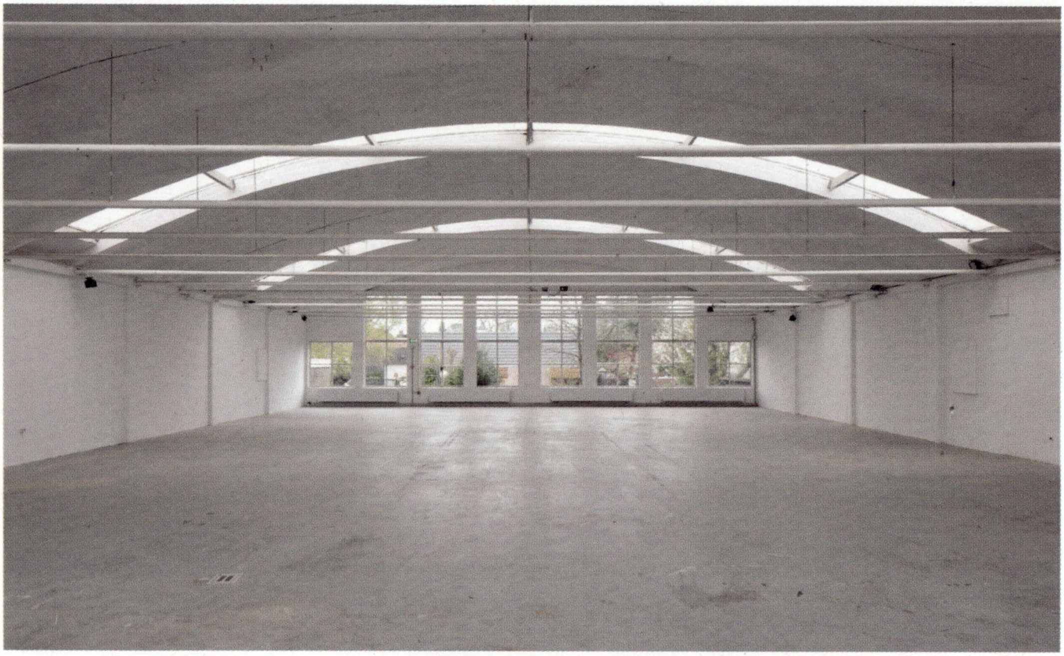

↑ **De Fabriek**, Eindhoven
Main workspace and exhibition space
De Fabriek is an artist-run space founded in 1980, situated in an old factory building from the '60s.
Photograph by Peter Cox

→ **KOP**, Breda
Dream On, 2012
Installation view
Photograph by Rachelle Delcroix

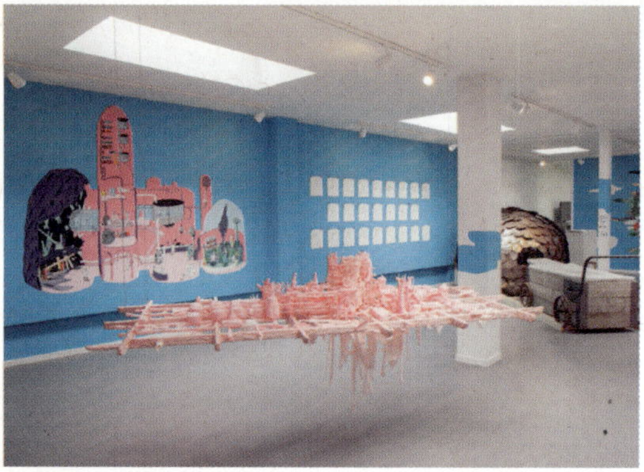

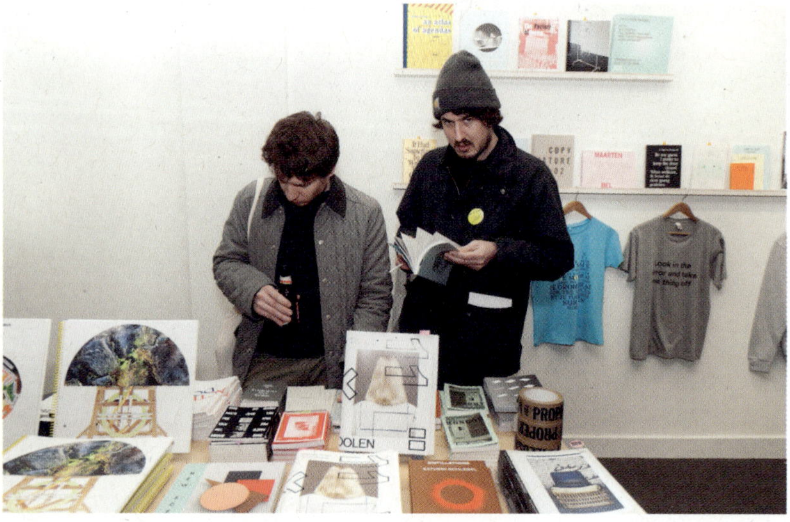

← **Onomatopee**, Eindhoven
Guys at the bookshop
Photograph by Fieke van Berkom

minimum wage, and when huge collections of public art were gathered, consisting of all too many locally produced works (many of which were recently dumped on the market or just put out with the trash). Even up to 2012, there was additional support in income for recent art school graduates. This was all inspired by notions of cultural capital, dominant within high-culture, when people visiting operas experienced historical legacies of revolutions after they drove in with leased cars, and after having purchased an artwork in a gallery, not knowing they were not part of society but were only part of a ruling class.

As a consequence of this top-down imposed idea of cultural uplifting (possibly a secret fear for radicalisation among smart dissidents to society), a minor part of policy made it all too easy for a complete social group of societal drop-outs called artists to give rise to their own economies in artist-run spaces. Their position was informed by motives such as (in our city) "inherent quality of arts" (I never knew what that motive meant) or, as (in our province), the "autonomous visual qualities of arts" (never knew what that meant either). Primarily these motives were the all-too-generic rules to fixate an art policy that supported the idea of emancipation through cultural uplifting. This bureaucratisation of bullshit motives turned out to be the gospel of a self-centred art world developed in parallel to the rise of the '80s yuppie culture of self-enriching kids that slowly, but gradually, took over the cultural authority of the post-war baby-boom generation; that of former hippies who effectively ended up being complete social democratic revisionists, too tolerant to see through the decadence of the third way.

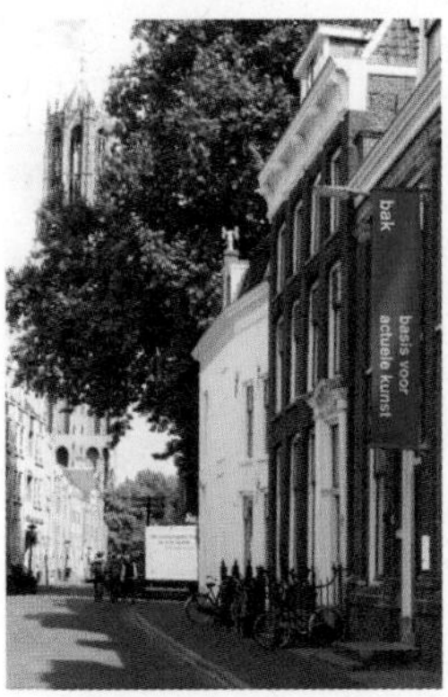

BAK, Utrecht
Exterior of the BAK building
Photograph by Victor Nieuwenhuijs

—

Over the course of the mid-'90s and into the early 2000s the Dutch art field slowly – very slowly in hindsight – started to change (no paradigm shift, simply little improvements). Pushed by the Mondriaan Foundation (founded in 1994), art spaces and artist-run spaces had to 'professionalise', and as their role shifted to mediation, the name label slowly changed to 'presentation spaces'. Artistically this meant that curating entered the field, and in managing terms it meant that policy became a more prominent factor in day-to-day management of these spaces. These changes were – and still are – considered a doom-scenario to those celebrating unconditional artistic autonomy (inherent value/autonomous qualities) within the art field itself. On the opposite end, even though there was a slowly growing awareness amongst policy makers that things should not to be taken for granted anymore, they did sustain a scene of independent art spaces. This proceeded for a while, as the former hegemonic political parties kept ruling the nation, even though the Catholic middle-of-the-road block lost position over the course of the 1990s.

But then something started to change, as in the early 2000s pioneering Dutch populist Pim Fortuyn stood up and the nation polarised, and polarised even more when a mentally troubled guy gunned him down. In hindsight Fortuyn seems the ideal Dutch citizen: outspoken, humanist, indifferent to authority yet tolerant to difference. What really changed was the turn to complete economic liberalism wherein the liberal idea of cultural uplifting stopped being a top-down public responsibility; while for Fortuyn, solidarity and cultural uplifting were apparent even if on an individual basis, this stopped being evident to his even more radical populist followers, resulting in a complete abandonment of respect for liberal research and development – formerly perceived as Cultural Capital – and instead opting for individual choice within capitalism under cultural protectionism inspired by a fear of the different. Over the course of the late 2000s, this idea completely put aside the cheap rhetoric of former-yuppie baby-boomers, rejecting the idea that public funding serves cultural uplift, that culture and arts has inherent quality, that there is something such as autonomous visual qualities.

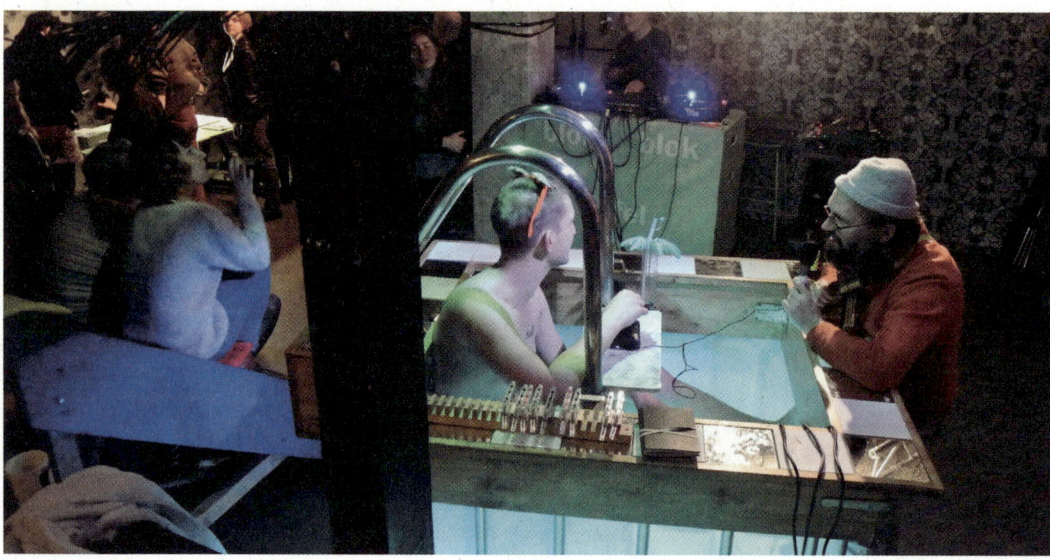

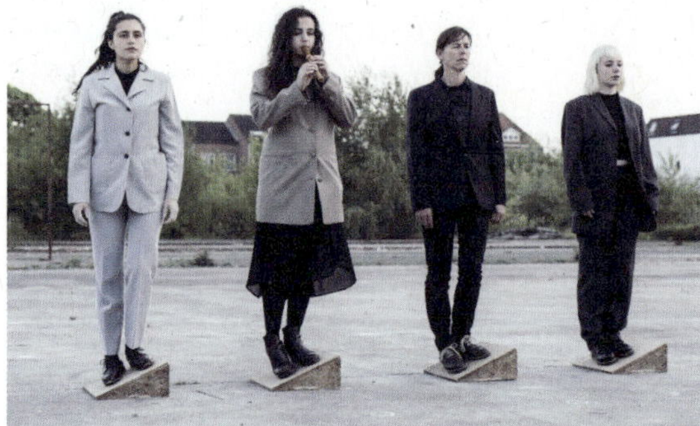

→ **KOP**, Breda
Gitte Hendrikx
Building Site/Building Sight, 2015
Photograph by Imara Angulo Vidal

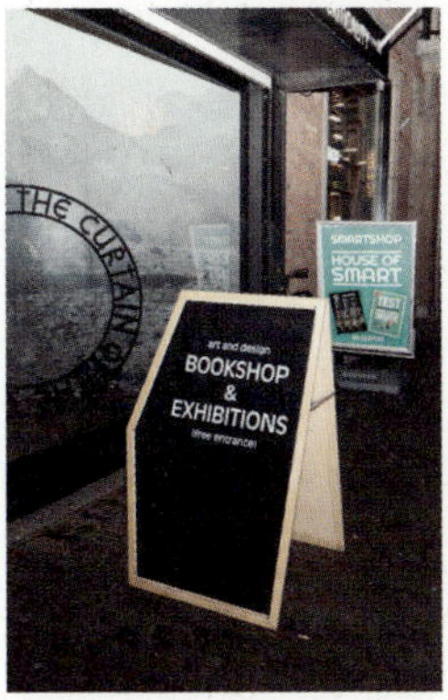

This is the point when government policy changed motivation: when belief for non-economic motivated research development and experiences were set apart by its prime investor. The objective turned to economic results, to independent, self-organised turnover, primarily via social segregation of target groups that divide culture among likes and un-likes. Although the arts, academic research and much alike, might have segregated from egalitarian access, it was primarily because mediation was supported too little in a society that simply did not respect cultural capital anymore, and turned to experiences. The citizen became a consumer and a producer. No greater cause in the arts is possible anymore, as the greater objective is no longer supported.

—

When, as a result of this change of perception, the arts were faced in early 2013 with their biggest budget cuts ever, they completely lost track of progressive public interest and had to turn to segregation even more, whether it be a focus for a segregated public fund to have blind people visit a museum of visual arts; or a focus for a segregated public by making profit via a party for youngsters during a museum night; or a focus for a segregated public with a high-end entrance fee to an afternoon with collectors. It is all market motivated and audiences will never blend anymore: the institutions will just change the interior, clothes and tongue to meet the demographics of their visiting consumers. But what this means most of all is that the perception of art will always be framed to the eye of the target group, and, as a result of this turn to the *target group* over the former humanist focus for cultural elevation, the economic basis for independent production for a greater cause of humanist man is abandoned. From now on, art will align itself with an agenda, with a subculture, with a segregated economy. There is no public good, there will only be publics of which some might survive and some might be ignored as unviable.

↑ **Onomatopee**, Eindhoven
Photograph by Fieke van Berkom

← **Extrapool**, Nijmegen
Maarten Bel making cassettes with sound and voice on the spot during a series called ***Landstaal***

The problem within resultant contemporary cultural consumerism is the lack of what's on offer, of access to ambiguity and doubt and of radical differences produced from a position standing above the cultural spectrum (as art effectively should). This leaves an inability to face the contemporary: to actively engage the doubtfulness of our being in the face of our history, and in facing our (lack of) opportunities. The idea that art is about joy and beauty f**ks up the capacity of art as a force of cultural empowerment and is a mindless capitalist construct exploiting a capitalist experience economy. Basically, this is a political choice, as we can also opt for other options.

—

I feel that it is out of a necessity to speak up for this humanist solidarity that independent spaces exist, stimulate production of a cultural meta-individual uniqueness, and try to deliver that with all the means available to an audience. It is for this reason, I feel, that Dutch independent spaces still call themselves presentation spaces – ranging from small spaces in the provinces such as Hedah in Maastricht, to established places such as Witte de With in Rotterdam – and have organised themselves in a union called De Zaak Nu (The Now Case), which is the equivalent of Common Practice in the UK. Likewise we see a new awareness among Dutch artists who organised themselves in Platform BK: a new collective way of organising work-spaces for art, design and architecture in ceramics, metal, graphics and more; and see growing awareness within a relatively a new type of organisation: art-clusters who rent out spaces, manage studio spaces and more. This is happening at various geopolitical levels: the city, the region and national.

I know many of my colleagues in the field will disagree, but for a long time, prior to the excessive budget cuts that forged a cultural paradigm shift, the art field, and the independent spaces in particular, felt they were tolerant to culture while they actually turned their backs to culture. Nevertheless the accomplishments within this all-too-segregated scene were remarkable in the way that it progressed our legacy of humanism into an era of increasing complexity. We need to be able to doubt within our horizontal proximity, and art does so within our experience, within direct encounters. It does so by demanding us to experience by our human capacity, positioned above taste, religion or anything whatsoever, and thus liberal in that sense. That is the biggest task for independent contemporary art spaces. It will never be unconditional or autonomous, even when the conditions might be vague, too experimental to legitimise in parallel to the experience of the work delivered, but that is exactly what living in the contemporary means. That is what true cultural production, true development means: setting hearts and minds, opening up. This implies the belief that we can all think for ourselves, and the necessity of battle while facing our present reality. It's a way to counter fear for eternal cultural shifts. As any other hegemonic culture we call democracy, it might be said that The Netherlands is simply changing one form of cultural dictatorship (that of an elite) for another (that of the silent majority, unwilling to emancipate). Yet what is most problematic is the fact that we ignore the use of the human capacity our parents have left to us as well. Why should we not finish the project of modernity, called emancipation and freedom, especially as hierarchy is abandoned and the individual is finally left on its own?

I'm active in local lobbying for small art spaces (K9 in Eindhoven), initiated provincial organisation, and am a board member of De Zaak Nu. It's a f***ing lot of volunteering work but together we can gain knowledge that helps us to inform others and ourselves. This knowledge can inform all stakeholders, either private or public, and convince them to invest. Locally we're too few spaces to come up with serious data, but nationally we can – and this data can be mirrored in a local setting and therefore be of representative value. Moreover, within the local scale, some organisations are featured who don't have paid staff (permanent or freelance), and might not even have a permanent office, and are therefore in a very precarious situation, while within the national context, some big organisations are featured. What I mean to say is that we should not be afraid of other leve ls, but should try and push for the right attitude in all levels. Whom if not us should do this? Nobody is going to care otherwise.

And if that would not work out, we can always turn to revolution, I once heard Rebecca Gordon-Nesbitt say. I would not dare to argue that.

Nieuwe Vide, Haarlem
Vito Willems,
video installation with sound
20 years of deferred value, 2015
20 1-day solo exhibitions
Photograph by Saskia Burggraaf

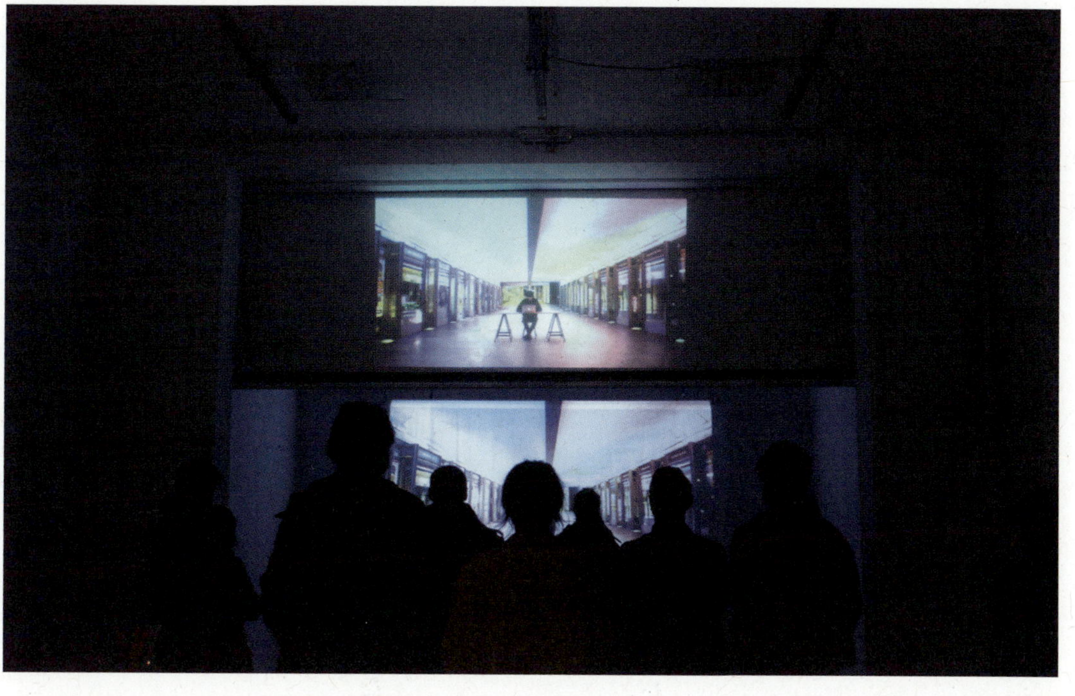

Handle with care

Artist-led spaces in Limerick

Noelle Collins

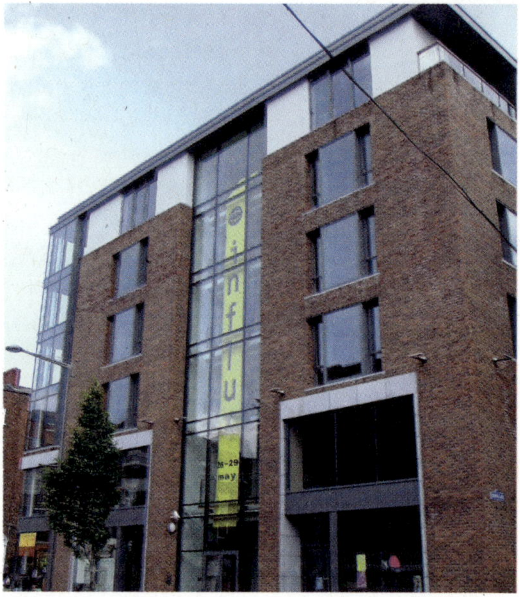

in_flux
Occupy Space, exterior of
Thomas Street Building
Photograph courtesy of Occupy Space

Space is seductive, a covetable asset that requires constant care, considerable attention, and a level of investment that is normally associated with institutions and commercial enterprises. The economic crisis and property market collapse that peaked in Ireland in 2008 had a severe impact in Limerick. Job losses hit the headlines[1] and many city centre businesses closed their doors, leaving a bleak streetscape. As rental prices dropped, spaces within the city became more affordable, and in 2009 a group of recent graduates from the local art college-Limerick School of Art & Design[2] were able to establish Wickham Street Studios in a domestic property that had stalled in the early stages of a drastic renovation. A five year lease was agreed, 1970s carpets were stripped out, and fresh plasterboard and strip lighting was installed creating rudimentary workspaces for a dozen artists. Wickham Street Studios launched publicly in September, 2009, populated by the founding members who were predominantly painters. As a resource WSS increased the available workspace for artists and, most importantly, offered reasonable studio rent that made it more feasible to continue the work of being an artist. This was a compelling reason for new graduates to live in Limerick, and perhaps the first marker to indicate a shift in the status quo.

Contrary to the economic climate, artist-led spaces experienced a kind of boom, Faber Studios, Occupy Space, Raggle Taggle, Like Studios and Ormston House were some of the artist-led initiatives that were established in the city's slack spaces between 2009 and 2011.

---

[1] In Jan 2009 Computer manufacturer Dell announced that it would move production from Limerick to Poland, with expected job losses of 1,900.

[2] Wickham Street Studios founded by Ramon Kassam in 2009 with Noelle Collins, Gerry Davis, Aoife Flynn, Sean Guinan, Emmet Kierans, Paraic Leahy, Laura McMorrow, Aislinn O'Keeffe, Kevin O'Keeffe, Tom Prendergast and Paul Rhatigan.

But how was this possible? How could local artists afford to operate exhibition spaces and workshops in the city centre? At this time property development was at a standstill and pockets of vacant commercial units throughout the city centre were of concern to Limerick City Council. In 2009 an initiative was set in motion to improve the appearance of vacant properties by displaying art, craft and design in the windows. This short-term solution was problematic but there were mutual benefits for all parties involved; vacant units were revitalised, they looked appealing to potential tenants and they also provided a platform for local 'creatives' to promote their work. The initiative was named "Creative Limerick – Connect to the Grid", a concept developed by Lise-Ann Sheahan that was coordinated through the Economic Development and Planning Department at Limerick City Council. Creative Limerick adopted the role of middleman between creatives and property owners. Spaces were initially provided rent free[3] and included public liability insurance from the Council. This is one of the main reasons why artist-run spaces were able to flourish in the city.

Faber Studios and Occupy Space were the first artist-led initiatives to redefine how this scheme was implemented by proposing to use not just the windows but entire units, extending into substantial vacant spaces to provide studio and exhibition facilities. The Thomas Street Centre, a new seven-storey development struggling to attract a paying tenant, was one of the vacant properties that provided considerable space for artists through the Creative Limerick initiative. The ground floor became a creative hub for the city with Faber Studios and Occupy Space promoting contemporary art practices alongside other grassroots organisations. Faber Studios was founded by four recent graduates from the sculpture department[4] who required studio and workshop facilities to continue their practices. Located on the corner of Catherine Street, their unit was primarily used as a studio space but members also programmed exhibitions, artists talks and events. Occupy Space was established by members of Wickham Street Studios, myself included, who were eager to provide a dedicated exhibition space for graduates and emerging artists from all disciplines[5]. A high turnover of events ensured visibility across national event listings, and as exhibition making and organisational skills were developed amongst the team we were able to secure funding for projects through the Arts Council.

[3] Limerick City Council charged reduced rates for the landlord and invited applications from 'creatives' to activate the vacant properties and to take responsibility for all utilities.

[4] Faber Studios founded by Clive Moloney, Chris Boland, Sarah Bolger and Stephen Neary in 2009.

[5] In 2009 Limerick City Gallery of Art and The Belltable Arts Centre, dedicated exhibition spaces, were operating offsite programmes while their respective homes underwent renovations. There were limited exhibition opportunities for visual artists which also motivated artists to organise exhibition programmes.

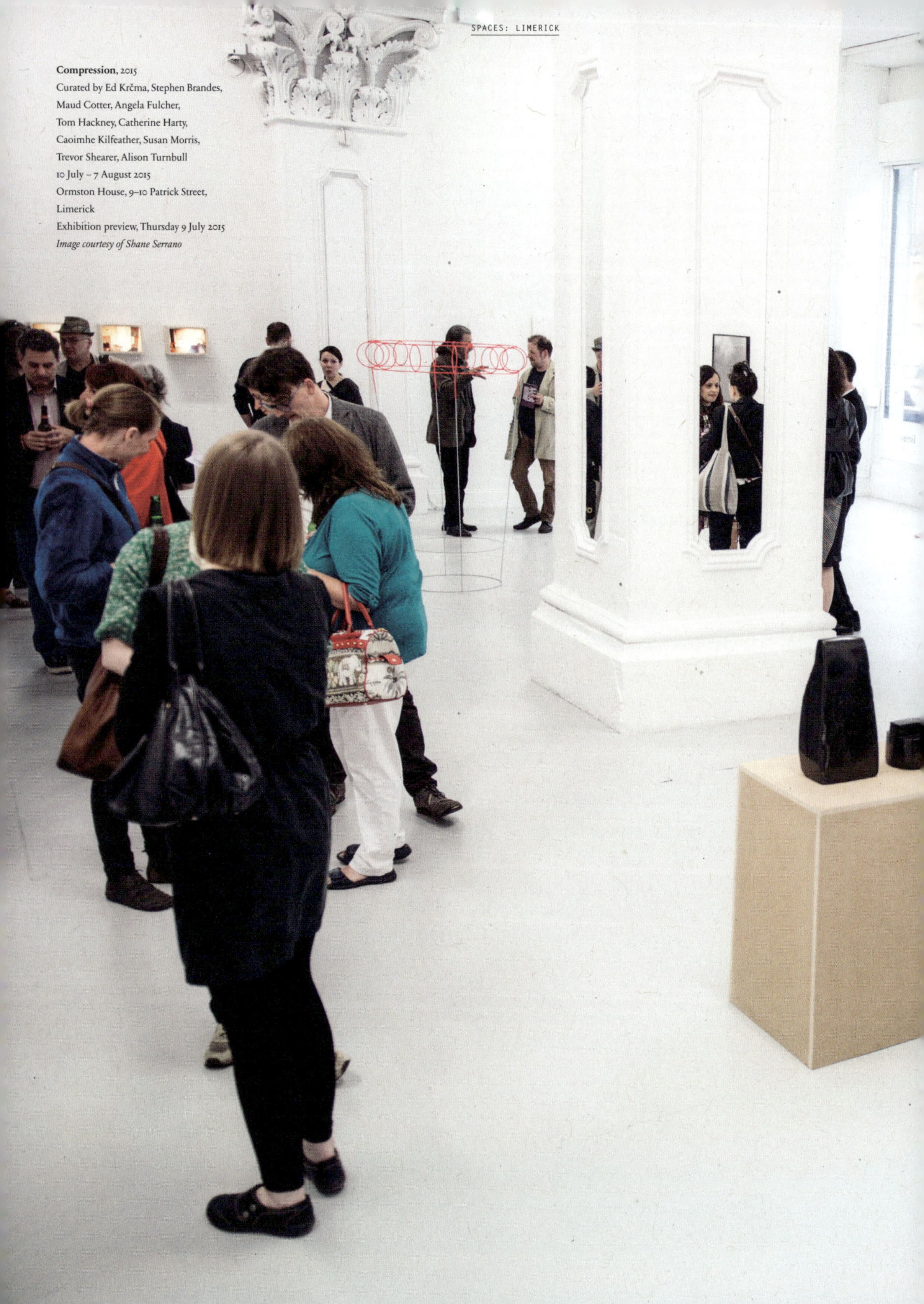

Compression, 2015
Curated by Ed Krčma, Stephen Brandes, Maud Cotter, Angela Fulcher, Tom Hackney, Catherine Harty, Caoimhe Kilfeather, Susan Morris, Trevor Shearer, Alison Turnbull
10 July – 7 August 2015
Ormston House, 9–10 Patrick Street, Limerick
Exhibition preview, Thursday 9 July 2015
Image courtesy of Shane Serrano

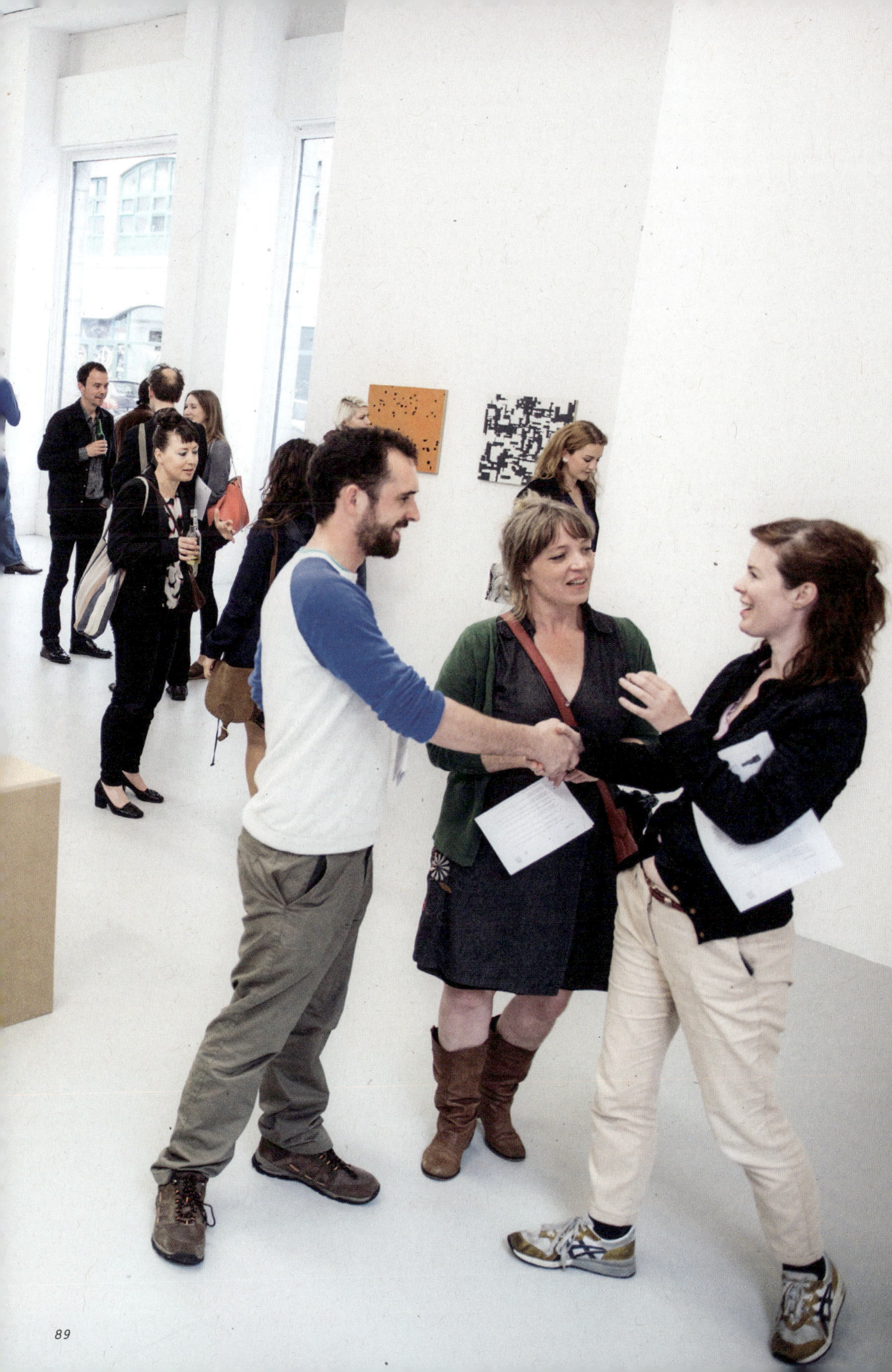

NOELLE COLLINS

→ Paul Tarpey
Like Clockwork, 2011
Video Installation
Exhibited at CatDig Festival 13 – 15 May 2011
Faber Studios, Thomas Street
Photograph courtesy of the artist

Emerging at the same time, Raggle Taggle[6], a hive of artist studios and a bookable ground floor exhibition space, was another prominent artist-run space to champion opportunities for emerging visual artists. Located in the National Irish Bank Building on Sarsfield Street, Raggle Taggle was working towards a more sustainable model – income generated through studio and exhibition space rental was used to cover utilities and to build storage facilities. The studio members, students and recent graduates exhibited their works in solo and group exhibitions. Local community groups and societies were eager to use the ground floor and this wide-ranging remit of activity contributed to a positive environment for creative practitioners.

The provision of artist-run spaces, alongside the existing visual arts facilities, unfolded the potential for live events, screenings, discussions, performances and experimental projects, established Limerick as a fertile testing ground for ideas. A highlight of this activity and an ambitious achievement for an artist-led space was *in_flux* which ran in May 2011. Occupy Space proposed *in_flux* as an artist-led alternative to commercial art fairs with the potential to occur periodically at other sites of artist-led activity. Ten such initiatives presented works throughout the remaining six stories of the Thomas Street Centre: 126 Artist-Run Gallery, Galway; Block T, Dublin; Transmission, Glasgow; Basement Project Space, Cork; Transition, London; Monster Truck, Dublin; Wolfart Projectspaces, Rotterdam; Catalyst Arts, Belfast; SOMA Contemporary, Waterford; and 1646, The Hague. The expansive exhibition celebrated the autonomy of artist-led spaces and was complemented by a social space on the top floor labelled the 'in_flux salon'. The salon hosted events including Pecha Kucha with participating artists and spaces, and 'What it is not/ New Works UK', a programme of new film and video works by UK based artists curated by Gil Leung, screened in partnership with Limerick City Gallery of Art and LUX Art Agency. EVA International[7] also supported the in_flux salon, creating a reading area with free copies of exhibition catalogues from previous years.

Some months later, in August, 2011, Ormston House[8] was established on Patrick Street and is evidently the final visual arts space to emerge through the Creative Limerick initiative. Ormston House operates a slightly different model: a Director/Curator runs the exhibition space with a team of students and recent graduates in supporting roles. This structure offers greater stability for planning, fundraising and programming as the position of Director/Curator is consistent from year to year. Ormston House is also a members' organisation, artists pay a membership fee which allows them to submit proposals to open call exhibitions twice a year.

[6] Raggle Taggle Consortium founded by Alan Crowley in 2009.

[7] Not unfamiliar territory for EVA International as they had utilised the Thomas Street building as an exhibition venue in 2010.

[8] Ormston House was established by Mary Conlon in 2011.

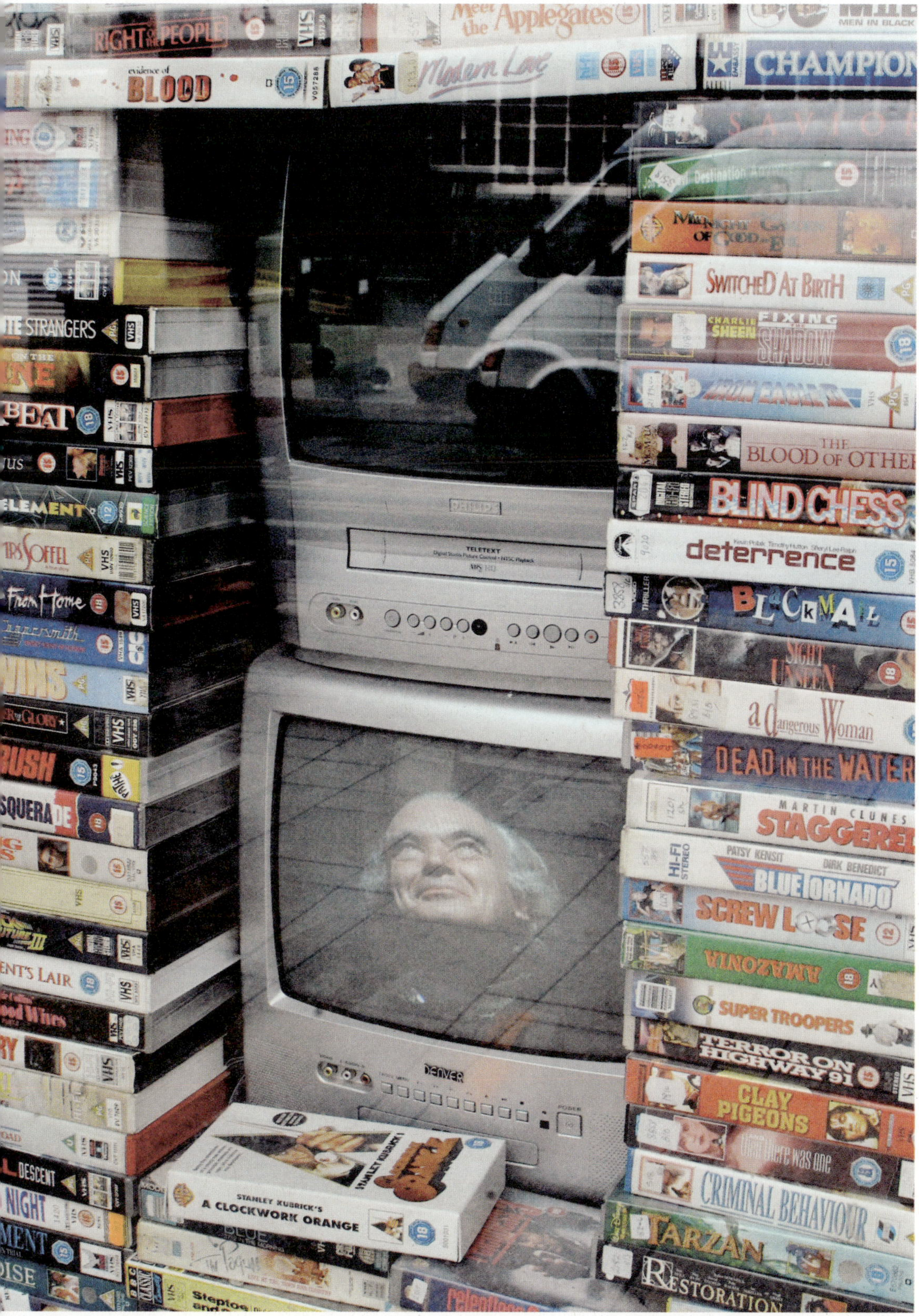
RIGHT TO THE PEOPLE
Meet the Applegates
MEN IN BLACK
evidence of BLOOD
Modern Love
CHAMPION
TE STRANGERS
Destination
SWITCHED AT BIRTH
CHARLIE SHEEN FIXING THE SHADOW
THE BLOOD OF OTHER
BLIND CHESS
TELETEXT
deterrence
Kevin Pollak Timothy Hutton Sheryl Lee Ralph
BLACKMAIL
SIGHT UNSEEN
a dangerous Woman
DEAD IN THE WATER
MARTIN CLUNES STAGGERED
PATSY KENSIT DIRK BENEDICT
BLUE TORNADO
SCREW LOOSE
AMAZONIA
SUPER TROOPERS
TERROR ON HIGHWAY 91
CLAY PIGEONS
CRIMINAL BEHAVIOUR
TARZAN
RESTORATION
DENVER
STANLEY KUBRICK'S A CLOCKWORK ORANGE
ENT'S LAIR
DESCENT
NIGHT
Steptoe

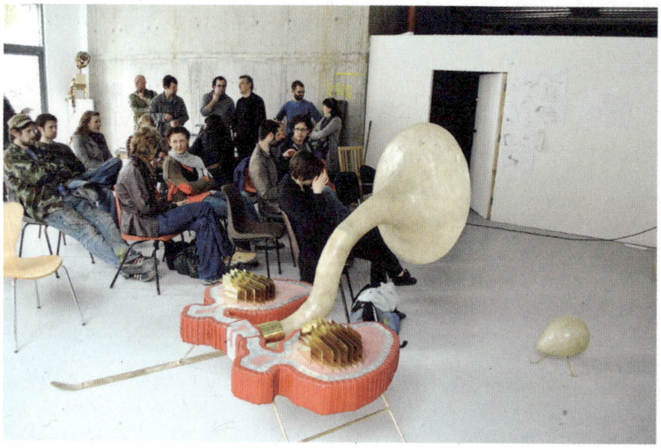

← **Artist's Talk with Seán Lynch**, May 2010
Artworks in the foreground by studio member Chris Boland
Faber Studios, Thomas Street
Photograph by Paul Tarpey

↓ **Stone Soup**, 2014
Ormston House, residency in collaboration with Basic Space
1 – 31 July 2014
The Sailor's Home, O'Curry Street, Limerick
BACK ROW L–R: Jason Dunne, Oisin O'Brien, Niamh Brown, Marta Slawinska, Patrick Leydon, James O'hAodha, Hannah Fitz, Paul Maguire, Niamh Moriarty, Ruth Clinton, Daniel Tuomey.
FRONT ROW L–R: Molly O'Leary, Eilish Murrihy, Alan James Burns, Katie Mooney Sheppard, Greg Howie, Suzanne Walsh
Final public event, Saturday 26 July 2014
Image courtesy of Daniel Tuomey

→ Deirdre O'Mahony
Public Works, 2015
Askeaton Contemporary Arts
Welcome to the Neighbourhood
artist residency, 13 – 25 July 2015
Photograph by Seán Lynch

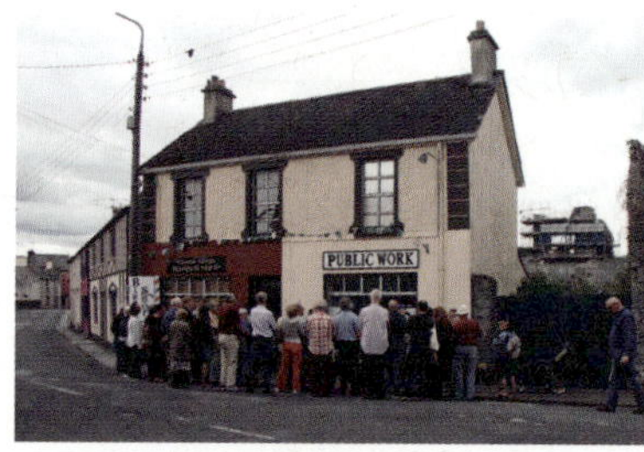

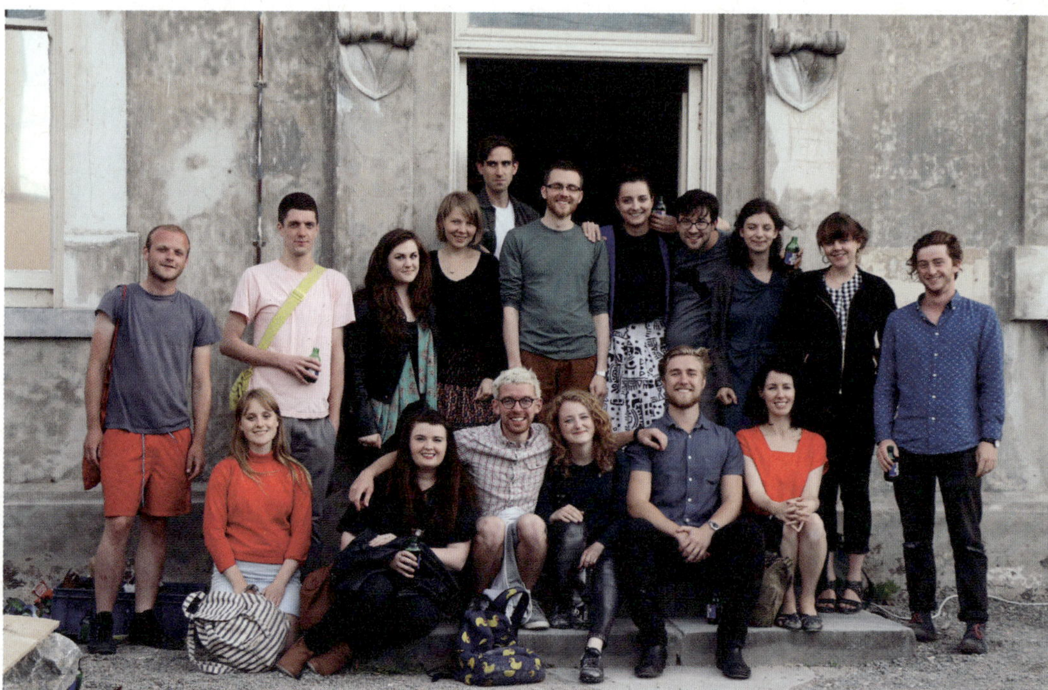

The diverse artist-led activity that revitalised Limerick's vacant spaces was contingent upon the availability of the slack spaces in which they operated. Paradoxically, one of the main objectives of the Creative Limerick initiative was to attract potential tenants to these slack spaces so the outcome is inevitable, a kind of *fait accompli*. City centre artist-led spaces, bright and inviting, attract potential tenants, and in 2012 the Thomas Street Centre was vacated to make way for a buyer. After almost three years of programming, presenting forty exhibitions and numerous events at that location, Occupy Space "deinstalled" and the building remained entirely unoccupied for a further four years. Occupy Space has since continued as a nomadic entity hosting temporary exhibitions in partnership with local venues and slack spaces. Artist-run spaces operating under the Creative Limerick initiative were constantly at risk of losing their premises, but without that support Occupy Space encountered the full burden of rent, rates and insurance. Uprooting and relocating for pop-up exhibitions has had a considerable impact on the general visibility and perceived stability of the organisation. Faber Studios relocated to Henry Street just ahead of the Thomas Street Building closure. The new location, a former furniture store was spacious, new members came on board, and partitions were constructed to provide studio and exhibition spaces. Improvements were made to the cosmetic appearance of the building, but the artists were not in a position to make long-term repairs and this became problematic for both the artists and the property owners. Almost a year later discussions opened around Limerick's designation as a national city of culture and requests were made to safeguard artist-run spaces for a fixed term. This request was unsuccessful, and by the end of 2013 both Faber Studios and Raggle Taggle had closed their doors.

In 2014, Limerick's designation as a national city of culture was evidence of a cultural rebranding. Some part of that resurgence must be credited to the recent history of artist-run spaces and projects throughout the city and county. However, it has also become increasingly difficult to access vacant spaces for visual arts events, and the Creative Limerick initiative seems to have disconnected from the grid. Many of the conditions that encouraged artists to establish spaces in Limerick are still present: it's an inexpensive place to live, graduate numbers are rising, and the existing arts infrastructure has more than a hint of artist-led heritage. An established network exists in Limerick, through visual arts organisations such as Contact Studios, The Limerick Printmakers, Askeaton Contemporary Arts and EVA International – Ireland's Biennial (all set up at different times by artists). Limerick is now competing for the 2020 European Capital of Culture; this is the time to look at sustainability, to support grassroots projects and to develop long-term strategies that support a healthy local arts ecology. As local government comes to terms with the value of arts and culture as factors in urban regeneration, perhaps a more sustainable solution can be developed.

AA Bronson
Notes from Berlin

FRIDAY, 24 FEBRUARY 2016, 7:09 PM

I am sitting in a first class compartment on the ICE train from Munich to Berlin. My husband Mark Jan Krayenhoff van de Leur is sitting opposite me, also on his computer, and behind him is a sliding glass door to the second-class compartment, which opens and closes rather randomly. Apparently its motion sensor is a little too responsive.

It is dark outside, which transforms the trip from something charming to something boring. When I look out of the window, I see Mark's reflection, tapping at his keyboard. Not a single light illuminates the landscape. The sound of the wheels on the tracks provides a relentlessly ambient soundtrack.

Last night my exhibition PLAID opened at Deborah Schamoni in Munich. A collaboration with Keith Boadwee, the exhibition features a series of apparently fairly conventional modernist paintings. However, a publication reveals the secret subtext of the works: page after page depicts Keith and I naked in the studio, clambering on ladders, spurting red, brown and green paint from our assholes. In full-page portraits, each of us proudly displays the douche-bag (so to speak) we use to fill our rectum with paint. This is a technique championed by Keith many years ago. I invited him to revisit the technique during a residency in Salzburg, as a form of collaboration and a kind of homage to Austria's history of both Actionism and Psychotherapy, Nitsch and Brus, Freud and Jung – and artists' collaboration itself.

8:45 PM

The history of artist-run organisations in the Germanic countries dates back to the early 1800s. Among the oldest art associations are the Albrecht Dürer Society in Nuremberg (1792), the Kunstverein in Hamburg (1817), and the Badischer Kunstverein in Karlsruhe (1818). It wasn't long before these kinds of associations, many formed by artists, existed in every major Germanic city. Their primary purpose was to take art out of the hands of the aristocracy and make it an aspect of public life.

Artist-run culture as we know it today began in 1897, when a group of artists broke away from the Vienna Artists' Society (founded 1861) and its Kunstlerhaus (built 1865–68) to form the Wiener Secession. Gustav Klimt was the first President, and their official magazine was titled Ver Sacrum. The Secession stood opposed to the historicism that prevailed in art-making of the time. In 1898, the group's exhibition house was built in the vicinity of Karlsplatz, on the ring-road that symbolised wealth and culture at the time. Designed by Joseph Maria Olbrich, the exhibition building still exists today, and the programming is still run by the artist-members.

To my mind, the Secession has an almost ideal structure. New artist members must be proposed and supported by existing members. They are voted in for life by the membership. An artist board and a President elected from the membership runs the programme of the Secession, although a professional staff runs the organisation on a daily basis. The President of the Board is responsible for maintaining the continuity of the organisation. The Board chooses programmes from proposals made by the membership. (Outside proposals are also occasionally accepted.) These are mostly solo exhibitions. Once chosen, they are handed over to a group of exhibition coordinators, employees who take on individual projects and see them through to completion. A professional administrative staff runs the finances, daily management, and upkeep of the building, the programme, and the membership.

TUESDAY, 1 MARCH 2016, 8:28 AM

While we were in Munich, our apartment was broken into, and although the thieves took a gold watch, some jewellery and papers, and an old computer, somehow none of it seems to have been of so much consequence. The carpenter has just arrived to repair the front door, which was badly damaged.

What is the difference between an artists' studio and an artist-run space? Not much, I would say. This morning we have four assistants arriving to work on a big project, which will be exhibited at Art Basel in June. They are all artists and designers of various types, and when they are all here at once it feels rather like Santa's workshop... but also very much like the artist-run spaces I remember from the early '70s, when we were beginning to set up such things.

In 1971, when we (meaning Jorge, Felix and me, of General Idea) came up with the idea of opening an artists' archive and distribution centre, the mood was much the same: a group of artists sitting around a big table coming up with a scheme, and then later, with the help of friends, seeing it through. Art Metropole opened in the front half of what was then our studio, and Art Metropole's first employees would wake us up each morning, as they arrived for their coffee. In other words there was an intimacy to the operation that belies the more professional, even corporate, face on Canada's centres today.

The first time I visited the Western Front, a gigantic sprawling old mason's hall in Vancouver, I was struck by the number of people living there in various arrangements. And in addition to the artists' living quarters, there were two immense meeting halls, an eating hall, a kitchen designed to feed hordes, and various other facilities. The feeling was of something midway between a commune and a co-op. In fact the earliest artist-run facilities have always been co-ops. Artists' co-ops date back to the late 1940s in Canada and probably earlier in the UK, where for some time they were the norm. When the Canada Council began to fund these centres however, they demanded of them that they be non-profit corporations, little simulacra of the funding organisation itself. I suppose that this was to satisfy the politicians, but in the end they sowed the seeds of a vast bureaucratisation, which to my mind has castrated the entire Canada-wide network of artist-run endeavours.

WEDNESDAY, 2 MARCH 2016, 10:46 AM

For the last three years I have been living in Berlin. My husband Mark and I came as a guest of the DAAD, to participate in their one-year residencies, which have transformed Berlin's art scene over the last fifty years. The art scene here is vast and sprawling and international, although the city itself is about the same population as Toronto. A curator friend estimates that there are more than 120 artist-run project spaces at any given moment; alternates to the alternates, if you will. Berlin has a history of do-it-yourself gritty culture-making, and it is refreshing to see artists taking matters into their own hands without the endless bureaucratic squabbling and fretting that seems to dominate Canada. Although most of these spaces have no funding at all, the Berlin Senate has been awarding €30,000 each to 20 spaces annually for exceptional work. Hopefully this programme will expand. Whether it does or not, artist-run culture is alive and well in Berlin, perhaps more so than anywhere else in the world.

As usual, in writing these semi-autobiographical texts, I am late. My deadline is long past and I have promised something by this morning. So this text may or may not continue. In the meantime, the racket of the carpenter's tools reminds me that the difference between property that is owned or shared is not so much, one way or another.

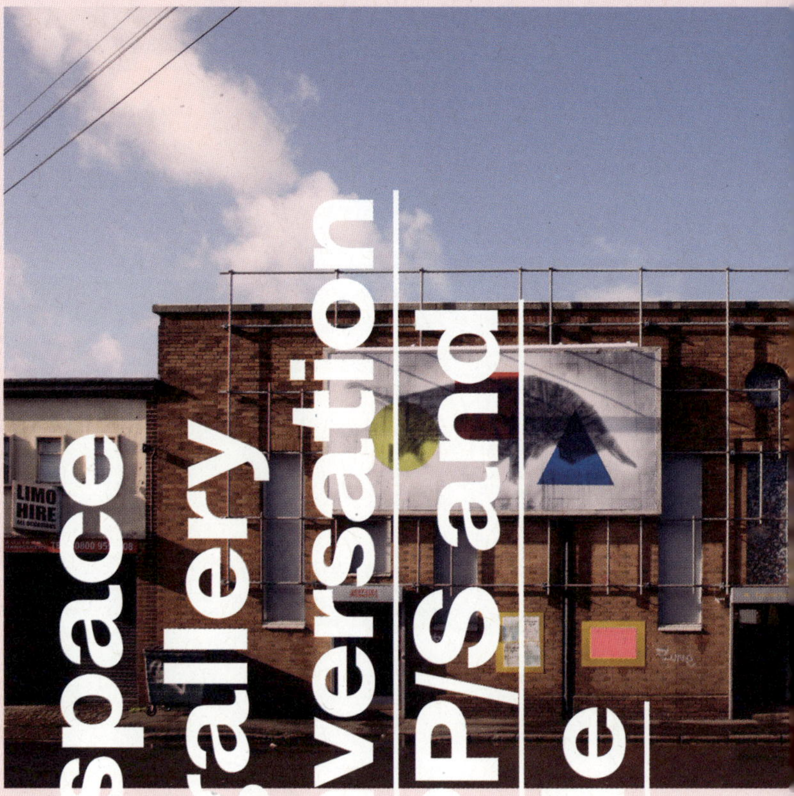

Artist-run space as public gallery
Edited conversation between P/S and Gavin Wade

NAME
Eastside Projects

LOCATION
Birmingham, UK

WEBSITE
www.eastsideprojects.org

YEAR
2008 to present

STRUCTURE
Artist-run, non for profit organisation, with six artist Directors and Council of Management, partnership with Birmingham City University

LEGAL STATUS
Not-for-profit company, limited by guarantee

TEAM
1 × Executive Director FT, 1 × Associate Director PT 0.5, 1 × ESP Programmer PT 0.5, 3 × Gallery Assistants (Operation/Distribution/Digital) PT 0.8, Volunteers

MISSION
Eastside Projects Makes Art Public

FUNDING
Arts Council England National Portfolio Organisation, in partnership with Birmingham City University. Other funding has included Paul Hamlyn Foundation Breakthrough Award, Esmee Fairbairn, Jerwood Charitable Foundation. EP is also commissioning agent for Birmingham Big Art Project, Chiltern Railways and others

PREMISES
Commercial lease, private landlord, supported by Birmingham City University

SELECTED PROJECTS
This is the Gallery and the Gallery is Many Things (2008); Liam Gillick: Two Short Plays (2009); Book Show (2010); Narrative Show (2011); William Pope.L: Child (2011); Caroline Achaintre/Sara Barker/Alice Channer (2012); Mike Nelson: M6 (2013); Cao Fei: Haze and Fog (2013); Bill Drummond: The 25 Paintings (2014); Susan Philipsz: Broken Ensemble (War Damaged Musical Instruments) (2014); Samara Scott: Silks (2015); Display Show (2015 – 16) Temple Bar Gallery, Dublin, Eastside Projects, Birmingham, and Stroom den Haag, Netherlands; Production Show (2016 – 2018)

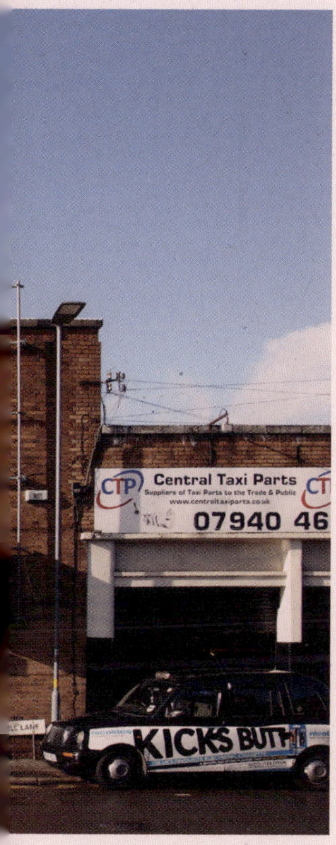

Gavin Wade
Bauhaus Bull, 2014
48 Sheet Billboard Poster (permanent billboard, exterior of Eastside Projects)
Photograph by Stuart Whipps

Mark Cullen: One of the ideas we're looking at is what is it that denotes an artist's practice if they're running an artist-run initiative; how increasingly this can be one and the same.
Gavin Murphy: It's an interesting alternative to the idea of compartmentalisation: putting on exhibitions, developing and programming work with other artists, and having your own practice which is outside of that, separate.
Gavin Wade: Quite different models, aren't they?
GM: You set up Eastside Projects very much with that in mind, it would appear.
GW: Yes, to show an artist-curator space. I think a lot of artist-run spaces aren't artist-curator models – they follow a standard divide between art-making and exhibition-making. It's not really perceived as part of the same practice. It's seen more as a means to develop the career of the artists running the space, as if the world of setting up a gallery isn't integral to what they might do as an artist. I wanted Eastside Projects to feel integral, that it is all bound up in the same reality as the one used to make art.
GM: Could it be almost considered a second-generation, or next-generation, artist-run practice space…
GW: That would be nice!
GM: Well, in generational terms Eastside Projects has obviously taken on board developments in curation over the last 20 years and the crossover between artists curating within their own practice, or doing both. Whereas with first-generation artist-run spaces there is a gap, and I think that's the case because these spaces changed and developed and responded to the needs of the scene or peer-group around them.
GW: When did PP/S start?
MC: It started in '96, so almost twenty years ago.
GW: That's the first year I curated a show.
MC: Is it? We're finding a lot of correlations with 1996, actually. We set up a studio; initially it was to have a space where we could work ourselves, but also to have a space where you're involved with your peers. We were just out of college, so that's one of the things you miss quite heavily: the peer learning that exists within college, so we figured out that that was something we'd like to set up in Dublin. From there it just became natural to start putting on exhibitions. For the first exhibition an artist came to us with an idea that they wanted to do a show. We took down a section of the studios, they put on their exhibition there and we thought, this is exactly what we'd like to be doing with artists and working for ourselves. And the two things correlate and intertwine.
GW: So quite an organic process...
GM: And responding to a definite lack – which I think is a key thing that comes into a lot of artist-run set-ups – where it's responding to a lack – be that, going back, it could be media-specific, or gender-specific, political, or just generational. In terms of Dublin, I think the lack was a

disjunct, a gap between finishing college and then actually maintaining a practice. There was no net to draw you from one stage to the other. And within my peer-group coming out of college, there was a massive drop-off with people just not being able to maintain a practice, and it just kind of dissipates.

GW: I think maybe the basic reason why a lot of artist-run spaces exist is to bridge that gap. You need to invent something when there isn't any structure supporting you.

MC: A self-made support network…

GM: But then you say that artist-run spaces aren't a stop-gap.

GW: Yes, a lot of people have referred back to that early statement I made at Eastside Projects – the artist-run space is not a stop-gap. The stop-gap structure is often the first thing that people do, and it serves a really vital purpose. But then ultimately the artist-run space becomes sacrificed. So you run an artist-run space until you don't need your stabilisers. I just thought, if that's the only reason for artist-run spaces, it's not good enough – to be a stabiliser. Or it's not enough for me. I think all big museums should be artist-run spaces. There's something very special about the artist-run space, something more than the idea of sacrificing your early career and going on to bigger things. I don't think there are bigger things – that's sort of what I mean.

MC: The artist comes first?

GW: That should be at the top of the pile, not the thing that gets sacrificed and thrown away.

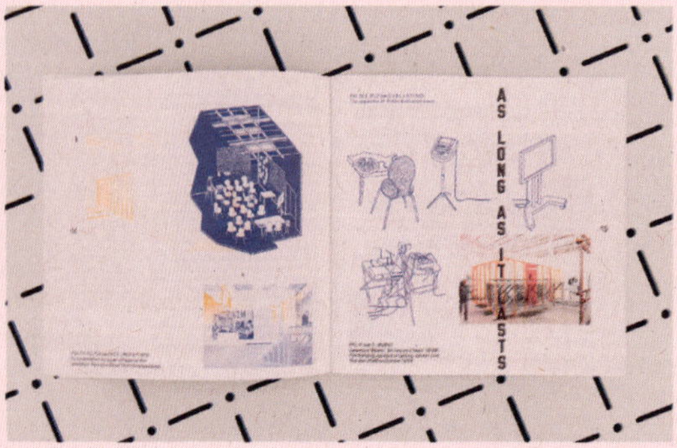

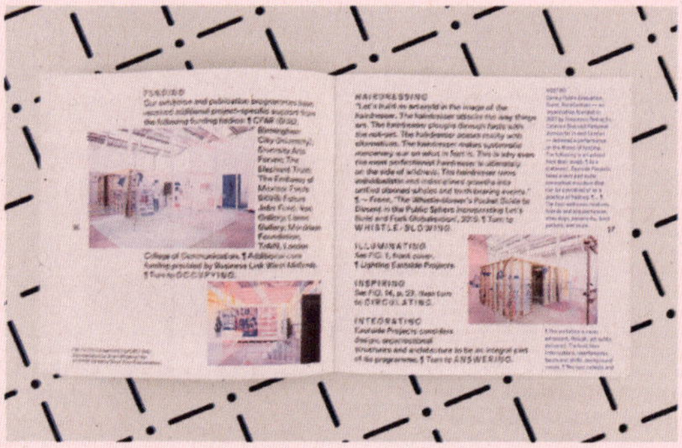

GM: If you look at many established spaces like Ikon in Birmingham, or Project Arts Centre in Dublin, these spaces were set up by artists, but at some point of the process – in order to continue or progress – artists are replaced by a director, a curator, a manager, and there's a gradual institutionalisation. So we're interested too in artist-initiated spaces, and questioning that perceived necessity: that if you're to be funded to the level where precarity doesn't become an over-riding factor in what you do – which certainly is something that we encounter a lot – that there should be a recognition of the viability of artist-run spaces to continue as artist-run. Take on some additional structure, or oversight – but not necessarily be made to change their structure, become institutions, and to be gauged on that basis.
GW: We feel like we're on the edge of that, because we're interested in being an institution. We're interested in being institutionalised, but on our terms. If the institution is just a structure for a group of individuals to support a bigger idea, then we'll be an institution. If we become a much bigger scale than we are already at Eastside Projects, then the natural force will be to become more bureaucratic, to try and become more efficient through certain administrative and managerial systems. And so always the pressure is to...
MC: You're not necessarily gaining efficiencies, you're just gaining processes.
GW: And so the question is back to that first point about transparency and reveal: how do you then make the managerial processes an artwork? Because that's always the bit to go back on. How do you still make that be part of it? And I think you can. I think you can run a city as an artwork. I think you can run the world as an artwork. You just have to think about it, and practice doing that, and experiment with it. And it's just that people don't do it because of the pressure to stick with rules that probably work nine out of ten times, but may not really lead to any significant reality. They just lead to a status quo reality.
MC: The rules are often suggested by funding though.
GW: It can be like that. You have to be effective, then. Your funders have to be affected by you. And in some cases, artists are affected by what we do, so it's a mutual thing. There isn't any division. So the idea of the gallery then is the same as the practice, it's not a default position that is other to the artist: the artist comes in, and then joins this 'other', does an activity and then leaves the 'other', and the 'other' returns to it's default. Instead it's like: the artist comes in, makes a gallery, and then goes away. And then another artist comes in, and that gallery is now part of that artist's work, so it's this ongoing process. And sometimes that doesn't click or work in the right way, and there is some opposition.
MC: At that point do the paint rollers come out?
GW: No, that's what I mean. The rollers don't come out back to a default... At the moment the gallery Eastside Projects is more white, but that's because Mike Nelson chose to do it. He wouldn't normally choose to make a room white. He did it because we weren't white. He did it

← **Eastside Projects User's Manual Draft #5**
Photograph by Stuart Whipps

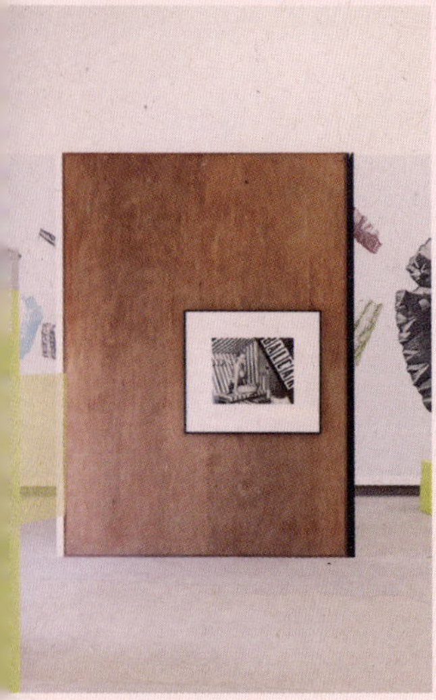

↑ Christopher Williams
TecTake Luxus Strandkorb grau/weiß,
Model no.: 400636
Material: wood/plastic
Dimensions (height/width/depth):
154 cm × 116 cm × 77 cm
Weight: 49 kg
Manufactured by Ningbo Jin Mao Import & Export Co., Ltd, Nigbo, Zhejiang, China for TecTake GmbH, Igersheim, Germany
Model: Zimra Geurts, Playboy Netherlands Playmate of the Year 2012
Studio Rhein Verlag, Düsseldorf, January 31st, 2013
(Zimra resting), 2013
Selenium toned gelatin silver print
Framed: 86 × 94.6 × 3.8 cm
Paper: 50.5 × 60.3 cm
Image: 46.4 × 56.5 cm
Edition 7 of 10, 4 AP
Certificate of Authenticity
WILCH0387
Photograph by Stuart Whipps

the opposite of what he would normally do. And that's not a standard. In some ways there are lots of elements of standard Mike Nelson because he responds to the context and he alters it. He looks at what the conditions are, the bigger context around the gallery, and introduces that into the space, and then connects it to things that he's fascinated with in the world. But there isn't an aesthetic fixed position for him to do that. In the gallery there are some fixed positions for periods of time, but they're not going to be default. And it's hard because you naturally want some kind of order to hang on to, and to build on, and to get your footing all the time, so it is quite difficult to be purposefully losing your footing. And that's the same with funding and all these other sorts of supports, that there has to be a place for the open brief in all aspects, which is when you probably need what I think public support is. Public support should be there for art to allow it to be completely open to do whatever it needs to do, and that's the reason why you have public support. Not public support to do the things the government thinks you should do.
MC: Certain types of art addressed to certain constituencies.
GW: It's a really hard thing to argue but I think it's quite important.
GM: And did you come up with much resistance on that point, in terms of your opening statement about Eastside Projects: you're not making art for "the public", but: "we are the public making art".
GW: No, because I think we did it in such a clear and, maybe, forceful way, that anybody who maybe doesn't agree with it, can't work out how to unravel it. People have a moment of shock that we've said that, and then consider it, and think, "there's some sense in that". I've never had a comeback that has argued the opposite thing. And the Arts Council seem to really find that interesting!
They've never challenged it. I mean, there are challenges to the way that we might offer interpretations to work or access to work, but what we say is that we are one of the organisations that are truly dealing with interpretation; that we help people to perceive what interpretation is, and to interpret perceptions of art. And so we put that back to them and say, "we do this, and you should do this". And they don't say, "no, we want you to do what we said in the first place". They just go, "okay". That's interesting.
That's what I've tried to do: tap into the foundational idea that they – funders, Arts Council, or government – are involved in a process of just exploring, and trying things out, and testing things, and trying to improve situations. I've found that they're quite good at taking advice, and taking on arguments for alternative ways of working outside of their own fixed parameters. I mean, maybe our scale allows us that slipperiness, because we still don't really spend a lot of public money. It's relatively a small amount. If we were spending £10 million, I think we'd get a lot more scrutiny. But because we're only spending £125,000 a year, and we do so much, there's no reason to criticise. It would only be an issue if something much more negatively extreme, culturally, happened – we might be one of the first to be clamped down on.

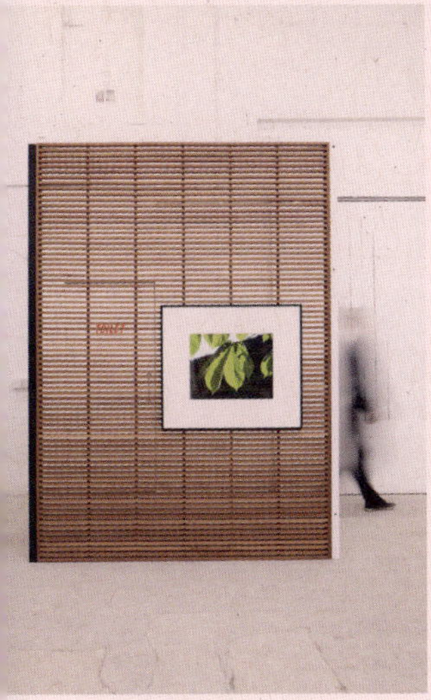

↑ Eastside Projects
↖ **Display Show**, 2015
Gavin Wade, ***Mobile Wall System with 4 permanent pole positions (After Krischanitz & Kiesler) (For Christopher Williams)***, 2015
4 powder coated aluminium poles 281.5 × 5 × 5 cm, 1 × solid panel with hard wood plugs, 1 hard wood slatted panel, both 281.5 × 197.5 × 5 cm, stainless steel bolts, stainless steel & brass floor inserts.
Function by Gavin Wade.
Execution by Queen & Crawford – Matthew Higginbottom, Matt Foster, Joseph Welden, Matthew Moore, Olly Jones, Avonstar Trading, Alex Bailey, Lee Stowers, Gene-George Earle, Jonathan Gordon, Rupert Pane, Laurence Price, Plane Structure, Tannad Williams, Andreas Kindler von Knobloch, and Gavin Wade.

↑ Christopher Williams
Tarten in Voigtmichelshof, Alpirsbach June 7, 2010, 2010
Archival pigment print on cotton rag paper
Framed: 83.2 × 94 × 3.8 cm
Image: 43.8 × 55.9 cm
Edition 3 of 10, 4 AP
Certificate of Authenticity WILCH0329
Photograph by Stuart Whipps

MC: And how do you sit with that ecology within Birmingham?
GW: Being more and more involved and implicated.
GM: Where did the impetus come from to set Eastside Projects up? Because it didn't proceed as per the usual artist-run: a perceived need, finding/setting up a space, and then applying for funding. Was there a perceived gap, culturally for a new space, artist-run or otherwise?
GW: Not from the political, not from the power in Birmingham itself, I don't think. They were quite happy with themselves, content with the very small cultural scene that there was. But even now, with us, we're one of only two Visual Arts National Portfolio Organisations of Arts Council England in the second-biggest city in the country: a city of 1.2 million, plus another 2 million people around the outside. Only two!
MC: And what does that mean?
GW: It just means that there is some investment, but not enough investment to make change happen. There has been investment over the last 20 years, 25 years, in high-end cultural activity like ballet and opera, dance and performance and theatre. And there has been a really small amount in visual arts, purely in one gallery. And then when we opened, that doubled the capacity for contemporary art in the city.
GM: Is that with the Ikon?
GW: Yeah, the Ikon has been there for 50 years. It was established by artists, but stopped being run by artists maybe five or ten years in.
MC: And did you go from having no building to having a building, and finance followed immediately, or was the finance in place to begin with?
GW: No, I think it was a very luxurious position. We opened with the building and knowing that I had three years' money, so in a very strategic way.
MC: From the Arts Council?
GW: It was a bit of two ways to it: the Arts Council was being really positive, and wanted to support a new space to happen, and then they hooked up with Birmingham City University, and I was research fellow at the university, so I was part of trying to provide a link: Arts Council and the university together. And they said together, "we'll support a new space to happen". I proposed Eastside Projects and they said, "great, that's what we want to do". But there was actually a moment where anybody could propose something to them.
GM: Was there an actual call-out?
GW: Yes, there was a call-out, which I knew about early on, with the idea that there is £100,000 a year, for three years. But what that was, was a very blurry framework.
MC: But it's not a huge amount.
GW: No, it's a modest amount, but it still seems like it was a huge jump. It's still a good opportunity. I wasn't thinking about running a space, so that didn't cross my mind at all. I was working with Celine Condorelli on our 'Support Structure' project, and we were looking to get the job of doing the architecture. That's what we were interested in at the time. We wanted to make a building. I saw it developing, and it

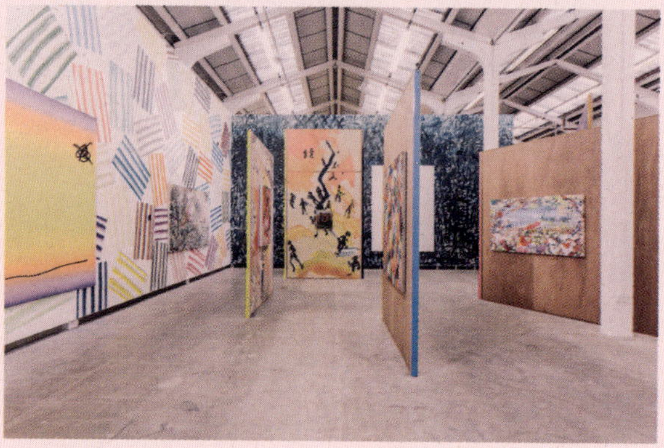

Eastside Projects
Painting Show, 2011–12
Curated By Sophie von Hellerman & Gavin Wade
WORKS L–R: Rob Pruit, Nicolas Party, Paul Newman, Tamuna Sirbiladze, Dan Rees, George Best, Alexis Marguerite Teplin, Brandan Cass
Photograph by Ashley Carr

was only really after another artist who I worked with challenged me, saying: "who's going to run this space? What's going to happen? This is a good opportunity. Why aren't you doing it?" And first of all I thought: I don't want to run a space. I've never really wanted to run a space. And I avoided it a little bit. Ultimately, I looked at the opportunity and changed my way of thinking about the gallery. With all of these things in place I realised I could test out many of the ideas that I had and could work to create a new situation, a new environment, for the production of art.
MC: In that context?
GW: Yeah, that's part of what I was doing. I thought, what about if I make a space that is context. And I make a space that is the same as a zoo, or a naval frigate, or a cathedral, or a somewhere else. I can make that interesting. I can try to develop the gallery as a new – a new universe in a way. And I'd been working the previous six or seven years towards that idea, and hadn't quite clocked that I should just get a space and start evolving it. Once that leap had been made, the next [one] was to expand the idea with my closest collaborators. Along with Celine, based in London, this was other Birmingham-based artists Ruth Claxton, Simon Bloor and Tom Bloor, and graphic designer James Langdon. The six of us formed the company of Eastside Projects as directors of a not-for-profit company, limited by guarantee.
GM: So was the space something that you brought to the equation then? That wasn't something as part of the call?
GW: We didn't have that space then. There was the idea of another space, which wasn't as good. So it took a year from proposing it to opening, and then we found this other space, so we were looking deep within Eastside, that area.
GM: So who owns that space? Is it a privately rented situation?
GW: It is. Very expensive rent.
GM: So would a good amount of your Arts Council funding go into that?
GW: Yes, it's taken between £30–40,000 a year.
GM: So the [city] council wasn't able to come on board, or there wasn't anything like that?

GW: We've never had any direct council funding. And they don't have any buildings in Digbeth. Our landlords are the Gray's, who set up The Custard Factory and other cultural regeneration things in that area. We knew that moving into that area you're part of a longer-term regeneration plan. It's only now, seven years in, that we're more savvy and really looking for how to own something there, how to control some of that area, which is going to be a real challenge because it's where the future HS2 train terminal comes in to Birmingham planned for 2027, so potentially it's a very profitable area, where a £35 billion national infrastructure project will come in and then that area around will be altered. But that still isn't for another ten years. But everybody's bought up the land already, so we're now altering the programme of what we do towards thinking about how we position ourselves, and we have been for a couple of years now: just thinking about how to get to that point. So the aim is, by 2018, to have created a next stage Eastside Projects as an artwork somewhere in that area of Birmingham, so we're more in control of our destinies. If such a thing is possible!

EDITED TRANSCRIPT OF A CONVERSATION RECORDED AT TEMPLE BAR GALLERY + STUDIOS
26TH JUNE, 2015

Eastside Projects
Display Show, 2015
Curated by Celine Condorelli, James Langdon, Gavin Wade.
WORKS L–R: Goshka Macuga, Gavin Wade, Leeds Weirdo Club, Charlotte Cullinan & Jeanine Richards, Yelena Popova, Gavin Wade, Christopher Williams, Amalia Pica, Celine Condorelli
Photograph by Stuart Whipps

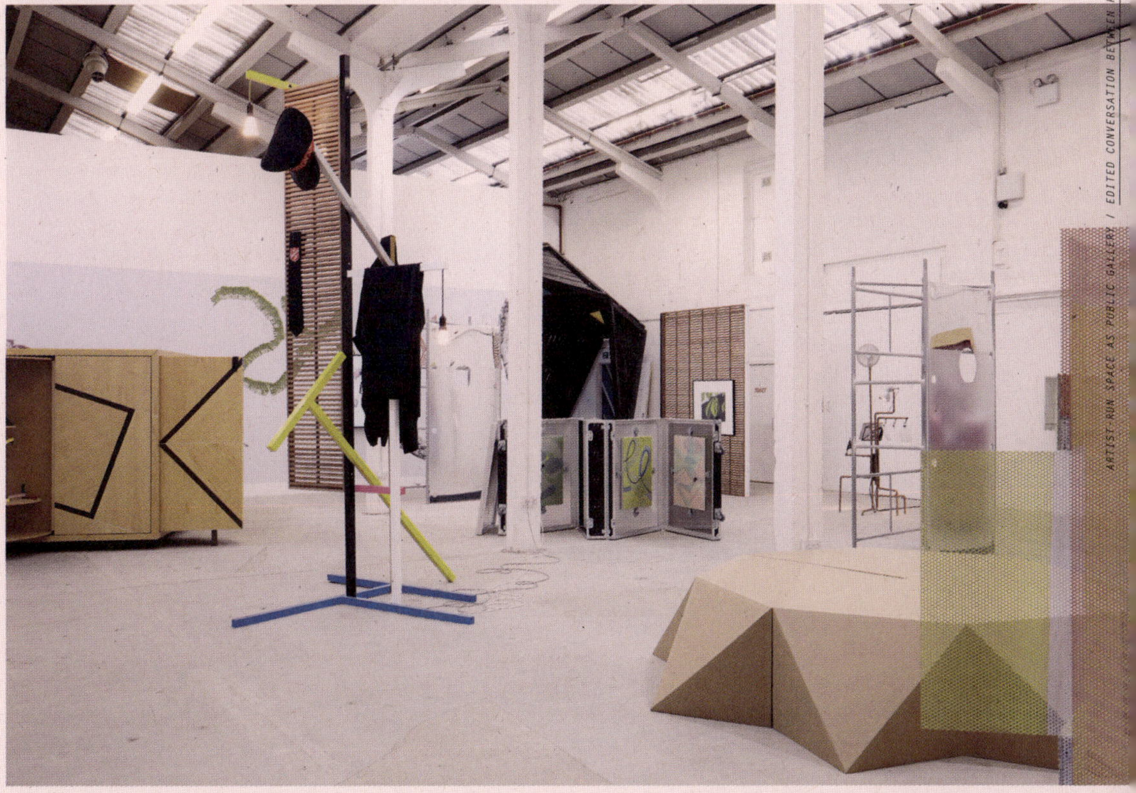

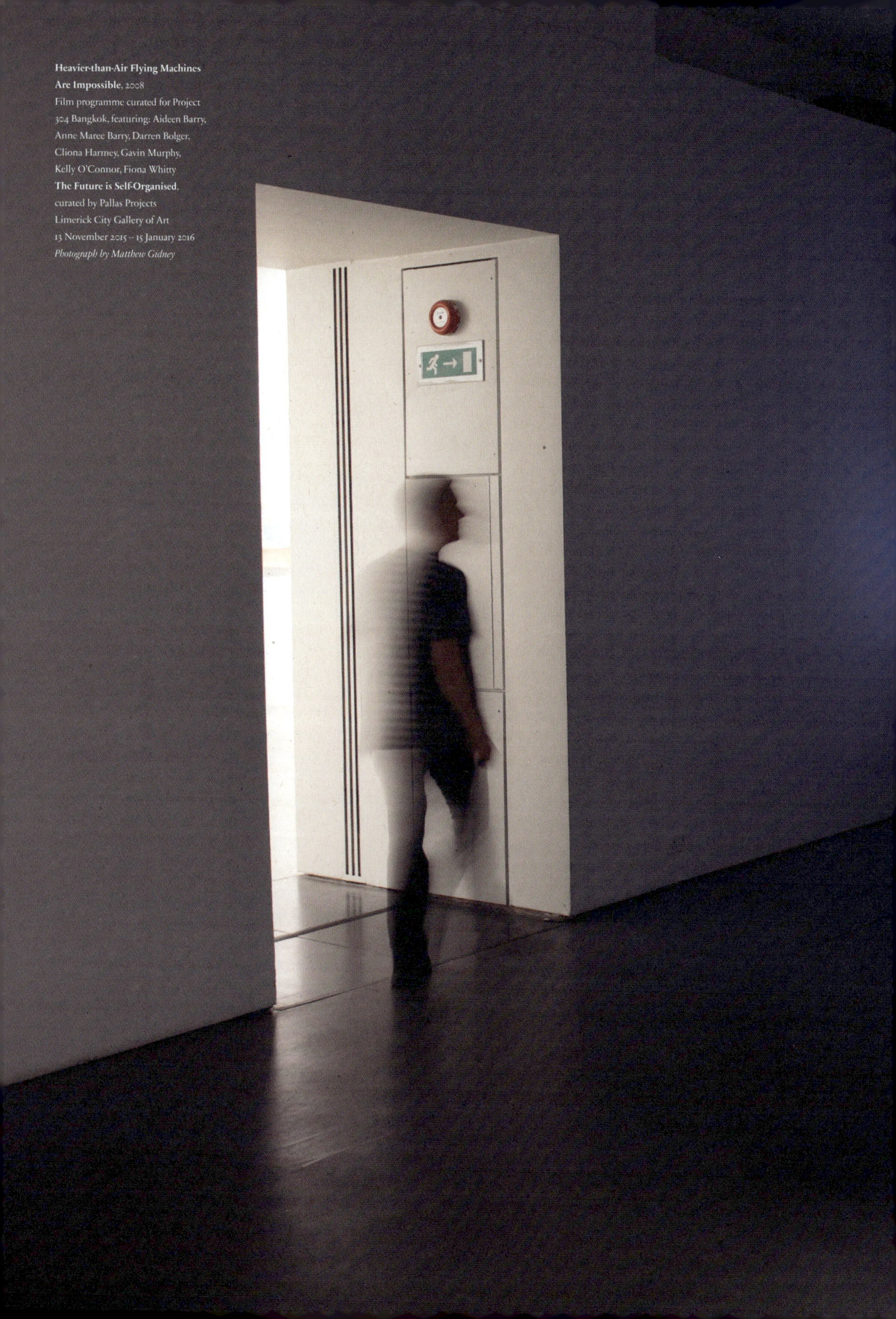

Heavier-than-Air Flying Machines Are Impossible, 2008
Film programme curated for Project 304 Bangkok, featuring: Aideen Barry, Anne Maree Barry, Darren Bolger, Cliona Harmey, Gavin Murphy, Kelly O'Connor, Fiona Whitty
The Future is Self-Organised, curated by Pallas Projects
Limerick City Gallery of Art
13 November 2015 – 15 January 2016
Photograph by Matthew Gidney

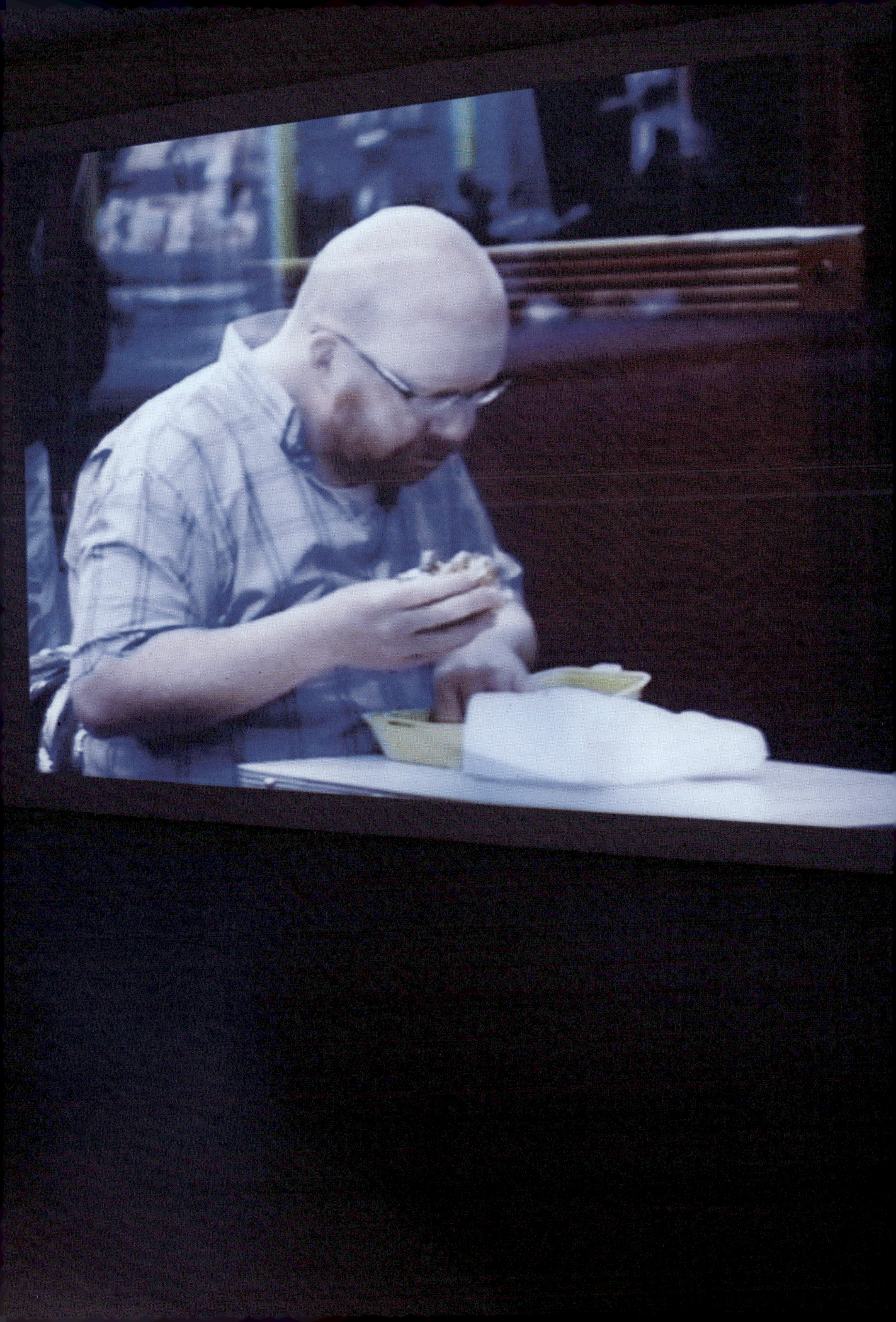

Jason E. Bowman

Midwest: an imagined settlement for the artist-led

In 2002 myself and two other arts workers, Rachel Bradley and Julie Crawshaw, responded to a tender circulated by Arts Council England to deliver a 'Project Shaper for Artists' Support' within the West Midlands region of the UK; a nebulous descriptor that nevertheless provided some key terminological nodes, these being Project, Shaping and for Artists, which effected what we consequently designed and delivered as an imaginary transposal of place: *Midwest – a catalyst for creative thought and action to complement the development of artistic practice in the visual arts*, which was active from 2003 until its intentional demise in 2008.

In this essay, produced eight years after our collective decision to halt Midwest, I will seek to describe it as a project and select aspects of its activity, while providing rationale for why it was shaped as it was and what it sought to shape. Hopefully this will represent the particularities of its contribution as a model within the cultures of artist-led activities by foregrounding a selection of its methods.

The initial contract with Arts Council England was for eighteen months, to succeed what had previously been offered to Junction, a subscription-based umbrella organisation working in artists' support, by that stage defunct. Their legacy passed on to us was a relatively modest database of artists who had previously subscribed to its services. We were informed that this would be the "last chance saloon" for a model of agency that would operate developmentally for "artists' support" in this region. Incremental extensions to the contract occurred several times, including discrete contracts to deliver specific enquiries that became elements within Midwest's programme.

Despite Arts Council England's supposed "arms-length" principle, Midwest may be understood not truly as an alternative to or independent of "the state", but possibly as generative within it through its capacity to be in receipt of the distribution of monies by a national agency for art and its development. Irrespective of being in receipt of state funding, Midwest operated as a project and was not constituted as a company until its final year of activity when Arts Council finally requested, as a condition of its funding agreement, that it become formalised. Consequently Midwest became a company limited by guarantee with not-for-profit status of which myself, Rachel and Julie were co-directors.

In his 2015 essay *How to Radicalise a Mouse*, curator Kuba Zsreder seeks to reconsider the nature of projects and projectarians, while acknowledging the problematics of precarity and the conditioning of the freelancer as opportunist within the neoliberal project, by proposing "radical opportunism" as a means to re-evaluate our understanding of those who conceive of project-based activities. He states:

> "Projects are not just means of production, neutral infrastructure which could be utilized for achieving one's goals. Every project is a material, temporal and localized embodiment of social apparatuses that regulate and support the making of these projects. The apparatus is not a thing, a machine, an institution or an organization, which could be controlled by any individual, class or social movement. ... In other words, the apparatus is both a systemic codification of the social relations and a tangible materialization of this code in the social form of projects, subjectivities and networks. The project-related apparatuses configure relations between such heterogeneous elements as the discourses of individual freedom and flexibility, the organizational formats of project-based management, the grant systems as embodiments of cultural policies, the legal acts in which they are embedded, the applications as interfaces linking applicants and funders, the values and subjectivities of project-makers, et cetera."[1]

As Zsreder identifies, projects are situational but also indicative of a profound meshing of multiple constitutive elements, agendas and conditions which have the capacity to shape, through themselves being configured from the numerous relations that consequently organise their existence and communicate their envisaged purpose or perceived usefulness.

In its initial identity as a project – as opposed to legitimised organisation – Midwest sought to emphasise the possibilities of discordant and harmonious relativity as a means to cooperatively identify the conditions for practice, its discontents and potentialities from the perspectives of artists, but also by engaging other practitioners such as art historians, cultural landlords, urban theorists, curators, policy and strategy makers, representatives of cultural and labour think-tanks, cultural theorists, directors of art institutions and bureaucrats,

[1] Szreder, Kuba. 'How to Radicalise a Mouse'. In *Mobile Autonomy Exercises in Artists' Self-Organization* Nico Docx and Pascal Gielen (Eds.). Amsterdam: Valiz. 2015. p. 199

for whom the prospect to discursively imagine transformation with artists in a given time and place, and as a mutual code that may associate them. Analysis and speculative elucidations surfaced through dialogic methods of analysis, conducted through collective and communal (though often facilitated) thinking that took place within an events-driven programme, orchestrated as a series of nodes within Midwest's itinerant and peripatetic programme.

Midwest did not explicitly found or manage a physical artist-run space. Equally, providing opportunities for exhibition was not one of its central missions, although both spaces and exhibitions were orchestrated during its term by many of the practitioners, who may also be considered as having *been* Midwest as much as its three instigators. Occasionally, we considered founding a dedicated physical space through which to host, orchestrate and debate the cultures of the artist-led though this was continuously assessed as potentially problematic. It may have isolated Midwest's activities from those initiatives and initiators that already existed, to whose work it aimed to be confluent whilst they pursued conceiving of, sustaining, or negotiating the survival of their particular initiatives.

By circumventing running a physical space we also eluded the conventions of exhibitionary practices as dispersed mediations of an organisational mission statement, in order to focus on developing more discursive methods by which to place greater emphasis on coterminous practices. Diversified modes of production and the multiplication of roles within artist-led cultures, such as artist-curator, artist-administrator, artist-organiser, artist-publisher, artist-distributor, artist-archivist, are still scarcely recognised as formations of "artistic practice", and thus often subjugated in a hierarchical framework of sanctification that prioritises the mediated artwork.

While he is not directly discussing the artist-led, it is relevant here to think through French sociologist Pierre Bourdieu's conclusion to *The Market of Symbolic Goods*, in respect to the question of autonomy and legitimisation through mediation of hierarchical power relations, but also in his qualification of "the restricted field" (producer to producer), and the "field of mass-production" (producer to reader/spectator, often through mediation by a third party such as a publisher etc.) He states:

> "… if the relative autonomy of the field of restricted production authorizes the attempt to construct a 'pure' model of the objective relations defining it and of the interactions which develop within it, one must remember that this formal construction is the product of the temporary bracketing-off of the field of restricted production (as a system of specific power relations) from the surrounding field of … power relations."[2]

[2] Bordieu, Pierre. The Market of Symbolic Goods. In *The Field of Cultural Production: Essays on Art and Literature*. New York: Columbia University Press. 1984. p 34

In Bourdieu's analysis of the coming into being of cultural legitimacy or "consecration", he has not quite imagined the potential interstice that may be originated through the diversification or divergence of roles and practices that the re-skilling embedded in artist-led practices may generate, in that within the artist-led significant precursors exist that re-calibrate the processes of mediation with artists being initiator, artist and mediator, and often through collectivised means.

We sought to position Midwest in ways that would accentuate and nuance such crucial but often concealed procedures and methods, which may be implicit to a more holistic understanding of the diversified and re-skilled forms of labour that those engaged in fostering artist-led cultures may generate, in order to vision alternate models or parallel practices to the dominant forms of mediation. A possible consequence of Midwest's accentuation of such practices and elusion of the exhibitionary-as-mediation, was the production of an interstitial interrogation of the hierarchisation of typologies of practices intrinsic to the *artist* in the *artist*-led, that could challenge the prevalent subordination of such forms of labour that result in them being rendered extramural or subordinate to the mediation of artworks through the sustained prevalence that the combined making and display of art is sui generis of artistic practice.

Following on from its canonised genealogical routes in the alternative space movement, to the various waves of institutional critique, to new institutionalism and successive discourse regarding other instituent practices, through to the discursiveness that is indicative of the speculative nature of "the curatorial", the currency of the profound oppositional or secessionary strategies of the historic foundations of the artist-led are now seen as questionable in terms of futurity. The usefulness of the term of artist-led, and its historic claims for alternativity, independence, secession and autonomy, is challenged by the necessity to acknowledge relationality, co-existence and reflexivity with other organisational, institutional and curatorial practices that also seek to re-purpose art, its means of production and its institutions, through speculative thought. As Stine Hebert and Anne Szefer Karlsen's 2013 anthology *Self-Organised* suggests, there is an intensified promiscuity by practitioners who shift between ideologically differing platforms, institutions and non-institutions, in ways which led them to respond to prior demarcations of alternativity through probing the interstices of self and organisation, as a means to re-orientate the discussion towards pluralities.

However, in accepting a correlated evacuation of the term "artist-led", along with meanings previously attached as key suffixes (artist-*led*, artist-*initiated*, artist-*run*, artist-*managed*) within its cultural history, we are also potentially discounting the possibility to benefit from – and argue for – at least half a century of incremental knowledge of organisation, built through contingent social, collectivised and collaborative working practices by artists and art workers, at a moment when key principles or modi operandorum such as horizontalisation, empowerment, self-determination, collaboration and co-participation, are now also shadowed by co-optation within neoliberal vocabularies.

Midwest, at its inauguration, did not invoke a pre-determined recall of the conceivability of linearity in the concept of artist-run or its efficacy, as termed by Jens Hoffman:

> "The concept of "artist-run" will not outlive its usefulness so long as it realizes the transformative potential that it holds within an increasingly professionalized and conformist artworld. Here lies the strength of artist-led initiatives, to propose meaningful and radical alternatives to the established art system."[3]

Hoffman calls to mind creeds which are recognised as prefatory to an understanding of the artist-led as an alternative to dominant cultures of capital effecting art, its institutions and structures; institutions that may be disregarding of particular progressive models of practice, or exclusion of practitioners in terms of race and ethnicity, gender-identification, age, cultural heritage or sexual orientation; mainstreaming and thus concerned with purposeful-marginalisation, and an overall concern to formulate initiatives that would be constituted by and operate along different doctrines and codification from those to which they were to be alternative to or independent of, but to which we must now consider being anxiously yet inexorably tied.

—

Midwest inaugurated with Saloons, which took place in 16 venues across the region's urban and rural conurbations with guest speakers including artist-initiators, educators, policy-makers, bureaucrats, commercial gallerists, institutional and independent curators, who referenced their own situations and experiences through discussion of the universal and provincial; networking models with digital case studies; working in non-urban centres; curatorial development; regionalised support structures; codes of practice for the visual arts; sustaining visibility as a form of agency; the art market and its value systems; self-organisation; research and intelligence gathering within the visual arts; artist-run spaces and initiatives, and expanded curatorial practices.

By addressing issues of infrastructure, art systems and their cultures of legitimacy, and discussing diverse exemplars of support systems, the Saloons were set out as refractive in that they resulted in an initial scoping and assembly of problems which artists perceived of as primary concerns, in relation to the stifling of their potential within the region, such as a limited recognition of their worth; inadequate

[3] Hoffman, Jens. In *decentre concerning artist-led culture*. Toronto: YYZ Books. 2008. p. 41.

access to quality studio provision; the proximity to London, meaning that people would travel through rather than stop, or not visit at all; and graduate retention being low, as it was understood that there were no distinct pathways post-art school. Primary among these concerns was the perceived inability for an artist-led infrastructure to be sustained, plus limited support at a local authority level. The latter was later expanded upon to be understood as a deficiency within policy contexts of social confidence in artists' capabilities to generate and self-manage initiatives, which in turn led to questions of probity, accountability and individualism versus communality.

The identification of these issues informed the consequent shape of Midwest's programme and the building of other mechanisms to assemble its imaginary settlement, including visually within its website which served as an incremental building of an imaginary settlement. Having firstly built the conviviality of a Saloon, we established the Ranch as a set of situations by which to communally corral, till, propagate, produce and harvest with a set of nomadic hired hands as hosts and facilitators. Operating by durational sociality, co-participation and co-learning, with systemic processes to encourage and facilitate conceptions of the artist-led, as a practice Midwest may be more accurately delineated as a means towards the founding of an imaginary which existed within the perceived problems, barriers, discontents and achievements of artists within the West Midlands region at its time.

By travelling to and organising collective events within multiple cities and across diverse spaces including Edinburgh, Glasgow, Newcastle, Manchester, Gateshead, Leeds and Sheffield, the community of Midwest expanded, and we were able to scope out different context-responsive models of artist-led cultures through dialogue with respective communities and discussion of their concerns and attainments, while identifying the strategies they had fostered to ameliorate precursory barriers and conceive of solutions through navigating and initiating within infrastructures, and to also discover compatibilities across the nation.

Between the sequences of Ranches other initiatives were generated, such as the seminar, *Should Black Art Still Be Beautiful?*, which sought to acknowledge the diversity of the region, but also recognise important antecedents within it regarding Black and Asian cultural and artistic practices, such as those originated by the globally influential Birmingham School for Cultural Studies, and *The First National Convention of Black Art* which had been organised in 1982 by a group of black art students and hosted at Wolverhampton Polytechnic to discuss the form, function and future of black art. From this arose the influential Blk Art Group, the members of which had studied within the region's art schools.

Intellectual Property was generated as a response to the dearth of artists' studios, particularly within Birmingham, but which had not been an acknowledged factor in the city's failed bid to become a European City of Culture. From across Europe, Midwest gathered together a series of economists, urban developers, human geographers, sociologists, urban theorists, artists and cultural landlords, to interrogate the interface of grassroots politics within the artist-led, and its relation to, disavowal through, and precarity within gentrification and regeneration processes, while Birmingham sought to develop Eastside as a cultural quarter.

Know Your Place posited the question: "Can policy be artist-led?", as a response to the remoteness and lack of knowledge that was perceived between artists and policy-makers, and to support artists as well as those responsible for the polices that affect their working lives, in co-analysing cultural, geographical and political contexts, while acknowledging the potential of artists as change-agents. Artists assembled to consider their perspectives on policy-making and identify key questions that were then posed face-to-face with significant policy-makers and influential strategists nationally. Subsequently, across a series of evenings, the policy-makers and strategists then re-assembled wwalongside those West Midlands artists who had originally questioned them, but also with a group of artists from across Europe, who had successfully intervened in cultural, artistic and environmental policy-making. Following these events a series of facilitated workshops took place to originate manifestos for the future of policy interaction from artist-led perspectives.

—

The request for organisational legitimacy from the Arts Council, which was internally struggling to recognise the benefits of project over organisation, provoked the necessity for Midwest's three initiators to undertake an extensive review to identify whether the project should continue or be dissolved, by appraising the originating aims of Midwest which were: to develop regional, national and international dialogue and partnerships within the visual arts profession; to develop the ambitions and capacity of artists and artist-curators within the West Midlands; to develop a critical mass of nationally and internationally active practitioners; and to support the development of the West Midlands region as a European centre for artist-led activity and debate. The decision was also informed by an analysis of a series of related rhetorical pronouncements which had been cumulatively instigated such as: Stake your claim; Manage your own change; Establish and re-establish self-determined criteria; Design your own decision-making processes; Negotiate your own knowledge; and Acknowledge your own redundancy. In finally deciding to reject future funding as a regularly funded organisation[4], we interrogated what it means when the flexibility, elusiveness, and indeed precarity, that may define a project is to be ended, by entering the logic of becoming an *apposite* organisation with its associative tendencies towards bureaucratic reproduction.

[4] Despite information to the contrary existing online, Midwest's funding was not cut by Arts Council England during its portfolio review in 2008.

In our appraisal of a demise we sought to also think through how Midwest had been made, with practitioners, as an imagined shape for artist-led culture over its five years, and to investigate our individual and collective considerations of whether Midwest had achieved one of its stated subsidiary objectives: a desire to become redundant. Or indeed, whether we may have become redundant to it in terms of our own individual trajectories as practitioners. We concurred that the Midwest website should have a wooden cross engraved with the project's name, and a vulture sitting on its horizontal bar, added to it as an announcement of its impending expiry.

In configuring the 2008 expiration of Midwest, its final event *Up, Up and Away* sought to concede and emphasise that it had been cooperatively developed in terms of both its imaginary (creative thought), and its agency (actions), by those whose engagement, whether durational, intermittent or even one-off, and presence within and to it, had co-founded, populated, wrought and informed what was a civic shape constantly being formed and contoured to negotiate and navigate the meaningful prospective of the artist-led within the complex of our organisational lives.

In providing these short examples of Midwest's activities and the points raised here, I have aimed to reveal that as a model of artist-led activity it was principled by the possibility of collective thought as a means by which to shape a reach towards a social epistemology that was to be generated through developing communicative – if at times inharmonious – interchanges. Midwest sought to identify, chart and map a complex picture towards alternativity through the interpretation of co-existing relations, whether these be towards funding agencies, geographic and administrative boundaries, policy, infrastructural cultural politics, existing institutional formats, counter-initiatives, and other instituent practices, whilst emphasising the necessity to re-evaluate our understandings of what may constitute the nomenclature of artistic practice within artist-led culture, and its capacity as a significant, but under-considered, mode of knowledge production – one that informs our civic cultures through its historic routes as a means to recalibrate the dominant politics of mediation and sanctification of artists' capacities to organise working practices within the cultures of the visual arts.

FOOTFALL: Articulating the Value of Artist-Led Organisations in Ireland

A research programme by 126 Artist-Run Gallery, Galway, Ireland

Joanne Laws

Understood in its commonplace sense, the term 'footfall' generally denotes attendance figures recorded during a particular timeframe. Aligning with the economic focus of cultural tourism, the monitoring of visitor footfall (including website visits) has become a widespread practice in contemporary art institutions and museums, aimed at quantifying organisations' reach and engagement. In a more literary sense, 'footfall' denotes the sound of footsteps, suggestive of activity occurring somewhere nearby. This definition reaches beyond numeric appraisal to describe activity in a richer, more poetic way. It is underscored by the process of 'attentive listening', to gauge the strength, pace and impact of this soundscape, how it resonates, where it can be heard, and by whom. In addition, it prompts reflection on what kind of physical impression or trail these footprints might leave behind. Positioning itself in the schism between these polarised definitions, the research project FOOTFALL aims to articulate the intrinsic value of artist-led organisations beyond econometrics and numbers[1].

FOOTFALL was initiated in 2013 by 126 Artist-Run Gallery, in response to a funding crisis that had almost resulted in its closure during the previous year. 126's Board devised the original research proposal, and was awarded funding under Strand 2 of the Arts Council of Ireland Project Award. As identified in the report, while self-organisation and

[1] For the purposes of the FOOTFALL research, artist-led organisations are defined as organisations which are directed and run by visual artists, in keeping with the professional and associate membership criteria outlined by Visual Artists Ireland. Such organisations might be staffed on a voluntary or paid basis and could be any size, although it was envisaged that the majority of participating initiatives would be categorised as small to medium non-profit organisations. Organisations currently operating, or closed within the last five years, were invited to take part in the research. It was also stipulated that participating organisations must have an exhibition or project display space and deliver an annual programme of contemporary visual art exhibitions and projects.

artist-led culture have become increasingly prominent formations within the visual arts in Ireland over the last 40 years, this diverse history remains only sporadically documented. Consequently, a review of existing literature for FOOTFALL focused largely on international precedents, in order to identify timely issues within the artist-led sector and methods that have previously been used in presenting this discourse to a wider readership.

FOOTFALL employed a range of data-gathering methods based on direct consultation with the organisations, practitioners and audiences within the artist-led sector in Ireland and Northern Ireland. A network of potential organisations was identified and Skype interviews were conducted with selected visual arts professionals. Organisation surveys provided detailed insights into the facilities, programming, audiences, organisational structures, finances and perceived sustainability of peer organisations. At macro-level, an audience survey was disseminated nationally, yielding hundreds of responses from 18 counties north and south of the border, while at micro-level, an ex-board member survey was conducted with former directors of 126 Artist-Run Gallery (2005–2014), providing regional insights.

In keeping with a methodology which acknowledges action research as an "important tool for generating collaborative inquiry and consulting with professionals from the sector"[2], a research session was devised as a forum for discussion and co-learning with representatives from artist-led organisations. The FOOTFALL symposium – coordinated by 126 and independent curator Megs Morley – took place on November 21st, in the Harbour Hotel, Galway, as part of TULCA Festival of the Visual Arts 2014. As one of the first research strands, the symposium functioned as a focus session and offered a tentative framework to organise subsequent primary data and findings.

In the morning session, presentations were delivered by invited speakers Jason E. Bowman (Midwest UK; University of Gothenburg, Sweden), Valerie Connor (NCFA chairperson 2012–15; independent curator) and Mikael Löfgren (writer and activist; Unga Klara Theatre; Kulturverkstan, Sweden). Keynote speaker Jason Bowman requested a show-of-hands from the audience, revealing that a large proportion of artists, artist-led workers, academics and curators were in attendance, but no political representatives, city or county Arts Officers, Councillors or policy-makers. Yet even within this concentrated assemblage, it proved challenging to agree on a common definition of 'we'.

[2] Reason, P. and Bradbury, H. (Eds.) (2001) Handbook of Action Research: Participative Inquiry and Practice, London: Sage Publications

Mikael Löfgren's presentation 'No Exceptions' outlined his research report of the same name, commissioned by Klister[3], on the conditions and challenges of small and medium-sized contemporary art centres in Sweden. With regard to the FOOTFALL research, Mikael advised that we should begin by "describing what you are actually doing in concrete terms: The daily work and what it consists of; what's worth it and what is not. Only then can discourse be formulated on what is of value". Valerie Connor's presentation 'On Our Watch: Artist's Time' considered artists as "non-commercial agent" labouring under a "socio-symbolic contract", which framed an in-depth discussion on volunteering in the artist-led sector. Whether this was mainly a "youthful activity", and whether voluntary labour can be traced, measured, recognised or valued, was debated at length. In one discussion, the volunteer was posited as the "site" (rather than the organisation or related events), with any "success" or favourable community perceptions being attributable to the skills, input and effort of the volunteering artists. In a similar vein, Jason Bowman's upcoming EU-funded research project 'Stretched' is grounded in the notion of "artists doing everything" (administration, public relations, curatorial/institutional considerations), while still determining these elements as practice. As stated by Jason Bowman during his keynote address:

> "Within these hybridised sets of behaviours that take place within artist-led cultures – artist as curator, artist as educator, artist as organiser etc. – most of these people fundamentally believe themselves to be doing all of those tasks, including the shitty ones, as artists. And yet when we consider what we think artistic practice to be, we quite often are willing to exclude all of that labour within that understanding of what the artist is ... In a sense, artist-led is one of the few distinct arenas that those types of things are determined as practice by artists."

[3] Klister (meaning 'Glue') is a nationwide network of small and medium-sized contemporary art institutions in Sweden, founded in 2012. The network wants to highlight contemporary art institutions' function in the community. Klister commissioned the research report 'No Exceptions' in collaboration with Swedish Exhibition Agency (Riksutställningar).

The English translation is available here: http://www.parainstitution.ie/relevant-articles/no-exceptions

Plenary Session: Alternative Values, Barriers & Aspirations

In the afternoon, a discursive plenary session was facilitated by Ailbhe Murphy and Ciaran Smyth of Vagabond Reviews, which provided a platform for discussion on key issues facing the sector. The consensus emerging from this session was that artist-led organisations are largely established in response to "some sort of void" or perceived need in the locality, relating to resources, supports, amenities or spaces for art. As noted by Jason Bowman, often artist-led organisations are "set up due to fear of infrastructures around them; it's a system with a history of fear". The lack of exhibition spaces in the locality was cited as one of the main motivations for a large proportion of the organisations. More specifically, there was a perceived lack of non-commercial exhibition spaces which could provide "platforms or channels for dissemination across local, national and international spectrums". Based on a desire for self-constitution, transparency and non-hierarchical formations, these spaces provide the "opportunity for artists to set the agenda".

A number of reoccurring issues within organisations were raised as constituting barriers to sustainability, namely: capricious and diminishing funding opportunities; overheads, maintenance and installation costs; political interference; precarious tenancy arrangements; relentless administration (which detracts from the core work of the organisation such as gallery programming); and an inability to pay staff, creating difficulties in securing long-term commitments from volunteers. Despite the fact that many artists sustain other jobs and a studio practice alongside volunteering, it was suggested that artists can often benefit from volunteering, in terms of the experience garnered for future careers. It was nonetheless agreed that without having to work additional jobs, artists could be more productive within artist-led organisations, and there would be "less turnover of staff and less chance of burn-out".

Aspirations for the Irish artist-led sector were also discussed at length. As well as defending the sector against (further) funding cuts and giving visibility to a legitimate occupation, a core aspiration for the sector is to be acknowledged and valued as an integral component of the wider arts eco-system. Furthermore, identifying new funding criteria – based on organisational model, reputation, trust, commitment and longevity – would provide the scope for organisations to compromise less on ambitious programming and develop long-term strategies. Securing the continuation of organisations (and their respective accumulated knowledge, experience and cultural contributions) for future generations emerged as the most urgent priority. To this end, a greater emphasis on archiving (to ensure continuity and to defend against institutional amnesia in organisations with rotating boards or high levels of staff turn-over) featured prominently among several recommendations for best practice (see FOOTFALL Report, p.p. 63–64).

fig.1
Audience & Ex-Member Survey
Question: 'What are the Strengths of Artist-Led Organisations?'

SURVEY COMPRISED OF 222 RESPONDENTS (AUDIENCE SURVEY), AND 43 EX-BOARD MEMBERS. RESPONDENTS COULD SELECT MULTIPLE ANSWERS.

Ex-Board Members Survey
Audience Survey

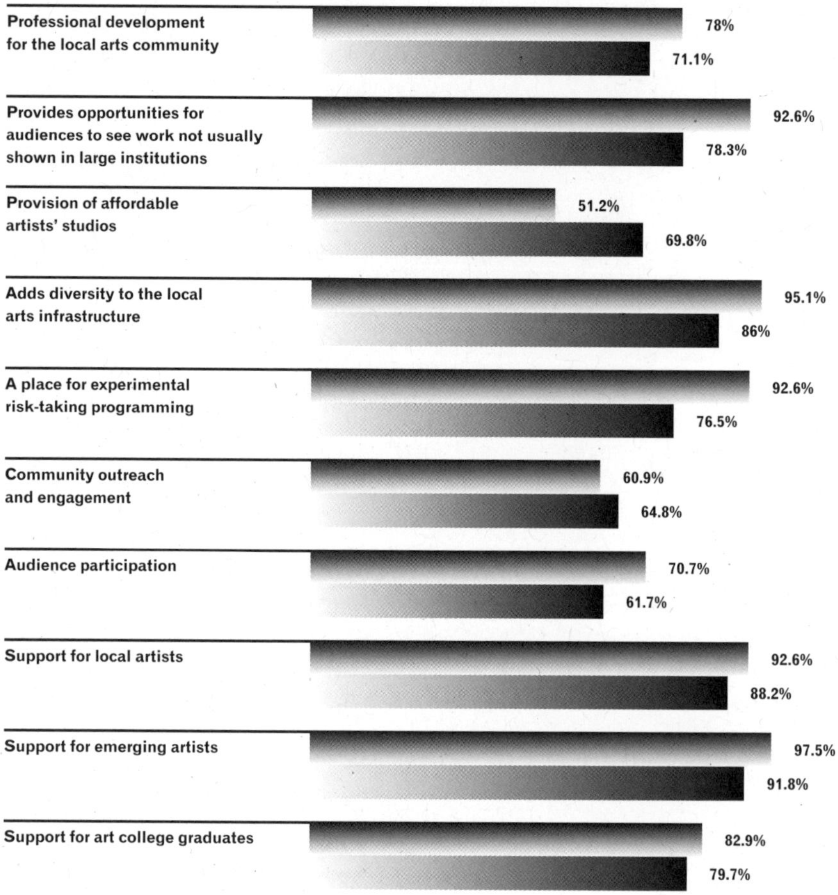

Research Overview: Perceived Strengths of Artist-led Organisations

As identified in *fig.1*, support for emerging artists[4] was revealed as an overriding strength of artist-led organisations across the data-gathering strands. The idea of a supportive cultural hub for recent graduates, which encourages art students to stay in a locality upon graduation, featured prominently in the qualitative data. Artist-led spaces were described as accessible exhibition platforms for emerging artists who might otherwise have nowhere to showcase work to gain exposure, recognition and feedback, and to connect with regional networks.

[4] For the purposes of the FOOTFALL research, an emerging artist is defined as someone who: has specialised training in the visual arts;
- is at an early stage in their career within the industry;
- has created a modest body of artistic work;
- has some evidence of professional achievement;
- does not have a substantial record of solo exhibitions, major publications or substantial funding;
- is not widely recognised (nationally or internationally) by other artists, curators or critics.

Furthermore, the training, mentorship and vocational opportunities offered by artist-led organisations generate a flow of people back into the local arts community with vastly enhanced experience and skill-sets. For similar reasons, support for local artists was cited as a key strength, with regard to the provision of resources, critical contexts and visibility for these artists. Experimental programming ranked highly as another perceived strength. Alternative forms of expression and participation were referenced, alongside the capacity to champion emerging practices, while exploring new media, innovative curatorial strategies and new approaches to engaging with theoretical discourse. In this way, artist-led organisations become platforms of exchange and sites of discourse and critique.

With the provision of alternatives to larger public or commercial galleries, artist-led spaces are perceived as adding diversity to the local arts infrastructures. It was suggested that these organisations give the public an extra dimension of cultural experience beyond the global art market, touristic events, and flash-floods of arts festivals, which permit only short-lived exchanges and reductive notions of what art can do. Numerous survey respondents commented that smaller organisations can capitalise on their lower running costs to develop projects quickly and more cheaply than larger institutions, whose overheads limit their scope for immediacy, therefore identifying agility and responsiveness as another key strength. An ability to connect to the 'local' is viewed as another perceived strength. Through the provision of regional cultural hubs, local artists and audiences can connect with national or global concerns, therefore emphasising their outward-looking perspective. As one respondent stated, these organisations "encourage new ways of thinking about life/community/the world: the more organisations operate [in a region], the more robust this conversation becomes".

The fidelity to practice-based activity emerged as the defining feature of the FOOTFALL research. As stated in the audience survey, "keeping artists' practice at the core of their activity" is exemplified in the programming of practice-specific agendas. Leading on from this, the level of care for artists and audiences offered by artist-led organisations was described as an additional strength. Given the fact that the volunteers running artist-led organisations are usually practising artists themselves, they tend to be more in tune with artists' needs and ambitions. These programmes of care are exemplified through attentiveness to artists' needs, attention to detail, providing feedback, forging long-lasting relationships, patience (to let art find the form it needs) and through advocacy, championing and seeking out development opportunities for artists.

The FOOTFALL report is available as a free downloadable PDF on the 126 website: http://126.ie/footfall-research-report

To purchase a hard copy, contact 126 Artist-Run Gallery at contact@126.ie

NAME
SUPERMARKET – Stockholm Independent Art Fair

LOCATION
Stockholm, Sweden

WEBSITE
www.supermarketartfair.com

YEAR
2007 to present (In 2006 called MINIMARKET)

STRUCTURE
Artist-run, not-for-profit organisation

LEGAL STATUS
Economic association

TEAM
3 permanent artist-directors, 4 part-time staff, volunteers

MISSION
The goal is to provide a showcase for artists' initiatives from all over the world and to create opportunities for new networks in the Swedish as well as the international art scene

CORE FUNDING
Swedish Arts Council and Stockholm City Culture Department: Project funding (non-recurring, applied for on project-to-project basis)

OTHER FUNDING
The Swedish Institute, Nordic Culture Point, The Swedish Arts Grants Committee's International Programme for Visual Arts: Projects within the project funding (non-recurring, applied for on project-to-project basis)

PREMISES
No permanent venue. Commercial or subsidized lease with Artists' Association/Private landlord/Hotel/Public Institution/Private landlord

SELECTED PROJECTS
Annual, Minimarket (2006), Supermarket (2007–2015)

Supermarket is an international art fair for artist-run spaces, created and managed by artists. Only artist-run galleries and similar artists' initiatives exhibit, and the focus is on the meeting between audience, art and artists from around the world as much as the exhibition itself. Over the years, Supermarket has featured exhibitors from more than 50 countries, all part of the growing international reach of artist-run galleries, project spaces, artist collectives and other artists' initiatives. Each year between 60 and 80 artists' initiatives from up to 30 countries participate.

Supermarket started on a small scale as MINIMARKET in 2006 at Konstnärshuset (The Artists' House) – an art nouveau palace owned by the Swedish Artists' Associations (SKF). The artists' initiatives in Stockholm came together to play around with the concept of an art fair in reaction to a new commercial art fair called Market. The following year, with an international presence, it became Supermarket.

One of Supermarket's biggest challenges has been to find sufficiently large spaces in Stockholm. In 2008 it moved to a run-down industrial space, then to a newly built first-class designer hotel, and in 2010 to the very heart of Stockholm – Kulturhuset (House of Culture) – where it stayed until 2014. In 2015 it took place in Svarta Huset, located next to Konstfack – the University College of Arts, Crafts and Design – at Telefonplan, an inner suburb of Stockholm. Supermarket returns to Svarta Huset in 2016.

By adopting the format of an art fair, Supermarket creates the framework for a large international exhibition where the participating galleries finance and produce their own contributions. The fair is financed with 50% municipal and national support, 25% participation fees and 25% entrance fees, in addition to a large number of unpaid work hours. The participation fee is kept at a low level in order to include interesting exhibitors who work on a not-for-profit basis and/or are un-funded.

Three artists – Pontus Raud, Andreas Ribbung and Meggi Sandell – act as creative directors, and together with a small team they work all year round, though the project team grows as the event approaches. A large team of volunteers, most of whom are art and art-theory students, work during the fair week. The programme includes the seminar series SUPERMARKET TALKS, the performance stage RED SPOT, the networking/knowledge exchange meetings SUPERMARKET MEETINGS, and much more. Since 2011 the catalogue is combined with the annual Supermarket Art Magazine.

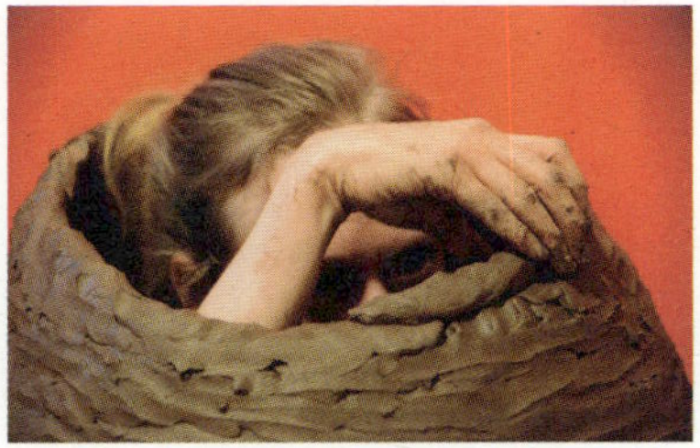

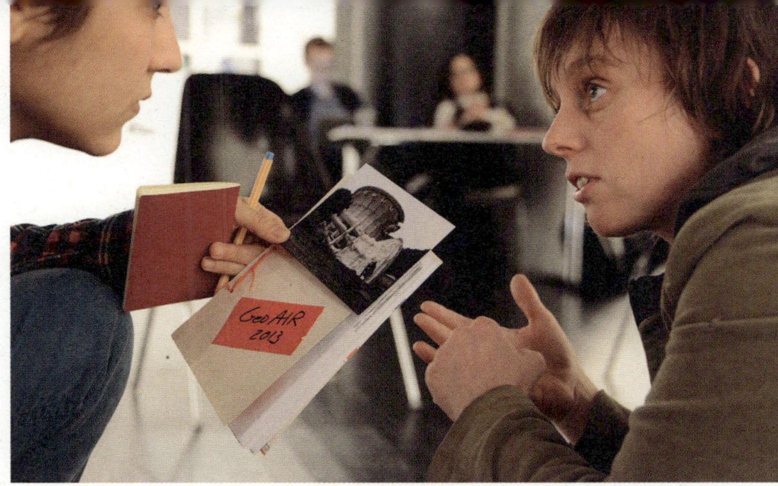

↑ Matilda Haggärde,
3rd floor, Gothenburg, Sweden
Supermarket 2014
Photograph by Joakim Erixon Flodman

→ Dolanbay
Untitled Singular Act
Supermarket 2014
Photograph by Joakim Erixon Flodman

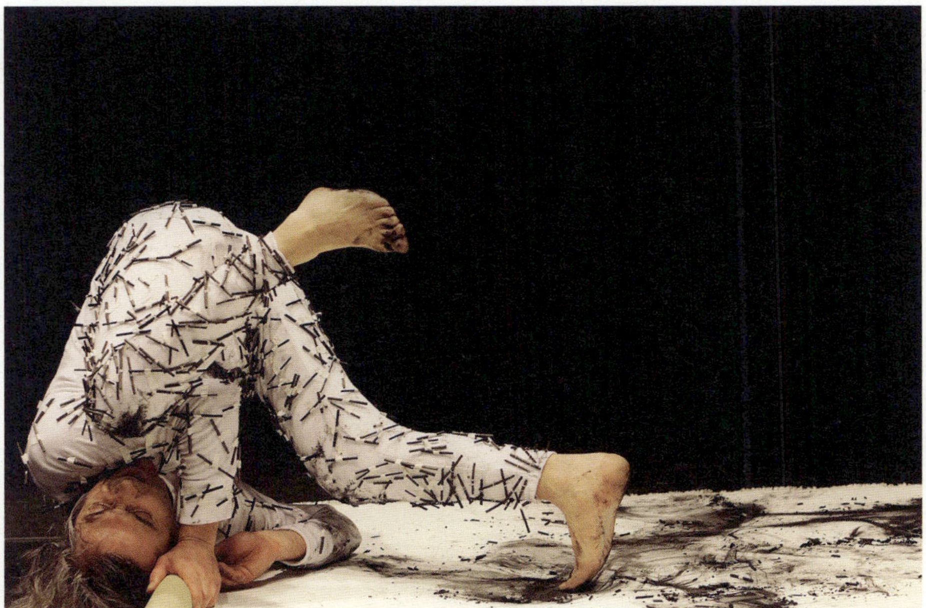

↑ Gallery Nectar / GeoAIR, Tbilisi, Georgia
Supermarket 2014
Photograph by Sarah Tehranian

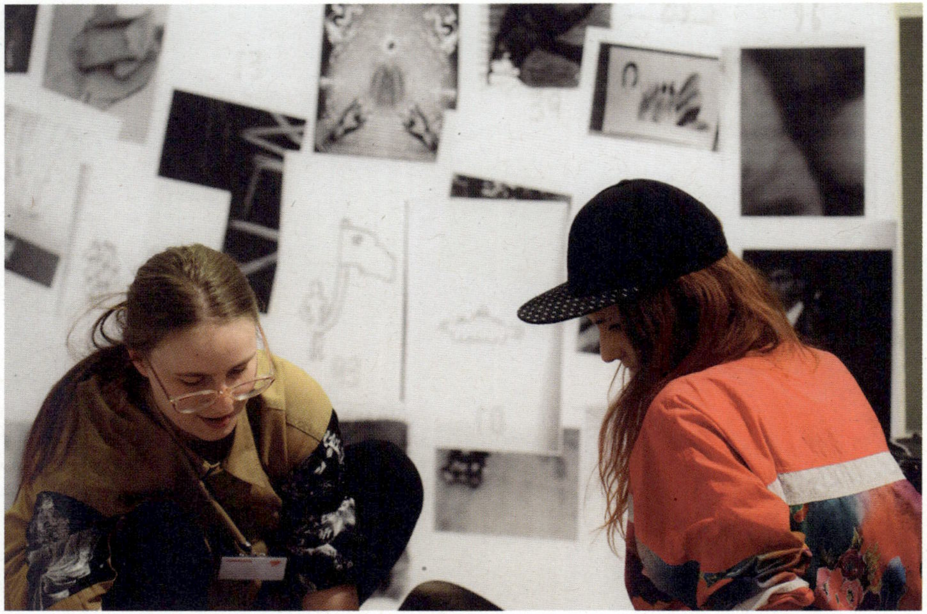

↑ A.M.180 Collective, Prague, Czech Republic
Supermarket 2015
Photograph by Kim Ventura

↓ Sever 7, St Petersburg
Supermarket 2015
Photograph by Mathias Persson

↓ Kunstschlager, Reykjavík, Iceland
Supermarket 2014
Photograph by Sarah Tehranian

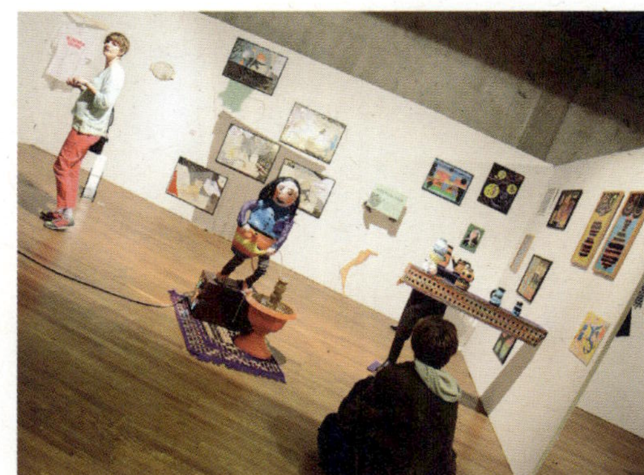

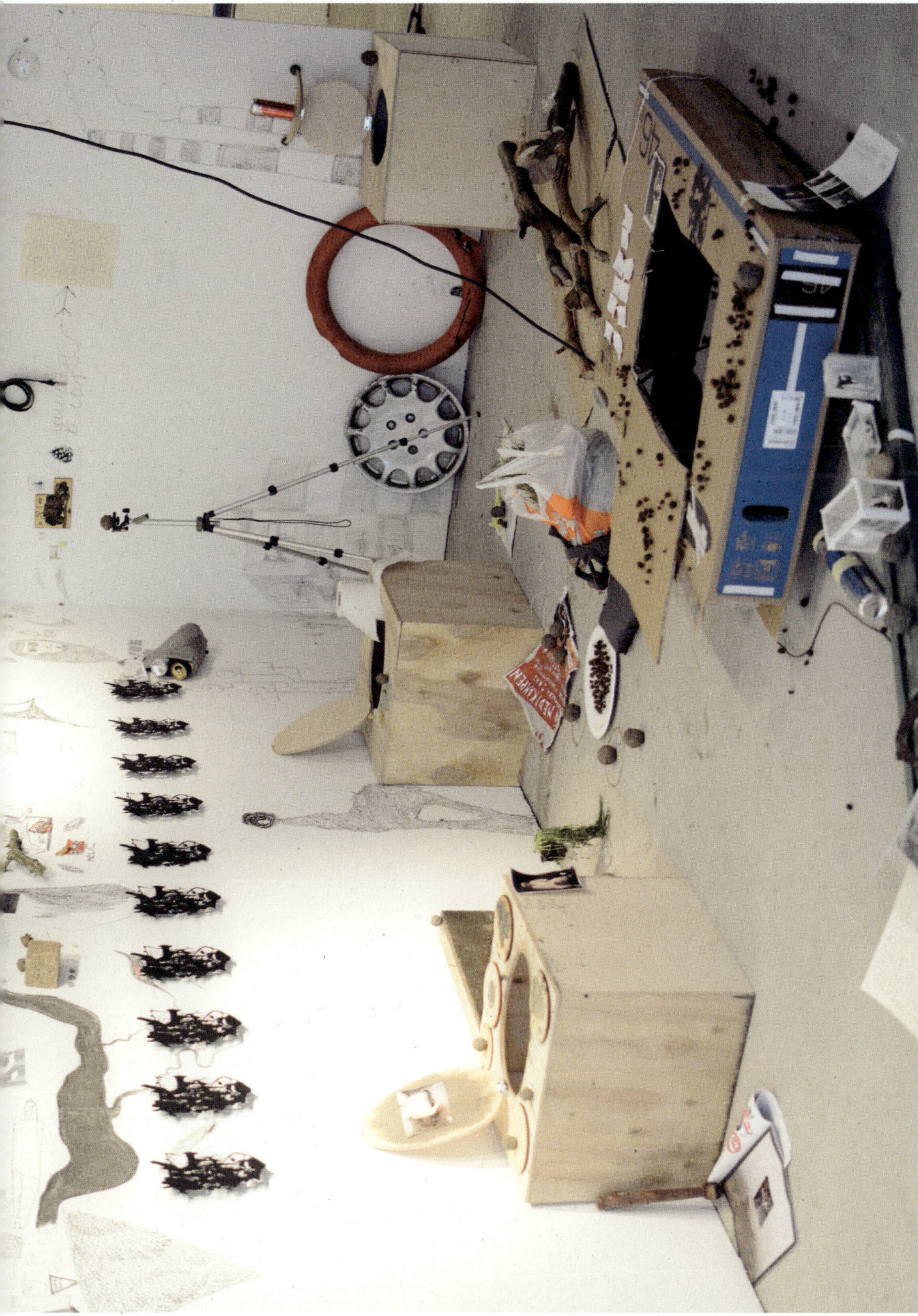

NAME
Vereinigung Bildender KünstlerInnen Wiener Secession (Association of Visual Artists Vienna Secession)

LOCATION
Vienna, Austria

WEBSITE
www.secession.at

YEAR
1897 to present

STRUCTURE
Artist-run, non-profit organization

LEGAL STATUS
Association

TEAM
13 voluntary board members including one president
3 curators, 2 employees for press and publications, 6 employees for administration and technical maintenance, 14 public service staff (mostly part time)

MISSION
To every time its art.
To art its freedom.

FUNDING
Public funding by the City of Vienna and the Austrian Federal Government (applied for annually), trustees, sponsors, operating revenues (entrance fees, shop)

OTHER FUNDING
Project sponsors, sponsors in kind, media partners

PREMISES
Building designed and financed by the founding members in 1898, on lease for a symbolic sum by the City of Vienna (owner)

The Vienna Secession is the world's oldest independent exhibition space explicitly dedicated to contemporary art. It was established in 1897 – and continues to operate today – as an institution run by artists. It occupies a unique position in the history of modern art, combining a contemporary, forward-looking programme with a building whose architecture is an icon of the spirit of imminent change around 1900.

The "Association of Visual Artists Vienna Secession" was founded by a group of artists who had split off from the conservative Künstlerhaus. Their leader, Gustav Klimt, became the first president of the association; other founding members included the painters Kolo Moser and Carl Moll, and the architects Josef Hoffmann and Joseph Maria Olbrich. The group needed a new exhibition venue, and so Olbrich directed the planning for an exhibition hall. The decoration scheme and interiors were finalised in close collaboration with other artists to create a *Gesamtkunstwerk* that embodied the group's new vision. In imperial Austria, the Secession represented not only a visual challenge but also a political one. Paid for mainly by the considerable proceeds from the First Secession Exhibition, with support from upper-class intellectuals like the industrialist Karl Wittgenstein, the art-nouveau Secession building occupies a prominent site. It stands as a confident symbol of an initiative launched by free spirits whose sole allegiance was to their art, as the manifesto – "To every time its art. To art its freedom." – emblazoned on the façade in golden letters proudly proclaims.

In keeping with the radicalism of its founding fathers, the Secession today hosts an international programme that explores current forms of artistic expression in solo and themed exhibitions. It is a sounding board for the aesthetic and critical discourses on art, culture, and society that define our era, and for the political significance they accrue. After facing a number of diverse challenges in the course of its history, including World War I, Nazi occupation, destruction by bombs in 1945, and the repressive cultural climate of the postwar years, it was not until 1985 that the Secession was able to undertake a general refurbishment and remodeling of the building, which was directed by the architects Krischanitz and Kapfinger. At the same time, Gustav Klimt's Beethoven Frieze (a remnant from the association's famous group show dedicated to Ludwig van Beethoven in 1902) was purchased by the Republic of Austria

↓ Laura Owens, 2015
Installation view
Secession
Photograph by Jorit Aust

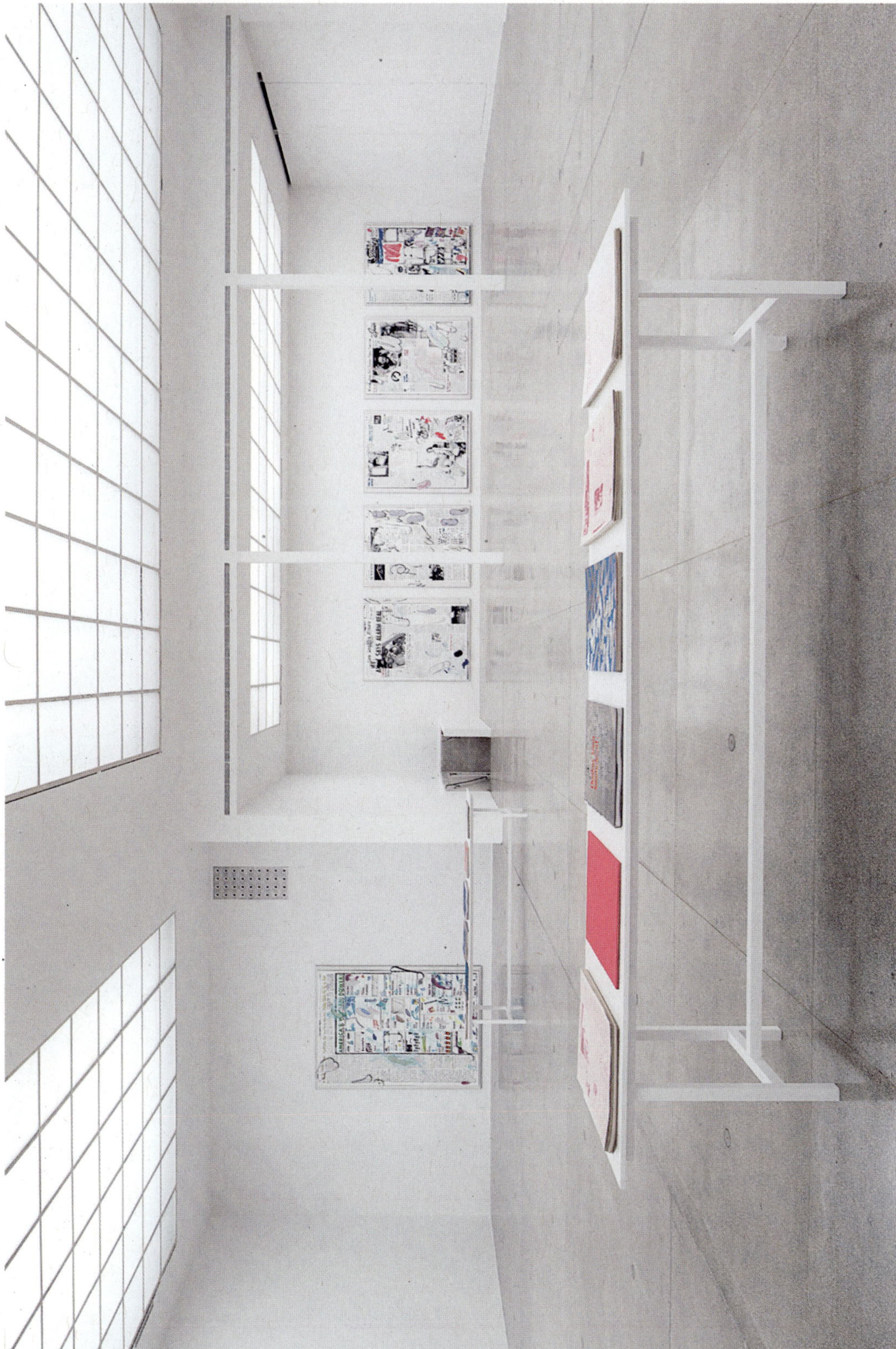

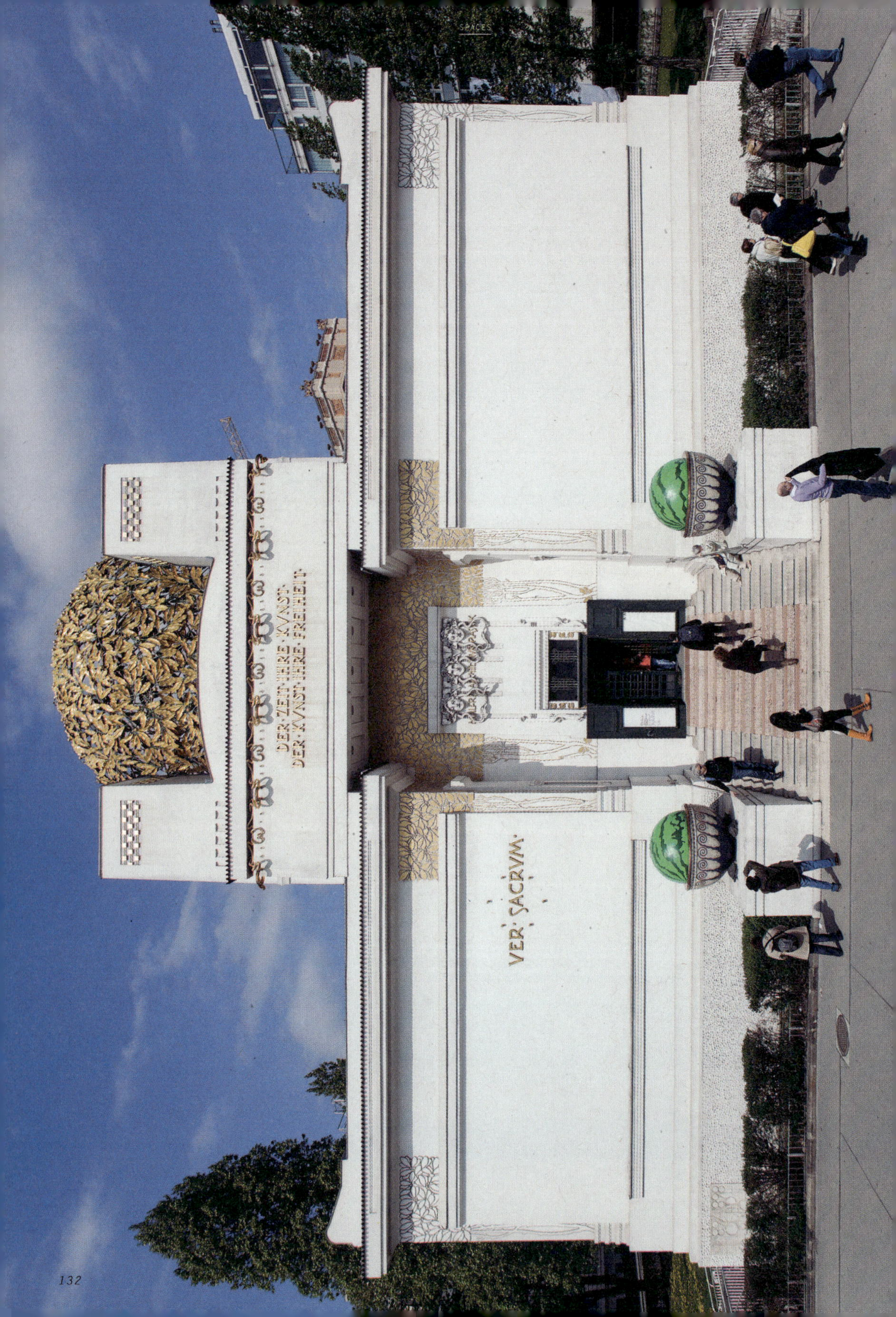
DER ZEIT IHRE KVNST.
DER KVNST IHRE FREIHEIT
VER SACRVM

and reinstalled in a specially designed room in the basement. The building's architecture – and especially the main gallery, which is often referred to as one of the very first "white cubes" – still provides excellent conditions for today's artistic practices.

The programme of ten to fifteen shows a year is put together in a democratic process by the association's thirteen-member board and based exclusively on artistic criteria. The Secession has almost four hundred regular members (working artists and architects), from whose ranks the board of directors and the president are elected to two-year terms of office. The association's funding is supplied by public subsidies, private partners such as the active and dedicated Friends of the Secession, and operating revenues in roughly equal parts. After more than a century, the Secession embraces as well as questions its role as guardian of the historic avant-garde and as an institution dedicated to critical engagement with tomorrow's art.

↑ Slavs and Tatars
Not Moscow Not Mecca, 2012
Installation view
Secession
Photograph by Oliver Ottenschlaeger

↓ Manfred Pernice, 2010
Installation view
Secession
Photograph by Oliver Ottenschlaeger

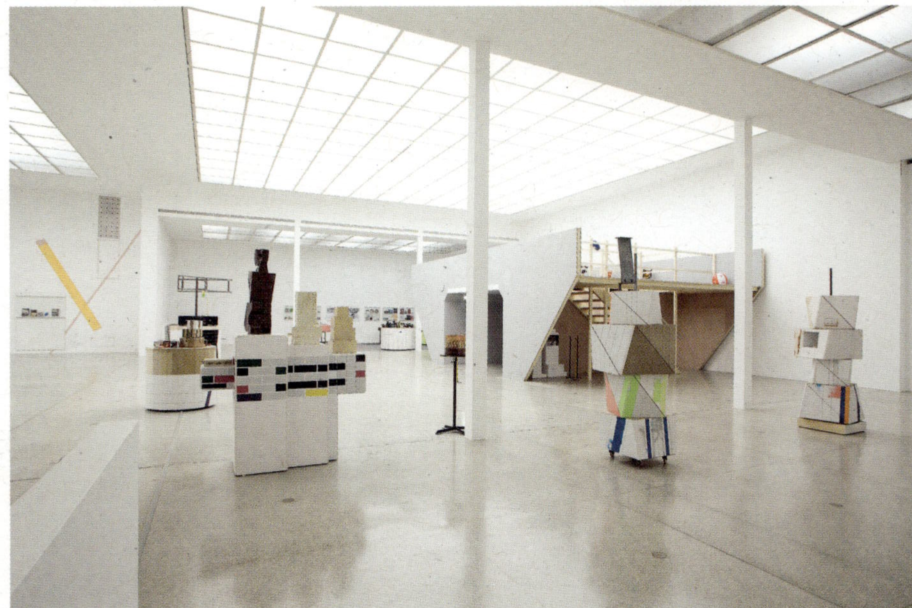

NAME
Transmission Gallery

LOCATION
Glasgow, Scotland

WEBSITE
www.transmissiongallery.org

YEAR
1983 to present

STRUCTURE
Artist-run, non-profit organisation with a voluntary committee

LEGAL STATUS
Charity

TEAM
Committee-led (6 volunteers on a term of up to 2 years)

MISSION
Transmission is an artist-run organisation that supports and is supported by its membership and surrounding communities in Glasgow and beyond. Transmission works with artists in the production of exhibitions, events, exchanges, residencies and publications. It also shares various resources with its membership in order to facilitate activities outside of its own programming

FUNDING
Creative Scotland funding, various other funding bodies and membership fees

PREMISES
Local authority subsidised

SELECTED PROJECTS
Index, Spike Island FILM OPEN 2015, presented at LUX Moving Images Festival, September 2015, Tramway, Glasgow; Johannes Paul Raether, *The Witch and the Swarm*, 16 June–18 July 2015; *Giving Up the Ghost*, Anna Zett, Basim Magdy, Steve Reinke, Transmission, 1 December 2015 – 16 January 2016

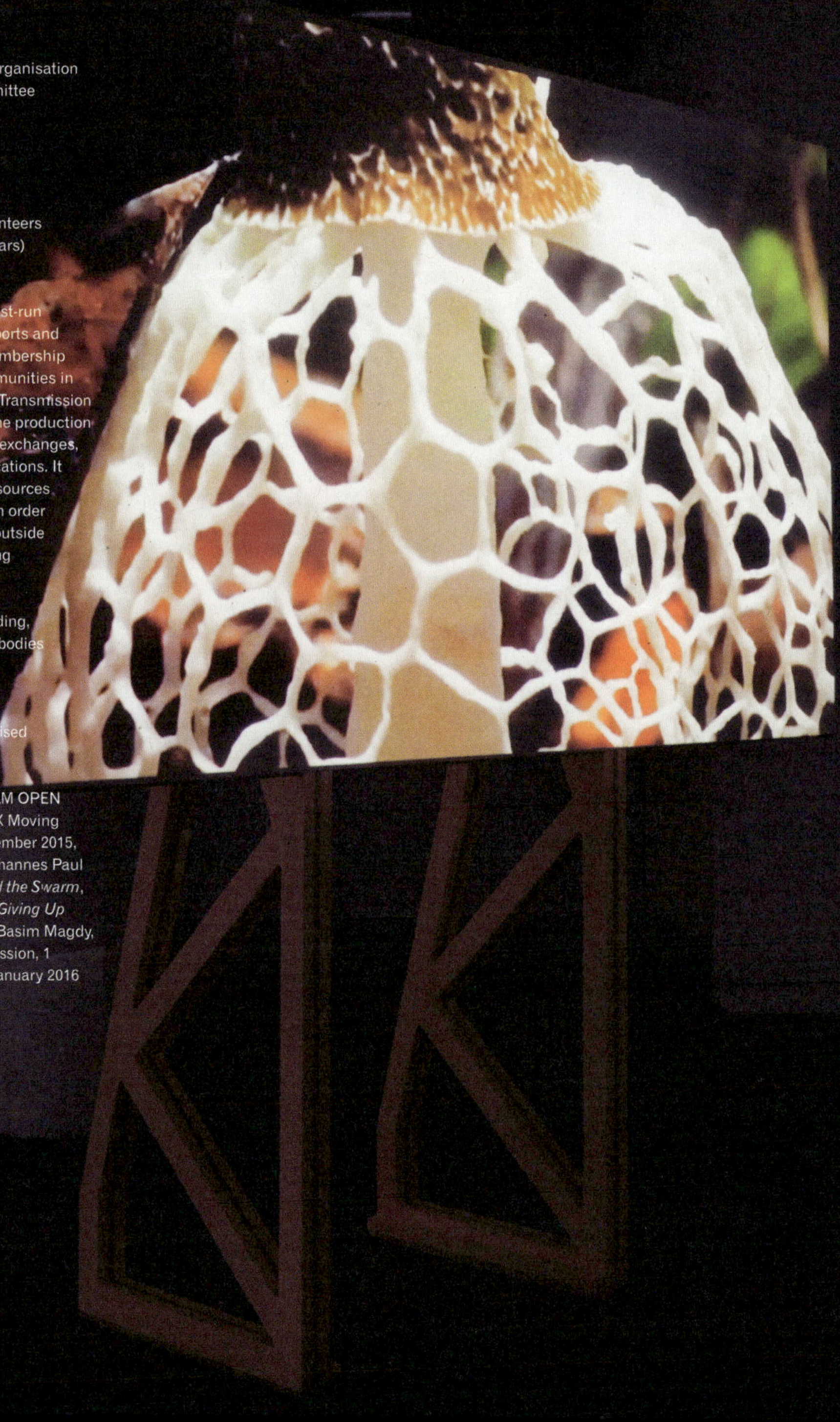

Transmission Gallery

I

I was wondering if you might like to make any changes to the section of the script that features Transmission:

> Looking to the left of Street Level we can see Transmission Gallery, which was set up in 1983 by graduates from the Glasgow School of Art who were dissatisfied with the lack of exhibition spaces and opportunities for young artists in Glasgow. The gallery is managed by a voluntary committee of six people, each of whom serves on the Transmission Committee for up to two years and is then replaced.
>
> The kind of art work associated with Transmission has changed over the years as the committee of artists who run the gallery change. In the gallery's earliest incarnation in the 1980s Transmission showed the politically motivated figurative painting of the 'New Glasgow Boys'; in the 1990s the gallery came to be associated with the neo-conceptualists coming out of the GSA Environmental Art course. Today the gallery exists as part of a network of artist-run spaces and initiatives, both within the city and further afield, but still functions as a focus for a community of artists and an independent space for the exchange of ideas.

...

Giving Up the Ghost
Video works by Anna Zett, Basim Magdy, Steve Reinke. Exhibition Design by Kevin Pollock
Transmission Gallery
1 December 2015 – 16 January 2016
Image: Steve Reinke, ***The Natural Look*** (36:32), Screen: Kevin Pollock, birch plywood and insulation foam, 2015
Photograph by Morwenna Kearsley & Erin Busswood

Having had a little bit of time to reflect on the script we thought there might be a few interesting titbits that could add some flavour to the description of Transmission [above]. It's a little bit longer than the suggested text but hopefully gives a little bit of an insight into the inner workings of the space:

> The basement of the gallery houses an archive which preserves the gallery's official history, but much of the folklore surrounding the space is only accessible through speaking to the members who constitute Transmission's community and primary audience.
>
> False walls in the basement are said to hide dusty but valuable artworks left over from previous exhibitions – kept as an alternative source of income in the eventuality of public funding cuts. A recent redevelopment of the building uncovered tunnels leading from the basement – used for unknown purposes in the '80s and forgotten by subsequent committees. The gallery is also the site of an occasional late-night speakeasy called 'The Cell,' advertised a week in advance by a photocopied mail-out to members. At a particularly difficult time for the space, committee member Hans Ahlgren attempted to sink Transmission by filing for bankruptcy, declaring the gallery "had sold out to the corporate art world and was kowtowing to state funding bodies", only for an anonymous private benefactor to provide an undisclosed bailout. At the 2009 AGM, visiting Czech feminist artists' co-operative OK Cabal railed against what they perceived as a gender bias in the programming, resulting in a period of instability with both all-male and all-female committees, finally resolving into a 50/50 split.

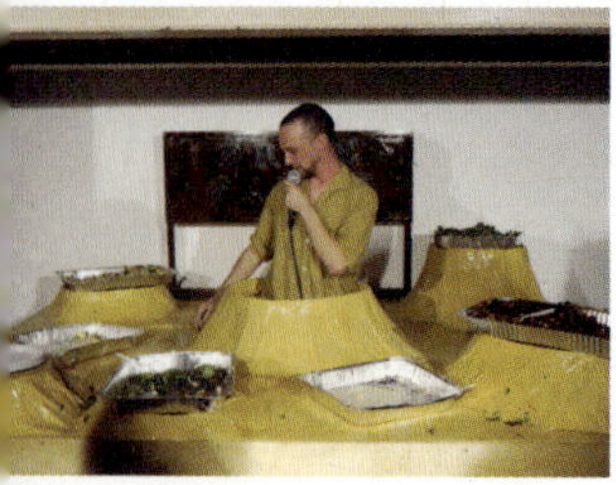

Patrick Cole
Free Salad
Performance event with sculpture and salad
Transmission Gallery
7 November 2014
Photograph courtesy of the artist and Transmission Gallery

Let us know what you think!
All the best,
Transmo

...

Hello,
That seems ok to me, I guess.

Personally, I would have more of an issue with the name: Glasgow Miracle City Walking Tour, but hey it's your thing.
Cheers,
X at Transmission

...

To those on the receiving end of my emails,

Please excuse my previous lapse in delicacy. I can only apologise profusely and renege on my prior approach to the emails.

As one of many, many emails that I was subject to that day, I treated it with an inappropriate level of dismissiveness and implied derision. I feel that this was another case of my being a bit too flippant and not seeming to take things seriously enough, and for that I am sorry.

I meant it though and if it was an email to my personal account I would have treated it in the same manner. Of course, in full understanding and acceptance of the error in responding this way as Transmission rather than simply as JS, I fully and sincerely apologise and will be more thorough next time.

Yours, ever-the-diplomat,

X

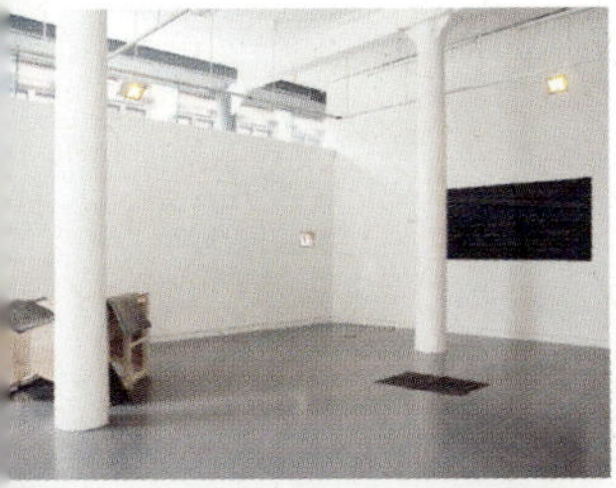

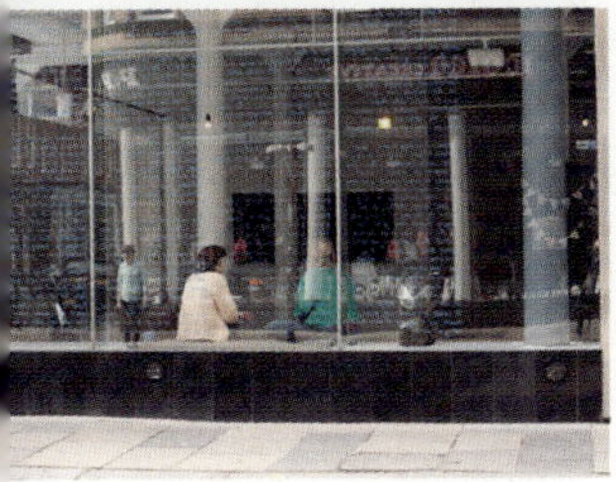

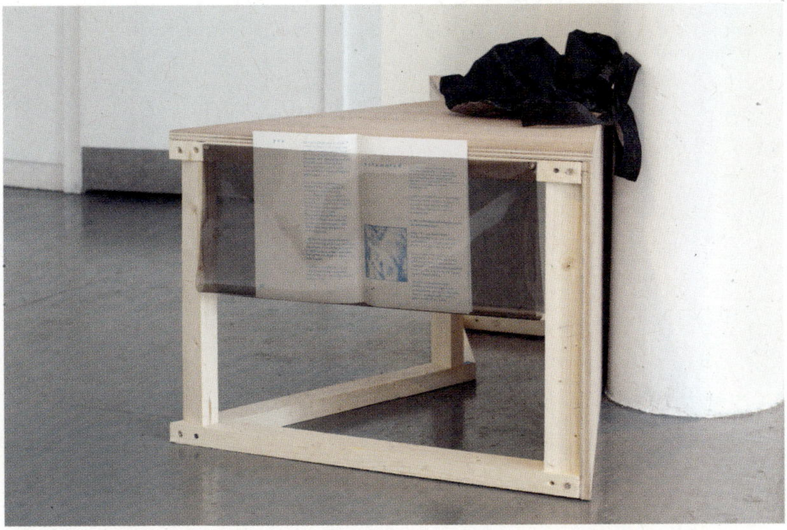

↖ Victor and Hester
↗ **VH-16-22-7-12-3-22-5 Dreams of Machines**
31 March – 25 April 2015
Transmission Gallery

A series of sort-of commissions; audio, text, screening, performance, and research using the domestic space as a structure for thinking through questions around a feminist reading of privacy, companionship, collaborations, language, labour, architectural space, and movement within and between these frameworks. Invocations of past practices; acts of collapsing definitions, a process of making non-spaces, dwelling in the domestic machine and dreaming past it.

Photographs by Tor Jonnson

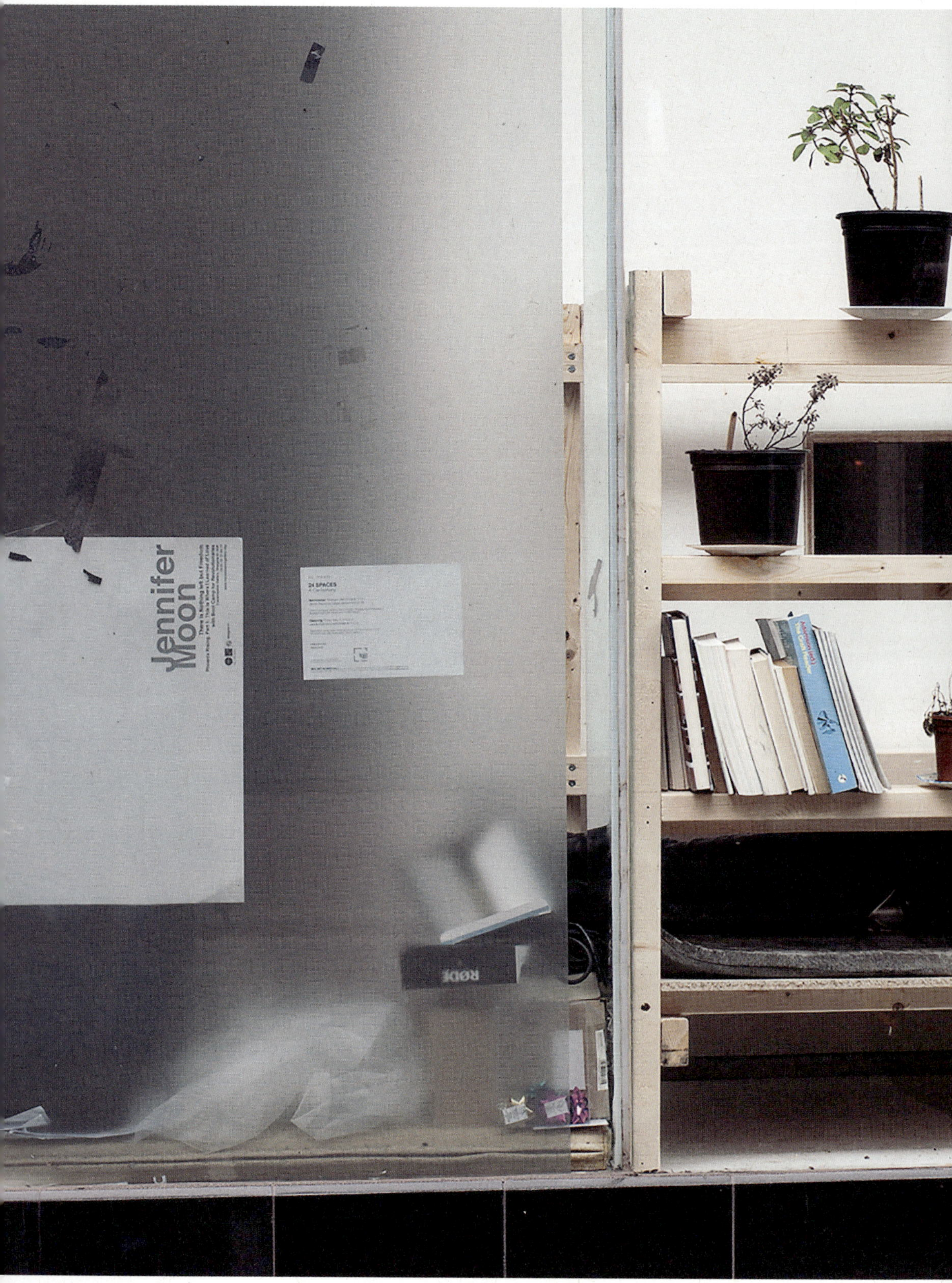
Jennifer Moon
24 SPACES

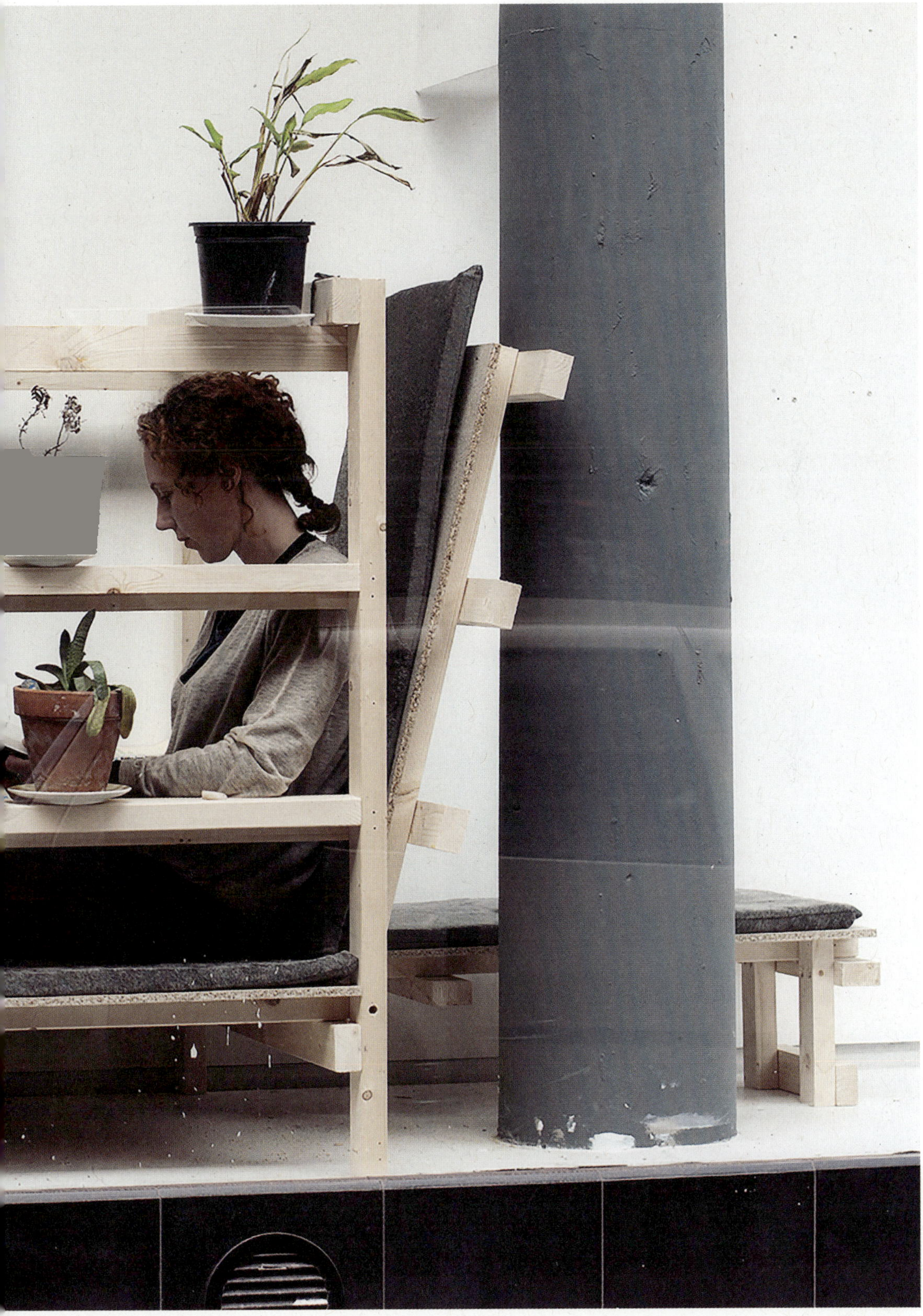

II

```
Hello all,
Please find email draft to XX, regarding their proposal and
our ill-defined interest.
Is it ok? Too long? Too vague? Too Toooooo?
     Love,
     X
```

How are you? We're really sorry that it has taken us so long to get back to you regarding the above proposal.

We look over them about once every 3–6 months, where we undertake close reading of the submitted material, considering them in relation to the existing programme, our ambitions and ideals for the space, and our individual interests as artists outside of Transmission. As such, it takes a while for us to get back to people either way, as we necessarily take our time. Slow processing and deep engagement is the ideal…

—

Working as volunteers, it is important for us that we have a genuine connection with the project, and as such, generally speaking, we're not always so interested in outsourcing shows to external curators. Having said that, we really value and encourage other voices, fresh perspectives and alternative formats and approaches to programming our programme.

At the moment, we are pretty committed to a programme of deeper, longer-term engagement with the development of each project from quite an early stage. This active investment in facilitating the creation of new work is important both for ourselves, and the people we work with. It offers a mutually beneficial approach that isn't simply about the final outcome, but values and supports the infinite amount of unrepresented background work (research, development, dialogue, crisis, etc.) that goes into every project.

—

In relation to your proposal, we were excited and intrigued about potentially developing a project alongside you rather than the simple administering/facilitating of a pre-packaged show...

As such, we are interested in counter-proposing you, to work in conjunction with us, towards producing something (an exhibition, a publication, a discursive event, a lecture, a meandering dialogue that goes nowhere. We want to keep it open).

—

If this all seems a bit vague, well, it is intentionally so, but I hope it finds you well and that you find it an appealing proposition. If you're open to the messiness of conjunction, the sharings and carings, the misunderstandings and mutations, the changing of ideas and perspectives that this entails, then we'd love to do something together!

Hope to hear back from you,

Transmission

III

Hi XXX,
So, we have no volunteering opportunities as such, no professional development or intern programme. In general we're against unpaid voluntary positions, especially ones that advertise themselves as 'opportunities' as the cultural sector runs on the exploitation of this intangible promise of a future 'pay off'.

Maybe to explain, the committee of six that runs this place all do it voluntarily and in a pretty 'unprofessional' way. I realise it's probably unclear why, as a volunteer myself, I am telling you that we're against volunteer positions in the arts, but it's a bit of a different set up here. The voluntary committee that runs Transmission aren't answerable to a manager or a boss or some higher authority that is using us to run their business for free: we run it for ourselves and for the membership (300 or so artists and interested people around Glasgow and across the UK). As such we have a lot of freedom to run the space as we see fit, according to our own values and ideals rather than by those of whoever would hypothetically be paying us (the art market if we were a commercial gallery, or Creative Scotland if we accepted wages from them – both have, to my mind, dubious value systems that I don't want to have to conform to). We do, however, make a point of fairly paying everyone that is asked to come and work with us (exhibiting artists, technicians, photographers for documentation, etc.).

Anyway, while we have no 'volunteer opportunities' you can (and should!) become a member! Being a member means you get (and can put things in) the 'monthly' mail-out, borrow any of our equipment (for free!), use the resource room and put your own work in the annual members' show, as well as all the other joys of being a part of a small, friendly community of artists. The membership make up the core of our audience, they are the users of the space and the resources, and they are the community that 'okays' the committee and how they're running the gallery. The committee is made up of members too, I should add, but that whole process is not so easy to explain in that there's no vote or anything, it works a lot more fluidly and discursively.

IV

Dear Members,
In the hope of opening up the process of committee member selection and making it more accessible to membership, the current committee would like to request nominations for consideration during upcoming committee vacancies. Discussions with members in the past few months have made us aware that the selection process for new committee members is somewhat opaque, and we'd like to remedy this by outlining the procedure in this message and making this request to the membership at large.

The nominations by members will support the committee in our effort to think outside of its immediate friends/ peer-group. However it is important to note that this issue is complicated by the fact that excluding people because of a pre-existing relationship with the committee is also problematic (there is something contradictory about the precedent of asking active members to be on the committee, whilst also trying to avoid any perceived nepotism). Above all, we believe it is fundamental to the spirit of Transmission that the process of appointing committee members not become a bureaucratic and competitive one. Having conventional applications would mean more paperwork for a volunteer committee who are already stretched, more paperwork for artists already filling out numerous application forms, and a professionalisation of the entire process that we want to avoid like the plague. So, the committee will continue to make our own nominations and will have the final say on who is asked. Usually we contact the person by phone to discuss their joining the committee.

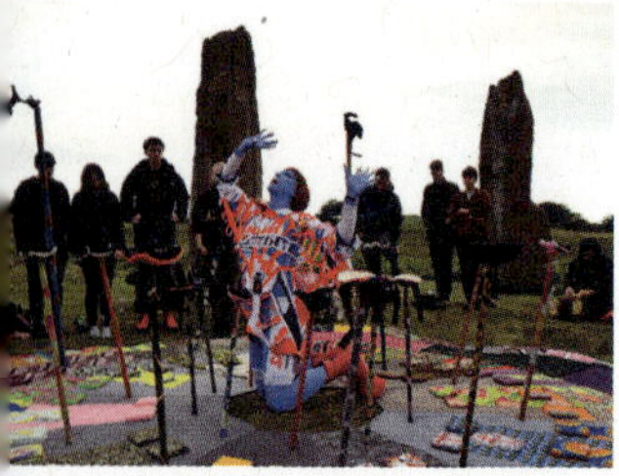

Transmission's constitution, which is handed out at each AGM and freely available from the gallery on request, defines the committee as follows:

> **Committee:** At the AGM the association will approve a Committee to administer the day-to-day affairs of the association. This Committee shall comprise of a Chairperson, a Secretary, a Treasurer and at least 2, but not more than 4, other ordinary members. The maximum period allotted to members of the Committee being two terms (two years). Any casual vacancy arising may be filled by the Committee. The Chairperson will preside at all meetings of the association, and in the event of their absence the Committee or the association, as the case shall be, shall appoint one of their number.

↙ Johannes Paul Raether
↘ **The Witch and the Swarm**
16 June – 18 July 2015

The Second Communisate with Protektorama, 2015
Sunset, 20–21 June (summer solstice), Machrie Moor Standing Stones, Isle of Arran (performance documentation image)

The Witch And The Swarm: a project in three parts. During normal gallery hours Transmission's white womb incubated an installation of devotional fetish-objects, a hoard of post-fordist swag lovingly collated and stitched together from the witches' past outings. The Witch And The Swarm could also be encountered dribbling out of the mouth of Glasgow's ex-industrial bloodline, the River Clyde – with the Swarm Being – and in the celestial setting of the Isle of Arran's ancient stone circles where we, together with Protektorama, celebrate the summer solstice.

Photograph by Tor Jonnson

"How do we get rid of you?"

Like I said, outside of the AGM, I don't presently know [how to get rid of a committee member]. Maybe as it's a members organisation, you'd have to get other members on board to propose an alternative committee, or failing that, if it's not run how you like, you should just relinquish your membership and set up an alternative. That's how Transmission itself started.

…members can call a special general meeting to dispose of the committee if they want to. There are some conditions they have to meet that I can't remember off the top of my head. It's all in the constitution (which is handed out at every AGM). My preference would almost be to reply with the constitution and mission statement attached and say that all the info needed is in there?

We're always open to feedback and you can talk to us in person or by email. (Most of the feedback we get is informal.)

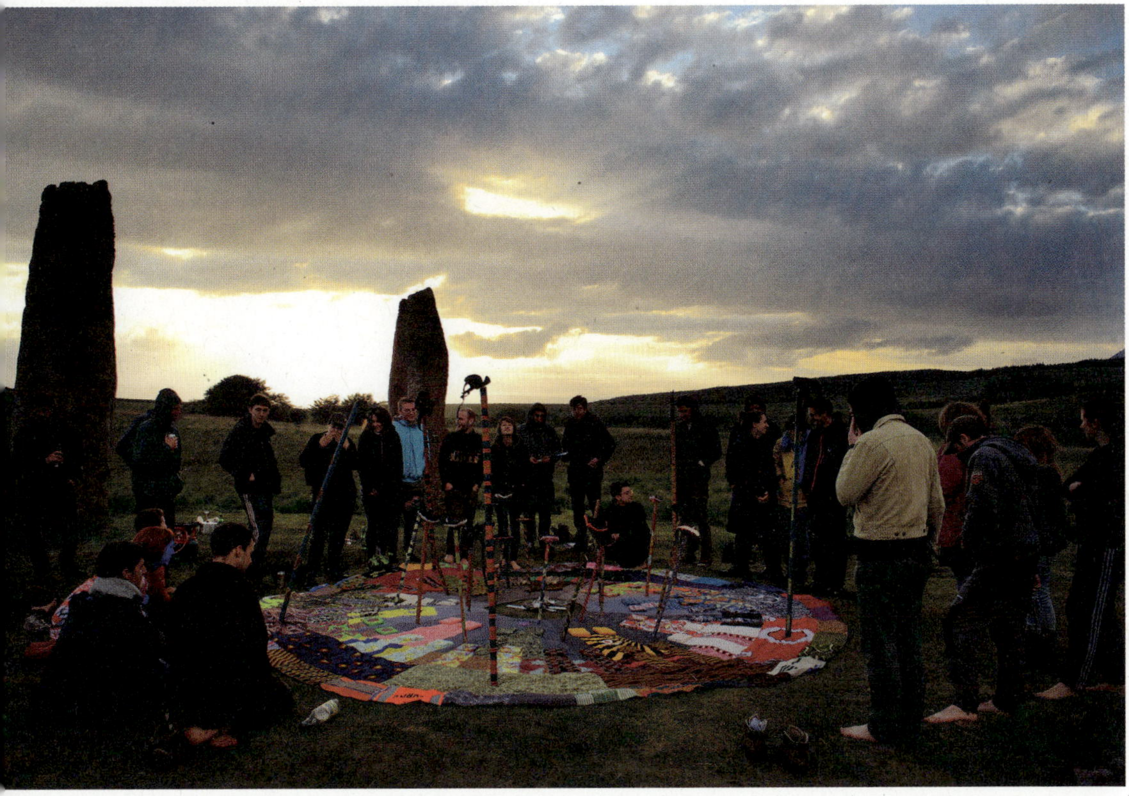

Katherine Waugh

Delicate Yet Deadly

"The Artist-Run Space of the Future is a mushroom, delicate yet deadly."[‡]

[‡] 'The Artist Run Space of the Future', 1st Edition, *Institute for Applied Aesthetics* Sept 2010 www.appliedaesthetics.org

Ekaterina Degot, in the Autumn 2015 edition of *Afterall*, acknowledged her ambivalent response to the Artist Organisations International (AOI) 'congress' which took place in Hebbel am Ufer (HaU) in Berlin in January of the same year, and which she helped moderate.[1] The 'hotchpotch' nature of the gathering was explicit: the assembly included dozens of 'artist organisations' sharing the widest of umbrellas, with many having incompatible and even contradictory agendas. Some were aggressively activist, others political only in the most tokenistic sense, and others again claimed a more performative, nebulous identity. The strong impression garnered by Degot from the event was that:

> "Institutional critique is over; instead the door is open to (re)construct the very thing that gives art scale, duration and – importantly – financial and organisational support: institutional activism."

Because criticality, which in the past had fostered such a sense of faith in its force, is now seen by many to be thoroughly instrumentalised, something else seemed to be needed, something more challenging.

Degot suggests that what we are witnessing is an 'ontological turn' in which a new emphasis is placed on modes of 'being' underpinning the explosion of what she refers to as 'righteous' artistic projects (yes, the thought of another 'turn' may have our heads spinning, the 'turn' machine endlessly churning out new variations as satirised by Lars Bang Larsen in *Turn Turn Turn* in Mousse a few years ago, asking: "Did somebody do the 'Whatever' turn yet?").[2]

---

[1] Ekaterina Degot 'The Artist as Director: 'Artist Organisations International' and its Contradictions', *Afterall* Autumn/Winter 2015

[2] Lars Bang Larsen, 'Turn Turn Turn', *Mousse* Issue 35 Oct 2012

Following Degot one has to admit the sheer level of incongruity seen between, on the one hand, the ostensible motivations and aspirations of many self branded 'radical' organisations and artists, and, on the other, the methodologies and means through which they choose to realise these aims, frequently encountering a Bartleby-like wall of ontological resistance.[3] When the relationship between form and content becomes a mere facetious structural obstacle, one often gets the impression of an immovable object coming up against an irresistible force within the artist-led community, producing, almost by default, this ontological desire for more cohesion backed by a grounded materiality. Echoing Bartleby again, Alan Bennett in a recent *Guardian* interview said he felt that all one had to do today to be radical was to stand still or, it could be added, just stick your thumb in the dyke to stem the relentless tide of self-promotion by many artist organisations and initiatives, constantly asserting their integrity yet undercutting that supposed integrity through the means used to defend that status.[4]

The open discussions which took place at AOI in Berlin displayed this simmering tension to be found between many artist-run organisations (AROs) today, with many participants contesting the choice of venue, the high entrance fee, and the formal structure and design of the event itself, demanding that the intense sense of conflict over such organisational givens was a "conflict which needs to be kept in our heads at all times", not just glossed over as a superficial difference.[5] Charles Esche, moderating the final discussion, asserted that he had no intention of "doing the social democratic option" of erasing differences in a false unity, and recognised that the imperative of specificity was crucial. The intensity of the differences which emerged at this event remind us of how difficult it is to speak about 'artist organisations' in any common language, and as Esche said, how important it is to maintain that sense of the complexity and singularity of each effort, each collaboration and its unique internal dynamic.

One interesting aspect of the event was that many present seemed to feel a distaste for the very process of calcification and institutionalisation involved in even constituting oneself as an 'organisation', and that an emphasis upon the activity of 'organising' instead allowed more fluidity and resistance at this point culturally.

***

[3] Herman Melville's 1853 story *Bartleby The Scrivener* has rendered the statement "I would prefer not to" as iconic in cultural terms as "I am Spartacus". Gilles Deleuze's essay 'Bartleby; or, The Formula' in *Essays Critical and Clinical* (Verso 1998 but originally published in France in 1989), initiated a new wave of interest in the story.

See also Tim Stott 'Not Saying No: Perverts, Melancholics and Bartleby', *Circa* 121, Autumn 2007

[4] http://www.theguardian.com/stage/2015/oct/31/alan-bennett-tories-govern-with-totalitarian-attitude

[5] See this and other contentious aspects of the event discussed in the online videos (more specifically the final debate) available at www.artistorganisationsinternational.org/#program6/

Looking more closely (and more critically) at the very nature of organisation itself has become the argument *du jour*, with the gauntlet thrown down by Dillemuth, Davies & Jakobsen in *There is No Alternative: The Future is Self-Organised* (1 and 2), the framing text used by Pallas Projects for the first gallery manifestation of its long term project *Artist Run Europe*.[6]

Barnaby Drabble's response in his essay *On De-Organisation* to both the initial text/manifesto and its follow up in 2012, recognises the pleasure to be found in polemical texts such as this, "like a surgeon listing malignant tumours for urgent removal."[7] He does however draw attention to an area that he feels isn't adequately addressed: the question of representational methodologies and their accompanying rationalities. Drabble reminds us that a central problem is that of institutions and AROs becoming "so caught up in the 'business' of representation and the expediency this entails that they have forgotten to pay attention to the nature of the practices they are tasked to look after."

The problem of the particular concept of 'self' that is being used in 'self-organised' initiatives is of primary importance since "the nature of self-organised activity often depends more on which particular 'self' is doing the organising than the activity itself". He argues that we need to take a very close look at the relationship between any idea of 'self' or 'subjectivity' and representational logic and aesthetics within culture, and we need to move away from the idea of 'representing' both culture and ourselves (even in seemingly 'radical' formats cultivated by many AROs) and focus instead on 'producing' culture, albeit outside of neo-liberal rationalities of production with set goals – whether those involve objects, performances/spectacles or fixed display models.

One particular criticism raised in *On De-Organisation* is one that any manifesto-like text leaves itself open to: that it may in fact end up like a "revolutionary tract with state managed footnotes" due to what Drabble suggests is the impression that Dillemuth, Davies & Jakobsen give of a post-institutional scenario where what was previously institutionally-directed public funding becomes re-distributed in a 'no-holds-barred' way to the true and worthy in the arts community (an impossible outcome in his mind). The core problem for Drabble, echoed by theorists such as Mark Fisher in his analysis of the psycho-social impact of excessive bureaucratisation in academia, is that of the new regime of the 'organisation of the self' forced upon us through the relentless techniques of time and resource management, structured in such a way as to construct very specific functional neo-liberal 'selves'

[6] See Stephan Dillemuth, Anthony Davies, Jakob Jakobsen, 'There is No Alternative: The Future is Self-Organised,' in *Art and Social Change: A Critical Reader*, (Eds.) Will Bradley and Charles Esche (London: Tate Publishing and Afterall, 2007), and "There is No Alternative: THE FUTURE IS (SELF-) ORGANISED PART 2, in *Self-Organised* (Eds.) Stine Hebert and Anne Szefer Karlsen, (London, Open Editions, 2013)

[7] Barnaby Drabble, 'On De-Organisation', in *Self-Organised* (Eds.) Stine Hebert and Anne Szefer Karlsen, (London, Open Editions, 2013)

(for Fisher the privatisation of stress within academia through an overwhelming 'audit culture' "forecloses any question of the systemic by focusing on the individual").[8]

In his call for de-organisation – an affirmation of the "ad-hoc, last minute and improvised", Drabble is attempting to introduce a more credible critique of the internal logic of organisation itself. Freelancers, those living by the new regime of precarity (including Drabble himself), should, he claims, "stop shoring up our craft in a rational and managerial way" and aim instead for different modes of production which may require turning off what he calls the "over heated machine" of artistic, discursive and institutional production as we know it. How much we find ourselves complicit in ushering in a regime of micro-management wherein we effectively bolster a culture based on the institutionalism of the self, is a subject returned to time and again by many writers and theorists looking at possible futures for AROs, demonstrating an awareness that a micro-political analysis is necessary before larger structural and political issues can be tackled.

The problem of negotiating the forces and calcifying effects of institutionalism within artist organisations is addressed again by Rachel Mader in her essay *How to move in/an institution* from *Oncurating*'s issue dedicated to *(New) Institution(alism)*.[9] Mader acknowledges the significance of Zurich-based philosopher and art theorist Gerard Raunig's "exemplary criticism" of Andrea Fraser and the 'second wave' of institutional critique, and echoes Brian Holmes' reservations about the theoretical weaknesses in Fraser's argumentation where, as Holmes writes elsewhere:

"Bourdieu's deterministic analysis of the closure of the socio-professional fields, mingled with a deep confusion between Weber's iron cage and Foucault's desire to 'get free of oneself' is internalised here in a governmentality of failure."[10]

Ultimately for Holmes (who has himself engaged in valuable collaborations with the artist-run space 16 Beaver St in New York) the limitations encountered in much of the second wave of institutional critique create a "dead end, with institutional consequences of complacency, immobility, loss of autonomy, capitulation before various forms of instrumentalisation."[11]

---

[8] Matthew Fuller 'Questioning Capitalist Realism: An interview with Mark Fisher' Jan 2010 www.spc.org

[9] 'Oncurating' Issue 21 Jan 2014 *(New) Institution(alism)*. Mader frames Raunig and Holmes problematisation of Andrea Fraser's theorising rather than practice thus: "Raunig predictably attacks Fraser based on her fatalistic-sounding statement that there is precisely no fleeing from the institution: "It is because the institution is inside of us, and we can't get outside of ourselves."[44] The configuration of this argument reveals much about the problematic jostling of positions that determines this debate as a whole and points to a lack of reflection on the interactions and struggles between different actors in their respective institutional dispositions." p. 7.

[10] Brian Holmes, 'Extradisciplinary Investigations. Towards a New Critique of Institutions', 2007 http://eipcp.net/transversal/0106/holmes/en

[11] See www.16beavergroup.org and Brian Holmes 'Articulating the Cracks in the Worlds of Power'.pdf of seminar with 16 Beaver 2006

Foucault's writings and lectures on governmentality have been re-invigorating much recent thought on art and politics, and both Raunig and Mader are among those who see value in drawing on their insights. It is seen as a body of work that provides tools to help get beyond an impasse many artists and activists feel they encounter when trying to think and act in new ways within the labyrinth of power and institutional structures stultifying radical aspirations. The relationship with a concept of the 'outside' is central, not the simplistic 'absolute' outside so often presented in careless readings of Foucault, but a constantly re-generating series of thresholds producing a dynamic of challenge and transformation as identified by Felix Guattari (and in tune with Foucault as read by Deleuze).[12] For Holmes, the drive to tap into a movement between disciplines has potentiality, accessing "the real critical reserve of marginal or counter-culture positions – social movements, political associations, squats, autonomous communities – which can't be reduced to an all-embracing institution". The extra-disciplinary emphasis of such artistic initiatives links to modes of expressivity and subjectivity that combine the analytical with the affective, in a process which helps resist codification. The value of such artistic initiatives and projects stems from the sense that "their analytic processes are at the same time expressive, and for them, every complex machine is awash in affect and subjectivity."

Gerard Raunig's promotion of an alternative to what he feels were the 'paralysing' and overly canonised strategies of institutional critique is articulated through his idea of "instituent practices" which exceed mere opposition to institutions. Instituent practice becomes a means to avoid simplistic characterisations of institutional power and practice, yet continues to "flee from institutionalism and structuralisation". Raunig insists we need a shift in our thinking about resistance and counter-strategies to conventional institutions, away from centralised notions of power towards a more immanent idea of a dynamic of power and its pathways, "a constant struggle on the plane of immanence".[13]

In *From Community to the Undercommons*, Christoph Brenner and Raunig find inspiration in many transversal micro-political movements emerging in Southern Europe, though many have been aggressively resisted since their text was written.[14] The rejection of the individual as the primary unit of capitalism, along with subjectivities aligned with ideas of creative entrepreneurship, remains central within any attempt to create alternative artistic structures. In their analysis of the concept of 'Undercommons' (as written about by Stefano Harney

---

[12] Félix Guattari, *Chaosmosis: an Ethico-Aesthetic paradigm*. Translated by Paul Baines and Julian Pefanis. Sydney: Power publications 1995

[13] Gerald Raunig, 'Instituent Practices: Fleeing, Instituting, Transforming' in Gerald Raunig and Gene Ray (Eds.), *Art and Contemporary Critical Practice: Reinventing Institutional Critique*, MayFlyBooks/eipcp, London, 2009, pp. 3–12

[14] Christoph Brunner & Gerard Rauning, 'From Community to the Undercommons : Preindividual – Transidividual – Dividual – Condividual' in *Communist Aesthetics Open! Platform for Art Culture and the Public Domain* www.onlineopen.org/download.php?id=470

& Fred Molten) Brenner and Raunig see new potentialities for re-conceptualising sociabilities and communities which, though primarily addressing politics *en sui*, bear much relevance for those AROs which position themselves within specific community contexts.[15]

Drawing on Deleuze and his work on Spinoza but also on Guattari's theorising of micro-politics, Brunner & Raunig also build upon concepts found in the work of Gilbert Simondon, a philosopher at the forefront of much thinking in artistic contexts in recent years due to his writing on emergence, individuation and the metaphysical complexity of subject/object relations.[16] The process of 'individuation' in Simondon is very much an active one (escaping the trappings and restrictions of 'individuality'), and related ideas of the 'dividual', preindividual and transindividual, provide means through which to rethink problematic and overly-simplistic relations between an individual and a community, an artist and an artist organisation, away from a logic of representation itself, towards thinking about constituent power of a more fluid, less hierarchical kind. A conceptual lineage, centred on the idea of the 'commons', has gained much leverage in art circles in the last decade, drawing most notably on the writings of Antonio Negri and Michael Hardt (whose book *Commonwealth* had dedicated extracts re-printed in *Art Forum*, followed by an exchange between David Harvey and the authors on its political significance). The emergence of this new paradigm of the 'commons' driven by a resistance to the commercialisation of culture and public spaces, a rejection of the commodification of knowledge through the digital commons, environmental activism and various Occupy struggles, resonated with aspirations to create an alternative world based on non-hierarchically organised movements found filtering into art organisations.[17]

However, Harney and Moten's concept of the Undercommons seeks to escape an overcodification of the 'commons', which for them retains a false and antagonistic dialectic between the individual and the community: a commons that requires base-line subjectivities subsumed into a 'community'. Rather, the struggle demands that, "One becomes unfit for subjection, because one does not possess the kind of agency that can hold to the regulatory forces of subjecthood and one cannot initiate the auto-interpellative torque that bio-power subjection requires and rewards."[18] Modes of collective individuation fostered by the

---

[15] Stefano Harney and Fred Moten, *The Undercommons: Fugitive Planning & Black Study* (New York: Minor Compositions, 2013)

[16] Gilles Deleuze, *Spinoza Practical Philosophy*, San Francisco: City Lights Books 1988. Felix Guattari, *Molecular Revolution* Penguin 1984. For Simondon, see for example Yves Michaud's essay 'The Aesthetics of Gilbert Simondon: Anticipation of the Contemporary Aesthetic Experience' in *Gilbert Simondon: Being and Technology*, Edinburgh UP 2012 and Gilles Deleuze 'On Gilbert Simondon' in *Desert Islands and other texts*, Semiotext(e) 2004.

[17] 'Commonwealth: An Exchange' *Artforum* Nov. 2009 David Harvey & Michael Hardt and Antonio Negri. See also Michael Hardt & Antonio Negri *Commonwealth* (Harvard University Press 2009) *Multitude* (Penguin 2004) and *Empire* (Harvard University Press 2001)

[18] Ibid, p28

Undercommons thus necessitate fugitive forms of planning rather than conventional forms of strategic organisation with "their usual habits and aesthetics of resemblance", and, further, resisting the logic of capital may now require "developing techniques of unruly subsistence, of a mutant proliferation of differences that hold internally through resonance."[19]

***

But in all of the philosophising about new structural models and formations for AROs and their foundational battleground of subjectivities, representation and power, we might ask 'where oh where does the art fit in?' Stephen Zepke's response to the 'third wave' of IC brings us back to the ontology of art itself.[20]

He argues convincingly that much of Guattari's writing has been selectively applied by proponents of IC3: that on some fundamental level 'art' has become overly identified with the institutions that house it; that art in itself is seen as inherently complicit with institutionalism. We are reminded that 'art' for Guattari was central in the aesthetic production of subjectivities and sensations of a resistant nature:

> "'Art' remains in its autonomy as much as its engagement, the most important mechanism of 'political' resistance."[21]

Guattari's attack is aimed at the institution of art (and here institution means any structural organisation of artistic activities), rather than art itself (which at its best upholds a force of immanent critique in society). His analysis of institutional power and rationalities insisted on a direct relation with social production and his 'ontological pragmatics' (*Chaosmosis*) has been a driving force behind artistic initiatives which attempt to resist institutional 'capture' – the desire to foster and activate a concept of aesthetics which for Zepke, "produces sensations that achieve a rupture in the model's (institution's) cohesion and create a transversal connection to an outside that enables the construction of a new dimension of being."[22] The question of how artistic initiatives and spaces can create conditions in which aesthetics can be manifested as a process of individuation prior to any instrumentalisation becomes a primary one relating to form and content: how does one create the conditions of possibility for maximum aesthetic potentiality and affectivity whilst steering through the problematic terrain of institutionalising structures which facilitate instrumentalisation by capital? For Zepke the capacity of art to "escape its institutional banalisation by introducing alterity into experience" remains paramount within any cultural assessment of how

---

[19] Ibid, p14

[20] Stephen Zepke, 'Towards an Ecology of Institutional Critique' in Do You remember IC? Transversal 2007)

[21] Ibid

[22] Ibid

art organisations and projects function. Guattari insisted that art "has never stopped being a vital element in the crystallisation of individual and collective subjectivities."[23]

In a discussion on new forms of subjectivation and political mobilisation in light of increasing bureaucratisation within the arts, which took place between Maurizzio Lazzarato, Kersten Stakemeir and Sarah Rifky in 2013, Rifky said: "We all want to be living systems more than machines… it evokes the role of being brokers between chaos and an organised cultural economy."[24] One could argue that being a living system inherently resists processes of 'brokering' which again falls back on a representational logic of translation: translating chaos (aesthetics) into economics.

In *The Future is Self Organised 2* we are reminded of the 'vulgarity' of the rise of the creative industries which promote a fantasy of liberation "in a process of creative self-realisation and autonomy". The precarity of both artists' spaces and artists themselves is in alignment with the latest capitalist dynamic of a 'proliferation of speculation'. Significantly, the text also echoes those who would argue that expedient notions of 'openness' towards a nebulous 'outside' have been utilised to disguise slashed budgets within institutions – the concept of porosity being conveniently appropriated for the purposes of drawing in more free labour and research. 'De-institutionalisation' in the worst neo-liberal sense is frequently a cover for very ruthless strategic organisational re-structuring completely at odds with the creation of new, more challenging possibilities. Porosity for many of us has simply expanded the boundaries of exploitability.

Resonating with Raunig's call for a disposition inclined towards the 'unruly' and Harney and Moten's summoning of the fugitive, *TINA (There Is No Alternative) 2* calls for a process of 'unlearning capital" and asks if we in the cultural and educational sectors, rather than feeding into destructive and competitive ideas of specialisation, can instead "contribute to post-capitalist, de-specialised spaces which enable cultural production and engagement in the *wildest* sense" (my emphasis).[25]

We begin to see common ground across the widest spectrum of writing and thinking about the future of artist organisations; a resistance to the slick and instrumentalised methodologies of corporate capitalism that inevitably reduce complex ideas and projects to servile crowd-funded, Eventbrited, Facebook-feted phenomena where the worst of communicative capitalism holds forth. What does it matter if an event or initiative has any of the radical potential or aspirations it claims to nurture if it can flaunt success 'virtually' with all the PR techniques at its organiser's disposal, feeding straight into the worst auditing criteria of new public funding assessments? 'To be is to be seen' as opposed

[23] *Chaosmosis* op. cit. p130

[24] 'No New "New Deal "' in *Texte Zur Kunst*, Globalism issue (91 Sept 2013)

[25] Ibid

to the philosopher Berkeley's more complex "to be is to be perceived". Projects that require in-depth research or more intellectually challenging frameworks struggle to differentiate themselves in such an environment.

TINA suggests that rejecting the vocabularies and modes of expression of self-promotion might be an important starting point for new artist initiatives:

"The desired outcome of self-organisation is not the affirmation of the self, the individual, the institution – it's in the negation of these relationships [...] experiment with yourself, get rid of yourself slowly".

Interestingly, Anne Siefer Karlsen notes the tendency of supposedly non-institutional and even anti-institutional organisations to "write themselves into history, ironically often employing the same strategies as their institutional cousins".[26] What role does self-mythologising play in how artist-run organisations situate themselves? We need to keep in mind that 'self-organisation' is in no way transformative in itself (suggesting a form of essentialistic virtuousness).

***

It is worth looking briefly at how some specific artist spaces and organisations engage with these thorny subjects and negotiate such territories for themselves. In an interview with *Paper Visual Art*, as part of its series on alternative and artist-run spaces, the space *55 Syndenham Road* in Sydney set out what, for them, was the most urgent and contentious subject amongst its members.[27] It was not, as might have been expected 30 years ago, the lack of artistic opportunities, or alternative exhibition strategies to the white cube format – pressing as these issues might still be – but rather, how to dismantle "the most pervasive and omnipresent ideological pretext in contemporary art", and the "protocol that informs all contemporary art production and reception: self promotion". They suggested replacing this protocol with one in which anonymity be substituted for the use of artists names, and artistic and textual authorship were completely avoided. The problem addressed by this particular project was that of resisting the "institutionalised compulsion for visual artists and institutions to gain greater public representation", at the cost of recognising the material force of art itself, but also the force of collective agency. Spaces such as this and more recent projects such as Ahmet Ogut's *Silent University* resist what 55

---

[26] Anne Szefer Karlsen in 'Self-Organised – an interview with David Blamey', *Kunst-Orte im Wandel*, No 5 March 2015

[27] *Paper Visual Art* (online interview consulted 2014). Proudly included on the 55 Sydenham website is the following 'damning' review www.55sydenhamrd.com/mission: "It represents the most conceited, convoluted and contrived contemporary art in Australia. It is an exclusive clique, full of wanky mumbo-jumbo types who claim a posterity they don't deserve. I of course understand the need for artist-run spaces, but most just make room for stuff we could do without, and such is the terrible fate of this gallery. Luckily, the public will only have to be subjected to their pestilent pretensions for a maximum two years, as it will no doubt sink under the weight of its own obscurity." — John McDonald, Sydney Morning Herald

Sydenham calls "the rule of corporate-capital individualism", and reject many of the often unarticulated (but nevertheless accepted) aspirations of AROs: the fostering of 'emerging' artists and artistic 'process' as a form of temporal rehearsal for success on an institutional level, and the methodological and structural compromises which end up "honouring hierarchy, singularity and competitiveness above and over all else, reducing art to nothing more than a campaign prop."[28]

Marina Vishmidt has sought to challenge the easy givens of 'alternative' art spaces, collectives and organisations in *Mimesis of the Hardened and Alienated* in which she confronts the 'non-politics' of a particular conceptualisation of 'inclusion' where "systematic variables cannot be questioned or changed but more and more people can be upgraded to 'participate' in the system, and political activism is nothing but an evening out of the playing field to improve the prospects of success for those temporarily 'excluded'."[29] Her analysis of the political technologies at work in the Foucauldian sense – the idea of artist spaces 'empowering' themselves in an entrepreneurial narrative ("getting on their bikes") – makes explicit the link with a 'kick-start' rationality whose function is to initiate a production business model:

"When applied to collectives, 'empowerment' denotes a non-antagonistic mode of advancing through power structures that are flexible enough to accommodate the claims of the thus-far marginalised. It implies a system that is in a position to grant 'power' to those claims or the people making them, rather than a system structurally hostile to equality or an 'equal' distribution of power."[30] Vischmidt finds the French project *Claire Fontaine* of interest in terms of the specific strategies utilised in the construction of their 'persona', as it sidesteps what we might see as typical modes of artistic collective agency and organisational formats. *Claire Fontaine* as a 'ready-made' artist/institution/phenomenon in itself performs the problematic of the "ethical and affective homogeneity that obtains between the subject and object of art, and in terms of the intensified role of abstract value over production in general and art markets in particular, between art and capital."[31] Though it could be argued that *Claire Fontaine* constitutes an artistic practice (albeit an anonymous collective one), rather than an ARO, the challenges they bring to problems of subjectivation within contemporary art organisations are important and well articulated.

They see themselves as "guerrillas" in the field of subjectivation and recognise their complicity in the system that produces them as subjects. Their strategy explicitly draws on Deleuze & Guattari's concept of 'Minoring' in *Kafka –Towards a Minor Literature*: that of becoming

[28] Ibid

[29] Marina Vishmidt, 'Mimesis of the Hardened and Alienated: Social Practice as Business Model', *E-Flux* Journal 43 , 2013.

[30] Ibid

[31] Ibid

foreign in one's own language, which for them is the language artists need to speak, and the "promise of any community rests solely in this impropriety" – an impropriety akin to Raunig's 'unruliness' perhaps or TINA's 'wildness'. They utilize the fiction of a proper name whilst retaining anonymity, they seek collective activity but without the imposition of formats such as 'artist initiative' or 'artist collective'. They declare that they maintain "laboratories of subjectivity" composed only of assistants with the management being "an empty centre."[32]

Dave Beech, in his critique of the participatory ethos of relational art, emphasises the need to go beyond what he sees as mimetic processes of corporatisation expediently using the vocabulary of participation. His criticisms of the way many participatory art projects function could equally apply to artistic organisations:

"Outsiders have to pay a higher price for their participation, namely the neutralisation of their difference and the dampening of their powers of subversion. Participation papers over the cracks. The changes we need are structural."[33]

The persistent bugbear of a form/content relation emerges again in Gavin Murphy's essay on pleasure and bureaucracy in artist-led organisations in which he laments the over-bureaucratisation of the arts and the far too readily assimilated rationalities of 'New Public Management'. For Murphy, the figure to contend with is that of the 'artocrat' who "promotes active citizenship, social engagement and extols democratic ideals in a manner easily absorbed and increasingly shaped by neo-liberal governance."[34]

Even much respected ethically-driven organisations such as *Casco*, with its commitment to fostering experimental and investigative forms of practice and contributing to "non-capitalist cultures and possibilities", recently initiated a project entitled *Site for Unlearning* as part of their *Composing the Commons* framework begun in 2013. Artist Annette Krauss unfolded a series of meetings and workshops aimed at 'unlearning' the social norms and structures which are internalised in artist-run organisations, challenging (with a diagrammatic instinct) and re-thinking the structural and hierarchical models often taken for granted as necessary evils; ideas of incessant productivity, promotion, the maintenance of achievement-based 'public profiles' etc. *Casco*'s intent was to try to create transversal rationalities within the very relations that constitute the organisation.[35] Looking at artists' spaces that exist completely outside standardising western frameworks can often prove very insightful, as it facilitates the recognition of significantly different dynamics and conditions of emergence. It also helps to break out of

[32] Claire Fontaine interview with John Kelsey Nov/2006 www.clairefontaine.ws

[33] Dave Beech, 'Include me Out' *Art Monthly* (April 2008)

[34] Gavin Murphy, 'Fantasy Island: Pleasure and Bureaucracy in Artist led Organisations' Available at: gavinmurphy.eu

[35] See cascoprojects.org

the relentless 'compare and contrast' name-dropping of competitive art spaces established using quite a predictable set of criteria. An essay by curator Clementine Deliss (*Afterall*, Summer 2014) on *Laboratoire AGIT'Art* and *Tenq* in Senegal (both entities she had close working relations with), proves particularly interesting as it demonstrates just how much the self-mythologising function and representational rationalities of most Western spaces are subverted in an African context.[36]

The methodologies chosen by *Laboratoire AGIT'Art*, based around collective performance and resisting commercial tropes of conventional exhibition-making, found their origins in the instincts and theories of experimental theatre influenced by Artaud. Its history conjures up the material intensity many curators and art theorists (Deliss included, going by the fervent tone of her essay) would appear to long for when considering the new possibilities that might exist for artist-run spaces of the future. Deliss rhapsodises about the "air of choreographed chaos" in the "alchemical laboratory" which was their new courtyard space after the military ambushed their original Village des Arts seafront location in 1983. It had a dense materiality, producing a unique sense of power according to Deliss: "I read into the scenario a deviant language of philological interpenetration, not dissimilar to the 'bas-materialisme' that Georges Bataille had evoked in his journal Documents."[37] Aware of her own role in producing new mythologies she adds:

> "However legitimate it may seem to disseminate information on former artistic methodologies, this procedure raises many questions about the language employed to do so, the status of the document produced, the ownership of the material, and with it the cannibalistic urge to accumulate the codes of other cultures as one's own."[38]

Much of this statement seems applicable to the present text. What function might the very concept of a meta-perspective have when dealing with the complicated relationships with capitalism negotiated by Degot's 'hotchpotch' of artist organisations? The temptation to write something utterly foreign to art-speak becomes very seductive, to enter into that *bas matérialisme* oneself and disregard any pretence to synthesising rationality or argumentation.

If the art space of the future is a fungus then spores floating in the air might be their only manifestation.

In the film *John Cage Mushroom Hunting in Stony Point*, directed by Jud Yalkut in 1972, we hear lines from a poem by Cage:

---

[36] Clémentine Deliss, *'Brothers in Arms: Laboratoire AGIT'Art and Tenq in Dakar in the 1990s'* in *Afterall*, Summer 2014

[37] Ibid

[38] Ibid

> "Our intention is to affirm this life, not to bring order out of chaos, nor to suggest improvements in creation."

Art spaces of the future are mushrooms... and the spores seek out crevices and cracks and just wait for their moment.... Perhaps all we can do is what *The Future is Self Organised (2)* recommends: "continue to widen the cracks."[39]

> *Cracks in the state of things, in the state of places, in the state of norms... Cracks leading us despite ourselves to new social practices and to new aesthetic practices which will reveal themselves as less and less separate from each other and more and more in complicity...*[40] —Felix Guattari

[39] TINA 2: "A key task now is to derail capitalist restructuring, continue to widen the cracks, block all attempts at reform wherever possible. We need to build, protect and defend the communes and commons that will make up post-capitalist life."

[40] Felix Guattari, 'Cracks in the Street', *Flash Art*. 135 1987 p.85

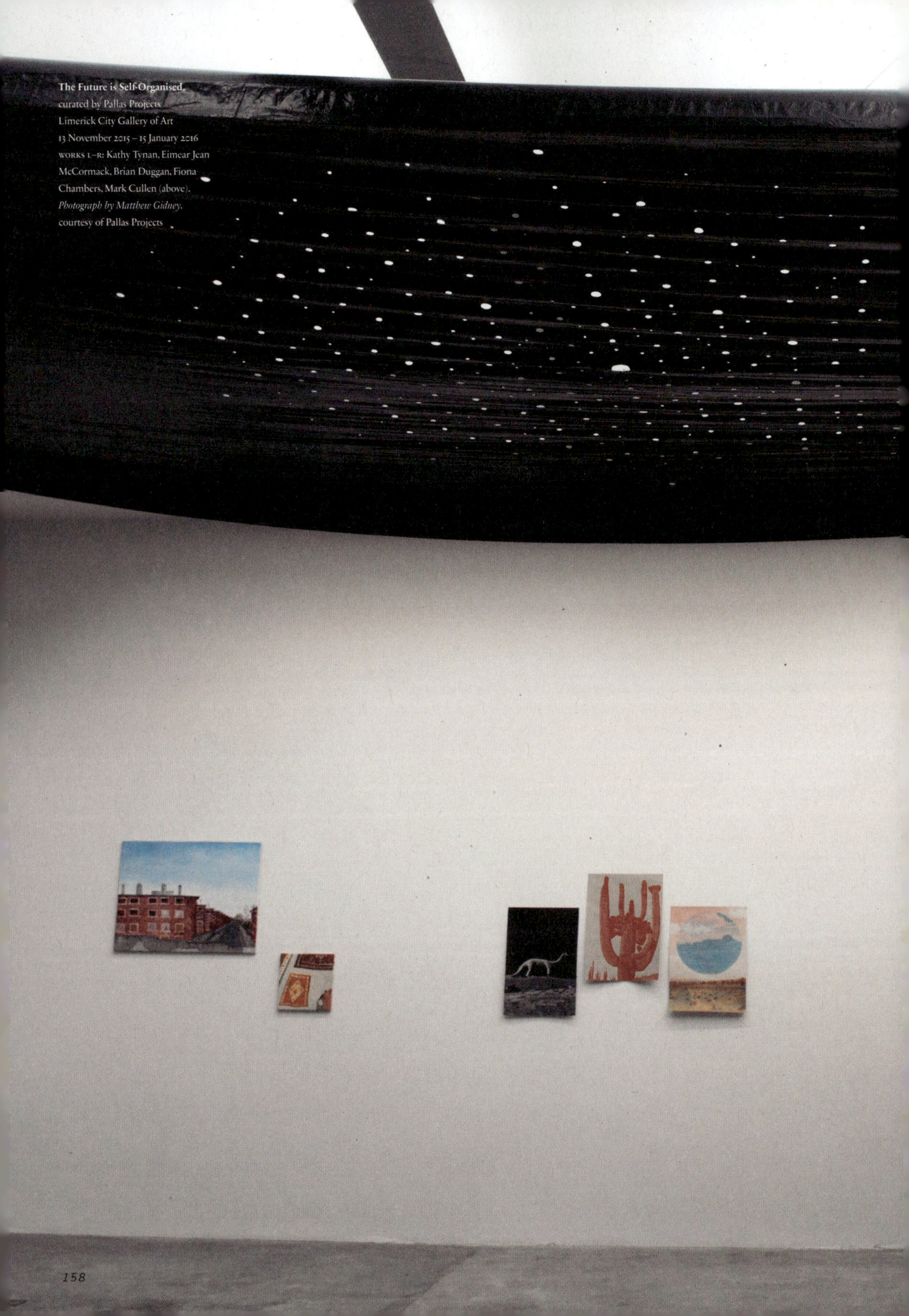

The Future is Self-Organised,
curated by Pallas Projects
Limerick City Gallery of Art
13 November 2015 – 15 January 2016
WORKS L–R: Kathy Tynan, Eimear Jean McCormack, Brian Duggan, Fiona Chambers, Mark Cullen (above).
Photograph by Matthew Gidney.
courtesy of Pallas Projects

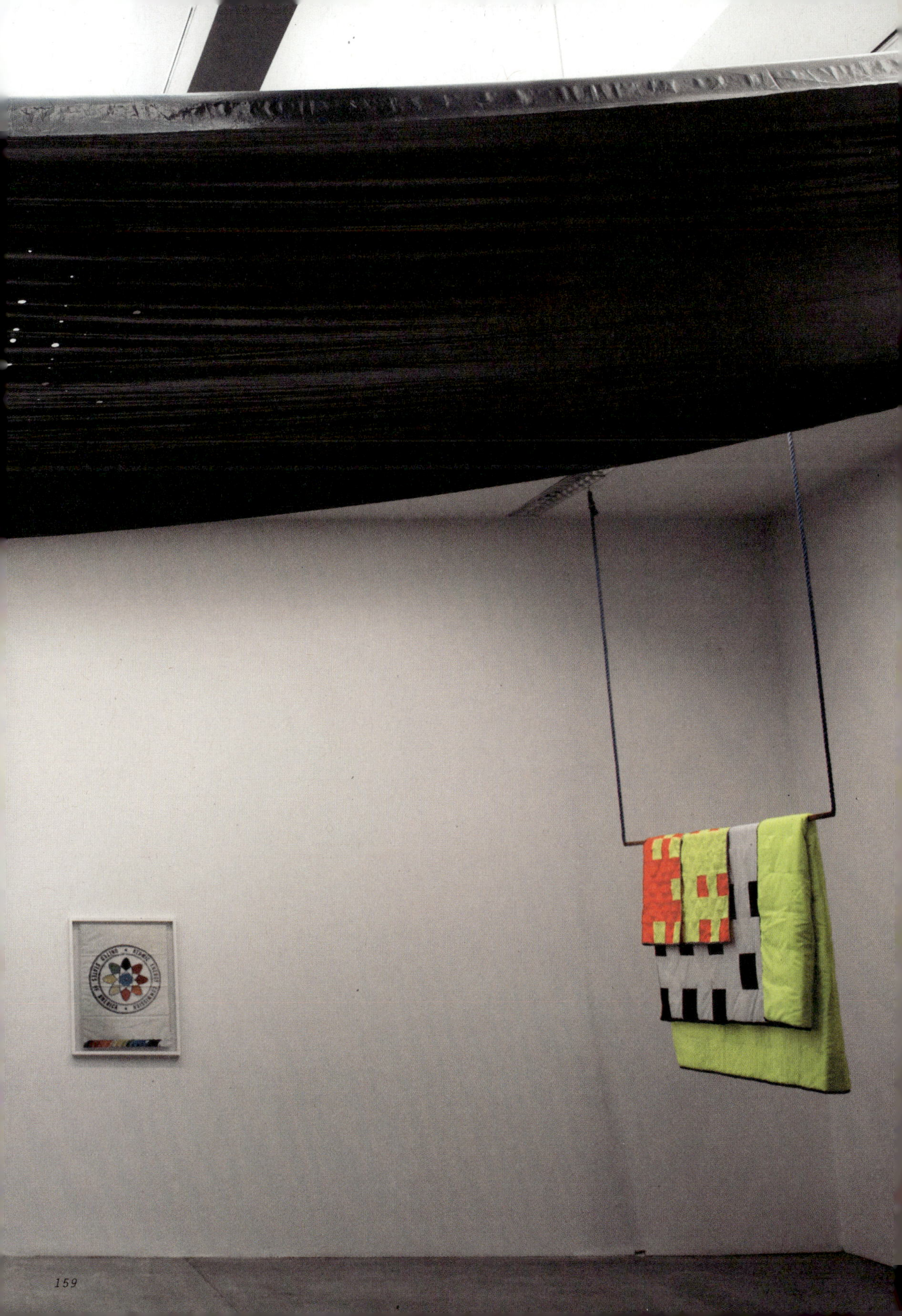

The Artist-Run Index

The Artist-Run Index and its Methodology

This index of artist-run spaces across Europe, which has been fully updated for this second edition, and expanded to include additional spaces, is envisaged as a tool to quantify and compare the disparate attributes, organisational models, funding structures and aims of a vast number of spaces in virtually every corner of the European continent. A lack of knowledge in this area – complicated by language barriers, differences in terminology (i.e. presentation spaces, project spaces, off-spaces, alternative spaces), the short timespan of many spaces, along with a scarcity of published accounts distributed beyond the city or country of origin – has meant that the level of artist-run activity from country to country, and its relevance and impact has previously been difficult to ascertain.

Over an initial 4-year period (2012–16) we attempted to research each country in turn, consulting exhibitions and publications relating to artist-run activity, organisations' websites, through individual contacts on the ground, and via artist representative organisations and funding bodies. A number of existing online sources were also consulted, including: artist-run-spaces.org (Glassbox, France), The New Museum's Art Spaces Map (since defunct), sluice.info (UK), supermarketartfair.com (Stockholm), artspaceguide.ch (Zurich), and arttransponder.net (Berlin), and for this edition: alternativeartguide.com, and artistrunalliance.org.

Our main parameters for inclusion were: artist-run spaces with a dedicated programme showing contemporary, alternative and critically engaged art practices. All spaces featured were contacted and encouraged to supply more information if necessary (and given the option to opt out of the index if desired). Certain artist-initiated spaces which are no-longer artist-run have also been included, as have those with expanded administrative and institutional structures but which remain artist-run or artist-directed. In countries where it has been difficult to ascertain specific artist-run spaces, we opted to include what we feel is nearest to an artist-run model.

A table graphic has been devised so that attributes and information can be viewed easily. The funding column indicates from where spaces receive their core or additional support, it cannot be assumed however that spaces are wholly funded from listed sources, with many spaces relying primarily on self-funding and voluntary labour, with varying degrees of support from public and private funding bodies. The designation of 'Non-profit/Project' has been given a dual role: where a space states explicitly that it is non-profit, or in a number of cases to indicate a non-profit/project space that exhibit artist-run characteristics, for instance in certain countries where artist-led and project spaces are not differentiated. It can be assumed however that most spaces in the index are non-profit.

When first compiling this index we were aware that much of it would quickly go out of date, and while certain regions and countries (Ireland, The Netherlands, and The UK, and cities such as Berlin and Zurich) were well represented, we acknowledge that many spaces, cities and regions may have been missed due to the difficulties listed above. This edition tries to rectify this in part, including more spaces from eastern Europe, the Baltic and Balkan regions, and by widening our parameters to include Ukraine. Added to this we found during our initial research that many spaces closed their doors in the course of our project, and the decision was made to retain these in the index. This is no less true today, and this edition denotes those which have become inactive since 2016 – 149 or more than 25% – making it an important record of these now-defunct spaces. In addition, any changes (names, location, website info, etc.) to the original index have been updated and noted.

Despite this constant flux, the index in its revised form – 625 spaces and counting – represents a valuable document that can continue to be added to, improved, and expanded over time.

Symbols

Nomadic ≈
Closed pre-2016 †
Closed/inactive since 2016 edition ‡
Updated since 2016 edition ◊
Added since 2016 edition §

Note

Every effort has been made to ensure the information in this index is correct and up to date. Please contact the editors regarding corrections, or to be included or removed from future reprints, or other published formats.

Albania

	LOCATION	WEBSITE	ARTIST-RUN	ARTIST-INITIATED	NON-PROFIT/PROJECT	INSTITUTIONAL	STUDIOS	FOUNDED	FUNDING	MISSION STATEMENT
OFFICE Tirana Art Center / Gallery On The Move §	Tirana	www.tiranartcenter.net, www.galleryonthemove.net	○	○	●	○	○	2007	Private, sponsorship	OFFICE Tirana Art Center / Gallery On The Move produces projects by local and international artists, focusing on time-based and site-specific projects that challenge perceived notions and stimulate debate, experimentation, and engagement.
MIZA Galeri ‡	Tirana	www.mizagaleri.com	●	●	●	○	○	2012–2018	Self-funded	Miza is a Tirana based, not-for-profit, non-governmental organisation working in the field of culture and contemporary art since its inception in November 2012.
Tirana Ekspres ◊	Tirana	www.tiranaekspres.com	●	●	●	○	○	2011	Public & embassies	Tirana Ekspres is a non-profit organisation initiated by artists, activists, environmentalists, policymakers, social-business and researchers whose purpose is to enhance the cultural and artistic perception and expression in Tirana and beyond.
ZETA Center for Contemporary Art §	Tirana	www.qendrazeta.com	●	○	●	○	○	2007	State/local government, International Institutions/ grants, sponsorship & self-funded	ZETA Center for Contemporary Art is a non-profit exhibition space founded in 2007 by Valentina Koça in downtown Tirana. ZETA functions as an autonomous cultural venue for multidisciplinary approaches to visual arts, including painting, sculpture, photography, video, installation, sound, and performance.

Austria

	LOCATION	WEBSITE	ARTIST-RUN	ARTIST-INITIATED	NON-PROFIT/PROJECT	INSTITUTIONAL	STUDIOS	FOUNDED	FUNDING	MISSION STATEMENT
bb15 §	Linz	www.bb15.at	●	●	●	○	○	2009	Public institutions	bb15 is an independent artist-run-space and curatorial collective that develops exhibitions, performances, and cultural events, fostering experimental approaches, international and local collaborations, and acting as a platform that supports emerging artists throughout their careers.
Periscope §	Salzburg	www.periscope.at	●	○	●	○	○	2006	Salzburg City Council and Austria City Council	periscope:project:space is an event-led artist-run space for young visual artists. Periscope stands for a glimpse of a new sphere, deliberately seeking contact, and readily connecting.
Kunstverein Galerie Arcade / kunstraumarcade §	Mödling	www.kunstraumarcade.at	●	●	●	●	○	1974	Ministry for Arts and Culture, Federal Government of Lower Austria, Town of Mödling	kunstraumarcade is situated in the courtyard of the Beethoven House, an early Renaissance building in the centre of Mödling. As opposed to presenting solo exhibitions, the programme places an emphasis on dialogue between different positions. In parallel, music and literary events are hosted, alongside published editions.
Adhoc Pad ‡	Vienna	www.adhocpad.com	●	●	○	○	●	2011–2018		adhocPAD is a creative hub for people who share their passion in different subcultures. An office, a showroom, a workshop. Not just another off-space, but a meeting point for the openminded.
Das Weisse Haus	Vienna	www.dasweissehaus.at	●	●	●	○	●	2007	Public & corporate	Das Weisse Haus is an art association, exhibition space and non-profit-organisation for the promotion and presentation of young art.
G U I M A R Ã E S §	Vienna	www.guimaraes.info	●	●	○	○	○	2016		Guimarães is an artist run space founded by Christoph Meier, Nicola Pecoraro & Hugo Canoilas in 2016.
HHDM ‡	Vienna	www.hhdm.eu	●	●	○	○	○	2012–2016	Public with cultural partner sponsorship	Hinter Haus des Meeres is an artist-run space, founded by Daphne Ahlers, Roland Matthias Gaberz and Philipp Timischl in April 2012.
Kunstraum SUPER ◊	Vienna	www.supersuper.at	●	●	○	○	○	2013	Public	Founded in 2013 by Viktoria Mayer, Andreas Perkmann Berger, Rainer Stadlbauer
Secession	Vienna	www.secession.at	●	●	○	●	○	1897	Public & private (corporate sponsors, media partners)	The Association of Visual Artists Vienna Secession is the world's oldest independent exhibition institution specifically dedicated to contemporary art. Artwork is selected on artistic criteria. Secession aims to present current developments in Austrian and international art.
See You Next Thursday	Vienna	www.seeyounextthursday.com	●	●	●	○	●	2012		A non-profit artist association that sees itself as a platform that supports artistic and curatorial working methods, trans-disciplinary interactions and lived art practice.

Austria *(Continued)*

Name	City	Website						Year	Funding	Description
Ve.Sch	Vienna	www.vesch.org	●	●	●	○	○	2008	Self-funded & public	An art room with a bar.
WochenKlausur ≈	Vienna	www.wochenklausur.at	●	●	○	○	○	1992	Institutional on a project-by-project basis	WochenKlausur, at the invitation of art institutions, develops and realises proposals for improving sociopolitical deficits. Artists' competence in finding creative solutions can just as well be applied in all areas of society.

Belgium

Name	City	Website						Year	Funding	Description
Netwerk Aalst ◊	Aalst	www.netwerkaalst.be/nl	○	●	○	●	○	Late 1980s	Provincial councils	Netwerk Aalst develops practice focusing on the visual arts, placed in a national and international context, delivering a programme of exhibitions, lectures, workshops, screenings, concerts and residencies, collaborating with international curators.
Extra City ◊	Antwerp	www.extracitykunsthal.be	●	●	○	○	●	2004	State & private	Extra City Kunsthal is a place for the production, presentation and debate of artistic practices. Focusing on contemporary art and historical positions that are of relevance for today's discourses.
Drop City ◊	Antwerp	www.drop-city.net	●	●	○	○	○	2014	Public & private	Drop City is an occasional public space, curatorial project and collaboration between Sam Watson and Eleanor Wright (co-founded with Paul Becker & Nadia Hebson), which began in Newcastle UK, and is now located in Antwerp.
Argos	Brussels	www.argosarts.org	●	●	○	●	○	1989	State & media partner	As intermediary between the artist and the public, Argos is a place for encounters, dialogue and exchange.
Constant	Brussels	www.constantvzw.org	●	●	●	○	○	1997	State	Constant is an incubator, artistic workplace, think-thank, content generator and media lab, supporting artists through production, exhibition, publication, research, financially, in-kind, in the broadest possible framework. We cherish an ethical approach and respect for cultural differences and gender.
De La Charge †	Brussels	www.delacharge.com	●	●	●	○	●	2012–2015		De La Charge is a place inaugurated by 19 artists, divided into workshops and an exhibition space.
Enough Room for Space	Brussels	www.enoughroomforspace.org	●	●	●	○	●	2005		A non-profit organisation that initiates and coordinates events, residencies, research projects and exhibitions. ERforS tries to act as freely as possible, always putting the context and the idea before the medium.
Etablissement d'en face ◊	Brussels	www.etablissementdenface.com	●	●	○	○	○	2003		A group of people, who are actively working in the visual arts came together in 2003 to create Etablissement d'en face projects.
Greylight Projects	Brussels	www.greylightprojects.org	●	●	●	○	●	2010		Greylight Projects is an artist-run organisation based in Brussels and Hoensbroek. It focuses on the development, production and presentation of contemporary art. The current location houses nine studios and residencies.
Island §	Brussels	www.islandisland.be	●	●	●	○	○	2012	Fédération Wallonie Bruxelles, Fondation Roi Baudouin, COCOF and Drogenbos Brewery	Island is a non-profit art space, founded by Belgian artists Sébastien Bonin and Brice Guilbert. Artists are allowed to experiment, not constrained by a curatorial lead. Therefore, every exhibition is unique, conceived according to its own criteria without referencing previous projects.
Komplot ◊	Brussels	www.kmplt.org	○	○	●	●	○	2002	Sponsors	A curatorial collective of variable composition and condition concerned with nomadic creative practices and trends of specialisation.
La Loge	Brussels	www.la-loge.be	●	●	●	○	○		Private	La Loge invites contemporary artists to develop projects engaged with questions of space, habitat and use. Driven by encounters between disciplines it aims to serve as a dynamic site for dialogue between its guests and public.

Belgium (Continued)	LOCATION	WEBSITE	ARTIST-RUN	ARTIST-INITIATED	NON-PROFIT/PROJECT	INSTITUTIONAL	STUDIOS	FOUNDED	FUNDING	MISSION STATEMENT
OKNO ‡	Brussels	www.okno.be	●	●	○	○	●	2013–2017	State & EU	OKNO is an artist-run organisation connecting new media and ecology. It approaches art and culture from a collaborative, DIY and post-disciplinary point of view, discovering new materials and aesthetics.
Rosa Brux ≈	Brussels	www.rosabrux.org	●	●	●	○	○	2012		Rosa Brux's activities are rooted in the understanding of art that is critically engaged with political and social issues. Conceived as a new type of institution, Rosa Brux provides an informal relationship between artworks and audience, leading to discussion, learning and experimentation.
(SIC) ‡	Brussels	www.sicsic.be	○	○	●	○	○	2005–2020	Fédération Wallonie-Bruxelles	(SIC) publishes a journal, books dedicated to the history and theory of modern and contemporary art, artists books and monographs. In its gallery space, (SIC) presents an annual exhibition programme.
019 §	Ghent	www.019-ghent.org	●	●	●	○	●	2013	City of Ghent (Cultuur Gent, Fonds Tijdelijke Invullingen), Government of Flanders	019 is a transdisciplinary platform that develops in-between spaces for intuitive experimentation, collaboration and encounter between architecture, graphic design and visual arts.
Croxhapox ◊	Ghent	www.croxhapox.org	○	●	○	○	●	1990	State	Interested in contemporary art and offer a working space for music, film, poetry and art criticism. In this way, we offer a large potential for experimenting.
Kunsthal Gent §	Ghent	www.kunsthal.gent	●	●	●	○	●	2018	City of Ghent and the Flemish Community, donations and sponsors	Kunsthal Gent is an experimental intersection for contemporary art, located in a monumental fourteenth-century Carmelite monastery. An exhibition space at weekends, on weekdays a workplace for artists, organisations, and public activities such as lectures, workshops, screenings and performances.
Werktank	Leuven	www.werktank.org	●	○	○	●	●		State	Our main mission is the realisation and distribution of installation art that investigates the relationship between technology and perception.
Voorkamer ‡	Lier	www.voorkamer.be	●	●	●	○	○	1996–2017	State, memberships & donations	Voorkamer provides an insight into the heterogeneity of today's visual art and encourages an active dialog between the artist, the public and themselves. Voorkamer's objective is to help artists carry out experiments without commercial pressure.

Bulgaria

	LOCATION	WEBSITE	ARTIST-RUN	ARTIST-INITIATED	NON-PROFIT/PROJECT	INSTITUTIONAL	STUDIOS	FOUNDED	FUNDING	MISSION STATEMENT
0mgs †	Sofia	www.facebook.com/0gmsgallery	●	●	○	○	○	2009–2014		0gms is an artist-run space based in Sofia, Bulgaria. The goal is to share experience and to develop a platform for art with Bulgarian and international artists.
Æther §	Sofia/The Hague	www.aether-artspace.com	●	●	●	○	○	2016	Self-funded	Æther Sofia/Haga are two sibling independent art spaces, whose activities and exhibitions create a possibility for experimentation and critical feedback on the contemporary obscurities of living through art, science, politics and activism. They organise SAW Sofia Art Week, and alternative education platform School of Kindness.
Gallery Gallery §	Sofia	www.gallerygallery.space/en	●	●	○	○	○	2019	Self-funded	Gallery Gallery is the first gallery in Bulgaria that is exclusively focused on digital art. The gallery operates two virtual exhibition spaces; a router-gallery for browser-based work and our public space Ploshtadka for Augmented Reality (AR) work. Both spaces are accessible non-stop, but only if you are at the physical location of the gallery.

***Bulgaria** (Continued)*

InterSpace †	Sofia	Sofia	●	●	●	○	○	1998–2011	Public and Private Sponsor	InterSpace founded as an association of artists, engineers and media makers has realised art projects, events in research and education, to attempt to contextualise and apply new technology to network and community building.
Swimming Pool §	Sofia	www.swimmingpoolprojects.org	○	○	●	○	○	2015	National Cultural Fund	Swimming Pool is a platform for contemporary art and research with a focus on intersectional and collaborative practices, art education, art politics, and institution-making. It is located on a central rooftop with an empty pool.
Water Tower Art Fest ◊	Sofia	www.watertowerartfest.com	●	●	●	○	○	2006	Sofia City Arts Council, Private sponsors	The organisation aims to work with artists, cultural organisations and arts projects in Bulgaria and abroad, and participate in the development and implementation of cooperative projects in the sphere of arts and culture.
Tsarino Foundation Air Project	Tsarino	www.tsarino.org	●	●	○	○	●	2009		Created by a collective based in Amsterdam, organises artist-run AiR programmes in the deserted village of Tsarino, Bulgaria. These are part of a long-term research project on art in such a remote place.

Bosnia & Herzegovina

CRVENA ≈	Sarajevo	www.crvena.ba	●	●	○	○	○	2010	Public & private	Our mandate is to act as transformers and mind triggers and to offer different and more critical ideas on the world around us, and the world in which we wish to live in.
Duplex100m²	Sarajevo	www.duplex100m2.com	●	●	○	○	○	2007	Agnès B. Endowment Fund & the Agency of Paris	Duplex100m² hosts numerous artists, enables production, exhibition and presentation of their works. It plans and organises exhibitions on the local, regional and international level.

Croatia

Delta 5	Rijeka	www.en.delta-5.org	●	●	○	○	●	2014	Self-funded	An artist-run space that is divided into a number of ateliers/studios and one project room which is used for presentation, production and social purposes of the members and associates of the organisation.
Drugo More §	Rijeka	www.drugo-more.hr	○	○	●	○	○	1999	Local and national Government and European	Drugo more (The Other Sea) is an interdisciplinary non-profit organisation working locally, regionally, and internationally in the field of arts and culture. Understanding art as an important cognitive tool, our artistic program addresses topics relevant to contemporary science and social theory.
Fokus Grupa ◊	Rijeka	www.fokusgrupa.net	●	●	●	○	●	2012		Fokus Grupa point to the power relations within the art system, as well as within the broader economic and social context, and are especially interested in the role of art within those relations. Our work extends over the neighbouring disciplines and borrows and learns from design, architecture, curating and literature.
SIZ ‡	Rijeka	www.g-siz.com	●	●	●	○	○	2009–2020	Public	SIZ or the Self-managed interest community is an association of authors approaching the art market collectively. Grounded in social reality, SIZ, confronts the problem of financing artistic practice on ideal and practical level through collective affiliation of equal individuals made in order to jointly approach the public and the market.
HDLU §	Zagreb	www.hdlu.hr	●	●	●	●	○	1868	Ministry of Culture and Media, City of Zagreb, sponsors, membership fees	The Croatian Association of Visual Artists (HDLU), Zagreb, was established in 1868 and consists of visual artists of all generations, with the aim to support and encourage contemporary visual expression. The exhibition program ranges from the experimental to large national and international projects.

***Croatia** (Continued)*

	LOCATION	WEBSITE	ARTIST-RUN	ARTIST-INITIATED	NON-PROFIT/PROJECT	INSTITUTIONAL	STUDIOS	FOUNDED	FUNDING	MISSION STATEMENT
What, How and For Whom ◊	Zagreb	www.whw.hr	○	○	●	○	○	1999	European Cultural Foundation & various other foundations	A curatorial collective whose projects have been conceived as a platform for socially engaged models of cultural production and reflection of social reality.

Czech Republic

	LOCATION	WEBSITE	ARTIST-RUN	ARTIST-INITIATED	NON-PROFIT/PROJECT	INSTITUTIONAL	STUDIOS	FOUNDED	FUNDING	MISSION STATEMENT
D.I.V.O. ‡	Kolin	www.divoinstitute.org	●	●	●	○	●	2008–2018	Donations & grants	D.I.V.O. Institute is a living institute where art is displayed, created and discussed. The Institute strives to overcome the boredom and disorientation that prevails in European contemporary art providing an exciting alternative.
35M2 §	Prague	www.35m2.cz	●	●	●	○	○	2006	Local and national public insitutions	The 35m2 is an artist run space and non-profit gallery for contemporary artistic activity. The gallery is focused mainly on progressive and young visual artists creating solo projects.
Entrance §	Prague	www.divoinstitute.org	○	●	●	○	○	2005	Ministry of Culture Czech Republic, Prague City Hall and Municipal District of Prague 6	Entrance Gallery is the first artistic space in Prague that focuses systematically in its long-term program on the issues of ecological sustainability and care for the environment.
etc. galerie §	Prague	www.etcgalerie.cz	○	●	●	○	○	2004	Local, national and European public insitutions and private institutions	Etc. gallery showcases the work of both Czech and international artists within exhibitions, screenings, discussions, and research projects. Its programme is currently focused on the presentation of artists who deploy the medium of moving image in their work and explore socially and politically engaged topics.
Karlin Studios ◊	Prague	www.futuraprague.com/en/karlin-studios	○	●	●	○	●	2005	The Ministry of Culture of The Czech Republic The City of Prague	A former factory hall in Prague. It includes a 500m² exhibition space curated by the FUTURA team, 17 artists' studios and 2 independently run galleries (KIV and K.ART.ON).
Meet Factory	Prague	www.meetfactory.cz	●	●	●	●	●	2001	Public (City of Prague) & self-funded	A not-for-profit international centre for contemporary art. Our mission is to foster a dialogue between individual genres and make the current art scene accessible to the widest public.
Petrohradska kolektiv z.s §	Prague	www.petrohradskakolektiv.com/Gallery-Galerie	●	●	●	○	○	2015	Local, national and European public insitutions	PETROHRADSKÁ KOLEKTIV is an artist-run initiative with it's own production, dramaturgy and spaces for experimental and contemporary art since 2015.
Trafo Gallery ◊	Prague	www.trafogallery.cz/en/	○	●	●	○	○	2006	Grants	Trafo Gallery is an exhibition space. Until recently it included residential studios and a large-scale studio open to projects of all kinds, but currently it operates solely as a project space.

Cyprus

	LOCATION	WEBSITE	ARTIST-RUN	ARTIST-INITIATED	NON-PROFIT/PROJECT	INSTITUTIONAL	STUDIOS	FOUNDED	FUNDING	MISSION STATEMENT
ARTos ‡	Nicosia	www.artosfoundation.org	●	●	○	○	○	2011–2016	Self-funded	The ARTos Cultural and Research Foundation was founded by the artists Achilleas Kentonis and Maria Papacharalambous. It is a contemporary arts and science centre dedicated to research and creativity.
Ground Artist Run Space ‡	Nicosia	www.groundartistrunspace.tumblr.com	●	●	○	○	○	2013–2015		Ground is an artist-run space operated by visual artists Lito Kattou and Leontios Toumpouris. Ground is an interdisciplinary platform open to all forms of artistic practice, willing to encourage dialogue and networking.

***Cyprus** (Continued)*

Name	City	Website						Years	Funding	Description
Neoterismoi ‡	Nicosia	www.neoterismoi.com	●	●	●	○	○	2011–2021	Self-funded	Neoterismoi Toumazou was a 1960s imported goods store that was turned into an art space. The group introduces fashion as everyday life, curates exhibitions and produces editions/multiples.
Stoa Aeschylou Association †	Nicosia	www.stoaaeschylou.blogspot.ie	●	●	●	○	○	2007–2010	State funded	Stoa Aeschylou Association is a non-profit organisation founded by Panikos Tembriotis and Demetris Neokleous with the aim of creating dialogue around contemporary visual arts through setting up art laboratories and experimental workshops.
Thkio Ppalies	Nicosia	www.thkioppalies.org	●	●	○	○	○	2015		Thkio Ppalies is a project space founded by Stelios Kallinikou and Peter Eramian. The space is committed to the facilitation and production of creative and intellectual endeavours across a wide range of disciplines and practices.

Denmark

Name	City	Website						Years	Funding	Description
Spanien19c	Arhus	www.spanien19c.dk	●	●	●	○	○	1998		A non-profit artist-administrated space showing high quality contemporary art. The space was established in 1998, and has 6–8 shows a year, presenting both Danish and international artists.
Antechamber ‡	Copenhagen	www.antechamber.dk	●	●	○	○	●	2012–2014		Antechamber functions as a platform with exhibitions, studio work and artistic experiments, the hoarding of material and literature, self-publishing, conversation and confabulation.
Beton ‡	Copenhagen	www.betonartspace.com	●	●	●	○	○	2014–2017		BETON is a non-profit artist-run exhibition platform for contemporary studies in matter. The base for BETON is contemporary sculpture, and key words are density, intimacy and reflection.
Green is Gold ‡	Copenhagen	www.gigstudio.dk	●	●	●	○	○	2011–2016		Green is Gold is a non-profit exhibition space, which was opened by Danish artists Amalie Bønnelycke Lunøe and Ditte Knus Tønnesen. The space focuses on exhibiting artists with diverse, progressive practices.
Koh-i-noor ‡	Copenhagen	www.koh-i-noor.org	●	●	●	○	○	2004–2016	Self-funded	As one of the oldest non-profit, independent, artist-run project spaces in Copenhagen, Koh-i-noor aims to provide a collaborative, process-related, informal platform for open thought, information exchange, experiments and interdisciplinary approaches.
New Shelter Plan ‡	Copenhagen	www.newshelterplan.com	●	●	●	○	○	2013–2015	Danish Arts Foundation & Copenhagen City Council	New Shelter Plan is a contemporary, non-profit exhibition space. In our 185m2 unusual exhibition space, we feature solo shows, group shows and collaborative exhibitions as well as shorter events – 'Shorts'.
OK Corral ◊	Copenhagen	www.okcorral.dk	●	●	○	○	○	2012	Danish Arts Council Committee for Visual Arts, and Frederiksberg Fonden	OK Corral, a self-organized exhibition space and studio community in the heart of Frederiksberg, creates a platform for recent graduates of the three Danish art academies, and foreign artists and curators who have not previously had significant solo exhibitions in Denmark.
SixtyEight	Copenhagen	www.sixtyeight.dk	○	●	●	○	○	2010	Public & Private	A non-profit exhibition space focused on exhibiting younger Danish and non-Danish artists in order to create networks and initiate dialogue between the different contemporary art scenes.
Sydhavn Station	Copenhagen	www.sydhavnstation.info	●	●	●	○	○	2012	Self-funded w/ help from Danish Arts Foundation	Sydhavn Station is established as an artist-run, DIY, and build-your-own experimental platform. It calls for experiments with quirky aesthetics and offers other ways to work seriously with art.
Toves Galleri ‡	Copenhagen	www.toves.dk	●	●	○	○	○	2010–2017		TOVES is an exhibition space and production unit based in Copenhagen, Denmark. Experimenting with co-production, and external exhibition projects, TOVES continue to develop and renew the organization of the production and exhibition of art.
TTC ‡	Copenhagen	www.ttcgallery.com	●	●	○	○	○	2006–2014		Since 2006 Emil Alsbo and Simon Højbo have worked together on various art, book and exhibition projects. From their studio at Gammel Kongevej 37, they have established their own gallery and independent publishing house TTC Books.

Denmark (Continued)

	LOCATION	WEBSITE	ARTIST-RUN	ARTIST-INITIATED	NON-PROFIT/PROJECT	INSTITUTIONAL	STUDIOS	FOUNDED	FUNDING	MISSION STATEMENT
Vermilion Sands §	Copenhagen	www.vermilionsands.net	●	●	●	○	○	2016	State funding, City funding, private foundations, self-funded	Vermilion Sands is an exhibition space for local and international contemporary art with an emphasis on experimental strategies of curation, mediation and access.
Years ≈	Copenhagen	www.years.dk	●	●	○	○	○	2012	Danish Arts Foundation	YEARS is an exhibition space run by Anna Margrethe Pedersen, Steffen Jørgensen, Søren Aagaard, Merete Vyff Slyngborg & Ditte Soria.
YNKB	Copenhagen	www.ynkb.dk	●	●	○	○	○	2002		YNKB wants to leave the elitist centres of Art and establish cultural and artistic activities where people live, seeing art as a collective research project on a global inter-relational and human scale.
teksas ◊	Græsted	www.teksas.dk	●	●	○	○	○	2011		teksas is a project space focusing on contemporary art and related matters. teksas gives an independant view on the art scene and is run by visual artists Karin Lind and Peter Holm.

Estonia

	LOCATION	WEBSITE	ARTIST-RUN	ARTIST-INITIATED	NON-PROFIT/PROJECT	INSTITUTIONAL	STUDIOS	FOUNDED	FUNDING	MISSION STATEMENT
MoKS	Mooste	www.moks.ee	●	●	●	○	●	2001	EU & State	Opened as an organisation dedicated to local and international cooperation in arts and environmental research in the rural context of post-Soviet Estonia. Main activities include artist residency programmes, art symposium, workshops, community and international events.
MAAJAAM ◊	Otepää Nature Park	www.maajaam.ee	●	●	○	○	○	2013	Self-funded	A project space in an old farm in Estonian countryside where art meets technology. Substituting the urban environment with a rural landscape allows us to observe technology in its pure form.
Culture Factory Polymer †	Tallinn	www.kultuuritehas.ee	●	●	●	○	●	1995–2013		Kultuuritehas/Culture Factory Polymer is a multidisciplinary centre for artistic creation and diffusion. This former toy factory became in 2003 one of the the main strong points for alternative un-institutionalised culture in Tallinn.
EKKM (Contemporary Art Museum Estonia)	Tallinn	www.ekkm.ee	○	●	●	○	○	2006		A squat that was transformed into an alternative museum. EKKM can be perceived as a certain counter-public institution that includes many traits inherent to normative public institutions, but its goal is to conceive of another kind of institutionalism.
Ptarmigan ‡	Tallinn	www.ptarmigan.ee	●	●	●	○	○	2011–2014		Ptarmigan is a project space operating in Helsinki, in 2011 another was opened in Tallinn. We try to create unique environments, support collaborative practices and focus specifically on international mobility and unusual educational forms.
Rundum ‡	Tallinn	www.rundumspace.com	●	●	●	○	○	2013–2018	Estonian National Agency for Youth in Action Programme	Rundum aims to react to gaps in the local art field, creating opportunities to relate to different locations, offering new exhibiting spaces, as well as more flexible and experimental formats.

Finland

	LOCATION	WEBSITE	ARTIST-RUN	ARTIST-INITIATED	NON-PROFIT/PROJECT	INSTITUTIONAL	STUDIOS	FOUNDED	FUNDING	MISSION STATEMENT
00130 Gallery ‡	Helsinki	www.00130gallery.net	●	●	●	○	○	2010–2018		The main idea behind the gallery's ideology is to support young contemporary artists and non commercial projects in all mediums.
Alkovi ◊	Helsinki	www.alkovi.site	●	●	●	○	○	2005		A display window style space, open 24 hours. Since 2009 the space has been organised by Arttu Merimaa and Miina Hujala, also producing workshops as well as other collaborative projects and art events.

***Finland** (Continued)*

Name	City	Website						Year	Funding	Description
Galleria Huuto	Helsinki	www.galleriahuuto.net	●	●	●	○	●	2002	Kone Foundation, Swedish Cultural Foundation, Ministry of Education and Culture.	Galleria Huuto is an independent artist collective. Huuto maintains two galleries. Galleria Huuto is focused on creating new institutional practices in art, promoting co-operation among artists and offering a platform for individual artists.
MUU	Helsinki	www.muu.fi	●	●	●	○	○	1987		MUU gallery has profiled itself as an non-commercial multiform stage for installations, video art, audio pieces and performance exhibitions. They present works that have yet to be seen in mainstream galleries and experimental art.
Oksasenkatu 11	Helsinki	www.oksasenkatu11.fi	●	●	●	○	○	2008	Foundations, State & self-funded	Oksasenkatu 11's aim is to showcase experimental and ambitious ways of presenting things without commercial attributes. The exhibition schedule is flexible: a longer period of time can be used for building when necessary, which enables artistic solutions beyond the norm.
Ptarmigan ‡	Helsinki	www.ptarmigan.fi	●	●	●	○	○	2009–2014		Ptarmigan is a non-profit initiative to house projects that exist outside of the realm of the traditional. We seek to provide space for adventurous and challenging scenarios.
SIC	Helsinki	www.sicspace.net	●	●	○	○	○	2012	Arts Promotion Finland & Finnish Cultural Foundation	SIC is a space for contemporary art founded in 2012 by a group of artists – Olli Keränen, Karri Kuoppala, Muriel Kuoppala, Kalle Leino, Maija Luutonen, Konsta Ojala, Sauli Sirviö, Timo Vaittinen and Laura Wesamaa.
Sorbus ‡	Helsinki	www.sorbus.fi	●	●	●	○	○	2013–2019	Kone Foundation	Opened in January 2013 and has since hosted exhibitions, performances, concerts and happenings from different art fields. The gallery tries to remain impulsive and adaptable to a variety of exhibition formats.
Kutomo	Turku	www.ehka.net	●	●	●	○	●	2009		Kutomo is a space, place, studio, gallery and a room in which performances from different art fields are organised year round.

France

Name	City	Website						Year	Funding	Description
Fabrique Pola ◊	Bordeaux	www.pola.fr	●	●	○	○	○	2000	Ministry of Culture, European Union, Bordeaux City, and others	An artistic and cultural association which aims to consolidate the activities and economy of its members, and to engage in a development project based on a diverse and inclusive economy for the cultural sector.
Mosquito Coast Factory ◊	Campbon	www.mosquitocoastfactory.com	●	●	○	○	●	2011		Thought of as a laboratory Mosquito Coast Factory is dedicated each year to welcoming the commissioner's exhibition, artists for exchanges, experimentations and collaborations. It is run by the artist Benoît-Marie Moriceau.
In Extenso ◊	Clermont-Ferrand	www.inextenso-asso.com	○	●	●	○	○	2002	Clermont-Auvergne-Métropole, Ministry of Culture-DRAC Auvergne-Rhône-Alpes, and others	Focused on three main activities: exhibitions, publications, and developing exchanges between contemporary art venues in the centre of France with the magazine La belle revue.
Castel Coucou ◊	Forbach	www.castelcoucou.fr	○	●	●	○	○	1983		Castel Coucou offers artists and the public exhibitions and remains in close contact with the regional art scene, in a desire to be part of a dynamic cross-border cooperation.
Le Générateur ◊	Gentilly	www.legenerateur.com	●	●	●	○	○	2006	Val-de-Marne Département utile, Mairie de Gentilly, and others	Le Générateur is run by artists for whom being an artist is a way of life, a way not to give up on life, seek solutions and other livelihood strategies, a way of production meetings where everyone is free and respectful about its subjectivity.
Khiasma ‡	Les Lilas	www.khiasma.net	●	●	○	○	○	2004–2018		The association is a production and distribution of artistic and cultural activities which question the relationship between art and social practices.

France (Continued)	LOCATION	WEBSITE	ARTIST-RUN	ARTIST-INITIATED	NON-PROFIT/PROJECT	INSTITUTIONAL	STUDIOS	FOUNDED	FUNDING	MISSION STATEMENT
La Malterie ◊	Lille	www.lamalterie.com	○	●	○	○	●	1995		La Malterie is focused on the place of the artist at the heart of the project, experimentation, and the artist's presence in a social environment.
Néon ‡	Lyon	www.chezneon.fr	●	●	●	○	○	2000–2019	Public	Producer and broadcaster of contemporary art. Néon sees exhibitions as tools of research and exploration. It proposes an electic programme, favoring the multiplicity of proceedings that generate artists projects.
Asterides ‡	Marseille	www.asterides.org	○	●	○	○	●	1992–2018		In 2018, Astérides merged with Triangle France, pooling the mission, programs and know-how of each of the two structures while respecting and continuing their unique histories in order to sustain their development. See below.
Triangle - Astérides	Marseille	www.trianglefrance.org	●	●	●	●	●	1995	City Council of Marseille, Ministry of Culture - DRAC Provence-Alpes-Côte d'Azur, and others	Through a program of artists' residencies, exhibitions, events, new commissions, and publications, Triangle - Astérides supports the production and presentation of new forms of artistic activity aiming to create dynamic relationships between art, artists, and audiences both locally and internationally.
Octave Cowbell	Metz	www.octavecowbell.fr	●	○	○	○	○	2002		Octave Cowbell is an exhibition association whose primary objective is to show young contemporary creation in all its various forms, in Lorraine and elsewhere.
Association Aperto	Montpellier	www.aperto.free.fr	●	●	○	○	○	1997		Association Aperto's vocation is to be a space for research, production and exhibition, open to artists, to participate in the richness and cultural diversity of the area by presenting works of art and artistic proposals worldwide.
Galerie RDV	Nantes	www.galerierdv.com	○	●	○	○	○	2007		The program covers various aspects of contemporary art, featuring renowned artists but also European and international emerging artists.
Tripode ‡	Nantes	www.tripode.fr	●	●	●	○	○	2002–2017	Public	Tripod invites artists whose practice is predominantly visual arts and produces solo exhibitions in general, duo sometimes, rarely collective in the field of contemporary art.
La Station	Nice	www.lastation.org	●	●	●	○	○	1996	Public	La Station offers an experimental platform within which up-and-coming artists can find conditions conducive to initiating projects and participating in the development, promotion and dissemination of their activities.
Le Pays où le ciel est toujours bleu ◊	Orléans	www.poctb.fr	●	●	●	○	●	2000		A creative label and contemporary art mediation installed in the workshops of artists Oulan Bator. This label is considered as a source of proposals and reflections on territories.
Glassbox	Paris	www.glassbox.fr	●	●	●	○	○	1997	Self-funded	Since 1997, Glassbox's mission has been to promote international and contemporary creation in visual arts, without technical nor theoretical borders.
Immanence et New Immanence	Paris	www.art-immanence.org	●	●	●	○	○	1997	Public & private partnership	Immanence is an artist-run exhibition space, a springboard for artists, linked to a network of international exhibition spaces. Its mission is to organise exhibitions, to offer artists *carte blanche*, and to host projects by young curators.
Plateforme / L'Entreprise ◊	Paris	www.plateforme-paris.com	●	●	●	○	●	1999		Dedicated to contemporary art diffusion, creation and resource, and works as a unifying and shared space, a place of exchanges between artists, curators and audiences. Plateforme is run by the parisian structure L'entreprise bringing together around fifty international artists
Shanaynay ‡	Paris	www.shanaynay.fr	●	●	●	○	○	2011–2020	Self-funded & private donors	Shanaynay is a cooperatively run contemporary art space founded by Jason Hwang and Romain Chenais. Projects are developed in a progressive and flexible manner, avoiding certain traditional modes of presentation and conventional formats associated with art institutions. It is now run by two artists and curators.

France *(Continued)*

Tonus §	Paris	www.tonus-yo.tumblr.com	●	○	●	○	○	2014		TONUS is a not-for-profit exhibition space founded in 2014 by the artist duo Jacent.
Treize (*formerly* Le Commissariat)	Paris	www.treize.site	○	●	●	○	○		Paris City Council & DRAC Île de France	Like an umbrella in Paris, Treize is a place for production and programming of exhibitions, concerts, lectures.
Brigitte Industrie ‡	Rennes	www.brigitteindustrie.over-blog.org	●	○	○	○	●	Closed 2012		Brigitte industry is a platform for research, production and artist-run distribution.
Standards ‡	Rennes	www.standards-expositions.com	●	●	○	○	○	2008–2013		Standards aim is to promote the emergence of young artists focusing on projects allowing them to produce new œuvres. The project is driven by the lack of local structures likely to host the work of students or young artists.
Look & Listen ≈	Saint-Chamas	www.lookelisten.blogspot.com	●	●	●	○	○	2014	Public	L&L started as a blog in 2010, became an art gallery in 2014 and has organised exhibitions, artist residencies, events and community projects since.
Le 6B	Saint Denis	www.le6b.fr	●	●	○	●	●	2010		Le 6B is born of the gathering of people and structures – for the most part artists – who have decided to pool their resources to create workspaces, and freedom of expression.
L'Assaut de la Menuiserie	Saint-Etienne	www. lassautdelamenuiserie. blogspot.ie	●	●	●	○	○	1995		Its purpose is to promote and develop the art and entertainment in the Rhône-Alpes region.
SuperStrat ◊	Saint-Etienne	www.superstrat.fr	●	●	○	○	○	1996	Institutional funding, regular artistic partners	Superstrate is a platform for research, production and dissemination artistic self-directed mission.
La Générale en Manufacture ‡	Sevres	www.facebook.com/ LaGeneraleEnManufacture/	●	●	○	○	○	2005–2010		The focus is on the shape of our investment unfolding in a place crossed by a project and acts in a given time.
Le Syndicat Potentiel	Strasbourg	www.syndicatpotentiel.free.fr	●	○	●	○	○	1992		The current artistic project focuses on the potential to generate new economic intersections between contemporary art and questions specific to the world today, be they social orders, political, environmental.
Collectif IPN ◊	Toulouse	www.facebook.com/collectifIPN	●	●	○	○	○	2012		Collectif IPN are studios of interdisciplinary production. In opening our space to diverse collaborations we support the emerging artistic scene.
Treignac Projet	Treignac	www.treignacprojet.org	●	●	●	○	●	2007	Self-funded & regional state	Treignac Projet is an off-centre, peer-initiated organisation, directed towards collaborative activity within the arts, modelled on the Academy rather than the Arts Centre. It revolves around a studio research programme, workgroups, and a schedule of exhibitions.

Germany

After the Butcher	Berlin	www.after-the-butcher.de	●	●	○	○	○	2007		As a project space created by artists for artists, After the butcher aims to present a platform for young and unknown creatives, to present their work.
All Girls ‡	Berlin	www.art.allgirls-berlin.org	●	●	○	○	○	1992–2015		Founded by three artists. A network of artists who do exhibitions.
Alpha Nova Kulturwerkstatt	Berlin	www.alpha-nova-kulturwerkstatt.de	●	●	○	○	○	1986		Alpha nova-kulturwerkstatt & galerie futura is a Berlin-based art space for exhibitions and cultural events with an explicit gender-critical perspective. The project was founded in 1986. One artist and one academic run it.
Autocenter ‡	Berlin	www.autocenterart.de	●	●	○	○	○	2001–2018	Private	"Showing" here is understood as an non-ideological gesture without economic pressures. Autocenter is about artistic experimentation in the fields of painting, sculpture, photography, video, etc. beyond the confines of curatorial concern and limitation.

Germany (Continued)	LOCATION	WEBSITE	ARTIST-RUN	ARTIST-INITIATED	NON-PROFIT/PROJECT	INSTITUTIONAL	STUDIOS	FOUNDED	FUNDING	MISSION STATEMENT
Apartment Project Berlin	Berlin	www.berlin.apartmentproject.org	●	●	○	○	○	2012		Apartment Project, based in Berlin since 2012, was established as an artist-run space in Istanbul in 1999 – an interdisciplinary project for sharing, communal living and collective production models that focus on process.
art.endart ◊	Berlin	www.facebook.com/art.endart	●	●	○	○	○	2012		Project Space set up by artist Lucyna Viale. The space collaborates with artists and other cultural workers.
Art Laboratory Berlin	Berlin	www.artlaboratory-berlin.org	●	●	○	○	○	2006		Art Laboratory Berlin was founded by an international team of art historians and artists and established as a platform for inter-disciplinary exhibition projects in an international context.
Atelierhaus Mengerzeile / Kunsthalle m3	Berlin	www.atelierhaus-mengerzeile.de	○	●	●	○	●	2001	State	The gallery was set up by the Swedish artist Thomas Henriksson. His goal was to create a space which artists would personalise and make their own, unlike existing spaces which were often formal and unapproachable.
Arttransponder ‡	Berlin	www.arttransponder.net	●	●	●	○	○	2004–2015		Arttransponder provides a platform for discussions and exchange, focusing on interdisciplinary, site specific, participatory and temporary art practices.
BERLIN-WEEKLY	Berlin	www.berlin-weekly.com	○	●	●	○	○	2010		The project space BERLIN-WEEKLY.COM was founded by Stefanie Seidl in June 2010. BERLIN-WEEKLY.COM is an arranged window on display for 24 hours a day – in the city and on the internet.
Bi'bak e.V	Berlin	www.bi-bak.de	○	●	●	○	○		Public & private (European & German)	A non-profit association for contemporary art and community-based projects founded by an artist, filmmaker and cultural anthropologist. Engaged in a variety of sociopolitical issues like migration, discourses on mobility, constructions of identities, consumerism, labour and cultural memories.
Capri Space for Contemporary Art †	Berlin	www.capri-berlin.de	●	●	○	○	○	2001		Until October 2006, CAPRI was a non-commercial artspace founded in 2001 by the artists Ina Bierstedt, Bettina Carl and Alena Meier, realising over 70 exhibitions and events. They continue their work as a collective of artists-curators.
Centrum	Berlin	www.centrumberlin.com	○	●	○	○	○	2009		Founded in 2009 by Kate Squires and David Moynihan, working with international and local artists, offering space and support for experimentation and the development of new work.
Circleculture	Berlin	www.circleculture-gallery.com	●	●	○	○	○	2001		A project space for urban art that was founded by Dirk Staudinger and Johann Haehling von Lanzenauer. It represents a group of artists standing for the rising urban art movement in Berlin.
COPYRIGHTberlin ◊	Berlin	www.copyrightberlin.de	●	●	○	○	○	1999		Founded by artists Ute Lindner and Patrick Huber. The space is an interdisciplinary platform for artistic positions and strategies. Formerly listed as COPYRIGHT Projektraum / LINDNER HUBER.
Dada Post	Berlin	www.dadapost.com	●	●	○	○	○	2008		Dada Post is an artist-run organisation, founded by Howard McCalebb, a sculptor and active figure on the international art scene. We contemplate artistic expression from the standpoint of pure inspiration emanating from the source – the artist.
die raum	Berlin	www.dieraum.net	○	●	●	○	○	2011	Self-funded	die raum is a 5m² exhibition space run by Jesper Dyrehauge (artist) and Lotte Møller (curator) in collaboration with BAR architects. Every project will be accompanied by an edition of posters in collaboration with the exhibiting artist.
Donau-Ecke Ganghofer ‡	Berlin	www.donaugang.wordpress.com	●	●	●	○	○	2010–2018	Private & public	Donau-Ecke Ganghofer is a department store window displaying artistic processes rather than products. We are interested in art beyond the image and non-commodifiable manifestations of the creative unconscious. We do resist gentrification.
Errant Bodies	Berlin	www.errantbodies.org	●	●	○	○	○	1995/2010		Errant Bodies is dedicated to supporting diverse discourses and projects in the fields of sonic and spatial practices, auditory culture and performativity, experimental writing and critical thought.

Germany *(Continued)*

Name	City	Website						Years	Funding	Description
exp12 ‡	Berlin	www.exp12.com	●	●	○	○	○	2010–2017	Private	exp12 is a collective of photographers aiming to develop contemporary photography through a space for meetings and exchange. We are open to different topics, styles and visual languages.
F60.4 ‡	Berlin	www.publiclook.com	●	●	●	○	○	2014	Self-funded	The project F60.4 is examining the common base of artist, curators, gallerists, collectors, critics. Testing the possibilities to show, experience, receive. Input instead of output.
Fenwarme ‡	Berlin	www.fernwaerme-berlin.net	●	●	○	○	○	2002–2007		Fernwaerme was founded as a production group by seven artists. It is the continuation of their long lasting cooperation in various performance projects having a special interest in artistic process research and cross genre exchange.
Flutgraben e.V	Berlin	www.flutgraben.org	○	○	●	○	●	2009		A not-for-profit space with 40 studios and several exhibition spaces. Along side their exhibition programme in the gallery, since 2009, they have invited artists to use their common spaces for art.
Freie Internationale Tankstelle (FIT)	Berlin	www.f-i-t.org	●	●	○	○	○	2003		FIT is based at a 2m² historic gas station, run by Dida Zende as an arts project, working with the symbol and situation of the gas station and its culture in the program.
Front Views	Berlin	www.frontviews.de	○	●	●	○	○	2012		Frontviews is a forum of international artists and theorists. Based on flexible collaborations and without a settled space, we develop concepts of contemporary art in Europe.
Galerie Crystal Ball ◊	Berlin	www.galeriecrystalball.de	○	●	●	○	○	2007		A space, exhibitions and projects run in co-operation with an artist and curator.
Galerie Invaliden 1 ‡	Berlin	www.invaliden1.com	●	●	●	○	○	2005–2017		Galerie Invaliden1 is the collaborative product of 6 Berlin-based artists. There is freedom for mutual exchange, experimental collaboration and reflexive dialogue amongst practitioners.
Galerie Kurt im Hirsch ≈◊	Berlin	www.kurt-im-hirsch.de	●	●	●	○	○	1999	Private	Since 2016 kurt im hirsch acts as an initiative for urban art and publications about site specific and community based art. The gallery space at the Hirschhof in Prenzlauer Berg is closed – the city is open.
Gallery Loris ‡	Berlin	www.lorisberlin.de	○	●	●	○	○	2007–2017		LORIS is a project by 11 artists from Berlin. Photography, video, and installation form the methodological interface of the participating artists. On Monday evenings there is free space for experimental lectures, screenings, and concerts.
General Public ‡	Berlin	www.generalpublic.de	●	●	○	○	○	2005–2020	Private	General Public is an independent project space run by a group of cultural workers. It aims to install and uphold a collaborative, process-related, informal platform for open thought, information exchange, spatial experiment and trans-disciplinary approach.
Gitte Bohr ‡	Berlin	www.gittebohr.de	●	●	○	○	○	2010–2016		Set up by Eva May (researcher) and Diego Castro (artist). They currently dedicate themselves to the German political landscape.
GlogauAIR gGmbH	Berlin	www.glogauair.net	○	●	●	○	●	2006	National & European	The non-profit organisation GlogauAIR hosts Artist Residencies. Founded by the Spanish artist Chema Alvargonzález with the intention of creating a meeting point between artists from all disciplines to work in collaboration and expanding their practice.
Grimmuseum	Berlin	www.grimmuseum.com	○	○	●	●	○	2010		GRIMMUSEUM is an independent not-for-profit organisation with a programme of solo and group exhibitions. GRIMMUSEUM is a organisational model to support contemporary art practice, a registered Community Interest Company (gUG) in Germany.
Group Global 3000	Berlin	www.groupglobal3000.de	○	●	●	○	○	2012		The artist group "Group Global 3000" work with different media such as object, installation, drawing, photography, video, land art, painting. Our subject is art and other sustainabilities.
Gruntaler 9	Berlin	www.gruentaler9.com	●	●	○	○	○	2006		Grüntaler9 is not a Gallery, a White Cube or a Black Box. Every performance leaves visible and invisible traces that remain for the next performance to come and take over and let go again.
Hilbert Raum ◊	Berlin	www.hilbertraum.org	○	●	●	○	○	2015	State Supported	An independent, non-commercial, artist-run project space. It is a group of 14 Berlin-based artists, who take turns curating and organising two-week exhibitions throughout the entire year.

Germany *(Continued)*	LOCATION	WEBSITE	ARTIST-RUN	ARTIST-INITIATED	NON-PROFIT/PROJECT	INSTITUTIONAL	STUDIOS	FOUNDED	FUNDING	MISSION STATEMENT
Infernoesque ‡	Berlin	www.infernoesque.de	○	●	●	○	○	2007–2013	Self-funded	Infernoesque is a free, non-commercial exhibition space for contemporary art under the guidance of four artists aiming to build a high-quality program of new artistic approaches in the field of sculpture and installation art.
Kotti Shop	Berlin	www.kotti-shop.net	●	●	●	○	○	2008		An experimental, not-for-profit, art project space established in 2008 by Annette Knol and Stefan Endewardt. It hosts international art exhibitions and art festivals. It also has a print workshop and prints artists' books.
Kreuzeberg Pavillion	Berlin	www.kreuzbergpavillon.tumblr.com	○	○	●	○	○	2010		An independent non-profit project space. The open process in this field of interests complies with the desire of all participants to establish the pavilion as a public non-excluding system of contemporary art.
Kroneboden ◊	Berlin	www.kronenboden.de	○	●	●	○	○	2008		The project space is run by the pinhole and theatre photographer Karen Stuke and focuses primarily on the intersections between visual and performing arts. Kronenboden also hosts readings, classical concerts and similar events.
KUNSTFAKTOR †	Berlin	www.kunstfaktor.de	○	●	●	○	●	1997	Publicly funded	KUNSTFAKTOR what founded in 1997 by Frank Benno Junghanns, Gerard Dekker and René de Rooze as to artists' cooperative gallery associated with their studio house in Berlin Mitte.
KUNSTrePUBLIK (ZK/U) ◊	Berlin	www.zku-berlin.org	●	●	●	○	○	2008		The ZK/U concept and practice were initiated by the artist collective and non-profit organisation KUNSTrePUBLIK e.V. Coming from non-institutional backgrounds, the founders aspire to continue exploring ways of collaborating, researching and creating.
Lage Egal	Berlin	www.lage-egal.de	●	●	○	○	●	2010	Private & public	LAGE EGAL is a place for production and exhibition. The founding artists aim to work with the mechanisms of presentation and marketing of artwork in an experimental and playful way.
Loge ‡	Berlin	www.loge-berlin.com	●	●	●	○	●	2006–2018	Self-funded	An historical and romantic 4m² space in a building constructed before World War I.
Loris ‡	Berlin	www.lorisberlin.de	●	●	●	○		2007–2018	Self-funded	LORIS is a project by 11 artists from Berlin. It is the goal to establish contacts to collectors, curators, institutions, and galleries and therewith realize exhibitions in Germany and abroad.
L'Oiseau Présente	Berlin	www.loiseaupresente.blogspot.de	○	●	●	○	○	2010		A non-commercial project initiative of artists Gunna Schmidt, Nicola Stäglich and Anke Völk who focus is on abstraction in cross-genre painting.
Manière Noire ‡	Berlin	www.manierenoire.net	●	●	○	○	○	2011–2019	Self-funded	Manière Noire hosts readings from authors, performances, discussions, and workshops. Currently involved with the Appropriating Language Series and Picture Window Series.
MEINBLAU Project Room	Berlin	www.meinblau.de	●	●	○	○	●	1997		The MEINBLAU project room is a location made by and for artists. It provides 125m² of exhibition and activity space on two levels being surrounded by ten studios.
Montanaberlin ‡	Berlin	www.montanaberlin.de	●	●	○	○	○	2006–2016		Montanaberlin is purpose, act, and space. In our work, we focus energy on the interface between nature and the space of human life. We invent a new reality, and organise it.
Mount Warning ‡	Berlin	www.mount-warning.de	●	●	○	○	○	1998–2016		
NGBK ◊	Berlin	www.ngbk.de	●	●	○	○	○	1969		An alternative Kunstverein, with a grassroots aproach towards art. Participation is open to everyone who is interested in the advancement of contemporary arts and theme-based exhibition projects.

Germany *(Continued)*

Or Gallery ‡	Berlin	www.orgallery.org	●	○	○	○	○	1983–2015		The Or Gallery is an artist-run centre committed to exhibiting work by local, national, and international artists whose art practice is of a critical, conceptual and/or interdisciplinary nature.
ORi	Berlin	www.ori-berlin.de	●	●	●	○	○			The everyday operations are organised by the ORi-collective, a group of constant change, always open to new members. Decisions are made on a grass-roots level with the aim of consensus.
OKK – Organ Kritischer Kunst	Berlin	www.kritische-kunst.org/de	○	●	●	○	●	2007		OKK/Raum29 is an atelier, experimental and exhibition space, a mediating platform for dialogue, an artist-run platform for cultural activism based in Berlin, Germany.
oqbo	Berlin	www.oqbo.de	●	●	○	○	○	2008		Gallery oqbo a space for image word and sound is an artist-run gallery in Berlin. The co-organisers are Michael Bause, Christian Bilger, Frank Eltner, Dirk Lebahn, Serpahina Lenz and Julia Ziegler.
Panke e.V	Berlin	www.pankeculture.com	●	●	●	○	○	2009		Panke is a creative multi-purpose space run by a collective of creative people and is registered as a non-profit members organisation. Its main aim is to promote experimental/fringe creativity in Berlin.
Pavillion am Milcof	Berlin	www.milchhofpavillon.de	●	●	○	○	○			Studio community in an old milking parlour, which has now moved to an old school. They currently have over 40 artists. There is a pavillion in the garden, used as an exhibition space.
Prima Centre	Berlin	www.prima-center.net	●	●	○	○	○	2004		Supporting artists in the realisation of their artistic concepts as well as in their promotion to the professional and wider public. It is in the Kolonie Wedding association of art project spaces.
Projekt 0047 ≈	Berlin	www.0047.org	○	●	○	○	●	2004	Norwegian Arts Council & Private	0047 is an organisation for projects in and in between art and architecture. Over 130 artists, architects and curators have been involved in over 30 exhibitions and projects, both in our space or collaboratively in others.
Rosalux	Berlin	www.rosalux.com	●	●	○	○	○	2007		Rosalux exhibits works of conceptual and performance artists who have not had the opportunity to present themselves in Berlin so far, projects rarely seen in commercial galleries, because they are at intersections between disciplines.
Salon Populaire ‡	Berlin	www.salonpopulaire.de	●	●	○	○	○	Closed 2013		Founded by an artist, an art historian and a critic, it is a meeting point in Berlin, inviting anyone interested in the arts and its reflection. It addresses Berlin's local context as much as issues of universal concern with space for anachronistic, indulgent, academic, individual engagement.
Scotty ◊	Berlin	www.scotty-berlin.de	●	●	●	○	○	2006	Senate Department for Culture and Europe	Organized by 10 artists, in the house with the smallest floor space in Kreuzberg SCOTTY provides an open platform for its member artists and curators as well as for guests, offering the greatest possible freedom while exploiting group potential to a maximum.
Scriptings	Berlin	www.scriptings.net	●	●	○	○	○			Showroom and publishing house run by artist Achim Lengerer.
SOMA Art Gallery	Berlin	www.somagallery.de	●	●	●	○	○	2014	Public	SOMA Art Gallery is an independent contemporary art and culture space and initiative. It encourages collaborations among networks between cultural professionals and artists and academics and social activists from all over the world.
Spor Klübü	Berlin	www.koloniewedding.de/sporkluebue	●	●	○	○	○	2003		Spor Klübü is a project space, that works mainly with international artists based in Berlin, offering them room to experiment with their work. Projects in cooperation with guest curators, NGO's and institutions are part of the space's activities.
Souterrain ‡	Berlin	www.souterrain-berlin.de	●	●	○	○	○	Closed 2014		Gallery run by art historians, cultural scientists and artists. The space is an experiment for how the theory and practice of art affect one another.
Sparwasser HQ †	Berlin	www.sparwasserhq.de	●	●	●	○	○	2000		A non-profit artist's project as well as space for projects characterised by a process-oriented practice – a group of participating artists and scientists influence together the outcome and the conditions of work.

Germany (Continued)	LOCATION	WEBSITE	ARTIST-RUN	ARTIST-INITIATED	NON-PROFIT/PROJECT	INSTITUTIONAL	STUDIOS	FOUNDED	FUNDING	MISSION STATEMENT
Stedefreund †	Berlin	www.stedefreund-berlin.de	●	●	●	○	○	2006–2013		Stedefreund was founded by 20 artists and has since been active as a project space nationally and internationally. The confrontation with physical, cultural, social and abstract spaces is the focus.
Super bien! ‡	Berlin	www.superbien.de	●	●	○	○	○	2007–2017		A project aimed at developing alternative strategies for the display of visual art functioning as a catalyst for the growing interest in exhibition spaces other than the 'white cube'.
SUPERUSCHI ‡	Berlin	www.superuschi.org	●	●	●	○	○	2013–2017		A not-for-profit artist initiative with a social vision. Jonny Star develops events as an exploratory artistic act to take place in specific venues (either within private or staged private living spaces).
takt	Berlin	www.taktberlin.org	●	●	●	○	●	2003	Self-funded	Takt Artist Residency and Takt Academy Berlin, Kunstraum Tapir, Tapir LAB, Okapi gallery are designed to host/support active artists. Takt is an artist residency project with a maximum number of 20 studios and three project rooms.
tête	Berlin	www.tete.nu	●	●	○	○	○	2012		tête is an experiment in how to run an art space, artist-run spaces usually being about collective decision making, tête is looking to create a cross section of artistic interests.
tamtamART	Berlin	www.tamtamart.de	●	●	●	○	○			tamtamART is an association for the advancement of Taiwanese Contemporary Art in Germany. We hope not only to create free, open, and diversified conversations, but also to develop a cross-culture and cross-field exchanging art center.
Unwetter ‡	Berlin	www.un-wetter.net	●	●	●	○	●	2002–2018	Art foundations, private & self-funded	UNWETTER's basic format is the Discursive Picnic that connects different contexts in an ongoing process of reciprocal exchange. It works as a potluck, where everybody is both guest and host at the same time.
Uqbar	Berlin	www.projectspace.uqbar-ev.de	●	●	○	○	○	2007		Founded as platform for interdisciplinary projects and international cooperation. Unbar is dedicated to the research and promotion of experimental, interdisciplinary artistic and cultural practices in the international context.
Zagreus Projekt / Koch / Kunst	Berlin	www.zagreus.net	●	●	○	○	○	2006		Zagreus Projekt functions as a gallery and gastronomic space. The chef, gallery owner and curator Ulrich Krauss organises exhibitions in relation to food or gastronomic concepts.
Freies Kunst Territorium ‡	Bochum	www.fktbo.blogspot.de	●	●	○	○	○	Closed 2017		The gallery should be a 'free safe haven for art'.
Kunstraum Unten ‡	Bochum	www.kunstraum-unten.de	●	●	○	○	○	Closed 2017		Exhibition space for young art with an art teacher running the space.
Projektraum Rottstr. 5	Bochum	www.rottstr5.de	●	●	○	○	○			Three important aspects of the orientation of Rottstr5 Art halls: the need for accessibility for the residents in the multicultural neighborhoods of Bochum West, supporting the academic young artists, and promoting innovative artistic approaches.
S.Y.L.A.NTENHEIM ‡	Bonn	www.kunst-bedarf-kunst.de	●	●	○	○	○	2012–2018		The S.Y.L.A.NTENHEIM is the ART SUPPLY VENUE. Everyone can occupy the space for the meaning of art. The concept was initiated by DEMECO & PASQUALE in April 2012.
Boutique – Raum für temporare Kunst ‡	Cologne	www.boutique-koeln.de	●	●	●	○	○	2011–2017	Self-funded	Established by Maximilian Erbacher in a sub basement as a "non-elitist" art space with a subversive and informal program focusing on conceptual and site-specific work.
Bruch and Dallas	Cologne	www.bruchunddallas.de	●	●	○	○	○	2009		An 'Off Space' for contemporary art which was founded by artists as an independent project space. The aim of this space is to show current, ambitious, critical and site specific positions.

Germany *(Continued)*

Salon Atelier	Dortmund	www.salon-atelier.de	●	●	○	○	●			A community of emerging artists in a former hair dressers. They have exhibitions at intervals in their studio space and occasionally do what they call, 'salon on tour' to other exhibition spaces.
Bautzener 69	Dresden	www.bautzner69.de	●	●	○	○	○	2003		The artist-run gallery exhibits young artistic positions from the domains of photography, video, installation and architecture, focussing on connecting young artists and initiating collaborations.
GEH8	Dresden	www.geh8.de	●	●	●	○	●	2007		Studio community of artists, architects, designers and city planners. It follows the non-commercial approach of the artist-run space. They show young artists, musicians and writers.
STORE Contemporary ‡	Dresden	www.storecontemporary.com	●	●	○	○	○	2010–2017		A non-profit art space with a focus on young contemporary art and boundary-pushing projects across disciplines. It shows a diversity of local and international artist and art projects.
CAPRI	Dusseldorf	www.capri-raum.com	●	●	○	○	○			CAPRI is a non-commercial exhibition space in Düsseldorf funded by Nina Höke and Alexander Sies and their Modern Collections-Foundation. The program is curated by Moritz Wesseler.
Parkhaus im Malkasten Dusseldorf ‡	Dusseldorf	www.parkhaus-duesseldorf.com	●	●	○	○	○	1997–2016		Parkhaus exhibits mainly young positions with location-specific work, organises film evenings and discussions. Once a year the work of renowned artists such as Gilbert & George is presented here so as to appeal to a wider audience.
RAUM Oberkassel	Dusseldorf	www.blog.raumfuerkunst.org	○	●	●	○	○	2009	Public	RAUM is an exhibition space that can be rented. They predominently show works from the Art Academy in Dusseldorf. It was founded by an artist and a curator.
Bildwechsel	Hamburg	www.bildwechsel.org	●	●	○	○	○	1979		An umbrella organisation for women, media culture and the arts. With bases in different cities, agents and friends making connections and collecting work.
Blinzelbar †	Hamburg	www.hierunda.de/blinzelbar.html	○	●	●	○	●	2009-2012		A former shopping centre until 2009 when 140 artists turned it into studios and a gallery space. However in 2012, it was pulled down and was replaced by an IKEA.
Dosenfabrik	Hamburg	www.dosenfabrik-hamburg.de	○	●	○	○	●	1995		Dosenfabrik operates 28 artists' studios. Its discourse relates to the public space, a starting point for the creation of temporary projects and actions by its individual artists.
Einstellungsraum	Hamburg	www.einstellungsraum.de	●	●	●	○	○	2001–2016		The Einstellungsraum is a non-profit art centre that mediates projects between car drivers and pedestrians. The exhibitions, focusing on one theme per year, address automobile transportation and traffic in a narrow or wider sense.
ELEKTROHAUS HAMBURG ‡	Hamburg	www.elektrohaus.net	●	●	●	○	○	2002–2016		Presenting young Hamburg and international artists working in media, concept, and action-art. Events are interdisciplinary and situated somewhere in the grey zones between art and literature.
FRISE Künstlerhaus Hamburg + Abbildungszentrum	Hamburg	www.frise.de	●	●	○	○	●	2003		FRISE has 40 artists in studios and an exhibition space. They work with media or concepts and have film and music production facilities. There is co-operation between the visual artists and the film and music producers.
Galerie Oel-Früh ≈	Hamburg	www.oelfrueh.org	●	●	○	○	○	2005		Galerie Oel-Früh has been exhibiting local and international artists since its foundation in 2005. They are encouraged to let the location of the space play a role in their general concepts.
Hafen + Rand †	Hamburg	www.hafenrand.com	●	●	○	○	○	Closed 2011		Hafen + Rand is a small gallery located close to Hans-Albers-Platz in Hamburg. As a project for contemporary arts, it works as an intervention into the mainstream, party and amusement atmosphere of the St. Pauli red light district.
Hinterconti	Hamburg	www.hinterconti.de	●	●	○	○	○	2000		The Hinterconti Off-Space gallery organises weekly shows with Hamburg-based and international emerging artists. Hinterconti offers a short-term exhibition period to realise ideas, which are not necessarily placed in the conventional fields of art.
KiöR – Kunst im öffentlichen Raum ‡	Hamburg	www.kioer-ev.de	●	●	○	○	○	2005–2011		Artist initiative concerned with art in public spaces. They bring art into areas that normally don't have contact with it. They aspire to making it into a public company.

	LOCATION	WEBSITE	ARTIST-RUN	ARTIST-INITIATED	NON-PROFIT/PROJECT	INSTITUTIONAL	STUDIOS	FOUNDED	FUNDING	MISSION STATEMENT
***Germany** (Continued)*										
KuBaSta — Raum für Kunst Bauen Stadtentwicklung †	Hamburg	www.kubasta.de	●	●	○	○	○			KuBaSta is situated in a former butcher shop operating as a gallery, bar, cinema and place for conferences. It was created as a reaction to Hamburg's city planning that plans past human needs.
Kunst Imbiss	Hamburg	www.kunst-imbiss.de	●	●	○	○	○	2005		A mobile gallery running in a food truck, it has had 90 contributing visual artists and writers.
Kunstverein St. Pauli ‡	Hamburg	www.kunstvereinstpauli.de	●	●	○	○	○	Closed 2018		Situated at a flat inhabited mostly by former arts students from Braunschweig in the middle of the red-light district of Hamburg and focused on showing exhibitions of emerging arts.
The Mars Patent †	Hamburg/Mars	www.mars-patent.org	●	●	○	○	○	1999-2010		THE MARS PATENT is an interplanetarian project founded by Helene von Oldenburg and Claudia Reiche. THE MARS PATENT invites you to experience culture on a fascinating and promising site on Mars.
Noroomgallery ‡	Hamburg	www.noroomgallery.com	●	●	●	○	○	Closed 2016	Public	They produce means of presentation. They present social artworks, or what they call 'object art'.
projekthaus | U.FO kunstraum ‡	Hamburg	www.projekthaus-hh.de	●	●	○	○	○	2004		An exhibitions venue, hosting events and creating space for thinking. U.FO kunstraum is located at projekthaus. The off-space gallery hosts 5 to 6 exhibitions per year, featuring painting, installation and video art.
SKAM ‡	Hamburg	www.skam.org	●	●	○	○	●	1992		The SKAM studio-community brings together 25 Hamburg-based artists: painters, sculptors, film animators, concept- and experimental-artists. Very recently SKAM became homeless. Future plans are yet to be announced.
target:autonopop	Hamburg	www.targetautonopop.org	○	○	●	○	○	Closed 2017		Examining the articulation between the market, gallery and institutional spheres, their cooptational and coercive instances, their aversion to any critique which has real consequences.
WESTWERK	Hamburg	www.westwerk.org	●	●	●	●	●	1986	Self-funded by artists & cultural activists	A group of artists and creatively-minded people maintain and program the space as an off-space, art gallery, music club, site for installations, performances, readings and events.
Kunstlerresidenz Blumen †	Leipzig	www.residence-blumen.de	●	●	●	○	●	2006-2013		*blumen* is a space for production of art, dedicated to advancing the work of emerging and under-represented visual artists through its artists-in-residence program, aiming to activate new discourses and impulses in the art field and local sphere.
Pilotenkueche	Leipzig	www.pilotenkueche.net	●	●	●	●	●	2007	City of Leipzig	An artist-run residency based in the Spinnerei complex fostering dialogue and exchange of ideas. Selected artists from around the world are invited to work in the space for 16 weeks.
Spinnerei	Leipzig	www.spinnerei.de	○	●	○	○	●	2004	Self-funded	A cultural hub initiated with artists and located in a former cotton factory, Spinnerei is the site of a multitude of artists' studios, workshops, project spaces and galleries.
Lost Weekend Gallery §	Munich	www.instagram.com/lost.weekendmeetsyoungart	●	●	●	○	○	2020	Local funding (Maxvorstadt) and self-funded	Lost Weekend Gallery focuses on exchange between two invited artists, one from Munich, one from another city/country, and totally open to gender, backgrounds and cultures. Collaborative exhibitions allow artists to develop connections/networks with artists from other cities/art scenes.
Greece										
Enterprise Projects	Athens	www.enterprise-projects.com	○	●	●	○	○	2015	Self-funded	Enterprise Projects, a project by Danai Giannoglou and Vasilis Papageorgiou. Created out of our need to express and share our point of view concerning contemporary artistic creation.

Greece (Continued)

Fokidos ‡	Athens	www.fokidos.tumblr.com	●	●	●	○	○	2013–2018		Fokidos is an artist-run space based in a domestic apartment.
Frown Tails ‡	Athens	www.frowntails.com	●	●	●	○	○	2010–2014	Private	Frown's objective lies in the familiarisation of the audience with the methods and practices of new art forms, working as platform for cultural collaborations through open calls.
Kunsthalle Athena ‡	Athens	www.kunsthalleathena.org	○	○	●	○	○	2010–2015	Donations	An artist-run, non-profit organisation based in Athens whose aim is to produce and promote cultural activities, with a focus on contemporary art.
LO AND BEHOLD ‡	Athens	www.loandbehold.gr	●	●	●	○	○	2008–2016	Membership, donations sponsorship & sales	An artist-run, non-profit organisation based in Athens whose aim is to produce and promote cultural activities, with a focus on contemporary art.
Radio Athènes	Athens	www.radioathenes.org	○	○	●	○	○	2014	Private, foundations & the Swiss arts council	Radio Athènes institute for the advancement of contemporary visual culture is a non profit organisation registered in Athens.
State of Concept	Athens	www.stateofconcept.org	●	●	●	○	○	2013	Outset foundation	Exhibits Greek artists without gallery representation, shows about two international artists per year, and offers free guidance and consultation services to art graduates.
The Daily Lazy ◊	Athens	www.daily-lazy.com	●	●	●	○	○	2011	Self-funded	Daily Lazy is an artist-run, independent art blog. Promoting contemporary exhibitions and fostering art discourse features a wide spectrum of shows from around the world.
Vital Space	Athens	www.vitalspace.org	●	●	○	○	○	2010		Built on belief in the power of art to change the world Vital Space strives to demonstrate that art has its finger on the planet's pulse.
Salon de Vortex ≈	Nomadic	www.salondevortex.wordpress.com	●	●	○	○	○	2009		We are concerned with the complementary relationship of the past to the present, with the playful scarification of history, a constant practice of our collective since its foundation.

Hungary

Budapest Art Factory	Budapest	www.budapestartfactory.com	●	○	●	○	●	2006		Budapest Art Factory (BAF) is a not-for-profit studio, exhibition and project space founded in 2006.
Dinamo †	Budapest		●	●	●	○	○	2003–2006		Founded by Hajnalka Somogyi and Katarina Sevic, Dinamo was an autonomous, non-profit artist-run-space, that functioned on the bases of organic 'self organisation'.
IMPEX †	Budapest		●	●	●	○	●	2006–2008	Self-funded	Founded by Katarina Sevic, IMPEX Contemporary Art Provider is an independent, flexible initiative for work, research and experiments in the field of art and culture.
MUTO §	Budapest	www.mutogroup.hu	●	●	●	○	○	2016		MUTO is an artist-run independent platform and art collective. Our mission is to create a physical space for young artists to experiment, to create diverse programs, and to build our community through a critical curatorial approach and democratic structure based on DIY culture.
Muvelodész ‡	Budapest	www.muszi.org	●	○	●	○	●	2011–2018	Self-funded & private	A complex cultural space, hosting community arts projects, creative workshops and various cultural and social events.
Pince §	Budapest	www.pinceproject.com	●	●	○	○	○	2014		PINCE aims at creating a social space for open communication, art discourse, and site-specific, experimental and installation-based collaborative projects with like-minded Hungarian and foreign collectives that take on a mediative role in their own local art community.

Iceland

Galleri BOX †	Akureyri	www.galleribox.blogspot.ie	●	●	○	○	○	2005		GalleriBOX is run by The Visual Artists Society in Akureyri. It exhibit the latest trend in the field of visual arts.

Iceland (Continued)	LOCATION	WEBSITE	ARTIST-RUN	ARTIST-INITIATED	NON-PROFIT/PROJECT	INSTITUTIONAL	STUDIOS	FOUNDED	FUNDING	MISSION STATEMENT
Geimdósin †	Akureyri	www.facebook.com/geimdosin								Workshop, gallery and coffee in a can.
Fjúk ‡	Husavik	www.fjukartscentre.com	●	●	●	○	●	2013–2017	Regional cultural funding	By inviting artists in residence to work here and through selected exhibitions, films, events, workshops and talks, Fjuk aims to challenge set ways of seeing and thinking.
BÚRIÐ/ The Tank †	Ísafjörður	www.facebook.com/B%C3%9ARI%C3%90-31641803642	●	●	●	○	○	2008-2012		Tiny exhibition space in a cage/tank.
Slunkariki ‡	Ísafjörður	www.facebook.com/Slunkariki	●	○	○	○	○	2012–2019		An artist-run gallery in the corridor of a bigger cultural centre called Edinborg. It is run by the local art club who were founded in 1985.
Ekkisens	Reykjavik	www.ekkisens.wordpress.com	●	●	●	○	○	2014	Self-funded & sponsorship	An artist-run space in a basement which aims to promote the work of emerging artists. It also is curating a series of squat exhibitions.
Gangurinn / Corridor ‡	Reykjavik	www.helgi-fridjonsson.com	●	●	●	○	○	1980		The main interest for the Corridor is to introduce new artists to Reykjavík art scene.
Harbinger ‡	Reykjavik	www.facebook.com/harbinger.is	●	●	●	○	○	2014–2020	Self-funded & sponsorship	Harbinger is an artist-run project space founded by Steinunn Önnudóttir and Kjartan Friðriksson. We select artists that challenge the local art practice and introduce new angles.
Kling & Bang	Reykjavik	www.this.is/klingogbang	●	●	●	○	○	2003		Kling & Bang gallery aim to participate directly in the process of creating the artworks, e.g. by producing the works in collaboration with the exhibitors.
Mengi ‡	Reykjavik	www.mengi.net	●	●	○	○	○		Self-funded	An operation created and managed by artists. Mengi hosts diverse art events, releases music by some of the nation's most ambitious musicians, operates an art store and hosts art exhibitions.
Nýló §	Reykjavik	www.nylo.is	●	●	●	●	○	1978	The City of Reykjavík, the Ministry of Culture and Business Affairs, Icelandic Visual Arts Fund and others	The Living Art Museum, or Nýló, is an artist-run museum and exhibition space with the aim of preserving and exhibiting contemporary art and being a forum for experiments and international discussion about art.
Skúrinn/The Shed †	Reykjavik	www.skurinn.com	●	●	●	○	○	2012-2014		The Shed is a multipurpose cultural centre and an artwork in and of itself. It has housed exhibitions by some of Iceland's finest contemporary visual artists as well as events and performances.
Wind & Weather / Window Gallery ‡	Reykjavik	www.windandweather.is	●	○	●	○	○	2013		The aim is to connect art in the urban setting of Reykjavik with the people on the street.

Ireland

Ireland	LOCATION	WEBSITE	ARTIST-RUN	ARTIST-INITIATED	NON-PROFIT/PROJECT	INSTITUTIONAL	STUDIOS	FOUNDED	FUNDING	MISSION STATEMENT
Sarah Walker Gallery	Cork (Castletownbere)	www.sarahwalkergallery.com	●	●	○	○	●	2000	Self-funded, Cork County Council	Sarah Walker Gallery is situated in an old stone carriagehouse, standing in the sea, at Castletownbere pier. It hosts exhibitions and concerts.
Sample-Studios ◊	Cork	www.sample-studios.com	●	●	●	○	●	2011	The Arts Council, Cork City Council & self-funded	Sample-Studios is an artist-led studio group based in Churchfield, Cork City, which presents an ambitious and diverse programme of visual arts exhibitions in The Lord Mayor's Pavilion, Fitzgerald's Park and St. Luke's Crypt.
The Basement Project †	Cork	www.basementprojectspace.wordpress.com	●	●	●	○	●	2009–2012	The Arts Council & self-funded	Basement Project Space is an artist-led initiative co-founded by three Cork-based artists Lorraine McDonnell, Stephanie Hough, and Rachel McDonnell.
The Black Mariah ‡	Cork	www.facebook.com/The-Black-Mariah-265003353523359	●	○	○	○	○		Closed 2014	

***Ireland** (Continued)*

The Guest House / Cork Artist Collective	Cork	www.theguesthouse.ie	●	●	○	○	●	2004	The Arts Council, Cork City Council & self-funded	An artist-led initiative whose objective is to create a place for production, meeting and cross-practice peer exchange that includes forms of public discourse and encounter. Cork Artist Collective was founded in 1985.
A4 Sounds §	Dublin	www.a4sounds.org	●	●	●	○	●	2009	The Arts Council	Based in north-inner-city Dublin, A4 Sounds provides facilities and professional development supports to 80 artists. Guided by feminist, anti-racist, anti-capitalist, and LGBT-inclusive politics, our mission is to transform the means by which cultural works are produced, accessed, and understood.
Basic Space ◊	Dublin	www.basicspace.ie	●	●	●	○	●	2009	The Arts Council, Dublin City Council & self-funded	Working primarily with emerging and early-career practitioners, Basic Space operates a representative programme, prioritising practices by women, black/brown, disabled and queer artists. The majority of projects are hosted or in collaboration with external institutions, where we act as a critical force, challenging attitudes and policy.
Block T	Dublin	www.blockt.ie	●	●	●	○	●	2010	Public & self-funded	An independent creative arts organisation and entrepreneurial hub.
The Complex §	Dublin	www.thecomplex.ie	●	○	○	○	●	2009	Arts Council of Ireland, Dublin City Council, and other public & private funders	The Complex is an artist led organisation committed to transforming vacant spaces into centres of professional arts practice, breathing creativity into the community, with a focus on theatre, visual art, studios and rehearsal space.
Eight Gallery ‡	Dublin	www.eight-gallery.com	●	●	○	○	○			Eight nurtures a constant platform on which to provide exclusive opportunities for emerging and intermediate artists, writers, curators, performers and musicians.
Flat Pack †	Dublin	www.facebook.com/flatpack.galleryandstudios	●	●	●	○	●	2012–2014	Self-funded	Membership ranges from recent graduates of visual arts, currently exhibiting artists and curators, to writers on contemporary art. The gallery & studios are seen as a critical platform.
FLOOD ≈	Dublin	www.flooddublin.com	●	●	●	○	○	2008	The Arts Council, Dublin City Council, Lismore Castle Arts	FLOOD is a not for profit contemporary art project directed and curated by Paul McAree. In 2012 FLOOD launched the first of 8 exhibitions in a successful partnership with Dublin City Council Arts Office as part of the Vacant Spaces initiative. From 2015 FLOOD will commission one-off projects.
FOUR Gallery †	Dublin	www.fourdublin.com	●	●	●	○	○	2005–2009	The Arts Council, Dublin City Council	Devoted to the development of an uninhibited artistic exploration of ideas, discourses and new trends in contemporary art and its practices.
Market Studios/Unit H †	Dublin	www.facebook.com/The-Market-Studios-83691744457	●	●	●	○	●	2008–2014	The Arts Council, Dublin City Council & self-funded	Providing workspace for artists, writers and curators who enjoy the benefits of peer and cross-disciplinary exchange. Our gallery space UNit H has held over 70 exhibitons and events.
MART	Dublin	www.mart.ie	●	●	●	○	●	2013	The Arts Council, Dublin City Council, Galway City Council, Culture Ireland & self-funded	Providing discourse and development of the arts in Ireland and abroad, partaking in fairs and promoting contributing artists internationally.
Monster Truck Gallery and Studios ‡	Dublin	www.monstertruck.ie	●	●	●	○	●	2006–2017	The Arts Council, Dublin City Council & self-funded	The project was initiated through a desire to respond to what seemed like an endless flow of creatives who wanted to produce work, have exhibitions and make things happen. Gallery now closed.
Moxie †	Dublin	www.mox.ie	●	●	●	○	●	2005–2014	Self-funded & private	Moxie Studios is a not-for-profit resource organisation providing technical training, event and exhibition space, materials and creative space for makers, artists and organisations.
Ormond Studios	Dublin	www.ormondstudios.wordpress.com	●	●	●	○	●	2009	The Arts Council & self-funded	Ormond Studios is a visual arts initiative. The studio was founded by a group of graduates as a self-managed, centrally situated, affordable working space for emerging visual artists.
Pallas Projects/Studios ◊	Dublin	www.pallasprojects.org	●	●	●	○	●	1996	The Arts Council, Culture Ireland, membership and fundraising	Pallas Projects/Studios is an artist-run organisation dedicated to the facilitation of artistic production and discourse, via the provision of affordable artists studios in Dublin city centre, curated projects, research, outreach, and international projects.

***Ireland** (Continued)*	LOCATION	WEBSITE	ARTIST-RUN	ARTIST-INITIATED	NON-PROFIT/PROJECT	INSTITUTIONAL	STUDIOS	FOUNDED	FUNDING	MISSION STATEMENT
Project Arts Centre	Dublin	www.projectartscentre.ie	○	●	●	●	○	1966	The Arts Council, Dublin City Council & private	Project Arts Centre is dedicated to protecting the independent sector and nurturing the next generation of Irish artists across all forms of the performing and visual arts.
Temple Bar Gallery + Studios	Dublin	www.templebargallery.com	○	●	●	●	●	1983	The Arts Council, Dublin City Council, Mason, Hayes & Curran & private	TBG+S have temporary exhibitions showing a cross section of contemporary Irish and international visual arts practice, as well as events and talks.
The Joinery †	Dublin	www.facebook.com/thejoineryd7	●	●	●	○	●	2007–2014	The Arts Council, Dublin City Council, fundraising & self-funded	The Joinery was a not-for-profit art space, which encompassed gallery/project/performance spaces and small studio/workspaces, providing a platform for emerging artists and musicians to experiment and explore.
Thisisnotashop †	Dublin	www.thisisnotashop.com	●	●	●	○	○	2006–2010/11	Self-funded	Thisisnotashop is an alternative, not for profit arts organisation. We are dedicated to supporting the work of emerging artists from both Ireland and abroad.
126 Artist-Run Gallery ◊	Galway	www.126gallery.com	●	●	●	○	○	2005	The Arts Council, Galway City Council, membership & private	126 curates and programmes an arts space including a contemporary exhibition programme, talks & workshops, residencies and research projects.
Engage Art Studios	Galway	www.engageartstudios.com	●	●	●	○	●	2004	The Arts Council, Galway County Council & self-funded	An artist-run studio space and provides an atmosphere of creativity, production, inspiration and opportunity for working artists in the Galway area.
Niland Gallery †	Galway	www.thenilandgallery.blogspot.ie	●	●	●	○	○	2010–2011	The Arts Council & private	The Niland Gallery was started and run on a voluntary basis by Engage Art Studios as a non-commercial project/space that promoted innovative contemporary artworks and events.
Solas Art Gallery	Leitrim (Ballinamore)	www.solasart.ie	●	●	●	○	○	2007	The Arts Council, Leitrim County Council	Solas runs three group exhibitions a year, a junior exhibition and a number of solo exhibitions. It aims to promote the arts in the wider local community.
Askeaton Contemporary Arts ≈	Limerick	www.askeatonarts.com	●	●	●	○	○	2006	The Arts Council	An annual residency programme situates Irish and international artists in the midst of Askeaton. With no 'white-cube' gallery spaces in Askeaton, artists work in public spaces throughout the town.
Faber Studios †	Limerick	www.faberstudioslimerick.blogspot.ie	●	●	○	○	●	2009–2013		An artist collective, studio and exhibition space, promoting and facilitating new directions in contemporary art.
Occupy Space ‡	Limerick	www.occupyspace.com	●	●	●	○	○	2009–2017	The Arts Council, Limerick City Council & private	Occupy Space is a not-for-profit artist-led organisation whose fundamental objective is to provide support and promote projects for graduate and emerging artists.
Ormston House	Limerick	www.ormstonhouse.com	●	●	●	○	○	2011	The Arts Council, Limerick City Council, membership	The gallery devises and delivers an experimental programme of multidisciplinary exhibitions and events, and research-based and archival projects.
Raggle Taggle †	Limerick	www.raggletaggleconsortium.blogspot.ie	●	○	○	○	○	2009–2010	Limerick City Council	
Engage Longford	Longford	www.facebook.com/engagelongford1	●	●	●	○	○		Longford County Council, self-funded & donations	Engage Longford is an artist-led not-for-profit initiative that provides a platform to promote Longford as a hub for contemporary visual art.
NeXus Arts ‡	Louth (Drogheda)	www.nexusarts.eu	○	●	●	○	○	2009	The Arts Council, Louth County Council	NeXus Arts is an artist-led independent curatorial duo. Our starting point is to advocate the work of artists we believe to be critically relevant to our times.
The Good Hatchery ‡	Offaly	www.thegoodhatchery.com	●	●	●	○	●	2007–2016	The Arts Council, Offaly County Council & private	The Good Hatchery is an experimental project that sets out to challenge the norms for the production and presentation of contemporary art in Ireland today.

Ireland *(Continued)*

Damer House Gallery ◊	Tipperary (Roscrea)	www.damerhousegallery.com	●	●	●	○	○	2013	The Office of Public Works (OPW)	A collaborative artistic research project, opening a new critical space within which to produce a platform for public awareness for art and criticism.
SOMA Contemporary ‡	Waterford	www.facebook.com/SomaIreland	●	●	●	○	○	2012	Waterford County Council & self-funded	SCG, as the people's contemporary art gallery, provides the city of Waterford with culturally relative art works.
The Rogue Gallery (formerly Hive Emerging Gallery and Studios) ‡	Waterford	www.facebook.com/TheRoguegallerywt	●	●	●	○	●	2015–2021	The Arts Council, Waterford County Council & self-funded	The Rogue Gallery is an artist-run, not-for-profit space and studios which hosts a programme of exhibitions, art classes and workshops.

Italy

BOCS (Box of Contemporary Space) ◊	Catania	www.bebocs.it	●	●	●	○	○	2008		BOCS is born from the need to create a landmark in the area, aiming is to contribute to the artistic and cultural growth of the place we live.
CHAN Contemporary Art Association ‡	Genova	www.chanarte.com	○	○	●	○	○	2009		As a non-profit collective curatorial space, CHAN represents different forms of expression and offers collateral activities such as video reviews and performances.
Fluxia Gallery †	Milan	www.facebook.com/Fluxia-gallery-151982099500	●	○	○	○	○	2009–2015		It is a miracle that curiosity survives formal education. (Albert Einstein)
Gasconade Gallery †	Milan	www.gasconade.it	○	○	●	○	○	2011–?		Gasconade is a non-profit art space founded in 2011 in Milan. Gasconade's program is devoted to presenting the youngest Milan-based artists and their foreign peers.
MARS (Milan Artist-Run Space)	Milan	www.marsmilano.com	●	●	○	○	○	2008		A deliberate accident, a physical space and above all a project in itself that decides not to be structured organically.
PAC Gallery	Milan	www.pacmilano.it	○	●	○	○	○	1947		In parallel to exhibitions, PAC promotes awareness of contemporary art with accompanying activities and events that foster understanding, deepening the topics discussed by the artist.
Flip Art Project ◊	Napoli	www.instagram.com/flip_project	●	●	●	○	●	2011	City council, private & self-funded	Flip is an artist-run project based in Napoli. Their new location is located the courtyard of a building in Via Giovanni Paladino near Piazzetta Nilo, in a 1950s noble chapel recovered after a long period of neglect.
Secondo Stile ‡	Nomadic	www.paolochiasera.org	●	●	○	○	○	2013–2015		II. STILE is a Nomadic Canvas-based Artist-Run Exhibition Space founded by Paolo Chiasera in 2013. It intend to activate a counter-discourse in the form of sustainable definition an exhibition space.
GUM Studio ‡	Turin	www.gumstudioinfo.blogspot.com	●	●	○	○	○	2008–2013		GUM studio began in November 2008 in Carrara as an independent gallery space, managed by artists for artists. From autumm 2011 moved to Turin.
Progetto Diogene	Turin	www.progettodiogene.eu	●	●	●	○	●	2007	Public & private (Compagnia di San Paolo)	Diogene is as an artistic self-identity group of people working together to create a place for reflecting and exchanging ideas concerning the issues and means of contemporary art practice.
La Rondine Gallery ‡	Tuscany	www.larondinegallery.com	●	●	○	○	○	Closed 2013		An artist-run space, open only when the *La Rondine* (sparrow) has arrived from Africa.
Studio Camnitzer ‡	Tuscany	www.studio-camnitzer.com	○	●	○	○	●	1971–2008		Studio Camnitzer is a studio residence for artists. The Studio is in an 18th century farmhouse completely equipped for printmaking, including the use of digital photography.
Yellow ≈	Varese	www.yellowyellow.org	●	●	○	○	○	2014	Associazione Stralis	Yellow is a new scenario for painting. It's a space where Italian and international painters are invited to meet, interact, experiment, present and discuss their own work.

Latvia

	LOCATION	WEBSITE	ARTIST-RUN	ARTIST-INITIATED	NON-PROFIT/PROJECT	INSTITUTIONAL	STUDIOS	FOUNDED	FUNDING	MISSION STATEMENT
427 §	Riga	www.fourtoseven.info/info-lv	●	○	○	○	○	2015		427 was opened in 2014 with the aim to frequently show contemporary art, to uncover signs, to cast nets, and to exchange with confabulations.
Kim? Contemporary Art Center §	Riga	www.kim.lv	○	○	●	○	○	2009	Self-funded, in-kind givers, technology lenders, long-term philanthropists and others	Kim? works with both emerging and established artists, theoreticians, curators, philosophers, translators and thinkers in other spheres, aiming to provide a responsive context to their work and to make critical practices accessible to a wider audience.
LCCA	Riga	www.lcca.lv	○	●	○	●	○	1993	State, international & private	Internationally active non-governmental culture organisation that offers an independent perspective on current topics and recent historical events through the looking glass of art.
Low Gallery §	Riga	www.low.gallery	●	●	●	○	○	2017	Latvian State Culture Capital Foundation	LOW connects local artists and audiences with the Baltic region and beyond through a diverse programme of events, talks, exhibitions and happenings, providing a safe space to connect and collaborate, and in doing so, dissecting, critiquing and celebrating both high and LOW culture, the soviet legacy, and our extreme present.
NOASS	Riga	www.noass.lv	●	●	●	○	○	1998	City council, ministry of culture, public & private	NOASS supports the realisation of contemporary arts projects in an urban environment, making art part of the daily lives of residents of Riga and visitors to the city.
RIXC	Riga	www.rixc.lv	●	●	○	●	○	2000	State & local	RIXC is a center for new media culture and an artists' collective, that initiates projects in the intersection of art, science and emerging technologies.
Totaldobze ◊	Riga	www.facebook.com/Totaldobze	●	●	●	○	●	2009		To bring together artists from different fields of disciplines and different countries. To focus on new art perspectives, keeping a close watch on the relation of matter and form.

Lithuania

	LOCATION	WEBSITE	ARTIST-RUN	ARTIST-INITIATED	NON-PROFIT/PROJECT	INSTITUTIONAL	STUDIOS	FOUNDED	FUNDING	MISSION STATEMENT
ARKA	Vilnius	www.arkagalerija.lt	○	●	○	○	○	1990	State, municipal and private funding	Working in the field of contemporary art and culture exchange projects, as well as solo, group, thematic, survey exhibitions.
Arts Printing House	Vilnius	www.menuspaustuve.lt	●	●	○	○	●	2002	EU, public & corporate	It aims to foster creativity and support emerging performing art.
Atletika §	Vilnius	www.atletikaprojects.lt	●	●	●	○	○	2019	Culture Council Lithuania and Vilnius city council	Atletika is a contemporary art space at the cultural centre SODAS 2123, which presents emerging and acclaimed artists from Lithuania and abroad. Its exhibition programme is open to experimentation, exploration of new processes in art and ideas.
Malonioji 6 ‡	Vilnius	www.echogonewrong.com/malonioji-6	●	●	●	○	○	2011–2016	European & public	Malonioji 6 was an informal art project space and artist-run initiative, founded by artist Žilvinas Landzbergas in the ground floor of an old wooden villa. It belonged to the Lithuanian Interdisciplinary Artists' Union 2014–2016.

Luxembourg

	LOCATION	WEBSITE	ARTIST-RUN	ARTIST-INITIATED	NON-PROFIT/PROJECT	INSTITUTIONAL	STUDIOS	FOUNDED	FUNDING	MISSION STATEMENT
21Art Street	Kehlen	www.21artstreet.com	●	●	○	○	○	2013		21Artstreet is a 225m² co-working space that can be rented for short term exhibition opportunities or on a weekly basis in order to create artworks on site.
Schlaiffmillen – Résidences d'Artistes ◊	Luxembourg	www.schlaiffmillen.com	●	●	○	○	●	1986		Artists' studio residencies and gallery

Malta

Name	City	Website						Year	Funding	Description
BLITZ ◊	Valletta	www.blitzvalletta.com	●	●	●	○	●	2013	Malta Arts Fund & others	An independent contemporary art space which supports experimental and radical arts practice in all its forms. BLITZ is a space to develop ideas, build relationships and nurture creative talent.
Fragmenta ≈	Valletta	www.fragmentamalta.wordpress.com	●	●	●	○	○	2013	Self-funded	FRAGMENTA is an NGO dedicated to showing great stuff in form of Pop-Up Exhibitions on the Maltese Islands. It has no physical space and is curated by Bettina Hutschek.
Unfinished Art Space §≈	Valletta	www.unfinishedartspace.org	●	○	●	○	○			Unfinished Art Space is a nomadic, artist-run, contemporary art space, a proactive project, that wants to re-mould the art scene in Malta into something that is more innovative, and open, giving artists a space to experiment within their community and to exhibit to a broad audience.

Netherlands

Name	City	Website						Year	Funding	Description
deSERVICEGARAGE ‡	Amsterdam	www.deservicegarage.nl	●	●	○	○	●	2007–2014		deSERVICEGARAGE is an art initiative in Amsterdam with exhibitions and studios.
Goleb	Amsterdam	www.projectgoleb.wordpress.com	●	●	●	○	●	2010	Self-funded	As an artist-led space that mixes both the living and the studio space, Goleb chose to blur the boundaries between the personal and the outside world.
Kulter ‡	Amsterdam	www.kulter.nl/KULTER..html	●	●	○	○	○	2009–2015		Kulter. is a gallery stimulating cross-overs between art, performance, music, words, spanning 6 locations to date. We create a home sphere wherein the artists and the public can discuss informally the work [process], sharing a meal and enjoying qualitatively relevant performances.
kunstenaarsinitiatief beyoncé ‡	Amsterdam	www.facebook.com/kibeyonce/timeline	●	●	○	○	●	2013–2015		kunstenaarsinitiatief beyoncé is a group that developed a way of being in the art world. kunstenaarsinitiatief beyoncé is Lot Meijers, Elke Baggen, Lukas Hoffmann, Susan Kooi and Nikki Oosterveen.
M4 Gast Atelier	Amsterdam	www.m4gastatelier.nl	●	●	●	○	●	2005	Amsterdams Fonds voor de Kunst, Mondriaan fund, private funding and sponsorship	Besides an Artist in Residence, M4gastatelier is a platform for the production, presentation and contextualization of contemporary art by means of a diverse range of disciplines.
OAZO AIR	Amsterdam	www.air-oazo.nl	●	●	●	○	○	1993		OAZO AIR invites artists working in one or more artistic disciplines from all over the globe to live and work temporarily in a lively, productive and creative environment in between the studios of several local artists.
Plan B	Amsterdam	www.planbprojects.nl	●	●	○	○	○	2006	Self-funded	Plan B is an independent artist-run platform by Tarja Szaraniec and Tomas Adolfs that initiates presentations for professional artists in various stages of their career.
PS Projects	Amsterdam	www.psprojectspace.nl	●	●	○	○	○	1999	Self-funded	PS aims to provide a platform for the work of upcoming international artists in an environment that exists between the conventions of an artist-run space and a commercial gallery.
Public Space with a Roof ‡	Amsterdam	www.pswar.org	●	●	○	○	○	2003–2012		Public Space With A Roof was founded by the artists Tamuna Chabashvili, Adi Hollander, Alon Levin, Wartan Aror Jiftian and Krzysztof Wegiel and initiated as a research project-space.
Rhizomatic †	Amsterdam	www.rhizomatic.nl	○	○	●	○	○	2009–2015		Rhizomatic is a platform for young artists and curators who are interested in interdisciplinary relationships, in cross-media and cooperative projects, in artistic experimentation outside the academic context.
RONGWRONG	Amsterdam	www.rongwrong.org	●	●	●	○	○	2011	Amsterdams Fonds voor de Kunsten and Mondriaan fund	Far from the inscrutable logics of sterile art trades and cultural branding, RONGWRONG supports and exhibits the work of both confidential and more rumoured artists.

	LOCATION	WEBSITE	ARTIST-RUN	ARTIST-INITIATED	NON-PROFIT/PROJECT	INSTITUTIONAL	STUDIOS	FOUNDED	FUNDING	MISSION STATEMENT
Stichting Kunsttraject	Amsterdam	www.kunsttrajectamsterdam.nl	○	●	●	●	●	1988	Amsterdam City Council, stadsdeel west and privately funded	Organising and initiating exhibitions, events and projects in the field of the visual arts in the broadest sense of the word.
Ukrop	Amsterdam	www.ukrop.nl	●	●	●	○	●	2009	Self-funded	Ukrop is an organisation run by and for artists who focus on international collaboration, centring on organising exhibitions throughout the world. The platform is used to (co-)create, exhibit, promote and reflect.
w139	Amsterdam	www.w139.nl	●	●	●	○	●		City council & private	Exploring the unknown; we value the freedom not to know. We develop site specific presentations.
Circa...dit	Arnhem	www.circadit.blogspot.nl	●	●	○	○	○			Circa...dit is three levels of fine arts with a program through the generations: new talent, established and reputable. Three floors for research, experimentation and talent.
Code Rood ‡	Arnhem	www.coderood.co	●	●	●	○	○	Closed 2018	Publicly and privately funded	CODE ROOD (RED ALERT) is an artist-collective of 6 people working together. It organises a cultural event every last Saturday of the month.
Motel Spatie ‡	Arnhem	www.motelspatie.nl	●	●	○	○	○	2010–2020		Motel Spatie is a project space inventing forms of engaged autonomy and D.I.Y urbanism always questioning: Who owns the city? It points to the unused places in cities.
Probe ‡	Arnhem	www.projectprobe.net/probe	●	●	○	○	○	2008–2019		Probe is an exhibition space, with walls no higher then 1,10m and a surface of 6m2. Its small and practical dimensions enables artists, to create works on scale, that are unthinkable in real life. Albeit a physical space, Probe is only accessible on the internet.
Club Solo	Breda	www.clubsolo.nl	●	●	●	○	○			Club Solo is an artist-run initiative that puts artists' work at the centre. Its solo exhibitions allow artists to show and discuss recent and older work from a new perspective.
KOP ◊	Breda	www.kop.nu/	●	○	●	○	○			Founded as an artists' initiative, KOP has now become a prized presentation setting for contemporary art and design. KOP's programs and projects are easily accessible and the perception of art and design is key.
MIKC/Kunststation Delden ◊	Delden	www.kunststationdelden.mikc.eu	●	●	●	○	○	1989		MIKC / Perron 1 / The-Counter is an international artists' initiative for visual art presentations. It represents and promotes young talent, international artists and collectives.
id11	Delft	www.id11.nl	●	●	●	○	●	2002	City council, European Union and Self funded	Artist initiative id11 organises artist residencies and provides exhibition spaces where artistic experimentation is nurtured.
Baracca	Dordrecht	www.baracca.nl	●	●	○	○	○	2004		Baracca combines the wildly divergent visions of two curators who are themselves working artists.
DeFabriek	Eindhoven	www.defabriekeindhoven.nl	●	●	○	○	○			An initiative led by professionals from the field of art and design, organising exhibitions and events on a voluntary basis, from idealism, and as an extension alongside their own professional practice.
Villa De Bank	Enschede	www.villadebank.nl	●	●	○	○	●	1985	Private sponsorship	Art Space Villa Bank brings young artists that make innovative work that is qualitatively high level and represent various disciplines and styles of modern art into the limelight .
Horizonverticaal	Haarlem	www.horizonverticaal.nl	●	●	○	○	○			We offer a program in which exhibitions are organised that cover cutting edge, 'high art', 'low art', film, design, cartoons and music.
Nieuwe Vide	Haarlem	www.nieuwevide.nl	●	●	●	○	○	1997	Public & private	Showing group and solo exhibitions of new media (video and sound installations).
Hotel Maria Kapel	Hoorn	www.hotelmariakapel.nl	○	●	●	○	●	2003	Mondriaan fund, Municipality of Hoorn, different art funds on project base, own income	Hotel Maria Kapel is an artist-in-residence, exhibition space and cinema for contemporary visual art. It is a non-profit organisation that aims to assist young as well as more established artists.

***Netherlands** (Continued)*

Peen en Ui	Leiden	www.peenenui.nl	●	●	●	○	○		Publicly and privately funded	Carrot and Onion provide a platform for encounters between people with different talents and knowledge that inspire each other to new insights and creative ideas.
B32 Artspace ≈	Maastrict	www.b32.org/archive/2015	●	●	●	○	○	2001	Maastrict City Council, Prins Bernhard Cultuur Fonds, Brand Cultuur Fonds Limburg, Mondriaan fund	B32 is an independent initiative for artists offering space for experimental, but especially fascinating art and culture. B32 is very flexible, open and interested in everything that has struggled in the established circuit to gain a place.
Beelden op het Vrijthof ‡	Maastrict	www.beeldenophetvrijthof.nl/2015.php	●	●	○	○	○	1981–2016		We approach the contemporary, society, and identify critical trends. We bring young artists together and activate exchange. We show art to the public and stimulate cultural expression.
ruimteCAESUUR ◊	Middelburg	www.caesuur.nu	●	●	●	○	○	1995	Self-funded	ruimteCAESUUR is a private initiative, without any profit, run by Willy van Houtum and artist Hans About Vliet.
Extrapool	Nijmegen	www.extrapool.nl	●	●	●	○	●	1983	Self-funded, city council & art foundations	Extrapool is a space for experimentation and discovery. It shows works from artists with small distribution networks, and who operate on the borders of art and music.
Collectief Derde Wal	Nimeguen	www.derdewal.nl/index.php/8-nieuwsflits	●	●	●	●	○	2009	Prins Bernhard Cultuur Fonds, ALTIJD NIJMEEN, Rabo Bank	Derde Wal is an initiative where young artist and young curators have possibilities to experiment en where they have opportunities to find new ways of working.
Whatspace ‡		www.whatspace.nl	●	●	○	○	○	2008–2012		The Dutch artists Koen Delaere and Bas van den Hurk set up Whatspace as an organisation that is an extension of their own individual artistic practice.
ADA Area for Debate and Art ‡	Rotterdam	www.adarotterdam.nl	●	●	○	○	○	2008–2019		A self-organised, independent artists initiative to support, nurture, stimulate and to create space for critical reflection and debate in and about art.
Bureau Voor Kunst PHK 18 ‡	Rotterdam	www.phk18.nl	●	○	○	○	○	2013	Initiated and supported by an Art Institute	PHK18 is a space for contemporary art and focuses on art and architecture. It is run by visual artists Marleen van Wijngaarden and Alexandra Roozen.
Foudation B.a.d	Rotterdam	www.foundationbad.nl	●	●	●	○	●	1994	Publicly funded and self funded	B.a.d's principal aim is to provide studios and a venue for presentations and events. Foundation B.a.d offers temporary guest studios for local and international artists.
Het Wilde Weten	Rotterdam	www.hetwildeweten.nl	●	●	●	○	●	1992	Rotterdam City Council	Het Wilde Weten functions as a studio and a public platform for all forms of contemporary art, cultural discussion and debate, with programmed exhibitions, presentations, artist talks, discussions, events.
Rib	Rotterdam	www.ribrib.nl	○	●	●	●	○	2015	Rotterdam City Council and Self Funded	Rib does exhibitions and long-term projects in collaboration with artists living and working both nearby and far. We perform art rather than present art.
Tupajumi	Rotterdam	www.tupajumi.com	●	●	○	○	○			Tupajumi is a foundation created for the promotion of artists by organising art related events and exhibitions. Its aim is to share art related networks and resources amongst the participating artists.
Upominki	Rotterdam	www.upominki.nl	●	●	●	○	○	2012		Upominki wants to create an alternative to the value of exchange and the gift-giving idea, and bases its practice on the ideas of hospitality and reciprocity.
Wolfart Projectspaces ◊	Rotterdam	www.cargocollective.com/wolfart-rotterdam	●	●	●	○	○	2008		A creative community who live, work and make use of Wolfart as a place of experimentation in many forms. It provides a regular program of performances, events and exhibitions.
Argument Vertoningsruimte †	Tilburg	www.argument-tilburg.nl	●	●	○	○	○	1993–2012		Its purpose is to offer art in all its aspects a place. Artists get time and space to tackle the experiment and to work on site. The starting point is – mental and physical – space.

Netherlands (Continued)	LOCATION	WEBSITE	ARTIST-RUN	ARTIST-INITIATED	NON-PROFIT/PROJECT	INSTITUTIONAL	STUDIOS	FOUNDED	FUNDING	MISSION STATEMENT
Park Platform for Visual Arts	Tilburg	www.park013.nl	●	●	●	○	○	2013	Tilburg City Council, MV/G Ontwerpes Breda and Social Label	Park is an art initiative founded by Rob Moonen in cooperation with six other artists living in Tilburg. Park focuses on current developments in contemporary art and on artists with extensive experience.
SEA Foundation ◊	Tilburg	www.seafoundation.eu	●	●	●	○	○	1993	Energie Anders, Gemeente Tilburg, Mondriaan Fund, Provincie Noord-Brabant	SEA Foundation is an artist-led contemporary art network. The program resembles an interchange in which interdisciplinary artistic practices combine, in connection to long term-research and dialogue on topics like sustainability, ecology, nature, and climate.
Billytown ◊	The Hague	www.billytown.org	●	○	○	○	●			Billytown is an artist-run gallery located in De Binckhorst.
Locatie Z	The Hague	www.locatiez.net	●	●	○	○	●	2009		Location Z is an initiative of a group of artists from The Hague. Originated (2009) out of the need for a place for research, experimentation, production and presentation.
Nest ◊	The Hague	www.nestruimte.nl	○	○	●	○	○		The Hague city council and Mondrian fonds	Nest is a contemporary art platform with a large exhibition space. Projects look at the artist, their work and role of artists and artworks within their social and functional context in society. 'One Nest Stands' allow artists and curators to visualise their own shows and projects for the duration of one night.
Quartair	The Hague	www.quartair.nl	●	●	●	○	●			Quartair initiates and supports exhibitions, projects and exchanges with artists and artist-run spaces at home and abroad. It pursues an emphatic cooperation with other cultural organisations.
1646	The Hague	www.1646.nl	●	●	●	○	○		Public & private	A dedicated space for experimental art practices and ideas, 1646 is a platform for new productions and presentations with special emphasis on encouraging artists to realise new projects.
BAK	Utrecht	www.bakonline.org	○	●	●	●	○	1989		A platform dedicated to thinking, researching, producing, presenting, and analysing contemporary art. Its philosophy is to make accessible the art of our own time and its developments toward tomorrow.
Expodium	Utrecht	www.expodium.nl	●	●	○	○	○			Expodium is a collective of three [Nikos Doulos, Friso Wiersum, Bart Witte]. We collaborated with and worked for housing corporations, local governments, museums, universities, festivals and art institutions.
Kuiperdomingos Projects ‡	Netherlands & Germany	www.kuiperdomingosprojects.blogspot.ie	●	●	●	○	○	2011–2017	Self-funded	Kuiperdomingos Projects is a an international artist-run mobile project where artistic reflection, production and presentation take place independently from commercial, academic or institutional criteria. Curatorial project by Hans Kuiper and Tiny Domingos.

North Macedonia

	LOCATION	WEBSITE	ARTIST-RUN	ARTIST-INITIATED	NON-PROFIT/PROJECT	INSTITUTIONAL	STUDIOS	FOUNDED	FUNDING	MISSION STATEMENT
KOOPERACIJA ◊	Skopje	www.o-p-a.org/kooperacija	●	●	○	○	○			KOOPERACIJA stands for shifting and redefining the borders between public and personal space, to unlock questions concerning the dynamic role of art in the context of centralised cultural politics and social discourse.
Raspeani Skopjani ‡	Skopje	www.youtube.com/user/PlostadSloboda	●	●	●	○	○	2009–2018		A singing collective who are affiliated with mental hygiene and have the slogan, Who sings, thinks.

Norway

Entree	Bergen	www.entreebergen.no	○	●	○	○	○		Arts Council Norway & Bergen Municipality	Entrée is an independent gallery promoting young international contemporary art.
Knipsu ◊	Bergen	www.knipsu.no	●	●	●	○	○	2010	Arts Council Norway and Bergen Municipality	An artist-run initiative, by Hilde Jørgensen and Maya Økland, that operates as a local art space and a mobile arena, producing exhibitions, events, screenings, concerts, workshops and publications.
Lydgalleriet	Bergen	www.lydgalleriet.no	●	●	○	○	○			Lydgalleriet is an experimental gallery for sound-based art practices. Lydgalleriet exhibits international sound-based art and initiates local art production in Bergen.
Kunsthall 3,14 (formerly Stiftelsen 3,14) ◊	Bergen	www.kunsthall314.art	●	●	●	○	○	1989	Local council & Arts Council Norway	Kunsthall 3,14 is a non-profit International Contemporary Art institution centrally located in the heart of Bergen, Norway, almost exclusively working with international exhibitions and partnerships, with an emphasis on contemporary art beyond the western discourse.
Atelier Nord	Oslo	www.ateliernord.no	○	●	○	○	○	1962		Atelier Nord is a project base for unstable art forms, such as electronic and new media art. Atelier Nord is a member of Production Network for Electronic Art, Norway (PNEK) and also teams up with other partners on several projects.
Pink Cube ≈◊	Oslo	www.pinkcube.no	●	●	●	○	○	2011	Public funding & self-funded	An art space founded and run by artist Anja Carr, it is now a nomadic space, with the possibility of traveling to different venues and countries with its unique wall-paint.
Unge Kunstneres Samfund	Oslo	www.uks.no	○	●	○	○	●	1921		Unge Kunstneres Samfund is a contemporary art gallery and a members' organisation for visual artists. It works for the economical and social rights of artists.
Kunsthall Stavanger	Stavanger	www.kunsthallstavanger.no	●	●	○	●	○	2013	Public	A contemporary art institution that serves as a platform for the production, exhibition, and distribution of artworks that are part of a large international discourse.
Prosjektrom Normanns ‡	Stavanger	www.prosjektromnormanns.com	●	●	○	○	●	2011–2020		Artist-run project space which also hosts events, workshops and seminars.
Rogaland Kunstsenter (RKS)	Stavanger	www.rogalandkunstsenter.no	●	●	●	●	●	1978	Public	As an independent, artist-run institution, RKS presents contemporary art exhibitions, hosts artist presentations, seminars and debates, facilitates residency programs, and develops art projects and public art commissions.
Studio 17 ◊	Stavanger	www.s17.no/oms17	●	●	●	○	○	2013		Frequently show exhibitions in order to maintain spontaneity, showcasing new artists and giving more established names the chance to show new and/or experimental work. The space is also used for lectures, talks and other events.
Kurant Visnigsrom	Tromso	www.facebook.com/kurant9000	●	●	●	○	○	2009		Kurant is an artist run space in Tromsø which has existed since 2009. Autumn 2021, Kurant is mutating. A new generation has moved into the Kurant body, a transition has begun.

Poland

Kolonia Artystów	Gdanska	www.kolonia-artystow.pl	●	●	●	○	●	2001		Artists' Colony popularises and promotes art including niche art, avant-garde and non-commercial, as well as supports and organises cultural initiatives, artistic, educational and social.
FUNDACJA SALONY	Góra	www.fundacjasalony.pl	●	○	○	○	●			We create platforms of understanding between visual arts and common life. We produce, support and distribute socially, historical and political engaged visual art practices.
The Hello Collective †	Jelenia Gora (Residency location)	www.cargocollective.com/hellocollective	●	●	○	○	○	2010		Hello Collective has run a vibrant and productive summer residency in rural Poland. The Hello Collective is an artist led collective that aims to engage in creative dialogue and collaboration between international artists.
Goldex Poldex ‡	Krakow	www.facebook.com/Spółdzielnia-Goldex-Poldex-146877842020632	●	●	●	○	○	Closed 2019		

***Poland** (Continued)*

Name	LOCATION	WEBSITE	ARTIST-RUN	ARTIST-INITIATED	NON-PROFIT/PROJECT	INSTITUTIONAL	STUDIOS	FOUNDED	FUNDING	MISSION STATEMENT
Silverado ‡	Poznan	www.galeriasilverado.pl	●	●	●	●	○	2013–2017		Silverado is an independent artist-run space focused on experimental activity within broad artistic and curatorial practices. We want to critically analyse established art circuit, aiming towards alternative ways of presenting art beyond predictable institutional strategies.
Galeria Rusz	Torun	www.galeriarusz.art.pl	●	●	○	○	○	1999	Public	We use a billboard – the symbol of the modern age consumption – and change it into an object of consideration, reflection and a deep insight into ourselves and the surrounding reality.
Galeria Nad Wisła ◊	Torun	www.culture.pl/pl/miejsce/galeria-nad-wisla	●	●	○	○	○	1991–2011/2015		A new artist group founded in 2015 out of an older space run by artist Marian Stepak. The gallery focuses on the promotion of young artists.
BRUD ‡	Warsaw	www.uvuu.xyz	●	●	○	○	○			The artist and writer Mandayam and the artist Ada Pola metamorphosed into the Indo-Polish art-parasite Brud. Operating out of a slaughterhouse in central Warsaw.
Czułość	Warsaw	www.czulosc.com	●	●	●	○	○	2010		CZUŁOŚĆ is an international movement in contemporary photography. CZUŁOŚĆ is a group of artists who explore the medium of photography and consciously limit themselves to the characteristics and meanings of the medium.
Ꝁem ‡	Warsaw	www.kem.space	●	●	○	○	○	2016		Ꝁem is an artist-run project space for choreographic and performative practices. Kem will host a programme engaged in researching embodiment, affect, new subjectivities and their stagings.
Poligon Artystyczny †	Warsaw		●	●	●	○	○	2015	Self-funded & private	
Stroboskop Art Space §	Warsaw	www.stroboskopartspace.com	●	●	○	○	○	2016	Self-funded	STROBOSKOP is an artist-run site for experimentation and risk-taking, providing opportunity for all individuals with whom we collaborate. Our mission is to promote new and challenging projects, and to initiate cooperation with other exploratory spaces/projects, both within Poland and abroad. programme engaged in researching embodiment, affect, new subjectivities and their stagings.
Galeria Entropia	Warsaw	www.entropia.art.pl	●	●	○	○	○	1988	City of Wroclaw	Entropia conducts intense exhibition and education activities. So far more than 500 events including screenings, lectures, concerts, workshops and meetings with artists have been organised.
WYKWIT	Warsaw	www.wykwit.tumblr.com	●	●	●	○	●	2015	Self-funded & private	WYKWIT is based in a century old post-German house with a large garden and a cellar space adapted for exhibitory purposes. Everyone who lives in the house is involved in giving it a new life.

Portugal

Name	LOCATION	WEBSITE	ARTIST-RUN	ARTIST-INITIATED	NON-PROFIT/PROJECT	INSTITUTIONAL	STUDIOS	FOUNDED	FUNDING	MISSION STATEMENT
Atelier Concorde	Lisbon	www.atelierconcorde.org	●	●	●	○	●	2010	EU, public & private	Artist collective and interdisciplinary workspace, with artists studios, occasional residencies and a project space for exhibitions and events.
Hangar	Lisbon	www.hangar.com.pt	●	●	●	○	●		Public & private	An independent space and a place for experimentation, research and reflection of artistic practices.
FarO (formerly Oporto) ◊	Lisbon	www.oportolisboa.blogspot.com	●	●	○	○	●			Oporto is now FarO! FarO is a non-profit space in Lisbon, operating in a theatre that parasites the external walls of a church.
Roundabout	Lisbon	www.roundaboutlx.wordpress.com	●	●	●	○	●	2012		Functions as an atelier, social and creative hub for an international and interdisciplinary group of agitators, facilitating residencies, artistic exhibitions, cultural events and other activities.
The Barber Shop ◊	Lisbon	www.thisisthebarbershop.blogspot.com	○	○	●	○	○	2009		A project space directed by Margarida Mendes that stimulates dialogue and reflection about the visual arts and surrounding fields of interest. One day events only, random dates.

Poland *(Continued)*

Transboavista	Lisbon	www.transboavista-vpf.net	○	○	●	○	●	2006		Transboavista is a cultural production and exhibition space, with the purpose of stimulating contemporary art through a program of temporary exhibitions, in the VPF cream art gallery and in the alternative venue PLATAFORMA REVÓLVER
Uma certa falta de coerência "A Certain Lack of Coherence"	Porto	www.umacertafaltadecoerencia.blogspot.ie	●	●	○	○	○			An artist-run space for the exhibition and discussion of art-related projects. This is done in tandem and in development with previous similar projects, a gesture we deem continuously essential.

Romania

1Zi Art Space ‡	Bucharest	www.facebook.com/1Zi-Art-Space-426568794138579	○	○	●	○	○	2013–2015		1-day Art Space exhibit art projects for a day.
Atelier030202 ‡	Bucharest	www.atelier030202.ro	●	●	●	○	○	2009–2015	Private	030202 Atelier Gallery is a platform for contemporary art dedicated to young artists, curators and art historians interested in the visual arts experiment and novelty of the moment.
Atelier35	Bucharest	www.atelier35.eu	●	●	○	○	○	1966		Cultivates an interest in socially and politically engaged projects, peripheral practices, collaboration and education.
PLATFORMA ‡	Bucharest	www.platformaspace.wordpress.com	●	●	○	●	○	2011–2015	The National Museum of Contemporary Art	Started as an independent artistic and curatorial project space with a self-constructed exhibitions program. It is interested in interdisciplinary strategies and methods of collaboration.
Lateral Art Space	Cluj Napoca	www.lateralartspace.com	●	●	●	○	○	2012	City council, private & self-funded	A non-profit artist-run exhibition and project space located at the Paintbrush Factory, dedicated to local, national and international emerging artists and founded by Dragos Badita, Cristina Curcan and Lucian Indrei.
Plan B	Cluj	www.plan-b.ro	●	●	○	○	●	2005		Plan B functions as a production and exhibition space for contemporary art; at the same time it is a research center focusing on the Romanian art of the last 50 years.

Serbia

Šok zadruga (formerly aer-Klinika) ◊	Belgrade	www.sokzadruga.com	○	●	○	○	○	2002		The Shock cooperative is redrawing the assigned institutional and disciplinary frames, formulating new, "wild", unconventional models of cooperation, replacing the periphery with center, basement with public space. Formerly known as aer-Klinika (2002–2012)
Art Space U10	Belgrade	www.u10.rs	●	●	○	○	○	2012		The fundamental point of the art space is to promote young artists at the beginning of their artistic careers who haven't had the opportunity to be adequately presented to the local public.
K42 †	Belgrade	www.facebook.com/pages/Studio-K42/334949895671	●	●	●	○	○	1988-2015		A non-governmental organisation whose main goal is to promote contemporary art.
Treci Beograd ‡	Belgrade	www.facebook.com/treci.beograd	●	●	○	○	○	2010–2018		Represents an initiative by a group of artists. Motivated by the need to explore autonomous artistic practice, members of the group actively test models of collective work.
U10 §	Belgrade	www.u10.rs	●	●	●	○	○	2012		U10 is a contemporary artist-run space founded to be a platform for young local artists. By collaborating with similar initiatives, U10 actively works on creating a culture of artistic education, debate and exchange between artists, curators, art theoreticians, writers and the wider public.
Art Association MOBA †	Kikinda	www.supermarketartfair.com/exhibitor/moba/2012	●	●	○	○	○	2010–2012		Art Association MOBA was founded by visual and video artists, painters, printers and sculptors, with the idea to share and spread art.
MAS Gallery †	Odzaci	www.infractionvenice.org/infraction-venezia-3/artists/1429709701.html	○	●	○	○	○	1998		Founded by Serbian artist Nenad Bogdanovic

Slovakia

	LOCATION	WEBSITE	ARTIST-RUN	ARTIST-INITIATED	NON-PROFIT/PROJECT	INSTITUTIONAL	STUDIOS	FOUNDED	FUNDING	MISSION STATEMENT
HIT Gallery	Bratislava	www.galeriahit.com	●	●	●	○	○	2003	Public & private	HIT Gallery emerged out of initiative of non-profit association KARTEL. Their aim is stimulate the local art scene, intercultural and international exchange and new projects.
Tranzit §	Bratislava	www.sk.tranzit.org	○	○	●	○	○	2002	ERSTE Foundation	Tranzit is a unique network of civic associations working independently in the field of contemporary art in Austria, the Czech Republic, Hungary, Slovakia and Romania and across the borders of a wider Europe.
KulturFabrik (Tabacka) ◊	Kosice	www.tabacka.sk	●	●	○	○	●	2006	State & EU	Aims to create an environment for the development of culture and creativity, residential activities and exhibitions, a centre of theatrical, dance, musical or multimedia productions.
Nástupište 1-12	Topolcany	www.nastupiste.sk	●	●	●	○	○	2011	Public & private	A civic association of several artists, graphic designers, psychologists, activists and cultural managers. They conceive and run projects aimed at art, culture and education.

Slovenia

	LOCATION	WEBSITE	ARTIST-RUN	ARTIST-INITIATED	NON-PROFIT/PROJECT	INSTITUTIONAL	STUDIOS	FOUNDED	FUNDING	MISSION STATEMENT
Conceptual Art Centre Bukovje §	Bukojve	www.cac-bukovje.com	●	●	●	○	○	2010	Private foundations	CAC Bukovje is a social art project in a Slovene hillside village, merging family life with contemporary art. Exhibitions are held in the living room, dining room and elsewhere throughout the house. Artists and curators are invited for talks in the shape of teatime with tea, coffee, cookies, cupcakes and more.
AQ Gallery	Celja	www.facebook.com/aq.galerija	●	●	●	○	●	2013	Self-funded	Contemporary art gallery.
CONA Institute for Contemporary Arts	Ljubljana	www.cona.si	●	●	●	●	○	2007	Municipal, national & EU	Creates and promotes contemporary art works relating to society, technology, space and sound.
Cross Community Creation Institute	Ljubljana	www.zavod-ccc.org	●	●	●	○	○	2006		An institute for multimedia art and projects in social research, working in the field of contemporary art with an aim to connect and research art in a broader social space.
KUD France Preseren ◊	Ljubljana	www.kud.si	●	○	●	○	○	1919	Donations	It is a place where as far back in 1919, individuals and groups formulate and express their interests in the cultural, artistic, educational, sociological and technical fields. Residencies available.
Metelkova Mesel	Ljubljana	www.metelkovamesto.org	○	●	○	○	●	1993		Autonomous cultural zone.
P74 Centre and Gallery	Ljubljana	www.zavod-parasite.si	●	●	●	○	○	1997		The P74 Center and Gallery program is focused on the presentation, study and promotion of contemporary visual arts, performance and time-related arts.
Projekt Atol	Ljubljana	www.projekt-atol.si	○	●	●	●	○	1992		Activities range from art production to scientific research and technological prototype development and production.

Spain

	LOCATION	WEBSITE	ARTIST-RUN	ARTIST-INITIATED	NON-PROFIT/PROJECT	INSTITUTIONAL	STUDIOS	FOUNDED	FUNDING	MISSION STATEMENT
Drap-Art	Barcelona	www.drapart.org	●	●	○	○	●	1995	State & private	Drap-Art is a non-profit organisation, dedicated to the promotion of creative recycling through the organisation of festivals, exhibitions, markets and workshops.
Eat Meat Raw †	Barcelona	www.facebook.com/eatmeat.cat/info?tab=page_info	●	●	●	○	○	2011–2014		To dissect contemporary art obsessions.

La Escocesa	Barcelona	www.laescocesa.org	●	●	●	○	●	1999	State & private	A self-managed artistic production centre that focuses on the visual arts with the public in mind. It aims to offer resident creators and collectives a series of different spaces at affordable prices.
Miscelanea	Barcelona	www.miscelanea.info	○	○	●	○	○			MISCELANEA is a multidisciplinary arts space that has as its aim the dissemination and exhibition of creative work and contemporary artistic expressions of the city.
The Green Parrot	Barcelona	www.thegreenparrot.org	○	○	●	○	○	2014	Private & self-funded	The Green Parrot is a non-profit space dedicated to contemporary art practices. It hosts a programme of four exhibitions per year and a series of other events derived from each show.
UntitledBCN ‡	Barcelona	www.untitledbcn.com	●	●	●	○	●	2008–2017		An arts organisation, with the objective to create a platform for early career multi-disciplinary artists, based in Barcelona we work with artists from all over the world.
AADK	Blanca	www.aadk.es	●	●	○	○	●	2008	International public & private	AADK Spain established a permanent space in the south of Spain. It is a space of investigation and artistic creation with the purpose of consolidating it as a pattern in our international networks.
Espacio Islandia	Madrid	www.espacioislandia.com	●	●	●	○	○	2011		A nomadic project dedicated to interdisciplinary artistic processes and encounters.
Naranjo ◊	Madrid	www.facebook.com/EspacioNaranjo	●	●	○	○	●			Naranjo is a space for the production and dissemination of art, made up of 7 studios and a showroom where we organise events, festivals, workshops and conferences streamings.
The Windor	Madrid	www.thewindor.com	●	●	●	○	○			A multifunctional space of interdisciplinary art, featuring the work of Spanish and international emergining artists every month.
Zape §	Valencia	www.zape.lol	●	●	●	○	○	2020	Self-funded	Zape is a non-profit, self-managed space that functions as an alternative framework located in Valencia, to carry out contemporary creative projects of general interest that flee from elitism, classism and the prevailing intellectual paternalism.

Sweden

Formverk ‡	Eskiltuna	www.formverk.se	●	○	●	○	○	2004		We are working on a domestic and international basis, to realise artistic exchange and cooperation.
Galleri 54	Gothenburg	www.galleri54.com	●	●	○	○	○	1954		Showing interesting and varied exhibitions of work by local, national and international artists, offering them the possibility to show their work without commercial pressure and influence.
Galleri Box	Gothenburg	www.galleribox.se	●	●	●	○	○	1998	Arts Council, City Council	Box is an artist-run space for contemporary art. The gallery aims at promoting contemporary Swedish artists, as well as introducing international artists to a Swedish audience.
Konstepidemin	Gothenburg	www.konstepidemin.se	●	●	●	○	●	1987	Self-funded, city council & the Arts Council	Konstepidemin is not a state or municipal institution. Konstepidemin's motto since the very beginning has been that art should infect society.
Martini Projects †	Gothenberg	www.martiniprojects.tumblr.com	●	●	○	○	○	2011–2012		
Galleri Syster	Lulea	www.gallerisyster.se	●	○	●	○	○			Our work is founded upon a feministic ground and we want to make a difference through investigating, challenging and deconstructing.
Cirkulations Centralen Project Space	Malmö	www.cirkulationscentralen.com	●	○	○	○	●	2003	Malmö City Council & Kulturrådet	An artist-run organisation for the production and presentation of contemporary art and culture. It has an artists' cooperative consisting of 24 studios and also houses a gallery.
Galleri 21	Malmö	www.galleri21.com	○	●	○	○	○	1985		One of Malmö's oldest artist-run galleries. Our ambition has always been to reflect the new in art.
Galleri Rostrum	Malmö	www.rostrum.nu	●	●	○	○	○	1985		Started in 1985 by a group of artists, the goal for Gallery Rostrum is to form a rich and varied exhibition program, which is not alien to any form of artistic expression.

Sweden *(Continued)*

	LOCATION	WEBSITE	ARTIST-RUN	ARTIST-INITIATED	NON-PROFIT/PROJECT	INSTITUTIONAL	STUDIOS	FOUNDED	FUNDING	MISSION STATEMENT
Signal – Center for Contemporary Art	Malmö	www.signalsignal.org	●	●	●	○	○	1998	Swedish Arts Council, Culture Administration of Region Skåne län, Culture Department of Malm	Signal is a center for contemporary art focusing on the production, presentation, discourse and promotion of contemporary art and culture, run by a group of artists and curators.
Skånes Konstförening – Skåne Art Association	Malmö	www.skaneskonst.se	●	●	○	○	○	1904/ 2008	Local & national councils	Skåne Art Association has a long tradition dating back to 1904. Today it has grown into an international scene of contemporary art in all forms.
Untendrunter ‡	Malmö	www.untendrunter.se	●	●	●	○	○			An exhibition space run by Trond Hugo Haugen, Michael Johansson and Henrik Lund Jørgensen. It shows every exhibition for two days, the opening night and the following Saturday.
The Pineapple Project Room †	Malmö	www.thepineapple.cc	●	●	●	○	○	1995–2005		The vision is to explore a continuous and ever changable open city space free from commercial interests focusing on the social aspects of art and its production in relation to the society.
Association for Temporary Art †	Stockholm	www.temporaryart.org	●	●	○	○	○	1993–2012		Association of Temporary Art was the result of a collaboration between the artists Åsa Andersson-Broms and Karin Hansson. They were looking for new forms and scenes for discussing and working with public art.
Candyland ◊	Stockholm	www.candyland.se	●	●	●	○	○	2004	Art Council, City Council, self-funded	Candyland is a non-profit art space that has arranged 120 exhibitions in the gallery space accompanied by gigs, performances, workshops and screenings.
Detroit ◊	Stockholm	www.detroitstockholm.info	●	●	●	○	●			Detroit Stockholm is a non-profit organisation. Aiming to create a free platform for artists, with 24 studio spaces in the basement below the gallery.
Fylkingen	Stockholm	www.fylkingen.se	○	●	○	○	○	1935	Swedish Arts Council, Stockholm Cultural Services Department, Stockholm County Council	Fylkingen is a venue and artists' society of over 250 members. Since its establishment in the 1930s, Fylkingen has been committed to experimental work in the contemporary performing arts, covering music, performance, video, film, dance, sound-text composition and intermedia.
ID:I galleri	Stockholm	www.idigalleri.org	●	●	○	○	○			An art scene where artistic integrity is reflected by exhibitors and their profiles.
Minibar ‡	Stockholm	www.facebook.com/ minibarstockholm	●	●	●	○	○	2011–2017		Non-profit project based exhibition space.
Platform Stockholm	Stockholm	www.platformstockholm.com	●	●	○	○	●	2010		Platform Stockholm is a hybrid arts organisation that manages Sweden's largest arts collective housing 100 artists and a 250 squaremeter experimental eventspace.
Studio 44	Stockholm	www.studio44.se	●	●	●	○	○	2002		Studio 44 wishes to develop its curatorial focus further, producing exhibitions that make connections between the members' work while also including a wider artistic community.
Tegen2	Stockholm	www.tegen2.se	○	○	●	○	○			
Galleri Verkligheten ◊	Umea	www.verkligheten.net	●	●	●	○	○	2001	Statens Kulturråd, Umeå Kommun and Region Västerbotten	Our concept is an experimental platform for various kinds of art expressions.
Kottinspektionen ◊	Uppsala	www.kottinspektionen.org	●	●	○	○	○	2014		An artist-run venue for art, choreography and theater.
United Net-Works †		www.sofiesweger.com/wp-content/ uploads/2011/06/newsletter20041.pdf	●	●	○	○	○			United Net-Works is an international network, platform and meeting place for contemporary artists, artists groups, independent curators, researchers and other arts professionals based in Stockholm.

Switzerland

Name	City	Website						Year	Funding	Description
Ausstellungsraum Klingental	Basel	www.ausstellungsraum.ch	●	●	●	○	●	1974	Association & council	An exhibition space, which provides a platform for artists living and working in Basel. We present, discuss and promote their artistic practice bringing it to public attention.
DOCK ◊	Basel	www.dock-basel.ch	○	●	●	○	○	2009	State & private	A project space with an emphasis on discussions and critical discourse, it also houses and ever-growing archive and also aims to integrate art more and more into society.
Kaskadenkondensator	Basel	www.kasko.ch	●	●	○	○	○	1994		Kaskadenkondensator plays a role in the context of the Basel art institutions – a flexible structure, artists and theoreticians working in common at the interface of art and communication.
SALTS	Basel	www.salts.ch	●	●	●	○	○	2009	Swiss Arts Council & foundation	Initially hosting exhibitions in a domestic set-up, SALTS supports young international artists to develop unique and exceptional projects. Since 2009, the exhibitions have often materialised site-specifically, with the goal to push beyond the artists' daily practice, while challenging the audience.
Forde	Geneva	www.forde.ch	●	●	●	○	○	1994	Municipal & Loterie Romaine	Every two years a new curator or curatorial team is selected who then design the programme for the space for the next two years.
BALTSprojects	Zurich	www.baltsprojects.com	●	●	●	○	○	2014	Canton of Zurich / Art Council, Ernst und Olga Gubler-Hablützel Foundation & private	It focuses on exhibitions by architects and artists who engage in some special way with architecture, whereby the subject is broadly conceived: BALTSprojects sees shows architecture from every different facet, points of view, and scale.
Box43 ◊	Zurich	www.box43.ch/wordpress	●	●	●	○	○	2011	Supported by Dienststelle für Kultur, Kanton Wallis	An independent, non-profit, artist-run venue. Marco Nicolas Heinzen and his sister Franziska Heinzen run the venue, which has realised a diverse program with national and international emerging artists in the last few years.
CCA / AZB	Zurich	www.plastiker.ch	●	●	●	○	●	1983	State & Nestlé Art Foundation	The CCA has the goal of improving working conditions of professional artists. This is done with the allocation of studios and work spaces on the one hand and the cultural promotion of the sculpture on the other.
Corner College ≈	Zurich	www.corner-college.com	●	●	○	○	○	2008	State & Nestlé Art Foundation	The Corner College Collective (CCC) are Amélie Brisson-Darveau, Alan Roth, and Dimitrina Sevova. They activate a space of micro-practices that operate in a network of immediate relations that resonate with what swarms around the edges (at the Corner).
Counter Space	Zurich	www.counterspace.ch	○	●	●	○	○	2013	Public funding (city of Zurich and canton of Zurich), private funding, as well as self-funding	Counter Space is an exhibition space dedicated to showing process-like methods in artistic work. Counter Space provides artists with an experimental platform for tentative forms, sketchy actions and ambiguous statements.
Die Diele	Zurich	www.diediele.ch	●	●	●	○	○		State funding and private/corporate sponsors	Pride themselves on giving artists carte blanche to create usually site-specific installations/ works, and trying to find a balance between newer and more estabished artists to exhibit. Also not interested in selling works.
DIENSTGEBÄUDE	Zurich	www.dienstgebaeude.ch	●	●	●	○	○	2009	State funding, private and corporate sponsors	DIENSTGEBÄUDE is an artist-run space in Zurich. The first exhibition took place in September 2009 in the former service building of the train company.
Hacienda ‡	Zurich	www.ha-cie-nd-a.ch	●	●	○	○	○	2013–2015		
Kiosk Tabak ‡	Zurich	www.kiosktabak.ch	●	●	○	○	○	2012–2018		This used to be a tobacco kiosk. Now, instead of selling tabacco, they have art.
Les Complices ◊	Zurich	www.lescomplices.ch	●	●	○	○	○	2003	Institutional and private support	A self-organised space and production office. Exhibitions, projects and events initiated and hosted by Les Complices are situated in and between the fields of contemporary arts, theatre and film, critical theory and activist practice.

Switzerland (Continued)	LOCATION	WEBSITE	ARTIST-RUN	ARTIST-INITIATED	NON-PROFIT/PROJECT	INSTITUTIONAL	STUDIOS	FOUNDED	FUNDING	MISSION STATEMENT
Message Salon ≈◊	Zurich	www.messagesalon.ch	●	●	○	○	○	1996	City council funding and private donations	It is stepping stone, platform, bar, shop and video club.
R57 ‡	Zurich	www.r57.ch	●	●	●	○	○	2007–2019		A non-commercial space for exhibitions, events, performances, installations and readings. Primarily for unestablished artists.
Shedhalle	Zurich	www.shedhalle.ch	○	●	●	●	○	1986	City of Zurich	The Shedhalle exhibition hall – with the shed roof – is located in the "Rote Fabrik," a compound within the city of Zurich that has been in use as a culture and recreation center since the early 1980s.
Sihlquai55 ‡	Zurich	www.sihlquai55.ch	●	●	○	●	○	2009–2017		Sihlquai55 presents itself with a newly developed concept, which is based on three basic principles of belonging, competence and networking.
Station 21 ‡	Zurich	www.station21.ch	●	●	○	○	○	2001–2015	Council and state funding	A space where art is produced and exhibited based on thematic cycles chosen and each lasting a few months at a time. The monthly developments in the works being shown attempt to promote a dialogue between artists and audience.
Tart	Zurich	www.tartart.ch	●	●	○	○	○	2014		Passionate about art of any form and shape, our aim is to introduce new, emerging artists in the Swiss art scene. Global in our outlook, we engage in tracing and promoting fresh, exciting, contemporary art.
Taylor Macklin ‡	Zurich	www.taylormacklin.com	●	●	○	○	○	2014–2018	Zurich University	Taylor Macklin is a Zurich-based project space and is currently run by Adam Cruces, Gina Folly, Michèle Graf, Selina Grüter, and Thomas Julier.
Up State ‡	Zurich	www.up-state.ch	●	●	●	○	○	2013–2016	Self-funded	A self-organised art space and part of the squatted industrial park 'Kochareal'.

Turkey

Name	LOCATION	WEBSITE	ARTIST-RUN	ARTIST-INITIATED	NON-PROFIT/PROJECT	INSTITUTIONAL	STUDIOS	FOUNDED	FUNDING	MISSION STATEMENT
5533 ◊	Istanbul	www.imc5533.blogspot.com	●	●	○	○	○	2008		5533 aims to create a platform where artists exchange ideas.
Apartment Project ‡	Istanbul	www.apartmentproject.com	●	●	●	○	●	1999		Since the very beginning, it has been committed to developing communication between artists and art operators, such as critics, researchers, and curators.
Caravasari ‡	Istanbul	www.caravansarai.info	●	●	○	○	○	2010–2013		An independent and loose group of artists congregating around Istanbul, Turkey.
Pasaj ◊	Istanbul	www.pasajist.wordpress.com	●	●	●	○	○	2010	Private	Pasaj offers an alternative to the ongoing commercial systems in the art world – it is not competitive but sincere and open to share the know-how.
PiST ‡	Istanbul	www.pist-org.blogspot.com	●	●	●	○	○	2006–2017		Interdisciplinary art space.
Sanatorium	Istanbul	www.sanatorium.com.tr	○	●	○	○	○	2009/2011	Privately owned	Enriching the art scene in Turkey with its perspective and vision as it was founded by artists, it searches for ways of increasing its contribution through collaborations in contemporary art.
Recollective ‡	Istanbul	www.reccollective.org	●	●	●	○	○			Rec, is an artists collective, working predominantly in the area of photography and film. Our aim is collective action and creation in collaboration with other collectives and artists.

UK – England

Eastside Projects	Birmingham	www.eastsideprojects.org	●	●	●	○	○	2008	Birmingham City University, Arts Council England, others	A free, public exhibition space that is being imagined and organised by artists.
Grand Union	Birmigham	www.grand-union.org.uk	●	●	●	○	●	2010	Arts council, local council & foundation	Run by a small group of artists and curators, Grand Union is part of a growing artistic community with the production of new art and ideas at its heart.
Stryx §	Birmingham	www.stryx.co.uk	●	○	○	○	●	2012	Public	Stryx is an female artist led residency, studios and exhibition space in Digbeth, Birmingham. Stryx focuses on supporting artists through residencies and artist development programmes, and engage with the public to experience the process of art making and exhibition production, creating an open platform for learning and growth.
Phoenix	Brighton	www.phoenixbrighton.org	●	○	●	○	●		Arts council & public	A gallery, an education programme, residencies, events, and provides over 100 artists' studios.
Spike Island	Bristol	www.spikeisland.org.uk	○	●	●	●	●		Arts council, local council & lottery	Spike Island is an international centre for the development of contemporary art and design. A vibrant hub for production, presentation and debate.
Turf Projects §	Croydon	www.turf-projects.com	●	●	●	○	●	2013	Friends scheme and supporters	Founded in 2013 by Croydon locals, Turf Projects is Croydon's homegrown artist space and the first entirely artist-run contemporary art space in the borough. It also provides studios and a community project space.
Workplace Gallery ◊	Gateshead	www.workplacegallery.co.uk	●	●	○	○	○	2005	Arts Council England, National Portfolio Organisation	A contemporary art gallery run by artists Paul Moss and Miles Thurlow that represents a portfolio of emerging and established artists.
RED Contemporary Arts ◊	Hull	www.redcontemporaryarts.tumblr.com	●	●	●	○	○	1997	Hull City Council Arts Unit, University of Lincoln, Arts Council England	Formerly known as RED Gallery (until 2016) RED Contemporary Arts is an independent arts initiative based in Hull, instigating new and accessible ways of experiencing contemporary arts by any medium necessary (public realm landscape, site specific, virtual).
Black Dogs ‡	Leeds	www.black-dogs.org	○	●	○	○	○	2003–2015		Black Dogs is an art collective formed in Leeds in 2003.
The Tetley/Project Space Leeds ◊	Leeds	www.thetetley.org	○	○	●	○	●	2006	Arts Council England, Leeds City Council	The Tetley is an organisation that engages creatively with the practice of contemporary visual art. An ethos of supporting, enabling and working collaboratively is central to our philosophy.
Threshold §	Leeds	www.thresholdsculpture.space	●	●	○	○	○	2020	Arts Council England, Leeds City Council	Threshold is an independent artist-led space for exhibitions of sculpture, located in the front garden of a traditional back-to-back house in Burley. Threshold is a relaxed space for experimentation, playfulness and engaging with sculpture in everyday situations.
Bidston Observatory Artistic Research Centre §	Liverpool–Wirral	www.bidstonobservatory.org	○	●	●	○	●	2019	Private funding, voluntary labour	Bidston Observatory Artistic Research Centre is a not-for-profit study site that focuses on providing individual users and groups with a low cost, temporary place to dictate their own methods of work. The Observatory also hosts seminars, events and workshops and is open to a range of academic and non-academic discourses.
Jump Ship Rat †	Liverpool	www.jumpshiprat.org	○	●	○	○	○			Jump Ship Rat is an artist-led organisation dedicated to the promotion of the visual and performing arts. We engage cultural dialogue, encourage experimentation and cultivate artistic production.
Metal	Liverpool	www.metalculture.com	●	○	○	●	●	2002	Arts council, local councils	We work to provide the catalyst that can transform the potential of people and places through great art and inspiring ideas. We support artists, working in all disciplines, at all career levels.
Output Gallery §	Liverpool	www.outputgallery.com	●	●	●	○	○	2018	Arts Council England	OUTPUT Gallery works exclusively with creatives who are from or based in Merseyside, delivering a programme of exhibitions to support to mobility, development and visibility of artists in the area. Alongside physical exhibitions we run regular postal exhibitions, a podcast and present work online and in the public realm.

UK – *England (Continued)*

Name	LOCATION	WEBSITE	ARTIST-RUN	ARTIST-INITIATED	NON-PROFIT/PROJECT	INSTITUTIONAL	STUDIOS	FOUNDED	FUNDING	MISSION STATEMENT
Static ◊	Liverpool	www.statictrading.com	●	●	●	○	●	1998	Self-funded, public funding, and private sector sponsorship	The Static organisation is concerned with the processes of creative production, exchange and trade and the structures that support these things.
The Royal Standard	Liverpool	www.the-royal-standard.com	●	●	●	○	●	2006		An artist-led gallery, studios and social workspace dedicated to promoting exchange, dialogue and experimentation, providing a supportive and critically engaged environment to work in.
Acme Studios ◊	London – Bow	www.acme.org.uk	○	●	○	○	●	1972	Previously Arts Council England, self-funded from March 2015	Acme supports over 700 artists and manages 573 studios in 15 buildings in Greater London, offering a wide range of high-quality, long-term and professionally-managed space including permanent new-build studios.
Bows Arts / Nunnery Gallery	London – Bow	www.bowarts.org/nunnery	○	●	●	○	●	1994	Self-funded 94% Arts Council 3% Foundations 3%	Our mission is to support community renewal in East London by delivering Arts and Creative Services through our financially sustainable social enterprise model.
WW Gallery ‡	London – Camden	www.wilsonwilliamsgallery.com	●	●	○	○	○	2008–2016	Self-funded	A contemporary art gallery established by artist/curators Chiara Williams and Debra Wilson, with a focus on consultancy and a limited number of specialist annual projects, such as the SOLO Award.
The Showroom	London – City of Westminister	www.theshowroom.org	○	○	●	○	○	1985	Arts Council	We commission and produce art and discourse; providing an engaging, collaborative programme that challenges what art can be and do for a wide range of audiences.
Almanac Projects ◊	London – Dalston Lane	www.almanacprojects.com	○	○	●	○	○	2013	English-registered charitable Community Benefit Society	Almanac Projects is a non-profit organisation founded and based in London since 2013 with a sibling, independent project in Turin, Almanac Inn.
Banner Repeater	London – Hackney	www.bannerrepeater.org	●	●	○	○	○	2009	Arts Council, borough councils, UK lottery fund	Project space and reading room.
Electra ≈◊	London – Hackney	www.electra-productions.com	●	●	●	○	○	2003	Regular funding from Arts Council England 2005-2015	Electra was founded by Lina Dzuverovic, Anne Hilde Neset, and Irene Revell. The organisation presented its last full annual programme in 2015, and is currently working towards a sustainable future structure, alongside one-off programmes.
not/nowhere ◊	London – Hackney	www.not-nowhere.org	●	●	○	○	○	2018	Arts Council England	not/nowhere is an artist workers' cooperative that programmes workshops, screenings, exhibitions and events. They were preceded by no.w.here (www.no-w-here.org.uk) a similar organisation which ran from 2004–2018.
Space Artists Studios ◊	London – Hackney	www.spacestudios.org.uk	○	●	●	●	●	1968	Arts Council and European Union	SPACE runs 18 artist studio buildings across 7 London boroughs, providing affordable creative workspace plus support programmes, such as exhibitions, artists residencies and training opportunities, to enable artists to be sustainable.
Studio 75 †	London – Hackney	www.studio75.org.uk	●	○	○	○	○	2011–2014		Studio 75 was founded to reinvigorate and renew the definition of "artist-run," exploring the relationship between artwork, artist and audience.
Transition Two (formerly Transition Gallery) ≈◊	London – Hackney	www.transitiongallery.co.uk	●	●	○	○	○	2002		Transition is an independent and innovative gallery and publisher founded by artist Cathy Lomax. In 2018 the gallery became Transition Two, and became an off-site project in 2020.
Working Rooms/Civic Room †	London – Hackney	www.civicroom.org.uk	●	○	○	○	●			Civic Room is the gallery component for Working Rooms, an artists-run organisation that provides studios for artists and designers
Welcome Screen †	London – Hackney	www.welcomescreen.biz/exhibitions	●	●	○	○	○	2013	Self-funded	WELCOME SCREEN was a London based contemporary art gallery. Founded and directed by artist Michael Pybus it focused on solo exhibitions by international artists most of whom have never shown in Europe or the UK before.

***UK** – England (Continued)*

Name	Location	Website						Year	Funding	Description
Lima Zulu ‡	London – Haringey	www.limazulu.co.uk	●	●	○	○	○	2008–2015		Project space.
Usurp Art Gallery	London – Harrow	www.usurp.org.uk	●	●	○	○	●	2010		Open to experimental ideas in all media, we support creatives to collaborate in research and action, and actively encourage a wide range of audiences to participate in the creation of artworks.
Kingsgate	London – Hampstead	www.kingsgateworkshops.org.uk	●	●	●	○	●	1978	Public	Kingsgate Workshops is a multi-use art space housed within a labyrinthine Victorian factory, providing affordable workspace for an exciting mix of artists, makers and designers.
Standpoint Gallery London ◊	London – Hoxton	www.standpointlondon.co.uk	●	○	○	○	●	2001		A leading artist-run gallery and studios in London. It does not represent artists, but curates shows from submission and invitation, concentrating on emerging/mid-career UK and international artists.
Cubitt	London – Islington	www.cubittartists.org.uk	●	●	●	○	●	1991	Arts Council England & Outset (philanthropic arts funding)	Cubitt is an artist-led organisation, which consists of a non-profit gallery, 32 artist studios and a locally-focused education programme.
Beaconsfield	London – Lambeth	www.beaconsfield.ltd.uk	●	●	○	○	○	1995		Three project spaces, very involved in curating and commissioning programmes.
Block 336 ◊	London – Lambeth	www.block336.com	●	●	○	○	●	2011	Public grants, voluntary support and private donations	It aims to promote engagement and critical discussion of contemporary art, with an emphasis on collaboration and cross-practice dialogue and is committed to providing a platform for artists.
Gasworks	London – Lambeth	www.gasworks.org.uk	○	●	●	●	●	1994	Lotto & Arts Council	Contemporary arts' organisation with artists studios and international residency programmes.
Space Station Sixty-Five	London – Lambeth	www.spacestationsixtyfive.com	●	●	○	○	○	2002		Space Station Sixty-Five (SS65) is an artist-run space co-directed by Rachael House and Jo David.
Studio Voltaire	London – Lambeth	www.studiovoltaire.org	○	●	●	●	●	1994	Arts Council & fundraising	Through an ambitious public programme of exhibitions, commissions, live events and offsite projects we play a key role in supporting emerging practices and ideas.
Enclave Projects (incl. News of the World and Res) ‡	London – Lewisham	www.enclaveprojects.com	●	●	●	○	●	2012		An experimental artist-run infrastructure that aims to promote contemporary, critical art practice. Hub space for galleries/projects.
News of the World ‡	London – Lewisham	www.thecentreofattention.org	●	●	○	○	●			Contemporary art/curators studio.
The Pigeon Wing †	London – Lewisham	www.facebook.com/thepigeonwing/	●	○	○	○	○	2005–2012		The Pigeon Wing is a space for experimentation and discussion. We host a series of exhibitions and events throughout the year.
Utrophia †	London – Lewisham	www.utrophia.net	●	○	○	○	○	2002		
Matt's Gallery ◊	London - Nine Elms	www.mattsgallery.org	○	●	●	●	○	1979	Arts Council England	Matt's Gallery is a contemporary art space, founded by Robin Klassnik (OBE), who opened the gallery in his studio. Now located in Nine Elms.
ALISN ‡	London City	www.alisn.org	●	●	○	○	○	2007		The Artist-Led Initiatives Support Network (ALISN) aims to foster community and collaboration between artist-led and other art galleries and projects, working across diverse platforms to deliver innovative exhibitions and events.
Arcadia Missa Project Space ‡◊	London City	www.arcadiamissa.com/arcadia-missa-project-space-2011-2014	○	○	●	○	○	2011–2014		In 2014 Arcadia Missa established as a commercial gallery after running as a project space since 2011.
Form Content ‡	London City	www.formcontent.org/about	○	○	●	○	○	2007	Arts Council & Henry Moore Foundation	A non-profit organisation founded by Francesco Pedraglio, Caterina Riva, Pieternel Vermoortel. After more than 35 exhibitions, it decided to close its space and work on a nomadic project.
Furtherfield	London City	www.furtherfield.org	●	●	●	○	●	1997	Arts Council & fundraising	We believe that through creative and critical engagement with practices in art and technology people are inspired and enabled to become active co-creators of their cultures and societies.

UK – *England (Continued)*

	LOCATION	WEBSITE	ARTIST-RUN	ARTIST-INITIATED	NON-PROFIT/PROJECT	INSTITUTIONAL	STUDIOS	FOUNDED	FUNDING	MISSION STATEMENT
Square Art Project ≈	London City	www.squ-are.com	●	●	○	○	○			Square Art Projects is an independent nomadic artist-run initiative which presents contemporary art exhibitions in non-gallery spaces on an international level.
The Old Police Station ‡	London City	www.theoldpolicestation.org	●	●	●	○	●	2009	Studio rents	A do-it-yourself arts centre with studios, converted cells for exhibitions, supper club and internet radio station. They also run an exhibition programme under the name of Cartel.
Assembly Point ‡	London – Peckham	www.assemblypoint.xyz	●	●	○	○	●	2015–2019		Assembly Point is a new contemporary arts space encompassing a gallery and studios and run by collaborative artists James Edgar and Sam Walker.
Alma Enterprises ‡	London – Southwark	www.almaenterprises.com	●	●	●	○	○	2004		A principal construct of working with individual artists showing singular pieces of work as a result of a lengthy engagement with the space.
ASC Gallery and Studios	London – Southwark	www.ascstudios.co.uk	○	●	●	○	●	1995	Artists Studio Company	Founded by two artists, Peter Flack and Jonathan Coombes. We provide affordable studio space for artists, providing a place to work to over 700 practitioners across Greater London.
Auto Italia South East	London – Southwark	www.autoitaliasoutheast.org	●	●	○	○	○	2007		Commissions and produces new work – collaborating directly with emerging artists. It aims to provide a framework for developing alternative approaches to production and exhibition formats.
Bermondsey Project Space †	London – Southwark	www.bermondseyproject.com	○	○	○	○	●	2010–2014	Crisis, homeless charity	A base for London Sculpture Workshop, London Community Furniture, over 140 artists studios, a gallery and cinema and Crisis Skylight Bermondsey – an arts and vocational college for ex homeless people.
Southwark Park Galleries (formerly Cafe Gallery Projects) ◊	London - Southwark	www.southwarkparkgalleries.org	●	●	○	●	○	1984	Arts Council England	An experimental contemporary visual arts venue with an established reputation as a test-site for ambitious artistic practice, founded in 1984 by a group of artists living in Bermondsey and Rotherhithe.
The Woodmill GP ‡◊	London – Southwark	www.archivesoftheartistled.org/projects/woodmill	●	○	○	○	○	2009–2011/12		Initiated by a group of artists and Southwark Council's Regeneration department. In October 2012 relocated and re-opened as 'The Woodmill GP'.
Vulpes Vulpes ‡	London – Southwark	www.vulpesvulpes.org	●	●	●	○	●	2009		Founded as an artist collective, studios and project space – hosting exhibitions, performances and educational workshops. The project is not for profit and is managed and run collectively.
Dolph ‡◊	London – Streatham Hill	www.dolphprojects.com	●	●	●	○	○	2014	Arts Council England and National Lottery	A not-for-profit visual arts group aiming to engage with artists, the public and neighbouring community by staging thought-provoking solo exhibitions with talks.
Cell Project Space	London – Tower Hamlets	www.cellprojects.org	○	○	●	○	●	2000	Self-funded	Cell is a self funding organisation, founded and directed by Milika Muritu & Richard Priestley with a non-profit seeking constitution. It presents an ongoing programme of exhibitions, projects, talks, screenings, and events.
Studio 1.1 London	London – Tower Hamlets	www.studio1-1.co.uk	●	●	●	○	○	2003		Studio1.1, an artist-run, not for profit space, we have evolved with a range of diverse shows, presenting artists at any stage of their career, from any country, in any discipline.
Studio One Gallery ‡	London – Wandsworth	www.studio1gallery.co.uk	●	●	○	○	●	2008		Four artists set up Collective Studios, an artists studio complex. We exhibit work from our own studio members, as well as local artist groups and selected early career artists.
Castlefield Gallery ◊	Manchester	www.castlefieldgallery.co.uk	○	●	●	○	●	1984	Arts Council England	Castlefield Gallery's vision is for the North to be a place where artists can live and produce work, while presenting their work in national and international contexts.
KRAAK †	Manchester	www.kraak.org.uk	○	●	○	○	○	2009–2015		KRAAK is committed to artist-led exhibitions where individual curators and groups of artists plan and produce the installation process, infusing their own personalities into the space.
Paper Gallery	Manchester	www.paper-gallery.co.uk	●	●	○	○	○	2012	Self-funded, commercial	PAPER is an artist-led, commercial gallery based in Manchester and represents a range of emerging and mid-career artists whose practice is based around the medium of paper.

UK – *England (Continued)*

Rogue Artists Studios & Project Space ◊	Manchester	www.rastudios.co.uk	○	○	●	○	●	1995		Rogue is a not-for-profit artists studios. Rogue runs a programme in the Project Space, which is used primarily for temporary exhibitions, residency and exchange projects and one off events.
The International 3 ‡	Manchester	www.international3.com	○	○	●	○	○	1992–2017	Public & private	With emerging and established artists, independent curators, galleries and organisations we produce a year round programme of new commissions, solo shows, group exhibitions and events both on and off-site.
The Penthouse	Manchester	www.thepenthouseng.com	●	●	●	○	●	2012		An independent not for profit artist-led work and project space. The Penthouse is the place to get your heads and hands dirty with ideas.
Gallery North ‡	Newcastle	www.gn.northumbria.ac.uk	●	●	○	●	○	2009	Public	The Gallery North Project Space showcases work by current students and staff as well as graduates of Northumbria University
Locus+	Newcastle	www.locusplus.org.uk	○	●	○	○	○	1993	Arts Council England	A visual arts commissioning agency that works with artists on the production and presentation of socially engaged, collaborative and temporary projects, primarily for non-gallery locations.
The Globe Gallery	Newcastle	www.globegallery.org	○	○	●	○	○	1995	Arts Council England, Newcastle City Council	Set up in 1995 Globe Gallery is a not for profit organisation. Our aim is to bring contemporary art to as wide an audience as possible and support artists through exhibition opportunities.
Vane	Newcastle	www.vane.org.uk	○	●	○	○	○	1997	Arts Council England	Vane was founded in 1997 in Newcastle upon Tyne in the North East of England. The gallery directors are Paul Stone and Christopher Yeats.
OUTPOST ◊	Norwich	www.norwichoutpost.org	●	●	○	○	●	2004	Arts Council England, Lottery	OUTPOST is an artist-run gallery committed to the uncompromising presentation of contemporary art. A core programme of 11 exhibitions per year.
Backlit ◊	Nottingham	www.backlit.org.uk	●	●	●	○	●	2008	Arts Council England	Backlit was established with an aim of supporting emerging artists with affordable studio space as well as developmental opportunities through participatory and collaborative exhibitions and events with arts and creative professionals.
One Thoresby Street	Nottingham	www.onethoresbystreet.org	○	●	○	○	●		Arts Council England	Comprising a collection of emergent and established artists, galleries, project spaces and studios. A partner of the Nottingham Artist-led Consortium with BACKLIT and PRIMARY.
Primary ◊	Nottingham	www.weareprimary.org	●	○	●	○	●	2012	Arts Council England, Nottingham City Council & Foyle Foundation	An artist-led space that exists to support creative research and to develop new ways of engaging with audiences, where artists and the public can share, experiment and learn about contemporary visual art.
Surface Gallery ◊	Nottingham	www.surfacegallery.org	●	●	●	○	●	1999	Lottery, Arts Council	We operate as a social enterprise celebrating and supporting the talent in our city, with a focus on engaging our immediate community and broadening participation in the arts.
ArtSpace Portsmouth	Portsmouth	www.artspace.co.uk	○	●	○	○	●	1980	Self-funded	Art Space's primary mission is to promote and develop contemporary visual arts by supporting emerging and professional artists' practice through the provision of affordable studios and facilities.
Bloc Projects	Sheffield	www.blocprojects.co.uk	●	○	○	○	●	2002		Bloc Projects is an artist-led project space with an annual programme of exhibitions, events, residencies, exchange projects and educational activity in our gallery and courtyard spaces.
S1 ArtSpace ◊	Sheffield	www.s1artspace.org	●	●	○		●	1995	Arts Council, Sheffield Council, Lottery	An artist-led organisation presenting an annual programme of contemporary exhibitions, commissions, screenings and events. S1 also provides studio space for contemporary artists at varying stages in their careers.
Airspace Gallery ◊	Stoke-on-Trent	www.airspacegallery.org	●	●	○	○	●	2006	Arts Council England, Stoke-on-Trent City Council	AirSpace Gallery is a collaborative, artist-led project in Stoke-on-Trent, providing professional development opportunities, studio and exhibiting space and support for artists.
Squid & Tabernacle †	Nomadic – itinerant gallery	www.georgemajor.com/squidandtabernacle.html	●	○	○	○	○	2008–2012		Squid & Tabernacle was an itinerant gallery set up by George Major and Hanna Sorrell that has staged exhibitions, live events and film screenings in a variety of spaces.

UK – N.Ireland

	LOCATION	WEBSITE	ARTIST-RUN	ARTIST-INITIATED	NON-PROFIT/PROJECT	INSTITUTIONAL	STUDIOS	FOUNDED	FUNDING	MISSION STATEMENT
Catalyst Arts	Belfast	www.catalystarts.org.uk	●	●	●	○	○	1993	Northern Ireland Arts Council, British Council	Catalyst Arts was formed in response to what was seen as a cultural vacuum. It is Belfast's primary artist-led organisation. In accordance with its constitution it is run by unpaid volunteers.
Platform	Belfast	www.platformartsbelfast.com	●	●	●	○	●	2009		Belfast Platform for the Arts is a voluntary organisation established to assist persons with artistic talents to promote themselves to the general public.
PS2 §	Belfast	www.pssquared.org	●	●	○	○	●	1993	Arts Council of Northen Ireland, Freelands Artist Programme	An artist-led collective, connecting art and society, in the centre of Belfast. We develop and support artists through Paragon Studios. We host project artists and welcome the public to our Project Space.
Queen Street Studios	Belfast	www.queenstreetstudios.net	●	●	●	○	●	1983	Public & private	QSS Studios currently provides subsidised studio spaces for artists who work in various mediums. The gallery was launched to fill an ever expanding need for gallery provision in Belfast.
Satis House †	Belfast	www.satis-house.com	●	●	●	○	○	2012–2014		Within a row of terraces, the space exists in the master bedroom. This room is transfigured on a monthly basis under the curatorial direction of Eoin Dara and Kim McAleese.
The Golden Thread Gallery	Belfast	www.goldenthreadgallery.co.uk	●	●	●	○	○	1998	Public & private	Golden Thread Gallery is a medium-scale, publicly funded, contemporary art gallery, recognised as having charitable status. The majority of its programme is engaged with offering the public a contextual experience of visual art.
CCA Derry~Londonderry ◊	Derry	www.cca-derry-londonderry.org	○	●	●	●	○	1992	Public & private	Centre for Contemporary Art (CCA) fosters a wide range of artistic, curatorial, and critical practices through five collaborative and process-driven streams: research and production, exhibition-making, public programmes, publishing, and residencies.
Void ◊	Derry	www.derryvoid.com	○	●	●	●	○	2003	Public & private	Void exists to present the contemporary visual arts and to support artists, through a programme of exhibitions, related educational and outreach activities from a national and international perspective.

UK – Scotland

	LOCATION	WEBSITE	ARTIST-RUN	ARTIST-INITIATED	NON-PROFIT/PROJECT	INSTITUTIONAL	STUDIOS	FOUNDED	FUNDING	MISSION STATEMENT
Gaada §	Burra Isle	www.gaada.org	●	●	○	○	○	2018	Public Institutions	Gaada works with communities in Shetland to develop meaningful and critical art activities, improving access to creative development through Gaada's well-equipped visual art workshop and specialist support from its experienced artists.
Generator Projects ◊	Dundee	www.generatorprojects.co.uk	●	●	○	○	○	1996	National Lottery, Dundee City Council	Facilitated by a rolling committee of volunteers, Generator was established to allow creative practitioners developing experimental, critical and autonomous work, the opportunity to exhibit.
Collective ◊	Edinburgh	www.collective-edinburgh.art	○	●	●	○	○	1984	Creative Scotland, Edinburgh City	Established as an artist-run organisation in 1984, Collective aims to foster, support and debate new work and practices in a way which is of mutual benefit to artists and audiences.
Embassy Gallery	Edinburgh	www.embassygallery.org	●	●	●	○	○	2004	Creative Scotland	EMBASSY is a non-profit making artist-run gallery. It holds a yearly programme of exhibitions and events and exhibits at off site projects.
Interview Room 11 ‡	Edinburgh	www.ir11.org.uk	●	●	●	○	○	2013		Interview Room 11 is an artist-run gallery and project space. Our programme consists of a mix of committee run projects, solo and group exhibitions and select invited curatorial projects.
Rhubaba Gallery and Studios	Edinburgh	www.rhubaba.org	●	●	●	○	●	2009	Public	An artist-run organisation that provides studio space for currently twenty-five artists across fifteen studios alongside an annual programme of exhibitions and events.

***UK** – Scotland (Continued)*

David Dale Gallery and Studios	Glasgow	www.daviddalegallery.co.uk	●	●	○	○	●	2009	Lottery/Glasgow Council	Provides innovative year-round exhibitions and events that promote international pioneering contemporary visual art and artists' studio spaces within a supportive peer group community.
Glasgow Independent Studio and Project Room ◊	Glasgow	www.gis.uk.com	○	○	●	○	●	1995		Glasgow Independent Studio and Project Room is a non-profit making charity. The organisation comprises of a large studio complex and contemporary art exhibition and project space.
Glasgow Sculpture Studios	Glasgow	www.glasgowsculpturestudios.org	○	●	○	○	●	1988	Creative Scotland, Glasgow Life	GSS is a unique centre for research, production, presentation and the dissemination of contemporary sculptural practices. It is our mission to place the artist, viewer, user and participant at the heart of all our activities.
LowSalt †	Glasgow	www.lowsalt.org.uk	●	○	●	○	○	2006–2010		We passionately believe that art offers empowerment, increases understanding and improves communication. All our collaborative projects, residencies and learning opportunities are about increasing participation.
SWG3	Glasgow	www.swg3.tv	○	●	●	○	●	2008		
Transmission Gallery	Glasgow	www.transmissiongallery.org	●	●	●	○	○	1983	Creative Scotland	Transmission works with artists in the production of exhibitions, events, exchanges, residencies and publications. It also shares various resources with its membership in order to facilitate activities outside of its own programming.

UK – Wales

g39	Cardiff	www.g39.org	●	●	○	○	○	1998	Arts Council of Wales	G39 focuses on contemporary work and consciously programmes a mix of work from Wales with work from further afield, placing work by established names alongside work by emerging artists.
SPIT & SAWDUST §	Cardiff	www.spitandsawdust.co.uk	●	●	○	●	○	2014		Spit & Sawdust is run by 3 artists and a skateboarder whose aim is to offer a unique and welcoming cultural, creative and social space in the city. We're located just off a busy dual carriageway through a bleak retail park, but when you find us, you'll forget all about that.
Mission Gallery ◊	Swansea	www.missiongallery.co.uk	●	●	●	○	○	1977	Arts Council of Wales, Lottery Funding	Mission Gallery is one of Wales' best-adapted spaces for the contemporary arts. It has developed a reputation for dynamic and distinctive programming, to present excellence across the visual arts, applied arts and crafts.

Ukraine

127 garage §	Kharkiv	www.127garazh.org	●	●	●	○	○	2019	Self-funded	127 garage's work is centred on different forms of knowledge exchange, new discursive lines, and challenging spatial narratives, developing new tools for understanding the condition today for a queerer tomorrow. 127 garage strives for a world of horizontal hegemonies, borderlessness, and borderlands, guided by our curiosity and urgency.
«HLEBZAWOD» §	Kyiv	www.artistrunalliance.org/initiatives/hlebzawod	●	○	●	○	○	2016	Membership	"Hlebzawod" art space was formed in an abandoned factory in the summer of 2016. Its mission is the promotion of contemporary art with social, historical and cultural significance. Educational activity is focused on expanding exhibiting activity and audiences for contemporary art in Ukraine, and developing and supporting young artists.
Institute of Automation §	Kyiv	www.artistrunalliance.org/initiatives/institute-of-automation	●	○	●	○	●	2020	Membership	The purpose of creation is to outline creative autonomy. The Institute of Automation directs its activities in search of forms and means of artistic expression in the field of contemporary art.
TU Platform §	Mariupol	www.tu.org.ua	●	●	●	○	○	2015	International foundations, Embassies, and fundrasing	The TU platform is a space in Mariupol created by people who were united by the war and who began to fight it through cultural initiatives. Our motto is: Everything that works for culture works against war. As a platform, we have become the only independent artistic space in Eastern Ukraine, where underground culture, innovative ideas, human rights and freedoms are our core values.

Acknowledgements

THE EDITORS WOULD LIKE TO THANK THE FOLLOWING FOR THEIR CONTRIBUTION TO THIS PUBLICATION:

Jason E. Bowman, AA Bronson, Noelle Collins, Valerie Connor, Céline Kopp & Alun Williams, Joanna Laws, Freek Lomme, Megs Morley, Transmission Gallery, Catalyst Arts, Gavin Wade, Katherine Waugh, Andreas Ribbung, Andreas Marti, Annette Süedbeck, Anja Carr, Amélie Claude, Lucy Watts, Róisín Hackett, Conor Nolan, David Wall, and all at WorkGroup.

Special thanks to Other Office (Simon Sweeney & Shauna Buckley); James Schofield (Exhibition Research Lab, Liverpool); Florence Gosset (Triangle–Astérides); Adi Levi (Artist-Run Alliance); Dymfy van Meel (Onomatopee); Maksym Mazur, Anton Tkachenko, Diana Berg, and all those who contributed to the updated Artist-Run Index; and The Arts Council of Ireland for their ongoing support.

We would also like to acknowledge the following for their help and support of the Artist-Run Europe project:

Jennifer Bailey, Josée Aubin Ouellette; Marie Redmond; Rayne Booth and Clíodhna Shaffrey, Temple Bar Gallery + Studios; Chris Fite-Wassilak; Katy Fitzpatrick; Dan Adler; John Holten; Dragana Jurisic; Matija Brumen; Frank Wagner; Stanislaw Welbel; Claire Power; Eve Woods; Steve Van Teeseling, Mondriaan Fund; Karl England and all at Sluice; Shirley Walsh, CONNECT; Janice Hough, IMMA ARP; Declan McGonagle; Anne Kelly, NCAD Gallery; Annie Fletcher, Van Abbemuseum; Katie Lowry and Audrey Keane, Creative Europe Desk, Dublin; Kathy Scott; Clare Lymer, NIVAL: The National Irish Visual Arts Library; Donna Romano, NCAD Library; Mary Conlon and all at Ormston House; Shelly McDonnell, Lucy Elvis and all at 126, Galway; Ian McInerney, The Black Mariah, Cork; Michaela, Edel, Anthony, Alessia and all at Catalyst Arts, Belfast; Scott Kiernan & Victoria Keddie, E.S.P. TV, New York; Occupy Space, Limerick; Toine Horvers, Suburban Video Lounge, Rotterdam.

Our Board: Our board: Caroline Cowley, Brian Duggan, Sarah Farrell, Clodagh Kenny, Brian Maguire, Paul McGowan, Della O'Donoghue, and previous board members: Fiach Mac Conghail, Linda Doyle, Helen Carey, Stephen Browne, Sarah Searson, Lisa Carroll, Patrick Ambrose, Gaby Smyth, Patrick T. Murphy, Garrett Phelan.

And for their support, and contribution to Pallas Projects/Studios:

Maeve Connolly, Sinead Hogan, IADT faculty and Degree year students and all who have contributed to the 'in the making' project.; Josip Zanki, Ivana Andabaka, Martina Milhovic, and all at HDLU; Nathan O'Donnell, Niamh Dunphy, Adrian Duncan at PVA Journal; Ángel Luis González, Julia Gelezova and Rita Hynes at PhotoIreland; Chris Hayes, James Merrigan, Celina Muldoon, Alice Butler, Seán Kissane, Workhouse Union, Aisling Prior, RGKSKSRG (Rachael Gilbourne & Kate Strain), Oonagh Young, Niamh Brown, Ailbhe Murphy, Marysia Wieckiewicz-Carroll, Paul McGrane & Mark O'Gorman, Dobz O'Brien, Simon Fennessy Corcoran, Linda Shevlin, Siobhán Geoghegan, Peter Richards, Tania Banotti, Tina McVeigh, Rebecca Moynahan, Patrick Costello, Joe Moreau, Channon Goodwin, Des Geraghty, Pat Cooney, Raymond Duggan, Elaine Leader, Philip Napier, Dominic Stevens; Louise O'Kelly, Artforum International; Bernadette Anderson & Femi Aiyegbusi at The Mercy Centre; James Yendole, James Kilgannon and all at Teeling Whiskey; Jason O'Connell & Galway Bay Brewery; Junior at Hopfully; John Mahon & Louis Scully (The Locals/Telephones); Marten Esko (EKKM); Barbara Dawson, Michael Dempsey and all at Dublin City Gallery The Hugh Lane; Sarah Glennie, Christina Kennedy, Irish Museum of Modern Art; Eamonn Maxwell, Paul McAree at Lismore Castle Arts; Mary McCarthy; Dublin Docklands Development Authority; Auto Italia South East; The Irish Georgian Society, and Seamus Hogan, City Assembly House Building Liaison; Sheena Barrett, Ray Yates, Dublin City Council Arts Office, and The Lab; Fire Station Artists' Studios; Gertrude Contemporary, Melbourne; Siobhan Geoghegan and Common Ground; Nathalie Weadick and all at the Irish Architecture Foundation; The Model, Sligo; Ian Whyte, Marianne Newman, and all at Whyte & Sons Auctioneers; Andrew Hetherington, Rowena Neville, and all at Business to Arts; Paul O'Kane and Dublin Airport Authority; Claire Doyle, the Visual Arts team, and all at The Arts Council; the staff of Limerick City Gallery of Art; Jacquie Moore, OPW; Visual Artists' Ireland; Christophe Neuman, Des Kenny, Niamh McCann, Darren Bolger, Mary Cremin, Paul Murnaghan, Emmet Ring, Mark O'Toole, Paul Maloney, Georgina Jackson, Seamus Kealy, Oliver Dowling, Jack Gilligan, Alex Caccamo, Jenny Haughton, Clodagh Kenny; Donall Curtin, David Smith and Oran Day at Atelier, Daniel Jewesbury, Paul Hallahan, Matt Packer, Michele Horrigan, Padraic E. Moore, Ruth Carroll, Carl Giffney; David Fitzgerald, Darragh Hogan & all at Kerlin Gallery; Green on Red Gallery; Kevin Kavanagh Gallery; Rubicon Gallery; mother's tankstation;

Rosa Abbott; Totally Dublin; Declan Long; and all those who have contributed to Pallas, our families and peers who have supported us, and all current and past studio members of Pallas Studios.

The team at Pallas Projects: Eve Woods, Gillian Lawler, Aoife Ward, Yusuf Amod, Jennifer Lena Harrington, Cristina Nicotra. Former staff members: Viktorija Kacanauskaite, Louise Dolan, Daire McEvoy, Vera Ryklova, Roisin Power Hackett, Lucy Watts, Tadhg Ó Cuirrín, Florence Gourret, Fiona Chambers. Previous and current PP/S interns and volunteers: Rachael Gilbourne, Tracy Hanna, Michelle Hall, Sharon Murphy, Imelda Barnard, Laura Carey, Jessica Foley, Emer Bermingham, Neil Ryan, Moya Revins, Emma Rowe, Niamh Dunphy, Aoife Doolin, Neil Ryan, Fiona O'Keefe, Katy O'Donoghue, Catherine Byrne, Chloe Brenan, Daniel Bermingham, Dary Gregg, Elizabeth Lyne, Emma Hogan, Jack Nyhan, Jenny Harborne, Lorraine Brannigan, Shannon Flaherty, Marian Balfe, Martina McDonald, Niamh Moriarty, Niamh Reynolds, Paddy Joe Rickard, Rachel Healy, Roya Miller, Sarah Devereux, Siobhain Boyle, Siobhán Mooney, Sofie Loscher, Sophie Behal, Susan Dunne, Susanna Galbraith, Ulla Juske, Vraja Lila, Loretta Moore, Catherine O' Keeffe, Sara Teckenberg, Holly Draper, Valeria Ceregini, Bartek Skrzyczek, Cará Donaghey, Megan Robinson, Chloë Nagle, Imogen Brady, Natalie Pullen, Max Rooney, Jennifer Ricci, Tara Ennis, Emily Geary, Frances Hennigan, Shane McInerney, Michaela Nash, Grace O'Boyle, Jonathan O'Grady, Jessica Daly, Catherine Ward, Aisling Clark, Méabh Hennelly, Steffi Kelly, Aoife O'Callaghan, Venus Patel, Olivia Throckmartin, Maria Krupa and everyone else who has helped at PP/S projects and events.

Special thanks to all the artists and artist-run spaces featured in this publication, and to all those artists who have exhibited, performed, spoken at, and collaborated with Pallas over the years, including:

Vito Acconci, ADF, Albano Afonso, Bassam Al-Sabah, Gayle Anderson, Antistrot, Dan Atkins, Bertille Bak, Marian Balfe, Robert Ballagh, Gustavo Barbosa, Imelda Barnard, Olive Barrett, Darren Barrett, Aideen Barry, Anne Maree Barry, David Beattie, John Beattie, Mark Beatty, Michael Beirne, Roisin Beirne, Stephane Bena Hanly, Kian Benson-Bailes, Terence Birch, Craig Blackwell, Bloodyends, Aisling Boland, Darren Bolger, George Bolster, Stephen Bourke, Anna Boyle, Joanne Boyle, Martin Boyle, Gráinne Brady, Jenny Brady, Lorraine Brannigan, Clare Breen, Chloe Brenan, Dermot Browne, Gemma Browne, Sarah Browne & Gareth Kennedy, Shane Bunnak, Karl Burke, Nicole Burke, Peter Burns, Sinéad Burt O'Dea, John Busher, Alan Butler, Eoin Butler, Jane Butler, James Butterworth, Fergus Byrne, John Byrne, Lorraine Byrne, Pat Byrne, Rhona Byrne, Peter Cabocky, Andy Cahill, Caroline Campbell, Rachael Campbell-Palmer, Merce Canadell, Nina Canell & Robin Watkins, Michael Canning, Laura Carey, Sarah Carroll, Judy Carroll Deeley, Andrew Carson, Colin Carters, Clare Cashman, Aoife Cassidy, Paola Catizone, Fiona Chambers, Gordon Cheung, Kraisak Chunahawan, Mark Clare, Declan Clarke, Click, Ruth Clinton, Nichola Coleman, Tobias Collier, Carol Anne Connolly, Michelle Considine, Amanda Coogan, Diana Copperwhite, Gavin Corcoran, Rachael Corcoran, Regina Corcoran, Garrett Cormican, Fiachra Corr, Rob Costello, Joseph Coveney, Gary Coyle, Anne Cradden, Daniel Cramer, Emma Crean, Jessica Crean, Liam Crichton, Kim Crilly, Alan Crosby, Martyn Cross, Diarmuid Crowley, Will Cruickshank, Mark Cullen, Sinéad Cullen, Mark Curran, Sinéad Curran, Maeve Curtis, Rajah Dagstani, Pamela de Brí, Niall de Buitléar, Gabrielle Deery, Anita Delaney, Fiona Galvin Delaney, Sophia Delavari, Ciara Dempsey, Aoife Desmond, Colm Desmond, Deviant, Johannes DeYoung, Brian Dillon, Craig Donald, David Donohoe and David Lacey, Vanessa Donoso López, Cian Donnelly, Ciara Donnelly, Aoife Doolin, Caroline Doolin, Mollie Douthit, Miranda Driscoll, Blaise Drummond, Brian Duggan, Joe Duggan, Nora Duggan, John Dummet, Adrian Duncan, Gabhann Dunne, Stephen Dunne, Niamh Dunphy, Brendan Earley, Aleanna Egan, David Eager Maher, Gardar Eide Einarsson, Neva Elliot, Clodagh Emoe, Kim Engelen, Haris Epaminonda, Gerard Erraught, Tim Etchells, Marie Farrington, Brian Fay, Morton Feldman, Emma Fisher, Hannah Fitz, Glenn Fitzgerald, Margaret Fitzgibbon, Fiona Fitzpatrick, Gemma Fitzpatrick, Jennifer Fitzpatrick, Johnny Fitzsimmons, Brendan Flaherty, Shannon Flaherty, Flatpack 001, Damien Flood, Michael Fortune, Pat Foster & Jen Berean, Sheen Frances, Alicia Frankovich, Matt Franks, Timothy Furey, Orla Galligan, Martina Galvan, Maurice Galway, Thomas Garrett, Mark Garry, Andreas Gefeller, Sheenagh Geoghegan, Rachael Gilbourne, Orla Gilheany, Alex Gillice, Kim Gleeson, David Godbold, Susan Gogan, Orla Goodwin, Gemma Gore, Richard Gorman, Brendan Grant, Eileen Gray, Aoibheann Greenan, Dary Gregg, Brian Griffiths, Seán Grimes, Saoirse Groves Murphy, Seán Guinan, Gretta Gunn, Stephen Gunning, Jennie Guy, Anthony Hackett, Michelle Hall, Tracy Hanna, Siobhán Hapaska, Seamus Harahan, Cliona Harmey, Andy Harper, Shona Harrison, Emma Haugh, Anthony Haughey, Cormac Healy, Laura Healy, Martin Healy, Lisa Heavey, Joseph Heffernan, Anne Hendrick, Charles Henihan, Diango Hernández, Brid Higgins, Anna Hill, Catherine Hildyard, Emma Hogan, Jacqueline Holt, Inge Hoonte, Katie Holten, Helen Horgan, Toine Horvers, Emma Houlihan, Allan Hughes, Helen Hughes, Jacinta Hughes, Ronnie Hughes, Sophie-Carroll Hunt, Angela Huntbach, Elaine Hurley, Santipab Inkong namg, Daniel Jackman, Candice Jacobs, Jakrawal, Daniel Jewesbury, Peadar Jolliffe-Byrne, Jesse Jones, Wendy Judge, Dragana Jurisic, Ulla Juske, Atsushi Kaga, Gillian Kane, Ramon Kassam, Allyson Keehan, Patrick Keiller, Conall Kelleher, Anne Kelly, Sally Anne Kelly & Kevin Gaffney, Mary Kennedy, Des Kenny, Denise Kevany, Caoimhe Kilfeather, Andreas Kindler Von Knobloch, Allan Kinsella, Ali Kirby, Vera Klute, Barbara Knezevic, Bartosz Kolata, Gereon Krebber, Grace Kristensen, Slavek Kwi, Nevan Lahart, John Lalor, Alan Lambert, Karen Land Hansen, John Langan, Tonia Larem, Niamh Laughlin, Gillian Lawler, Craig Lawlor, Richard Lawlor, Paraic Leahy, Kakyoung Lee, Jamie Lemon, Dylan Lennon, Jinx Lennon, Aisling Leonard, Kevin Lindsay, Namara Lindsay, Conor Linsky, Daniel Lipstein, Clive Lissam, Jane Lives, Owen Llewellyn, Loitering Theatre, Sofie Loscher, Stephen Loughman, David Lunney, Breda Lynch, Sean Lynch, Elizabeth Lyne, Catherine Lyons, Ingrid Lyons, Ruth E. Lyons, Colm Mac Athlaoich, Áine Macken, Maggie Madden, Dave Madigan, Brian Maguire, Darragh Maguire, Dee Maguire, Alice Maher, Tea Makipäa, Jack Marmion, Fiona Marron, Colin Martin, Fergus Martin, Alex Martinis Roe, Steven Maybury, Paul McAree, Niamh McCann, Hugh McCarthy, Eleanor McCaughey, Mary McClelland, Eimear Jean McCormack, Louise McCormack, Alex McCullagh, Angela McDonagh, Ciara McDonald, Eilis McDonald, Fiona McDonald, Martina McDonald, Siobhan McDonald, Ross McDonnell, Dave McGinn, Nina McGowan, Yvonne McGuinness, Eoin McHugh, Ian McInerney, Deirdre McKenna, Lucy McKenna, Paul McKinley, Brigid McLeer, Donna McLoughlan, Michael McLoughlin, Bea McMahon, Ciara McMahon, Róisín McNamee, Carly McNulty, Dennis McNulty, Tadhg McSweeney, Jordan McQuaid, Tracey McVerry, Sandra Meehan, Nathaniel Mellors, Jules Michael, Nicolas Milhé, Nick Miller, Yvette Monahan, Kevin Mooney, Siobhan Mooney, Ashley Moore, Loretta Moore, Madeline Moore, James Moran, Sally Anne Morgan, Niamh Moriarty, Stephen Morris, Jago Moulton, Ann Mulrooney, Paul Murnaghan, Aileen Murphy, Alex Murphy, Claire Murphy, Clive Murphy, Gavin Murphy, Jillian Murphy, Kate Murphy, Lorcan Murphy Gilligan, Lynn Murphy, Shane Murphy, Sharon Murphy, Adriette Myburgh, Chloe Nagle, Nawapol, Eszter Nemethi, Olarn Netrangsri, Cris Neumann, Jo Neylin, Aisling Ní Chlaonadh, Rićí Ní Chleirigh, Laura Ni Fhlaibhin, Sinéad Ní Mhaonaigh, Isabel Nolan, Nontawa, Not Abel, Cian Nugent & The Cosmos, Kathy Nugent, Jack Nyhan, Fiona O'Brien, Margaret O'Brien, Sarah O'Brien, Liam O'Callaghan, Noel O'Callaghan, Damien O'Connell, Lesley-Ann O'Connell, Kelly O'Connor, Meadhbh O'Connor, Siobhan O'Connor, Helen O'Dea, Blaine O'Donnell, Eoin O'Dowd, Alison O'Flynn, Mark O'Gorman, Beth O'Halloran, Eamon O'Kane, Catherine O'Keeffe, Ciarán O'Keeffe, Sarah O'Keeffe, Mark O'Kelly, Kathy O'Leary, Siobhán O'Leary, Deirdre O'Mahony, Fergal O'Mahony, David O'Mara, Paul O'Neill, Sinéad Onora Kennedy, Magnhild Opdøl, David O'Reilly, Vanessa O'Reilly, Paul Rooney, Catriona O'Rourke, Seamus O'Rourke, Sam Ruscica, Oran O'Siochan, Seoidin O'Sullivan, Sarah O'Toole, Florence Paule G, Alice Peillon, Ailish Phelan, Alan Phelan, Garrett Phelan, Alison Pilkington, Laragh Pittman, Andrew Pollard, Deirdre Power, Ruth Proctor, Richard Proffitt, Roma Przedpelska, Liliane Puthod, Linda Quinlan, Ann Quinn, Mary Quinn, Anna Rackard, Arnulf Rainer, Fiona Reilly, Sheila Rennick, Moya Revins, Abigail Reynolds, Jim Ricks, Patrisha Robertson, Erica Roche, Jason Roche, Alex Rose, Paul Rosser, Eva Rothschild, Emma Rowe, Sam Ruscica, James Ryan, John Ryan, Neil Ryan, Elvira Santamaria Torres, Sathit Satarasart, Joe Scullion, Leda Scully, Dana Sederowsky, Marinella Senatore, Margrét Helga Sesseljudóttir, Seán Shanahan, Gary Shaw, Gerard Shanahan, Paddy Sheehan, Zoe Sheehy, Sonia Shiel, Dan Shipsides, Christian Sievers, Chulayarnnon Siriphol, Suchada Sirithanawuddhi, Laura Skehan, Ian Slattery, Berndnaut Smilde, John Smith, Padraig Spillane, Joe Stanly, Amy Stephens, Hito Steyerl, Rich Streitmatter-Tran, Suthirat Supaparinya, Stephen Sutcliffe, Mark Swords, Stephanie Syjuco, Hussein Tai, Joyce Tansey, Cathy Taylor, Serena Teehan, Patomporn Tesprateep, Cornelius Thalbridge, Nitipong Thinthubthai, Jason Thompson, Kieran Tierney, Dave Timmons, Sally Timmons, Mark Titchner, Helena Tobin, Samuel Tobin, Sanja Todorovic, Moniek Toebosch, Stephen Toomey Gina Tornatore, Daniel Toumey, Josephine Turalba, Ann Turpin, David Turpin, T-woc, Ivan Twohig, Kathy Tynan, Stephen Usher, Suzannah Vaughan, Maria Vedder, Katie Waine, Ruby Wallis, Naomi Walsh, Chanelle Walshe, Freek Wambacq, Tom Watt, Lee Welch, Orla Whelan, Fiona Whitty, Jack Whycherly, Keith Wilson, Mick Wilson, Simon Wood, Nicki Wynnychuk, and the hundreds more we have worked with since our first edition.

Author Biographies

Jason E. Bowman is an artist with a curatorial practice, a writer and educator. He is MFA: Fine Art Programme Leader at the Valand Academy at the University of Gothenburg where with Julie Crawshaw and Mick Wilson he is researching into the expanded nature of practices generated within artist-led cultures and specifically in relation to issues of 'the curatorial'. With Crawshaw and Rachel Bradley he co-founded the now-defunct initiative *Midwest*, which was an imaginary for the artist-led active from 2003 until 2008.

AA Bronson (b. 1946 Michael Wayne Tims in Vancouver, Canada), lives and works in Berlin, Germany. In 1969 he formed the artists' group General Idea with Felix Partz and Jorge Zontal. Since his partners died in 1994, AA has worked and exhibited as a solo artist, often collaborating with younger generations, most recently in his performance series Invocation of the Queer Spirits. Since 1999 he has worked as a healer, an identity that he has also incorporated into his artwork. From 2004 to 2010 he was the Director of Printed Matter, Inc. in New York City, founding the annual NY Art Book Fair in 2005. In 2009 he founded the Institute for Art, Religion, and Social Justice at Union Theological Seminary in New York City, which he now co-directs. In 2013 he was the founding Director of Printed Matter's LA Art Book Fair. He has taught at UCLA, the University of Toronto, and the Yale School of Art.

Noelle Collins is an Irish Curator working at Towner Eastbourne (UK), and on the Board of Devonshire Collective (CIC). Her curatorial experience ranges from grassroots organisations to international arts institutions, including Arts Council Collection (UK), and EVA International – Ireland's Biennial of Contemporary Art. She has curated exhibitions and events independently and held the position of Director at the artist-led organisation Occupy Space, Limerick (2011–2013). Recent projects include: Ayo Akingbade, *Duette*; David Blandy, *The Edge of Forever*; Rita Evans, *Tuning in a Vacuum*; Jananne Al-Ani, *Timelines*; Melissa Gordon, *Liquid Gestures*. Past roles include: Curatorial Assistant for Ireland at Venice, 56th Venice Biennale; Project Coordinator NWCI: Legacy Project in Limerick; Curatorial Assistant AGITATIONISM, EVA 2014; Project Manager of "Artistic Justice", Limerick/Marrakech/Dublin; Curator of Amharc Fhine Gall IX: Eternal Light, Draíocht, Dublin; Project Manager of Curating Partnerships; Assistant Curator at Askeaton Contemporary Arts.

Valerie Connor is a freelance contemporary visual arts curator and lecturer in photography at the Dublin Institute of Technology. She is a member of the Advisory Board of PhotoIreland, Advisory Panel of the National Irish Visual Arts Library and, previously, a board member of the Irish Museum of Modern Art and Adviser to the Arts Council. She was the Commissioner-Curator for Ireland at the 50th Venice and 26th São Paulo international art biennials, and former Chairperson of the National Campaign for the Arts in Ireland. Projects and publications include *Still, We Work* for the National Women's Council of Ireland (2012–2015), GPO Witness History Permanent and Temporary Public Art Commissions (with Ruairí Ó Cuív, 2016), 'Reshape When Damp' in 126 Quarterly (Vol.2, 2015), 'Contemporary Art IRL, 2000–2010', in Art and Architecture of Ireland, Royal Irish Academy and Yale University Press (Vol.5, 2014), and *Local Authority*, Fingal County Council Arts Office (ed. with Daniel Jewesbury, 2015).

Mark Cullen works with various media as an artist, curator and a cultural instigator. In 1996 he was co-founder of Pallas Studios and is currently co-director and co-curator of PP/S. In 2007 he was co-editor of the ICAD gold award winning *Pallas Heights 2003–2006*, published to mark a programme of exhibitions and projects in a Dublin City Council semi-derelict housing block. In 2005 Cullen co-curated *Offside* at Dublin City Gallery The Hugh Lane. In 2006 he co-curated *MAIM XI*, part of the exhibition *.all hawaii eNtrées / luNar reGGae* at the Irish Museum of Modern Art. From 2005–2007 he was the International Representative of Visual Artists Ireland (VAI), representing Ireland at the 16th General Assembly of the International Association of Art held at Beijing Biennial, China, 2005, and the VAI at The World Summit on Arts and Culture held in The Sage Gateshead, Newcastle/Gateshead, UK 2006. Cullen curated the visual art section of Darklight Festival from 1999–2004 working with international artists such as Desperate Optimists, Al and Al, Ben Pruskin, and Cleary and Connolly. He was artist in residence in the School of Physics, University College Dublin in 2013–2014. He has exhibited internationally and throughout Ireland as a solo artist and as part of the artist group Difference Engine.